Exploring the Southeast States through Literature

Exploring the United States through Literature Series

Kathy Howard Latrobe, Series Editor

Exploring the Northeast States through Literature
Edited by P. Diane Frey

Exploring the Southeast States through Literature
Edited by Linda Veltze

Exploring the Great Lakes States through Literature
Edited by Kathy Howard Latrobe

Exploring the Plains States through Literature
Edited by Carolyn S. Brodie

Exploring the Southwest States through Literature
Edited by Pat Tipton Sharp

Exploring the Mountain States through Literature
Edited by Sharyl Smith

Exploring the Pacific States through Literature
Edited by Carol A. Doll

Exploring the Southeast States through Literature

Edited by Linda Veltze

State Editors

Judith V. Lechner, Alabama

Carolyn Brodie, Arkansas

Henrietta M. Smith, Florida

Priscilla Bennett, Georgia

Vandelia VanMeter and Linda Esser, Kentucky

Gayle E. Salvatore, Louisiana

Charjean Laughlin-Graves and Sid F. Graves, Mississippi

Linda Veltze, North Carolina

Pamela Barron, South Carolina

David Mielke, Tennessee

Suzanne Sprenger, Virginia

Harold M. Forbes, West Virginia

Exploring the United States through Literature Series

Kathy Howard Latrobe, Series Editor

Oryx Press
1994

The rare Arabian Oryx is believed to have inspired the myth of the unicorn. This desert antelope became virtually extinct in the early 1960s. At that time several groups of international conservationists arranged to have 9 animals sent to the Phoenix Zoo to be the nucleus of a captive breeding herd. Today the Oryx population is over 800 and nearly 400 have been returned to reserves in the Middle East.

Copyright © 1994 by The Oryx Press
4041 North Central at Indian School Road
Phoenix, Arizona 85012-3397

Published simultaneously in Canada

Printed and Bound in the United States of America

∞The paper used in this publication meets the minimum requirements of American National Standard for Information Science—Permanence of Paper for Printed Library Materials, ANSI Z39.48, 1984.

Library of Congress Cataloging-in-Publication Data

Exploring the Southeast states through literature / edited by Linda
  Veltze.
     p.   cm. — (Exploring the United States through literature
series)
  Includes bibliographical references and indexes.
  ISBN 0-89774-770-4
  1. Southern States—Juvenile literature—Bibliography.
I. Veltze, Linda. II. Series.
Z1251.S7E97   1994
[F209.3]
016.975—dc20   93-40813
                                                    CIP
                                                    AC

Contents

Series Statement

The *Exploring the United States through Literature Series* comprises seven annotated regional resource guides to selected print and nonprint materials for grades K-8. Each regional resource is divided into state sections identifying materials that relate to the history, culture, geography, resources, industries, literature and lore, and famous figures of the states in the region. The seven volumes cover the following regions and states:

- *Exploring the Northeast States through Literature:* Connecticut, Delaware, District of Columbia, Maine, Maryland. Massachusetts, New Hampshire, New Jersey, New York, Pennsylvania, Rhode Island, Vermont.
- *Exploring the Southeast States through Literature:* Alabama, Arkansas, Florida, Georgia, Kentucky, Louisiana, Mississippi, North Carolina, South Carolina, Tennessee, Virginia, West Virginia
- *Exploring the Great Lakes States through Literature:* Illinois, Indiana, Michigan, Minnesota, Ohio, Wisconsin
- *Exploring the Plains States through Literature:* Iowa, Kansas, Missouri, Nebraska, North Dakota, South Dakota
- *Exploring the Southwest States through Literature:* Arizona, Oklahoma, New Mexico, Texas
- *Exploring the Mountain States through Literature:* Colorado, Idaho, Montana, Nevada, Utah, Wyoming
- *Exploring the Pacific States through Literature:* Alaska, California, Hawaii, Oregon, Washington

The materials included in these resource guides were selected because they can be used by teachers and librarians to enrich young people's understanding of the histories and contemporary cultures of the 50 states, and because they are suitable for use with young people from any of the regional or ethnic groups of the contemporary United States. Each annotation includes a brief description of the particular work, a comment on its usefulness or appropriateness, and at least one learning activity compatible with the identified interest level of the resource.

Purpose

The *Exploring the United States through Literature Series* offers teachers, school library media specialists, and public librarians valuable assistance in resource selection and user guidance. The suggested activities demonstrate each title's potential for involving young people in creative thinking and problem-solving and for inspiring teachers and librarians to invent other imaginative uses for the title. The series can also be used effectively by school library media specialists and teachers as they work together to develop curricular units and plan learning experiences on the geographic regions of the United States or on specific states. Reading, language arts, and social studies teachers will find the series particularly useful.

The series addresses needs created by the following recent and important educational trends:

1. The whole language approach to learning, especially the integration of literature, the arts, and social studies curricula
2. Rapidly changing social environments that demand flexible curricula and multiple learning resources
3. Multicultural education with an emphasis on multicultural diversity and a recognition of the importance of leading young people to accept and appreciate diversity
4. The position of the Curriculum Task Force of the National Commission on Social Studies (NCSS) that the social studies curriculum should include both breadth and depth

The NCSS emphasizes the discovery approach to learning and maintains that young people should develop an overview as well as immerse themselves in the details of history and social studies.

Scope

Each regional editor coordinated the contributions of state editors who brought to the series a familiarity with and understanding of the notable and special features of their states and regions. The state editors used their own judgment in selecting materials that could most effectively assist young people in learning and understanding the many dimensions of each state. The editors' goal was not to include a predetermined number of entries, but rather to select pertinent items of merit. Because there are similarities across the regions, a few titles appear in more than one state bibliography. These duplicate entries serve to reinforce students' experiences with the region or to take the title in a new direction with a different activity. Also, some books listed under only one state may be appropriate for other states as well.

Each state editor valued diversity—in subject matter, in time period, and in media. The editors sought to capture the past and present of each state by including not only books, but also such items as periodicals, computer programs, sound recordings, and videocassettes. A major goal of the series is to bring alive to young people each state's sights, sounds, tastes, music, stories and legends, natural environment, and people.

Activities

The state editors, who are professionally involved either directly or indirectly with the education of young people, have devised learning activities that can appropriately extend the work being described. Denoted by a diamond (♦) in each entry, the activities are designed to enhance young people's understanding of each state and to encourage further exploration of the topic at hand. The activities relate the work to young people themselves, to specific geographic areas, to associated disciplines and subjects, or to broader concepts within social studies.

Sources of Materials

Because of the diversity and regional or state focus of materials, no single jobber can deliver all the included items upon request. Therefore, a "Directory of Publishers and Vendors," including specialized sources for state and regional materials, has been included in each volume. The agencies and departments of state and local governments, state and local historical societies, and other state and local organizations are also excellent sources of informational materials.

Organization

Each volume is organized first by the states within the region (arranged alphabetically). Each state section is then subdivided into Nonfiction (by Dewey Classification), Biography (collective biography, then individual biography, alphabetically by author), Periodicals, and Professional Materials (by Dewey Classification). Reference works listed in the Nonfiction section are identified immediately following the Dewey number.

In general, each bibliographic entry identifies Dewey Classification number, author, title, publisher or producer, ISBN or ISSN, date of publication or release, number of pages, black-and-white or color illustrations, cost of nonprint materials, any special purchasing information, and running time and format specifications for nonprint items. Each entry also includes an interest level designation and relevant subject headings, which are based on the *Sears List of Subject Headings*.

Three indexes provide access by author, title, and subject. The state-by-state division allows teachers and librarians to access materials by state, and the Subject Index provides access to materials appropriate to more than one state and to topics with regional significance.

The Dewey Decimal Classification numbers, while appropriate for each volume's organization, are not offered as recommendations for cataloging/classification purposes. Many items are open to classification in more than one area.

—Kathy Howard Latrobe
Series Editor

Preface

Alabama

Many great writers of both adult and children's literature have hailed from Alabama—Truman Capote, Richard Chase, Vicky Covington, Fanny Flagg, Harper Lee, Walker Percy, Anne Rivers Siddons, Margaret Walker, Dennis Covington, Faye Gibbons, James Haskins, Angela Johnson, and Katherine Tucker Windham. Nor is the list of Alabama greats confined to writers. It includes scientists such as William Gorgas (yellow fever), Percy Julian (cortisone and glaucoma medication), and Frederick Chapman Robbins, (Nobel Prize in microbiology); musicians such as Nat King Cole, W.C. Handy, Lionel Richie, Dinah Washington, and Hank Williams; athletes such as Hank Aaron, Bo Jackson, Joe Louis, Willie Mays, Jesse Owens, and Satchel Paige; statesmen and political leaders such as Rev. Ralph Abernathy, Justice Hugo Black, Senator Lister Hill, and Coretta Scott King; and champion of the disabled, Helen Keller. Sadly, the operative phrase is "hailed from." Some great achievers, such as Nat King Cole and Dinah Washington, had to be omitted from this resource guide because they left the state before they entered first grade; school and peers do shape us. For others, no children's biographies have been written. Fortunately, many have stayed and others who came here have made it their home. Most notable among these were George Washington Carver and Booker T. Washington. Compiling this resource guide has been an adventure of discovery, not only of Alabama's famous sons and daughters, but also of its rich folk heritage in stories, crafts, and religious and secular music.

Arkansas

An interesting selection of materials represents Arkansas' uniqueness, beauty, and character. A number of historical resources, both fiction and nonfiction, are available for upper levels, but information on contemporary Arkansas is harder to locate for younger audiences. Only a few biographies were available at press time, though others are forthcoming from publishers. There are, however, several audiovisual selections on a variety of topics, from the Old State House to an Arkansas Almanac.

Although there is certainly a need for more fiction, easy books, and contemporary biographies that focus on the lives and people of Arkansas, many unique and worthwhile items were located for this resource guide.

Florida

Florida, the twenty-seventh state to be admitted to the Union, can be called a state of contrasts; its topographical make-up beckons visitors seeking a wide variety of adventures. Dubbed the "Sunshine State" because there is usually so little rainfall, Florida's climate can vary from cold in the Panhandle to steamy hot and muggy along the Gold Coast and in the swampy areas of the Everglades.

In the Panhandle there are long stretches of glistening white beaches and sand-dunes topped with wild oats. A few miles down the east coast, the topography changes, and the climate is warmer and the beaches beckon again. Nature lovers, however, may bypass the beaches for the uniqueness of the Everglades. This natural resource, the largest sub-tropical area in the United States, is the home of alligators, osprey, spoonbills, the endangered black panther, and other wildlife. Central Florida is the home of Disney World and the NASA Space Center. The east and west coasts play hosts to several professional baseball teams during spring training season. For the above topics it was not at all difficult to find quality material, at all reading levels, to include in the resource guide.

Many personalities who have made a mark in history call Florida home: entrepreneurs Arthur Vining Davis, Henry Flagler, Mary Brickell; educator Mary McCleod Bethune; artist James Audubon; and novelist Zora Neale Hurston, to name a few. Several presidents, including Herbert Hoover, Grover Cleveland, Harry Truman, and Franklin D. Roosevelt, chose Key West as their place of rest and relaxation.

In preparing this resource guide, an intense search was made for materials that would represent the Cuban and Haitian populations. Unfortunately, such materials are limited.

Georgia

Georgia, the largest state east of the Mississippi, harbors great diversity in geography, history, population, weather, outdoor pursuits, and cultural opportunities. Unfortunately, certain places, people, or times are well represented in available material, while others are all but ignored. For example, Atlanta is strong in nonfiction, but fiction titles are primarily set in rural Georgia and predominately historical in nature.

Although there are many biographies of Martin Luther King Jr., and a scattering of sports and historical figures, few of Georgia's fine performing artists, musicians, or artists are presented in biographies for children. Most are given one line, if that, in surveys of the state.

Georgia's rich landscape from mountain to seashore is well represented in guide books for travelers and handbooks for outdoor enthusiasts. Although many of these are not written for children, most are accessible and interesting to intermediate and middle school children and can serve as springboards to further study in history, geography, and science.

The Georgia Department of Natural Resources has also produced a library of videotapes. They include historical, recreational, and ecological topics that provide a strong audiovisual component for learning about Georgia.

As might be expected, the Colonial period and the Civil War dominate the historical literature. So teachers will need to supplement the available historical materials with adaptations and creativity.

Kentucky

Kentucky is divided into three distinct social, cultural, and geographical regions: Western Kentucky, a rolling landscape of fertile fields and farm buildings; Central Kentucky, often called the Bluegrass and known throughout the world for its thoroughbred horses; and Eastern Kentucky, rich in the scenic beauty and venerable folklore of the Appalachians. All three regions, however, share a common bond. In all walks of life, from farmers to coal miners to urban dwellers, all are Kentuckians—and for Kentuckians, the family is the heart of community life, and the

welfare of the family, or "kin," is of paramount importance. From its earliest days to the present, the state has been well represented in a body of literature, written primarily by native sons and daughters, who speak of their home in a distinctive voice that reflects this intense commitment to family.

Louisiana

Louisiana is truly a multicultural state and has celebrated this heritage for many years. Tourists come to Louisiana to enjoy its history, listen to its music, and taste its cuisine. Louisiana has retained some of its distinctive European flavor and its residents have kept their allegiance to the French language through the patios of the region, through interest in things French, and through the daily reference to food and places. The vast amounts of materials on specific topics, such as festivals, the Cajuns, natural resources, Mardi Gras, ethnic populations, geographical features, politics, and traditions, resulted in a title selection as varied as possible among the extensive works considered.

Mississippi

Geographically and ethnically diverse, Mississippi is made up of five distinct regions and contains a wealth of unspoiled natural and distinctive beauty. The Magnolia State is unrivaled in excellent writers, artists, and musicians, such as William Faulkner, Eudora Welty, Tennessee Williams, Jimmie Rodgers (the "Father of Country Music"), Elvis Presley, B.B. King, and opera legend Leontyne Price. Lives of important Mississippians, from sports figures to authors, are well documented. The civil rights movement is also well represented in the literature. There is a need for more easy books, more young male characters for children and juveniles, and more fiction with contemporary settings. But with Mississippi's unique heritage, many exciting and worthwhile materials were located for inclusion in this resource guide.

North Carolina

North Carolina is the location of the "lost colony" and Virginia Dare, one of the 13 original colonies, one of the early ratifiers of the Constitution, home of the Eastern Band of the Cherokee, and site of Orville and Wilbur Wright's momentous flight at Kitty Hawk.

The materials provided in this chapter will lead the user (whether teacher, media specialist, or student) to learn more about the above and to see the state in its full richness and complexity. Multicultural materials on North Carolina are growing in number, but the surface has only been scratched. As such materials become more valued in our society, publishers will be encouraged to make them available in the schools, and then students will learn that there are more Native American tribes than just the Cherokee, that there was more to the North Carolina Civil Rights Movement than the Greensboro sit-in, and that women have contributed more to the making of the fabric of society than it would appear.

Why has there been such a change in the types of materials available for the study of North Carolina over the last several years? Historians continue to uncover new materials on African Americans in North Carolina, from slavery to civil rights days, and interest is rising in other types of African-American contributions—folklore, literature, music, poetry, and dance. All these contributions can now be experienced in nonprint as well as print forms.

Discovering Appalachia and the richness of its culture is possible due to media that has chronicled clogging, fiddling, singing, and storytelling. We've become even more broadminded about language and dialects. Children's books now help to bestow validity and significance on the dialects that arose from the isolation of the Appalachians.

The hunt for the "real" North Carolina was made possible by the rich resources that exist in the state. University presses, state library and archival resources, and the North Carolina Department of Public Instruction's Curriculum Laboratory all yield ample materials. The existence of a jobber, Broadfoots, that specializes in North Carolina materials, is also advantageous.

The tourist's interest in North Carolina has created a market for many new books that enable the student to take a trip without ever leaving the school. The Smokey Mountains and the Blue Ridge have provided opportunities for study for botanists, biologists, and ecologists who have written books that can be used by children and adults alike.

South Carolina

South Carolina's rich and diverse cultural heritage is portrayed in a rather limited fashion for children, especially children below third grade. There are no picture books set in South Carolina and no children's biography of Francis Marion, one of South Carolina's greatest heroes. Fort Sumter, near Charleston, played a critical role in the Civil War, yet only adult titles are to be found about it. With the exception of books that present an overview of the state's geography, more children's books about every aspect of South Carolina, historical as well as contemporary, need to be written.

Tennessee

Tennessee was one of the frontier areas adjacent to the 13 original colonies. Tennessee literature is rich with the biographical legends of Davy Crockett, Daniel Boone, John Sevier, Sam Houston, Andrew Jackson, and countless other frontier personalities. Prior to statehood, the territory was a frontier gateway that received individuals who desired to escape the "civilized states." Tennessee literature offers many accounts of frontier exploits, and the task of choosing among them was difficult.

Few states can match the pronounced sectionalism of Tennessee. Indeed, until a few years ago, signs greeted visitors to the state by proclaiming, "Welcome to the Three States of Tennessee." Beyond historical literature, the juvenile books on Tennessee tend to belong to one of these sectional divisions.

The first group of Tennessee sources relates to Tennessee's portion of the Appalachian Region. May Justus, Rebecca Caudill, and others have interpreted the East Tennessee experience as essentially "Appalachian mountain" by focusing on folkways and coal mining. The second group of important Tennessee books concerns the music industry which grew up around Nashville. Many books chronicle the lives of country musicians. The third group of Tennessee books focuses on life along the Mississippi River and the life experiences of Tennessee's African-Americans.

In literature, there is a tendency to stereotype Tennessee in terms of these three divisions. Very few published works other than anthologies and histories attempt to focus broadly on the state. Tennessee is represented prominently in children's literature by and about minorities. Beginning with early accounts of Native Americans through the "Trail of Tears" and the founding of the Eastern Cherokee Band, Tennessee writers have produced many child and juvenile interest accounts. African Americans are also liberally represented among Tennessee children's writers.

Virginia

The Commonwealth of Virginia is recognized as the "Mother of Presidents," with a rich history that forms a major part of America's beginnings.

So much has been produced about the state and its patriots, that it was a difficult task to make the final selections for this resource guide. An effort was made to represent the geographic areas of Virginia, major historical events that have occurred within the state, and notable Virginians who have contributed in many ways to the state and country. Easy reading materials about the wildlife of Virginia were difficult to locate for the primary student. Several excellent reference selections are included about the flora and fauna of the state and it's endangered species.

The earliest history of Virginia deals with the Native Americans and can be explored through short stories, biographies, maps, and historical fiction. The settlements at Jamestown, Yorktown, and Williamsburg can be visited through video, nonfiction, and historical fiction selections. The Revolutionary War and Civil War are represented in many works, including those about Virginia's early patriots, military leaders, and little-known heroes. History is brought alive through mysteries set in Virginia during the Revolutionary and Civil Wars, through realistic fiction dealing with the Depression era, and through the story of orphans of a Vietnam soldier. Biographical selections include many historical Virginians, as well as artists, sports figures, and entertainment notables who are native Virginians. The fiction books offered can be related to nonfiction selections for regional geographical studies. Examples of this correlation would be using *Grandpa's Mountain* with *Shenandoah National Park*, or *Misty of Chincoteague* with research on Assateague Island as a National Seashore. The correlations between the works suggested are only a beginning for an exciting study of this wonderful commonwealth.

West Virginia

Although West Virginia books and films for children are not abundant, West Virginia history and culture are well documented in the limited number of fiction and nonfiction works that are available. Virtually all the books and films in this resource guide are appropriate for children in grades 4 through 8. In addition, the availability of many excellent in-print adult materials provides resources appropriate for the professional collection. Materials for children in grades K through 3 are quite scarce.

Recurrent literary themes are West Virginia's mountainous terrain and natural beauty, traditional Appalachian culture, folklore and folk music, the Civil War and the birth of the state, and coal mining and miners. The state's rugged terrain and deep forests have influenced and molded West Virginia history and culture. Far from being a homogeneous state, paradoxes abound: progressive towns in the rugged and isolated mountains, colleges in coal mining communities, industry in rural settings, poverty amidst scenic splendor. A succession of ardent folklorists have avidly collected and preserved West Virginia's music, lore, and traditional culture. This long-lasting fascination with traditional culture has resulted in a paucity of writing on contemporary culture. Readers of all ages enjoy West Virginia historical and literary works, especially because they are so well populated with numerous historical characters of legendary or heroic status.

Most newly published West Virginia books are genealogical reference works and histories of specific families, communities, and counties. Numerous juvenile West Virginia history textbooks are in print but are not included in this resource guide. Several booksellers listed in the Appendix specialize in West Virginia materials and provide a wide variety of both current and out-of-print publications.

Contributors

Regional Editor

Linda Veltze is assistant professor and coordinator for the library science program in the Reich College of Education at Appalachian State University, Boone, North Carolina. She has recently authored reviews for the *Advisory List of Instructional Media—North Carolina* published by the North Carolina Department of Public Instruction and written articles in the *Reference Librarian* and *Resource in Education*. Her most recent research was reported on in "Current Research," *School Library Media Annual, 1993.*

State Editors

Pamela Barron is associate professor at the College of Library and Information Science at the University of South Carolina. She was the content and research supervisor for the award-winning telecourse "Jump Over the Moon: Sharing Literature with Young Children," and is the coauthor of *Collection Analysis for the School Library Media Center: A Practical Approach* (ALA, 1991) and *Writers on Writing for Young Adults* (Omnigraphics, 1991). She is currently at work on another telecourse, "West of the Moon: Exploring Literature with Children."

Priscilla Bennett is associate professor in the Department of Media Education at West Georgia College in Carrollton, GA. She is a long time reviewer of children's material for *School Library Journal*.

Carolyn Brodie is assistant professor in the School of Library and Information Science, Kent State University, Ohio. She is coauthor of *Many Faces, Many Voices: Multicultural Literary Experiences for Youth* (Highsmith Press, 1992), a book based on the Virginia Hamilton Conference held each spring at Kent State University. She

contributed the Ohio chapter and edited the Plains States book for the *Exploring the United States* series.

Linda Esser was formerly assistant professor, Department of Library/Information Science, at Spalding University, Louisville, KY. She is currently pursuing doctoral studies at the University of Kentucky, exploring gender difference in young adult literature and studying differences in reader response.

Harold M. Forbes is associate curator of the West Virginia and Regional History Collection, West Virginia University Libraries, Morgantown. He has been the West Virginia bibliographer for the West Virginia University Libraries for 20 years and has edited several publications on West Virginia historical sources. His family has lived in the region he has written about for many generations.

Charjean Laughlin-Graves is a middle school librarian at West District School, West Tallahatchie School District, Sumner, Mississippi. She was also consultant for the federally funded workshop entitled "Information for Tomorrow" in Fall, 1991, held at the University of Southern Mississippi.

Sid F. Graves is executive director of the Carnegie Public Library of Clarksdale and Coahoma County, Mississippi and the founding director of the Delta Blues Museum. He has authored several articles on Mississippi authors and on Mississippi Delta blues music.

Judith V. Lechner is associate professor of Educational Media in the Department of Educational Foundations, Leadership, and Technology at Auburn University, Alabama. She teaches courses in children's literature and reference and has published articles on multicultural/global children's literature, art in picture books, and award winning science trade books.

David Mielke is professor of Foundations of Education in the Reich College of Education at Appalachian State University in Boone, North Carolina. His high school through doctoral studies were done in Tennessee. He is author of several publications on the Appalachian region.

Gayle E. Salvatore is library directory for Brother Martin High School in New Orleans, Louisiana. She is the editor of *Sinfully Good* (CLA, 1985). Her recently completed doctoral research was on women administrators.

Henrietta M. Smith is professor emerita from the faculty of the Division of Library and Information Science at the University of South Florida, Tampa. Her main areas of expertise include children's literature, young adult literature, and storytelling. She is a reviewer for *The Horn Book Guide* and has contributed articles to *Book Links* and *School Library Journal*.

Suzanne Sprenger is an elementary and middle school librarian and developer of the statewide Virginia Young Readers program with over 100,000 student participants. She is a member of the executive board of the Virginia State Reading Association, contributor to the *Whole Language Catalog*, and reviewer for *School Library Journal*.

Vandelia VanMeter is associate professor and chair of the Department of Library/Information Science and Library Director at Spalding University, Louisville, KY. She is author of *American History for Children and Young Adults* (Libraries Unlimited, 1990) and *World History for Children and Young Adults* (Libraries Unlimited, 1992).

Exploring the Southeast States through Literature

Alabama

by Judith V. Lechner

Nonfiction

299.761
Oliver, Louis Littlecoon. "Chasers of the Sun" in *Chasers of the Sun: Creek Indian Thoughts*. Greenfield Review Press (0-912678-70-4), 1990. pp. 3-13. (Interest level: 7+).

Littlecoon Oliver, a Muscogee (Creek) poet, tells of the origins of the Creek tribe in Georgia and Alabama. Oliver does not claim to be a scholar but tells the origins of the Creeks (who now live in Oklahoma) in terms he has learned from his parents and grandparents, making these legends more immediate and compelling.
♦ Students may read other accounts of origins and compare them with the one retold here. On a map, students can follow the route of the Creek peoples in search of a home.
1. Creek Indians—Religion 2. Indians of North America—Alabama—Religion 3. Indians of North America—Oklahoma—Religion.

305.5
Working Lives. (Recording). Archives of American Minority Cultures, University of Alabama, 1985. Contact Special Collections, W.S. Hoole Library. 7 audiocassettes, (373 min.). (Interest level: 7+).

Describes in words and songs rural African-American farmers' lives and their migration to the cities, such as Birmingham. The combination of reminiscences by the people whose experiences are described with the songs of the era, such as "Boll Weevil," makes this set of tapes both interesting and authentic, and the clear, well-recorded sound track makes it enjoyable listening as well.
♦ Students can reconstruct the era in plays, paintings, and short stories after listening to one of the tapes.
1. Blacks—Alabama—History.

323.1
Haskins, James. *The Day Martin Luther King, Jr., Was Shot: A Photo History of the Civil Rights Movement*. Scholastic (0-590-43661-9), 1992. 96p. B/W photos. (Interest level: 4-8).

The civil rights movement is presented, beginning with the earliest fighters for freedom on the slave ships, through the events of the 1950s and 1960s in Alabama and other southern states, to recent political victories of such African-American candidates as Mayor Dinkins of New York City and Governor Wilder of Virginia. Haskins' clear writing makes the ideas accessible to young children without oversimplifying issues or situations, while the photographs portraying people and events greatly extend the discussion.
♦ Each specific era in the civil rights movement could be researched by small groups of students; this book's brief but excellent bibliography should aid research.
1. Civil rights—History 2. Blacks—Civil rights.

353.99761 (Reference)
Alabama Directory of State Government: A 1991-1994 Roster of the Alabama Legislature, Governor's Cabinet and State Judiciary. Edited by Darryl Gates. Alabama Rural Electric Association, 1991. 64p. B/W photos. Free. (Interest level: 4+).

Although this reference work introduces rural electrification, the bulk of the directory gives names, titles of address, addresses, and phone numbers of members of the executive, legislative, and judicial branches of the Alabama state government. It is useful for identifying individuals, and helpful for contacting elected officials.
♦ Students can identify their own state senator and representatives and can plan a class letter to express their opinions about a bill in front of their state's legislature, or a bill they think would be important to propose.
1. Alabama—Government—Directories.

398.2
Bang, Molly Garrett. *Wiley and the Hairy Man*. Macmillan (0-02-7083705), 1976. (Ready-to-Read). 64p. B/W illus. (Interest level: 1-3).

If Wiley can fool the Hairy Man of the swamp by the Tombigbee River three times, the Hairy Man will go away forever. Bang's adaptation of this Alabama folktale is retold in a controlled vocabulary, but is nevertheless enjoyable, and the suspenseful plot, accompanied by Bang's soft grey charcoal and pastel illustrations, should keep beginning readers turning the pages.

♦ Students can find on a map the Tombigbee River and the swampy forests around it. They can also examine the illustrations for images of rural Alabama homes and furnishings.

1. Folklore—Alabama 2. Blacks—Folklore.

398.2

Hamilton, Virginia, ed. "Tappin, the Land Turtle" in *The People Could Fly*. Illus. by Leo and Diane Dillon. Knopf (0-394-96925-I), 1985. pp. 20-25. B/W illus. (Interest level: 3-6).

Seeing that Eagle has no trouble feeding the Tree Children, Tappin tries flying with Eagle to obtain food for the Land Children, who are starving. He lands in the bottom of the ocean where the King of the Underworld first helps him in his quest but ends by punishing him—since then Tappin continues to wear marks of beating and lives in the mud. This "why" tale, first told in Alabama, is retold in dialect and includes African spells that African-Americans continued to repeat long after they lost the meaning of the words.

♦ Students may compare this African-American explanation of the markings on the terrapin's shell with the explanation of the Cherokee given below in *How Rabbit Tricked Otter and Other Cherokee Animal Stories (see* following entry).

1. Folkore—Alabama 2. Blacks—Folklore.

398.2

How Rabbit Tricked Otter and Other Cherokee Animal Stories. (Recording). Told by Gayle Ross. Harper Audio (1055994-542-7), 1991. 1 cassette, (50 min., 58 sec.). $11.00. (Interest level:1-4).

Rabbit (a typical trickster, boastful and resourceful, and sometimes foolish or mean), Turtle, Otter, Possum, and Bear are the heroes in this set of gently told "why" tales and legends. These authentic stories range from the humorous tales, ideal for younger children, which teach values such as cooperation and kindness, to legends, which must be interpreted with an adult's guidance within the context of Native American beliefs about the kinship of all living beings.

♦ Students may compare Rabbit, Otter, and the other animals with the characters who people the Br'er Rabbit tales.

1. Cherokee Indians—Legends.

398.2

Searcy, Margaret. *Alli Gator Gets a Bump on His Nose*. Illus. by Lu Celia Wise. Portals Press (0-916621221-4), 1978. 55p. (Interest level: K-3).

Alli Gator, the boastful bully of the swamp, tells the animals he will be their chief and will lead them to victory in the ball game against the birds, but even the animals cheer when Eagle bumps him on the nose, making him lose the ball and the game. This traditional southeastern Indian story is given a lively, realistic, if slightly modernized, rendition in the illustrations, with Alli Gator wearing a baseball cap.

♦ This story is ideal for dramatization, offering children many animals to represent both through words and movement.

1. Indians of North America—Southern states—Legends.

398.2

Searcy, Margaret. *Race of Flitty Hummingbird and Flappy Crane*. Illus. by Lu Celia Wise. Portals Press (0-916620-21-2), 1980. 32p. Color illus. (Interest level: K-3).

Though this traditional southeastern Indian folktale is not unique to Alabama, the author is an Alabamian expert on Native American archeology and cultures of this region, and the illustrations of the birds Hummingbird and Crane encounter on their race to the sea are typical birds of Alabama: cardinal, bluebird, wood thrush. The verse, unfortunately, is somewhat strained, but this may be the only version of this tale in picture-book format.

♦ Students may compare this story to "The Tortoise and the Hare." The class can set up a hummingbird feeder and a feeder for seed-eating birds and compare flight patterns and other behaviors.

1. Indians of North America—Southern states—Legends.

398.2

Searcy, Margaret. *Tiny Bat and the Ball Game*. Illus. by Lu Celia Wise. Portals Press (0-916620-19-0), 1978. 50p. Color illus. (Interest level: K-3).

Tiny bat doesn't fit in when the sides are chosen for the big ball game; he is neither "animal" nor bird. This southeastern Indian legend teaches cooperation and that everyone, no matter how "different," has something to offer, while also showing through both text and pictures some of the ways people classify animals.

♦ Children can classify the animals depicted in the story in a variety of ways, showing that different teams could have been drawn up for the ball game.

1. Indians of North America—Southern states—Legends.

398.2

Solomon, Jack and **Solomon, Olivia**. *Ghosts and Goosebumps: Ghost Stories, Tall Tales, and Superstitions from Alabama*. University of Alabama Press, 1981 (out of print). 202p. (Interest level: 7+).

This brief narrative, collected in central Alabama, includes family stories of hauntings, well-known tales, such as "The Big Toe" and "Raw Head, Bloody Bones," and commonly told superstitions. The authentic speech of the storytellers is captured, reflecting variety in storytelling styles, with hand motions accompanying some of the stories.

♦ Students can collect superstitions and other sayings from members of their community, comparing them with those from central Alabama.

1. Folklore—Alabama 2. Superstition—Alabama.

398.2

Windham, Kathryn Tucker. *Jeffrey's Latest Thirteen: More Alabama Ghosts*. University of Alabama Press (0-8173-0380-4 pbk), 1987. 147p. B/W illus. (Interest level: 5+).

Windham's ghost stories are more than good tales; they provide a picture of the lives of nineteenth and twentieth century people from all across Alabama.

Windham retells the stories and provides background details in a conversational style, allowing readers to get to know folks like Granny Dollar of DeKalb County, who could not rest in her grave after thieves stole the money for her tombstone.

♦ Students can create hypotheses about naturalistic explanations for the occurrences cited, which include a photograph of Ms. Windham's personal poltergeist, Jeffrey.

1. Folklore—Alabama.

398.2
Windham, Kathryn Tucker and **Figh, Margaret Gillis**. *13 Alabama Ghosts and Jeffrey*. Illus. by Delores E. Atkins; photos by Laury A. Egan. University of Alabama Press (0-8173-0376-6 pbk), c1969, 1987. 120p. B/W photos. and illus. (Interest level: 5+).

These first 13 of Windham's ghost stories recall antebellum mansions and lifestyles, while the accompanying photographs of each house provide the actual setting. The author has skillfully woven legend and fact together into suspenseful, slightly wistful, but never sentimental stories of elegant homes and parties, lost loves, tortured souls, and unfulfilled dreams.

♦ Despite their fanciful nature, these are good stories for introducing children to Alabama geography, antebellum architecture, and pre- and post-Civil War history.

1. Folklore—Alabama.

553
Alabama's Ancient Treasures. (Video). Produced by ADECA and Alabama State Museum of Natural History, 1989. (Discovering Alabama Series). Order from the museum video recording. VHS, Color, (30 min.). $10.00. (Interest level: 7-9).

Alabama's wide range of mineral deposits are explored region by region, with the history and present methods of extracting, as well as the uses of the various minerals discussed and demonstrated. Although to some extent a promotional film, this is an excellent source for learning about Alabama's geography, geology, and industry.

♦ Both science and social studies classes can use the film as a supplement to text material.

1. Geology—Alabama 2. Mines and mineral resources—Alabama.

574.529
Alabama's Vanishing Ecosystems; A Project of Mary Moten's Fifth Grade Class, 1991-1992. (Chart). E.P.I.C. Elementary School, Birmingham School System, 1992. Available through Alabama Conservancy. Color Chart, 25" x 35". Includes companion guide, 28p. $10.00. (Interest level: 4-7).

Students in Ms. Moten's class developed this pictorial chart and accompanying study guide, which shows 36 different species of endangered animals, from the snail darter to the mountain lion. The chart and study guide give each animal's scientific classification, endangered status, and other data. The chart is both attractive and informative.

♦ Students can use this project as a model for discovering and documenting endangered species in their own states. Students can create a table showing the frequency of occurrence of the various environmental threats and the types of animals each threat affects.

1. Endangered species—Alabama.

582.13
Dean, Blanche E., **Mason, Amy**, and **Thomas, Joab L**. *Wildflowers of Alabama and Adjoining States*. University of Alabama Press (0-8173-0147-X pbk), c1973, 1983. 230p. Color photos.; Map. (Interest level:7+).

Aimed at the amateur naturalist, this book describes and illustrates with photographs 392 of the most common and interesting of Alabama's more than 3000 species of wildflowers. The descriptions are clear, with a minimum of technical terminology. The photographs are also useful, and some helpful charts show parts of flowers and define technical terms.

♦ This book is ideal for student field trips near Alabama schools or when going on a longer field trip to a historic Alabama site, such as Moundville State Park or Horseshoebend National Monument. Students in other states may study a state park or national monument in their area.

1. Wild flowers—Alabama. 2. Wild flowers—Southern states.

596
Wildlife Pamphlets. Alabama Department of Conservation and Natural Resources, Game and Fish Division, Wildlife Section. 15 pamphlets, 4p. each. B/W photos. Single copy free. (Interest level: 5+).

Each four-page pamphlet is devoted to a single species of mammal, bird, or reptile, providing description, general background, life history/reproduction cycle, food distribution, economic status, hunting (where applicable), food quality, and bibliography. The pamphlets are valuable because they discuss Alabama distributions of animals from the point of view of bird watchers, hunters, gardeners, and farmers, thus making the information personally meaningful.

♦ Students may use these pamphlets for research projects on specific species. A whole class could create an animal distribution map of Alabama.

1. Mammals—Alabama 2. Birds—Alabama 3. Reptiles—Alabama.

629.45
Alston, Edith. *Let's Visit a Space Camp*. Photos by Michael Plunkett. Troll (0-8167-1743-5 lib bind; 0-8167-1744-3 pbk), 1990. 32p. Color illus. (Interest level: 2-5).

The U.S. Space Camp at the Space and Rocket Center in Huntsville, Alabama, is described, with background information on rockets and Skylab, and on the training of astronauts. The pictures, as well as the descriptions, especially of the training in weightlessness, make this book an invitation for children to go to the Space Camp.

♦ An exciting account of the work of an astronaut, such as Michael Collins' *Flying to the Moon and Other Strange Places* (Farrar, Straus and Giroux, 1976), would make a good companion reader.

1. Space flight—Study and teaching 2. Space flight—Models.

629.45
Baird, Anne. *Space Camp: The Great Adventure for NASA Hopefuls*. Morrow (0-688010227-1), 1992. 48p. Color photos. (Interest level: 4-6).

This day-by-day account of the week at Space Camp in Huntsville, Alabama, describes the objectives and activities of the camp, explains the functions and missions of the historic space crafts and training devices, and discusses future technology. Readers are likely to catch the spirit of excitement of Space Camp as they read about the children's experiences, with the excellent close-ups and action photographs reinforcing the mood.

♦ Students can do further research on space technology, from Goddard's earliest rockets to those still in the planning stage.

1. Space flight—Study and teaching.

629.45
Bankson, Ross. "Space Camp" in *National Geographic World* (ISSN 0361-5499), March 1992. pp. 3-6. Color photos. (Interest level: 4-6).

What it is like at Space Camp, who can attend, and how to apply are all covered through quotes from youngsters who have attended the camp in Huntsville, Alabama. The children's enthusiasm for their experiences, through which they learn about the excitement of being an astronaut, as well as the need for knowledge and teamwork, is apparent from the quotations, as well as from the lively photographs.

♦ Children can build models of rockets, such as Saturn V and Apollo 16, and a space shuttle, such as the Pathfinder shown in the article.

1. Space flight—Study and teaching.

633
Carver, George Washington. *How to Grow the Peanut and 105 Ways of Preparing It for Human Consumption*. 7th ed. Experimental Station, Tuskegee Institute, 1940. (Originally published as Bulletin no. 31, June 1925). Available through the George Washington Carver Museum. 30p. (Interest level: 6+).

Carver provides 14 basic facts about peanuts, including nutritional information, instructions for growing and harvesting them, and 105 different recipes, literally from soup to nuts, using peanuts. This historic agricultural extension bulletin from Tuskegee Institute is more than a curiosity; both the background information and the recipes are still useful.

♦ After reading one of the many Carver biographies (*see* Alabama "Biography," below), students should try doing the recipes and have a peanut luncheon (party) similar to one served by Carver. (Have some alternatives for people with peanut allergies.)

1. Peanut 2. Peanut cookery.

641.59761
Durham, Katherine and **Rush, Susan**. *The Alabama Heritage Cookbook: A Complete Menu Cookbook*. Alabama Heritage Cookbook Publications (09612868-A-4; 09612868-0-6 spiral), 1984. 164p. Color photos. (Interest level: 6+).

Photographs and descriptions of 24 Antebellum and Reconstruction era houses are followed by recipes for complete meals served at the houses, including such specialties as Alabama deviled crab, fried catfish, fig cake, and mint juleps. The photographs are lovely, and the recipes are clear, explicit, and easy to follow.

♦ Besides trying to reproduce some of the recipes, students can "furnish" the dining rooms of each mansion, using cut-outs from magazines, or can write scenarios for a dinner party.

1. Cookery—Alabama 2. Historic buildings—Alabama.

641.59761
Gulf City Cook Book: Compiled by the Ladies of the St. Francis Street Methodist Episcopal Chuch, South Mobile, Alabama, 1878. Introduction by George H. Daniels. University of Alabama Press (0-8173-0508-4), 1990. 252p. B/W photos. (Interest level: 6+).

The introduction describes the history of ordinary people's cookery and domestic lives in nineteenth century Mobile; the recipes are arranged by food types, from fish and crabs, to catsup, sauces, and pickles. This fascinating look at cooking styles of the last century includes such intriguing recipes as terrapin au gratin, bird-pies, and "excellent" vinegar.

♦ Students can study recipes to compare then and now for culinary habits and use of ingredients, and can identify ingredients that are no longer available or are now usually bought ready-made. Students can try to follow recipes and note difficulties with directions.

1. Cookery—Alabama 2. Mobile (Ala)—History.

641.59761
Marshall, Lillian B. *Cooking Across the South: A Collection and Recollection of Favorite Regional Recipes*. Oxmoor House, Inc. (0-8487-0505-X), 1980. 272p. Color photos; B/W illus. (Interest level: 5+).

This modern cookbook is arranged by six basic types of foods, from soups to desserts. Each section begins with an introduction to the food type's historic treatment and a few representative recipes, such as pit-barbecued pig; modern recipes with amounts and complete instructions and yields follow. The appetizing color photos, wide margins, clean lay-out, clear instructions, and historic introductions make this a practical, as well as appealing, book, and a must for introducing southern regional cookery.

♦ Students can create recipes for a southern feast.

1. Cookery—Southern states.

759.1761
A Symphony of Color: The World of Kelly Fitzpatrick, 1888-1953. Montgomery Museum of Fine Arts, 1991. 71p. Color and B/W illus. (Interest level: 7-8).

The introduction to this exhibit catalog sets Alabama artist Kelly Fitzpatrick in historic perspective, showing Thomas Hart Benton's influence on Fitzpatrick's work as a painter, art professor, founder of the Dixie art colony in Mobile, and visual chronicler of Alabama's New Deal era. The text is readable, and the reproductions are of good quality, with the colors faithfully rendered.

♦ Students can contrast Fitzpatrick's visions of Alabama with those of photographer Walker Evans in

Let Us Now Praise Famous Men (Houghton Mifflin, 1941).

1. Fitzpatrick, Kelly, 1888-1953 2. Art—Alabama.

769.92

Breeskin, Adelyn Dohme. *Anne Goldthwaite: A Catalog Raisonne of the Graphic Works.* Montgomery Museum of Fine Arts, 1982. 141p. B/W photos. (Interest level: 6+).

The works of this late nineteenth/early twentieth century Montgomery painter/print maker are reproduced in this catalog, with the artist's memoirs of growing up in Montgomery included in the introduction. The memoirs are written in an easy, conversational tone, capturing the mood of an era now long gone.

♦ Children can examine life in early twentieth century Alabama for people from different walks of life by comparing Goldthwaite's comfortable life with that of David Avant's in *Like a Straight Pine Tree* (*see* page 8).

1. Goldthwaite, Anne, 1869-1944—Catalogs 2. Montgomery, (Ala)—Social life and customs.

781.62

Possum Up a Gum Stump: Home, Field and Commercial Recordings of Alabama Fiddlers Past and Present. (Recording). Brierfield Ironworks Park Foundation, 1988. Pamphlet of historical notes by Joyce Cauthen, 24p. 33 1/3 rpm, (46 min.). $13.00 plus $2.00 shipping and handling. (Interest level: 4+).

Historic recordings from the 1920s and 1930s have been re-recorded (not remastered) on side one, while modern fiddlers play on side two. People of any age would have trouble keeping from tapping their feet and dancing to this recording. The historical notes explain how Alabama's rural isolation made it a great fiddle playing state.

♦ Listening to the record while clapping, foot stomping, or dancing could be part of a country festival, complete with syrup soppin' and other foods; students could also create crafts for the festival after researching traditional crafts of the Southeast.

1. Folk music—Alabama.

781.6296

Music from the South. Volume 5. Song, Play, and Dance. (Sound recording). Recorded by Frederick Ramsey. Folkways Records (FA 2654), 1956. Order through Smithsonian Recordings. 1 sound disc, 33 1/3 rpm, (42 min.). $10.95. (Interest level: 7+).

When children joined some adults in Perry County, Alabama, for an evening of singing and dancing in 1954, Ramsey taped these lively old timey songs. Some are still sung today, such as "Asked my mother for fifty cents," while others, such as "Blind child" or a buck dance are now of greatest interest when trying to understand the historical development of the music of the South. The recording is clear, the lyrics understandable, and the mood lively.

♦ Students may compare the music in mood and expressiveness to the music and lyrics of rock or rap.

1. Folk music—Alabama.

781.6296

Music from the South. Volume 10. Been Here and Gone. (Sound recording). Recorded by Frederick Ramsey. Folkways Records (FA 2659), 1960. Order through Smithsonian Folkways Recordings. 1 sound disc, 33 1/3 rpm, (40 min.); Pamphlet, 32p. Illus. $10.95. (Interest level: 6+).

In this "musical survey," Ramsey attempted to convey the music and sounds of the rural South of the late 1950s, including bird songs, the mimicry of hunting sounds, and the roar of cars and a tractor in a nearby field. Train imitating pieces, such as "The Frisco" and various bands' renditions of "The Saints," make this a lively musical tour from Perry County, Alabama, to New Orleans.

♦ After listening for the songs and sounds recorded by Ramsey, students can predict which sounds have vanished since the time of the recording, and what new ones have taken their places.

1. Folk music—Alabama.

781.6296

Negro Folk Music of Alabama. Vol. VI. Ring Games Songs & Others. (Record). Recorded by Harold Courlander. Folkway Records, 1955. Available through the Smithsonian Folkways Library. 33 1/3 rpm, (40 min.). $10.95. (Interest level: 1+).

This is one of a series of authentic recordings from 1950s rural Alabama; it features children from several church and secular schools singing such old favorites as "Loop de Loo," "Charlie Over the Ocean," and "Green, Green, Rocky Road." The spirited singing would be a good resource for dance and movement, rather than quiet listening, because the words are not easy to understand.

♦ After obtaining the words to the songs, children can be taught the songs and games associated with them in an effort to preserve a fast disappearing tradition—children singing and playing.

1. Folk music—Alabama.

781.642

Alabama's Greatest Hits. (Sound recording). RCA (ALL1-7170RCA), 1986. 33 1/3 rpm, (24 min.). $10.95 (Interest level: 5+).

This recording includes some of Alabama's most popular songs, including "Forty Hour Work Week,"which honors the working man, and "Mountain Music," "Tennessee River," and "My Home's in Alabama," which talk about home and roots. The slightly defiant tone of "Forty Hour Work Week" and the nostalgia of "Tennessee River" and "My Home's in Alabama" make this an especially appropriate record for gaining an impression of modern-day Alabamians and their values.

♦ Students may compare Alabama with Hank Williams (*see* following entry) for lyrics and themes.

1. Alabama (Musical Group).

781.642

Hank Williams' Greatest Hits. (Sound recording). PolyGram Records (422-823291-4). Audiocassette, (37min., 52 sec.). $8.55. (Interest level: 5+).

Some of the 14 Hank Williams hits included on this cassette are: "Your Cheatin' Heart," "Jambalaya,"

"Hey Good Lookin'," and "Honky Tonkin'." This lively collection is representative of a past era, in which Alabama's greatest country singer made country music a nationally celebrated phenomenon.

♦ Comparing and contrasting Hank Williams' themes and style with those of country singers today may be a way to introduce children to changing societal values, especially in relations between men and women.

1. Williams, Hank 1923-1953 2. Country music.

781.642
Morris, Edward. *Alabama*. Contemporary Books (0-80902-5306-2), 1985. 109p. B/W and Color photos. (Interest level: 5+).

Morris portrays each member of the country music group Alabama separately and then presents their collective rise to success and their philosophy of life and of music. Analytical rather than adulatory in tone, the book connects Alabama's rise to success with social forces that changed popular culture in the United States during the 1970s and 1980s.

♦ Have the students discuss why people listen to Alabama, and predict whether their appeal will last.

1. Alabama (Musical group) 2. Country musicians—Alabama.

781.643
Louis Armstrong Plays W.C. Handy. (Sound recording). Columbia (CL591), c1954. 33 1/3 rpm, (56 min.). $8.95. (Interest level: 6+).

This recording contains some of Handy's most famous blues: "St. Louis Blues," "Memphis Blues," "Beale Street Blues," "Yellow Dog Blues," and "Atlanta Blues." Handy's southern origins are reflected in folk songs, such as "Careless Love," which he adapted for "Loveless Love," and in themes he incorporated into the blues—all of it magnificently sung by Louis Armstrong and Velma Middleton.

♦ Have students listen to Hank Williams (*see* page 5), who was influenced by the blues, and W.C. Handy (*see* page 13) for similarities and differences in themes and styles. Have students draw or paint scenes elicited by the lyrics and music.

1. Handy, W[illiam] C[hristopher] 1873-1958 2. Armstrong, Louis 1900-1971 3. Blues.

782.27
Birmingham Boys Sound Recording: Jubilee Gospel Quartets from Jefferson County, Alabama. (Sound recording). Alabama Traditions (Alabama Traditions 101), 1982. Contact Special Collections, W.S. Hoole Library. 33 1/3 rpm, (50 min.); Pamphlet, 20p. Illus. (Interest level: 5+).

African-American a cappella gospel quartets from Birmingham, whose fame had gone far beyond Alabama in the 1930s, were recorded in 1982: The Sterling Jubilee Singers, The Shelby County Big Four, The Delta-Aires, The Four Eagle Gospel Singers, and The Ensley Jubilee Singers. The harmonies are beautiful, and listeners are likely to enjoy hymns, such as "Low Down Chariot," "Go Where I Send Thee," and "Steal Away."

♦ This is a good record for learning about Birmingham and the population movement from the country to the city during the early part of this century.

1. Gospel music 2. Black musicians—Alabama.

782.27
White Spirituals from the Sacred Harp. (Sound recording). Recorded at the Alabama Sacred Harp Convention at Fyffe, AL, 1959. New World Recordings (CD 80205-0), 1977. 1 sound disc, CD, (46 min., 33 sec.). $15.99. (Interest level: 8+).

This historic recording of the Alabama Sacred Harp convention captures some of the best loved hymns of *The Sacred Harp* hymnal, as well as the personal testimonials and mood at the all-day Convention. Full of spiritual and vocal energy, the hymns, with their four-part harmony and powerful words, provide a moving experience for the listener.

♦ Reading about this tradition before listening to the record will allow students to better understand the importance of Sacred Harp music for the singers as a social event, as well as religious expression.

1. Hymns—Alabama.

782.27
Wiregrass Notes: Black Sacred Harp Singing from Southeast Alabama. (Sound recording). Alabama Traditions (Alabama Traditions 102), 1988. Audiocassette, (30 min.). Historical notes by Henry Willett, 15p. Photos. (Interest level: 8+).

An important religious-social tradition in Alabama, shaped note or sacred harp singing is here performed by an African-American group, a rarity among sacred harp singers. The recording is clearly a performance but a performance for members of the group, not an outside audience, with the genuine spirit of the occasion evident from the tape.

♦ Listening to both this tape and to *White Spirituals from the Sacred Harp* (*see* preceding entry) is valuable for experiencing a tradition that continues to be important in rural Alabama.

1. Hymns—Alabama.

782.2709
Every Time I Feel the Spirit. (Video). Produced by Dwight Cameron. University of Alabama, Center for Public Television (Alabama Experience #771-A), 1992. 1/2" video, Color, (28 min.). $29.00. (Interest level: 7+).

The life and music of famous African-American composer William Dawson is commemorated through performance of his arrangements of African-American spirituals by the Tuskegee University choir, and through discussion by Professor John Price of Tuskegee University. The choral performances, discussion, and reminiscences by Dawson's contemporaries place the composer's work in perspective with respect to both past and present African-American musical developments.

♦ Besides music appreciation and history classes, this tape can be used in conjunction with choral and other music classes, both as instruction and as inspiration.

1. Dawson, William Levi, 1899-1992 2. Spirituals (Songs) 3. Folk music—Alabama.

912.19761

State of Alabama. (Shaded relief map). U.S. Geological Survey, compiled 1964, 1970 edition. 1:500,000 (1"=8mi); 31 1/2" x 47." $4.00. (Interest level: 4+).

This map shows physical features, such as mountains, rivers, creeks, swampy areas, and lakes; political features, such as county lines and county seats; and cultural features, such as dams. In spite of the large amount of information it presents, this map is highly readable and useful for an overview of Alabama's terrain.

◆ Students can use it as a reference for creating their own raised maps.

1. Alabama—Maps.

912.19761

State of Alabama. (Topographical map). U.S. Geological Survey, compiled 1989. Contours on topographic edition modified from 1:500,000 State Base Map, 1966. 1:500,000 (1"=8mi); 30" x 47." $4.00. (Interest level: 4+).

Though certain political features, such as population and highway designations, are dated, much of this map is still reliable and useful. It shows counties, towns and cities, physical features down to the level of creeks, state parks, military reservations, wildlife areas, and elevations. The map is clear and readable, except for elevation contour lines, which are light.

◆ Besides identifying political and physical features, this map can be used in conjunction with the relief map (above) to learn about the use of contour lines in designating elevations.

1. Alabama—Maps.

917.l61 (Reference)

Foscue, Virginia. *Place Names in Alabama.* University of Alabama Press (0817-30410-X), 1989. 175p. Maps. (Interest level: 6+).

The bulk of the book consists of an alphabetical listing of place names: cities, towns, and streams, with locations by latitude and longitude, linguistic origin (Choctaw, Muskogee, Creek), name changes, and pronunciation given for each place. The historic introduction, explanation of research methodology, and the maps showing name changes all make this a valuable resource.

◆ Have students look up sources of the names of each of Alabama's major cities, rivers, and mountains and, if relevant, of the students' home town.

1. Names, Geographical—Alabama—Dictionaries 2. Alabama—History—Local.

917.6

Discovering Alabama: Natural Diversity. (Video). Produced by Alabama Museum of Natural History, 1991. VHS, Color, (30 min.). $22.00. (Interest level: 5+).

This overview of Alabama's diverse natural environments shows the state's wilderness regions, from the northern mountains to the Gulf of Mexico. The narrator's obvious love of the natural beauty of the state, and the photographer's equally loving views of rivers, forests, and marshes make for an enjoyable introduction to Alabama's geography. The other programs in this video series are most appropriate for

Alabama teachers; the series is broadcast on Alabama Public Television.

◆ Have students map each of Alabama's many great rivers from its source to its final destination, showing the changing environment along its banks.

1. Alabama—Description.

917.6

Official Alabama Highway Map, 1991-1992. State of Alabama Highway Department, 1991. Obtain free from Alabama Bureau of Tourism and Travel.

The highway map shows towns and cities from under 1000 residents, paved and unpaved roads, state parks, points of interest, rest areas, airports, public lakes, and universities. An index of cities and county seats and inserts of eight of the largest cities are also provided. The reverse side shows photographs of the state's significant scenic landmarks, the state seal, flag, etc., as well as traffic rules, a mileage chart, and a state parks and national forests chart. The information included is useful and the map is clean, readable, and attractive.

◆ Students can use the map to develop a plan for a "vacation" or for a schedule of Alabama high school football games.

1. Alabama—Maps.

917.6

Richardson, Jesse and **McGraw, E. L.** *Geography of Alabama: Her Land and People.* Viewpoint Publications, Inc., 1986. 119p. Maps; B/W photos. (Interest level: 4-8).

Divided into 16 chapters, this book covers surface features, weather and climate, water resources, soils, forests, population, agriculture, minerals, transportation, industries, major cities, and recreation in Alabama. This is a serious but accessible book for young readers; its many detailed maps and systematic treatment of each topic make it suitable as a reference work, although the data are 20 years old and population figures are, therefore, out of date.

◆ Students can use this book to expand on information gained from textbooks on Alabama, and to gain practice in reading maps.

1. Alabama—Geography.

917.61 (Reference)

Reed, William. *Indian Place Names in Alabama.* University of Alabama Press (0-8173-0230-1; 0-8173-0231-X pa), c1937, 1984. 107p. (Interest level: 7+).

The 231 entries in this dictionary give location and description of the place or the history of its name changes. The introduction covers Native American languages spoken in Alabama. Though scholarly, this is a highly readable resource; anyone living in the Southeast would find this a useful and fascinating guide.

◆ Students living in the Southeast can use this dictionary to derive the meanings of Indian place names in their area.

1. Indians of North America—Alabama—Names
2. Names, Geographical—Alabama—Dictionaries
3. Alabama—History—Local.

917.612
Estes, James [Buddy] L. *Alabama's Youngest Admirals*. J.L. Estes (0-9628-6340-8), 1991. 125p. B/W photos and illus. (Interest level: 4-9).

The author describes a raft trip he and five other teenage friends took down the Alabama River from Montgomery to Mobile during the summer of 1958. In plain language the author retells the boys' adventures, describes their personalities, and gives a good picture of life in the 1950s in Alabama—dancing to Elvis, keeping cool before air conditioning, telling scary stories, and hunting and fishing illegally without a license.
♦ Students can trace the boys' river trip and calculate how much it would cost today to build a raft and buy the provisions for such a trip.
1. Rafts 2. Alabama River (Ala.)—Description and travel.

973
Spirit of America with Charles Kurault; Part 6, Florida, Alabama, Mississippi. (Motion picture; Video). CBS News Production (71700), 1982. 16mm; VHS, (17 min.). $350.00 for 16mm; $25.00 for VHS. (Interest level: 7).

Kurault selects one significant aspect of each state and creates an essay around it; in Alabama, the focus is on Tuskegee University. Kurault's choices are thought-provoking vehicles for introducing the historic events or conditions that made us who we are today.
♦ Students can use Kurault's model to brainstorm ideas on aspects of their state's history that were significant or influential in defining the present.
1. Tuskegee University 2. Alabama—Higher education 3. Florida—History 4. Mississippi—History.

975.00497
Brown, Virginia Pounds and **Owens, Laurella**. *The World of the Southern Indians*. Illus. by Nathan H. Glick. Beechwood Books (0-9122211-00-3), 1983. 176p. B/W photos and illus; Maps. (Interest level: 4-9).

This thorough and systematic description of southern Native American tribes covers the Chocktaws, Chickasaws, Creeks, Cherokees, Seminoles, and smaller tribes; although each tribe is treated separately, distinctions and similarities between tribes are clearly shown. This account is both factual and compelling; the author expresses the hopes, sorrows, courage, and resignation of the past and the renewed tribal consciousness of the present .
♦ Students can listen to or read the folktales of these tribes and can discuss the commemoration of tribal customs and values in these tales. Have students look for poetry, speeches, and other writings of southeastern Indians of the past and present.
1. Indians of North America—Southern states 2. Creek Indians 3. Cherokee Indians 4. Chocktaw Indians 5. Chickasaw Indians 6. Seminole Indians.

975.00497
Mancini, Richard E. *Indians of the Southeast*. Facts-on-File (0-8160-2390-5), 1992. (The First Americans). 96p. Color and B/W photos. (Interest level: 4+).

The history, religion, work, play, warfare, and other aspects of the southeastern tribes' way of life in the past and today are described, with images provided by early European representations, nineteenth century paintings, and modern photographs. This book provides a good overview and balanced account, treating Native American history and culture with respect and without sentimentality.
♦ Students can do further research on specific tribes, such as those belonging to the Creeks and the Chickasaw, and on individuals, such as Nancy Ward, Alexander McGillivray, Menewah, and Sequoyah.
1. Indians of North America—Southern states.

976.1 (Reference)
Alabama County Data Book 1990-1991. Alabama Department of Economic Affairs, Planning and Economic Development. 95p. Annual. (Interest level: 6+).

Divided into 12 broad categories, such as Government, Education, and Transportation, this book contains data in 53 tables, 20 maps, and 3 directories. It offers such diverse facts as the average educational attainments of people in a given county, the distribution of lakes and wildlife, and the migration patterns of people in and out of each county. Small print and tabular format make this an adult reference work, which nevertheless can provide a wealth of up-to-date statistics and locations on different aspects of Alabama.
♦ Students can look for patterns of migration and hypothesize about the reasons behind them based on other data from the handbook.
1. Alabama—Handbooks, manuals, etc. 2. Alabama—Statistics.

976.1
Alabama Experience: Our Humanities Heritage. (Video). Written by Jerry Brown. Directed by Jerry Brown. Auburn Television, 1982. Color, 1/2", (30 min.). $9.00 (reproduction cost). (Interest level:8+).

A narrator introduces the history of Alabama through the arts as he goes to different sites and discusses different art forms from early to modern literature to folk music and art. A good overview, the video includes scenes from historic places and book illustrations, as well as singing, to enliven the narrative.
♦ Students can follow up any of the many writers and personalities mentioned, such as Zelda Fitzgerald, W.C. Handy, Walker Percy, and Booker T. Washington.
1. Alabama—History 2. Authors, Alabaman 3. Musicians, Alabaman.

976.1
Avant, D.A. *Like a Straight Pine Tree: Stories of Reconstruction in Alabama and Florida 1855-1971*. Illus. by David A. Avant, Jr. L'Avant Studios (0-914570-03-X), 1971. 124p. B/W illus. and photos. (Interest level: 7+).

Avant wrote this memoir for his children and grandchildren in order to preserve the memory of a way of life that has completely disappeared. Though a private story, the detailed description of life in rural Alabama is interesting, as the author describes such incidents as helping his father shear a lamb and watching his mother make his first woolen suit from the wool.

♦ Students can read different chapters and then create crafts and utilitarian objects based on the descriptions the author gives.
1. Alabama—History—1865-1898 2. Alabama—Social life and customs.

976.1 (Reference)
Clements, John. *Alabama Facts, More than an Almanac: A Comprehensive Look at Alabama Today County by County*. (Flying the Colors) Clements Research II, (1056-2168), 1991. 342p. Available through Title Books. B/W photos; Maps. $60.00. (Interest level: 4+).

This reference work begins with an introductory overview of Alabama's land, people, climate, economy, transportation, community services, and other aspects. The introduction is followed by county-by-county descriptions covering the same categories, a chronological description of each county's historical developments, and demographic tables taken from governmental sources based on 1990 Census projections. Comprehensive and informative, this work updates the now 30-year-old *Alabama Encyclopedia* (*see* page 9), though the latter is more discursive and is still useful for a closer description of the histories of each county.
♦ Students can use this volume to obtain current facts about Alabama.
1. Alabama—Handbooks, manuals, etc.

976.1
Fradin, Dennis. *Alabama: In Words and Pictures*. Children's Press, (0-526-03901-6), 1980. (Young People's Stories of Our States). 48p. (Interest level: 2-4).

The first half of this book tells the story of Alabama from 9000 B.C. to the George C. Marshall Space Flight Center at Huntsville, Alabama, emphasizing Alabama's unique role in the larger events in U.S. history. The second half of the book is mostly a travelogue featuring famous landmarks and sites of the state. Though the author overuses the passive voice, this book is a good survey of the state of Alabama, providing sufficient names and events for further research.
♦ Children can create a travel guide for Alabama using pictures from postcards, travel brochures and magazines, and background information from this book and others.
1. Alabama—History 2. Alabama—Description.

976.1 (Reference)
Richardson, Jesse M. *Alabama Encyclopedia*. Alabama Southern Publishing., 1965. 1051p. Available through Title Books. Maps. $9.95. (Interest level: 4+).

The *Encyclopedia* contains the state constitution; a description of state history and geography county by county; the state flag, bird, holidays, etc.; agriculture; cities; forests and forest products; mineral deposits; water and water development; industry; business; and natural environment. It also prints the complete text of Julia Tutwiler's 1873 poem "Alabama," which was later adopted as the state song. Although dated, this work is still the most thorough and accessible resource on each county for school age children.
♦ Class discussions can cover such topics as how to evaluate information sources for accuracy and cur-

rency, and what the conscientious researcher can do to supplement dated resources.
1. Alabama—History—Dictionaries 2. Alabama—Geography—Dictionaries.

976.1
Stewart, John Craig. *The Governors of Alabama*. Pelican Publishing. (0-88289-067-0), 1975. 232p. B/W photos. (Interest level: 7+).

The first governor mentioned is Chief Tuscaloosa, who fought de Soto in 1541; the last is George Wallace. Information is given about each governor's birth, education, and political career as these facts bore on the larger contemporary issues of politics and government. This is a highly readable account of the major shifts in governance of the region that has been Alabama since 1819.
♦ Students can select governors and write "newspaper" accounts as if written during the governor's era. Students can research the missing recent governors since Wallace and write similar biographies; this book offers a good opportunity for discussing biography and political science research techniques.
1. Alabama—Governors—Biography.

976.1
Thompson, Kathleen. *Alabama*. Raintree (0-86514-451-3 lib bind; 0-86514-536-9 pbk), 1988. (Portrait of America). 48p. Color and B/W photos. (Interest level: 4-6).

The strength of this brief introduction to the economic and cultural history of the state, and to its people today, lies in its focus on individuals, such as Booker T. Whatley, professor of agriculture at Tuskegee University; Kathryn Tucker Windham, representative of the many great storytellers of this state; and Dr. Charles Bugg, medical researcher at the University of Alabama's renowned medical center.
♦ Students can brainstorm about selecting representative citizens of their state to interview and write about.
1. Alabama—Description.

976.1
Windham, Kathryn Tucker. *Alabama: One Big Front Porch*. University of Alabama (0-8173-0526-9 pbk), 1991. 158p. B/W photos and illus. (Interest level: 5+).

Windham takes the reader on a rambling journey from Mobile to the Tennessee River, recounting historical events, such as the visit by General Lafayette to the state's first capital at Cahaba, the meteor that fell through Mrs. Hodes' roof in 1954, and the legendary adventures of Railroad Bill. These entertaining tidbits add up to an impression of the lives of Alabamians (rich and poor, though mostly white).
♦ Students can research local legends and stories to create a many layered history of their own town or neighborhood.
1. Folklore, Alabama 2. Alabama—History.

976.1004
Discovering Alabama: Mound State Monument. (Video). Alabama Museum of Natural History, 1991. VHS, Color, (30 min.). $22.00. (Interest level: 5+).

Viewers learn about the history of these Native American mounds and about the goals and techniques of modern archeologists who work there to discover more about the everyday lives of the mound builders. The nature photography and the visuals of Indian vases, pots, and homes, as well as the interviews and monologues by scientists, make this a useful extension to the books children find on mound-building technology.

♦ Have the students create a classroom mural of Moundsville and the surrounding countryside, including the Black Warrior River and the forests.

1. Mounds and Mound builders 2. Indians of North America—Southern states.

976.1004
First Frontier. (Motion picture; Video). Auburn Television, 1986. 16mm; VHS. Includes viewer's guide. (60 min.). $595.00 for 16mm; $195.00 for VHS. (Interest level: 7+).

This award-winning video begins with the passage of de Soto through what is today Alabama and ends with the Indian removal from the Southeast, following Andrew Jackson's victory at Horseshoe Bend, Alabama. Dramatic reenactments are based on historical evidence, with the help of the Mississippi Band of Choctaw Indians, the Poarch Band of Creek Indians, anthropologists, and historians.

♦ Students can trace de Soto's route on maps, as well as the paths of epidemics, and the spread of technology, from the use of guns to the use of European tools and other goods.

1. Indians of North America—History 2. Creek Indians—History 3. Cherokee Indians—History 4. de Soto, Hernando, 1500?-1542.

976.1004
Holland, James W. *Andrew Jackson and the Creek War: Victory at the Horseshoe*. University of Alabama (0-8173-5101-9), c1968, 1990. Order from Horseshoe Bend National Military Park. 46p. B/W illus. and photos. (Interest level: 6+).

The political background and the events of the "Forgotten War" of 1813-1814, characterized as "a war to punish the Indians, a war among the Indians, and a war within the War of 1812," are described in a straightforward style, which, though aimed at an adult audience, presupposes a minimum of background knowledge. Contemporary portraits of Andrew Jackson and Chief Menewa, scenes from the Massacre at Fort Mims and the Battle of Horseshoe Bend, and a map of the battle from Jackson's report are included.

♦ Students can compare the lives of the Creeks, Cherokee, Chocktaw, and Chickasaw in Alabama and in Oklahoma, where they were forced to resettle. They can start by comparing place names.

1. Jackson, Andrew, 1767-1845 2. Creek Indians—History 3. Indians of North America—Wars.

976.1004
Lost in Time. (Motion picture; Video). Auburn Television, 1983. 16mm; VHS. Includes viewer's guide. (30 min. and 60 min. versions). $385.00/$595.00 for 16mm; $125.00/$195.00 for VHS. (Interest level: 4-7 for 30 min. version; 8+ for 60 min. version).

From 12,000 B.C. to the arrival of de Soto in 1540, *Lost in Time*, an award-winning video, shows prehistoric Native American life in the Southeast. This live action reenactment is combined with explanations of the archeologist's methods to provide insight into the changing environment and consequent lifestyles of Paleo hunters and Mississippian Mound Builders.

♦ Students can simulate the methodology of the archeologist, pretending they are future scientists, by studying "an archeological site," such as a waste paper basket or a city dump, from which they can reconstruct a culture.

1. Indians of North America—Antiquities 2. Stone age 3. Mounds and Mound builders.

976.1004
Wimberly, Christine Adcock. *Exploring Prehistoric Alabama Through Archeology*. Explorer Books (0-9605938-1-0), 1980. Available from Mound State Monument. 96p. Maps; Color illus.; B/W and Color photos. Includes teachers' guide, 23p. (Interest level: 4+).

Wimberly introduces both the science of archeology as it has been pursued in discovering prehistoric Native American cultures in Alabama, and the cultures themselves through text, informative cartoons, paintings of Native American life as imagined by researchers, and photographs of artifacts, archeologists at work, and archeological sites. This work is an excellent combination of information, humor, challenging questions, and creative ideas for further exploration, and can be used with fourth graders, as well as ninth graders.

♦ The author provides numerous valuable suggestions for further activities at the end of each chapter and in the *Teacher's Guide*.

1. Archeology 2. Indians of North American—Alabama—Antiquities.

976.1'45
Miller, Marilyn. *The Bridge at Selma*. Silver Burdette (0-382-06326-2; 0-382-06973 pbk), 1985. (Turning Point in American History Series). 64p. (Interest level: 4-8).

This journalistic account brings alive the facts and emotional tensions of the 1965 voting rights march from Selma to Montgomery. Archival photographs from UPI and other newspaper sources, a copy of President Johnson's speech urging passage of the Voting Rights Act, and inserts explaining background facts, should help young readers visualize the events and gain an appreciation for the people who dedicated themselves to the goal of achieving voting rights for African-American people.

♦ Have students look for newspaper accounts (on microfiche) of the events preceding, during, and following the march.

1. Protests, demonstrations, etc.—Selma (Ala.) 2. Blacks—Civil rights 3. Civil rights—History.

976.1'47
Siegel, Beatrice. *The Year They Walked: Rosa Parks and the Montgomery Bus Boycott*. Four Winds Press (0-02-782631-1), 1992. 103p. B/W photos. (Interest level: 5-8).

Rosa Parks didn't know that her individual act of courage would set in motion the Civil Rights Movement. In this lively account, Siegel focuses on Parks' and other Civil Rights workers' feelings and actions during the Montgomery Bus Boycott, using quotes, photographs, and newspaper headlines gathered from the State Archives in Montgomery.

♦ Have students compare this account to Rosa Parks' own account in *Rosa Parks: My Story*, (*see* page 16).

1. Parks, Rosa, 1913- 2. Blacks—Civil rights 3. Civil rights—History.

976.1'47

Stein, Conrad. *The Story of the Montgomery Bus Boycott*. Illus. by Nathan Greene. Children's Press, 1986 (out of print). 31p. Color and B/W illus. (Interest level: 3-5).

"My feet are tired, but my soul is at rest" is but one of several well chosen quotes from people involved in the Montgomery Bus Boycott of 1955 to be found in this brief but compelling account. Although few names are mentioned besides those of Rosa Parks, Martin Luther King, Jr., and E.D. Nixon, the initial organizer of the boycott, this book places the boycott in the larger context of the Civil Rights Movement.

♦ Students can write suggestions on how they could get to school if they could not use the school bus, or their own families' cars.

1. Protests, demonstrations, etc.—Montgomery (Ala.) 2. Blacks—Civil rights 3. Civil rights—History.

Biography

920

Alabama Women of History: Courage, Compassion, Conviction. (Poster) Sponsored by Alabama Women's Commission, 1992. 22" x 34"; B/W photos on blue background. $5.00. (Interest level: 4+).

The 16 women whose portraits are reproduced have contributed to the people of Alabama through their leadership in governmment (Dixie Bibb Graves, Hallie Farmer), education (Margaret Murray Washington, Julia Tutwiler), the law (Annie Lola Price, Maud McClure Kelly), nursing, the arts, and humanitarian work. The photographs are clear and distinct, contrasting well with their blue background, while the captions are informative.

♦ Small groups of students can further explore the lives of each of these women through magazine sources (*see Alabama Heritage*, page 19).

1. Women—Alabama—Biography.

920

Alabama Women's Hall of Fame: Installation. (Program notes). Bowling Library. Judson College, annual. 3-4p. each. (Interest level: 5+).

A one-page biographical sketch, which emphasizes the achievements of the woman honored, is included in the program notes for the annual installation of one to three of Alabama's outstanding women philanthropists, educators, government leaders, etc. This may be a unique resource for many of the less known women who have contributed to Alabama public life in the last 150 years.

♦ These brief biographies are a natural for women's studies, and, when taken together, they reveal that contributions can also be viewed as a reflection of concerns and issues of importance in the state throughout its history.

1. Women—Alabama—Biography.

92 Aaron, Henry

Haskins, James. *Babe Ruth and Hank Aaron: The Home Run Kings*. Lothrop, Lee and Shepard, (0-688-41654-3) 1974. 124p. B/W photos. (Interest level: 4-7).

This parallel biography of the two great sluggers starts with their early childhoods (Aaron's in Mobile, Alabama), through their years in baseball, ending with a chapter on their respective baseball records. Haskins presents each man's career, as well as anecdotes illustrating facets of their lives and personalities: the most memorable licking Hank ever got from his protective mother or the time he befriended a new Dominican rookie on the Braves team.

♦ Students comparisons of backgrounds and records through lists, charts, and tables are naturals for this book.

1. Ruth, George Herman 1895-1948 2. Aaron, Henry 1934- 3. Baseball.

92 Black, Hugo

Cooper, Richard. *Hugo Black*. Creative Productions (0-89136-064-6), 1987. 48p. Color illus.; B/W photos. (Interest level: 4-6).

The Supreme Court justice's life is described, focusing on the forces and ideas that shaped him while growing up in Ashland, Alabama, and on his beginning law practice in Birmingham. Though the language is simple, the author's style and information on African-American roles in fighting for social justice make this book interesting reading.

♦ Students can write a campaign speech for Hugo Black's senate race, based on information in the book.

1. Black, Hugo, 1886-1971 2. United States—Supreme Court—Biography.

92 Capote, Truman

Moates, Marianne. *A Bridge to Childhood: Truman Capote's Southern Years*. Henry Holt (0-8050-0971-X), 1989. 240p. B/W photos. (Interest level: 8+).

This highly readable adult biography should appeal to students who have read *A Christmas Memory* (*see* page 17) or *The Thanksgiving Visitor* (*see* page 17), as the reader now gets to meet the rest of the family, as well as Capote's childhood friend Harper Lee, the author of *To Kill a Mockingbird* (*see* page 18). This is a fascinating look at the backgrounds of these two famous Alabamans.

♦ After students read *A Christmas Memory*, *The Thanksgiving Visitor*, or *To Kill a Mockingbird*, they can compare the novelists' versions with the versions of these stories as told by relatives and friends.

1. Capote, Truman, 1924-1984 2. Lee, Harper, 1926- 3. Authors, American—Biography 4. Monroeville (Ala)—Social life and customs.

92 Carver, George Washington
Adair, Gene. *George Washington Carver: Botanist.*
Chelsea House (1-55546-577-3), (0-7010-0234-9
pbk), 1989. B/W photos. (Interest level: 7+).

One of the best among many children's books about
Carver, this is a serious, objective account of Carver's
entire life, presenting all aspects of his work while
evaluating its importance for science and the farmers
of Alabama. Adair avoids sentimentality, not hiding
Carver's weaknesses, yet shows the many reasons
Carver was both loved personally and admired as a folk
hero.
♦ After reading this and other accounts of Carver's
  life, students can create dramatizations of specific
  aspects of his life, paying close attention to the social
  context of each episode.
1. Carver, George Washington, 1864-1943 2. Scientists
3. Blacks—Biography.

92 Carver, George Washington
Aliki. *A Weed Is a Flower: The Life of George Wash-*
ington Carver. Simon and Schuster (0-671-66118-3),
c1965, 1985. 32p. Color illus. (Interest level: K-3).

This biography depicts the life of George Washington Carver through simple but effective words and
beautiful water color illustrations. Still one of the finest
biographies for the intended age group, the author/il-
lustrator conveys both Carver's life and contributions.
♦ Students can hold a peanut and sweet potato party,
  using each food in many ways, from boiled peanuts
  to roasted sweet potatoes.
1. Carver, George W., 1864-1943 2. Scientists
3. Blacks—Biography.

92 Carver, George Washington
George Washington Carver. (Motion Picture). Kaw
Valley Films, 1984. 16mm; VHS; Color, (29 min.).
$550.00 for 16mm; $385.00 for VHS. (Interest level:
5-8).

This narrative of the life of Carver illustrates his life
through excellent photography and an occasional direct quote from his own memoirs. A bit too adulatory
in tone, the film accurately conveys Carver's spiritual
nature, as well as his scientific/educational activities.
♦ Use this film as a follow-up after students have read
  a good biography or two of Carver, as well as
  portions of his own words, as recorded in Gary
  Kremer's, *George Washington Carver in His Own*
  Words (University of Missouri Press, 1987).
1. Carver, George W., 1864-1943 2. Scientists
3. Blacks—Biography.

92 Carver, George Washington
Gray, James Marion. *George Washington Carver.*
Silver Burdette (0-382-09964-7; 0-382-09969-0 pbk),
1991. 138p. B/W photos. (Interest level: 5-8).

Similar in tone and organization to Adair's biography of Carver (*see* preceding entry), this book covers
Carver's entire life and work. Gray uses somewhat
simpler vocabulary and sentence structure than Adair,
and includes quotes from Carver to illustrate his point
of view on specific events and people, making this
book more readable for younger students and more
personal.

♦ Students may compare Gray's account to more
  dramatized versions, such as Arna Bontemps's *Story*
  of George Washington Carver (Grosset & Dunlop,
  1954)
1. Carver, George Washington, 1864-1943 2. Scientists
3. Blacks—Biography.

92 Carver, George Washington
McKissack, Patricia and **McKissack, Fredrick**.
George Washington Carver: The Peanut Scientist.
Enslow (0-8949-0308-X), 1991. 32p. B/W photos and
illus. (Interest level: 2-4).

Carver's life from birth to death, with greatest
emphasis on his scientific and agricultural contributions at Tuskegee Institute in Alabama, is described.
Although meant to be read by transitional readers, the
book has a varied style. Detail is limited, but the book
provides facts about Carver while conveying his spirit.
♦ The class can grow sweet potatoes and herbs in
  hanging baskets, reinforcing Carver's message to
  teach children the joy of growing plants, especially
  edible ones.
1. Carver, George Washington, 1864-1943 2. Scientists
3. Blacks—Biography.

92 Carver, Geroge Washington
Moore, Eva. *The Story of George Washington Carver.*
Scholastic (0-590-42660-5 pbk), 1971. 96p. (Interest
level: 3-5).

Moore's straightforward narrative includes most of
the highlights of Carver's life and manages to convey
some of his joyful creativity and philosophy of service
to God and people. Greater emphasis is placed on
Carver's early life than on his work at Tuskegee Institute, but sufficient information is given to show the
significance of his work for the agrarian South.
♦ Children can compare this version with Teresa Rogers' *George Washington Carver: Nature's Trail-*
  blazer (*see* following entry).
1. Carver, George Washington, 1864-1943 2. Scientists
3. Blacks—Biography.

92 Carver, George Washington
Rogers, Teresa. *George Washington Carver: Nature's*
Trailblazer. Illus. by Antonio Castro. Twenty-First
Century Books (0-80502115-9), 1992. (Earth Keep-
ers). 72p. B/W illus. (Interest level: 3-6).

In keeping with the series title, this biography focuses on Carver's role as an agriculturalist close to
nature and "the man furthest down the line." The
narrative is lively, and the background information
about the problems of land degradation due to poor
agricultural practices is valuable.
♦ Students can experiment with the effect of compost-
  ing on soil friability or with different soils, including
  clay, as growing media.
1. Carver, George Washington, 1864-1943 2. Scientists
3. Blacks—Biography.

92 Gorgas, William Crawford
Epstein, Beryl Williams and **Epstein, Samuel**. *Wil-*
liam Crawford Gorgas: Tropic Fever Fighter. Messner, 1953 (out of print). 184p. (Interest level: 5-8).

Gorgas, an army doctor from Alabama who helped
rid Havana, Panama, and, by extension, the South of

yellow fever, is the subject of this suspenseful biography. The authors present a very human, even lovable picture of the doctor in a well-researched, slightly fictionalized biography that is fast paced and interesting reading and is informative about the social, political, and scientific issues surrounding Gorgas' life.

♦ Students may hypothesize how people today would deal with a resurgence of the yellow fever-carrying mosquito.

1. Gorgas, William Crawford, 1854-1920 2. Physicians—Biography.

92 Handy, W.C.
Cooper, Richard. *W.C. Handy: Doctor of the Blues*. Creative Productions (0-89136-065-4), 1987. (Famous Alabamians). 47p. Illus. (Interest level: 3-6).

This brief but involving biography, based on Handy's autobiography, presents his life and work from his earliest days in Florence, Alabama, to his success as the first composer to use the African-American musical idiom of the blues. Though sketchy, the book is nevertheless successful in conveying both Handy's contribution to American music and life and the times in which he lived.

♦ Students can listen to "Memphis Blues" on *Louis Armstrong Plays W.C. Handy* before or after reading the biography, and sing "Camptown Ladies Sing this Song," which is incorporated into this piece. They can also read "My Daddy Plays the Blues" in Eloise Greenfield's *Nathaniel Talking* (Black Butterfly, 1988) and, using the instructions in the back, learn the beat of the blues.

1. Handy, William Christopher (1873-1958) 2. Musicians, American 3. African-American musicians.

92 Handy, W.C.
Handy, W[illiam] C[hristopher]. *Father of the Blues: An Autobiography*. Edited by Arna Bontemps. Da Capo, (0-306-76241-2; 0-306-80421-2 pbk), 1985. 317p. B/W photos. (Interest level: 8+).

Handy describes his life and the musical influences on his work, starting with his strict upbringing in Florence, Alabama, where school singing and sneaked cornet lessons were his chief sources of music, through his peregrinations throughout the South as a musician, ethnomusicologist, and composer. This engrossing account sheds light on life in Alabama and the South during the late nineteenth and early twentieth centuries.

♦ Students may listen to *Louis Armstrong Plays W.C. Handy*. Compare the lyrics and music of the blues with those of rap for content, tone, and rhythm.

1. Handy, William Christopher (1873-1958) 2. Musicians, American 3. African-American musicians.

92 Jackson, Bo
Jackson, Bo and **Schaap, Dick**. *Bo Knows Bo*. Jove Books (0-515-10741-7 pbk), 1990. 279p. B/W photos. (Interest level: 8+).

This candid autobiography gives insight into Bo's early childhood, including his tough and rough life without a father, his changing attitudes about life and sports, his career as a two-sport athlete and professional, and his goals and ideals for himself and his family. The frank discussions of sex and the occasional use of swear words do not overshadow his idealism,

warmth, and conscious effort to become a positive role model for other young people.

♦ After reading the biography, students can discuss turning points in Bo's life and the reasons for his successes.

1. Jackson, Vincent Edward (Bo), 1962- 2. Football 3. Black athletes.

92 Jackson, Bo
Raber, Thomas R. *Bo Jackson Pro Sports Superstar*. Lerner (0-8225-0487-1), 1990. 64p. B/W photos. (Interest level: 4-6).

This book focuses on Bo's professional career as a baseball and football player, with just one chapter devoted to his childhood, high school, and college days. The style is simple but readable, and though the author emphasizes Bo's sports career, he includes quotes by Bo about his personal goals and values, such as doing charity work, that make this book more than a catalog of scores and plays.

♦ The statistical charts at the end of the book can give students an opportunity to practice graphing Bo's averages over several years.

1. Jackson, Vincent Edward (Bo), 1962- 2. Football 3. Black athletes.

92 Jackson, Bo
White, Ellen Emerson. *Bo Jackson: Playing the Games*. Scholastic (0-590-44075-6 pbk), 1990. 86p. Color photos. (Interest level: 5-8).

The focus of this biography is Bo Jackson's career as an athlete, with most emphasis placed on his professional career rather than high school and college experiences. Generally, White uses a light, lively, conversational style: "He had achieved one of the rarest levels of celebrity: instant recognition on a first name basis. People know Madonna, and Cher, and Magic, and—Bo."

♦ Students may use recent newspapers and magazines to research the athlete's career and practice statistics using his baseball scores.

1. Jackson, Vincent Edward (Bo), 1962- 2. Football 3. Black athletes.

92 Julian, Percy
Haines, Gail Kay. "The Brown Bean Mystery" in *Micromysteries: Stories of Scientific Detection*. Putnam and Sons (0-399-61270-X), 1988. pp 96-107. B/W photos and illus. (Interest level: 5-8).

Percy Julian's career and his discovery of synthetic glaucoma medicine is described. The focus is on Julian's attempts to obtain an education, first in his native Alabama, then at northern universities, where he still had to fight prejudice, and on his scientific work and successes.

♦ This article, along with "Percy L. Julian: Soybean Chemist" in *American Black Scientists and Inventors*, edited by Edward S. Jenkins (NSTA, 1975); and James Haskins' "Health and Safety: Percy Julian and Garrett Morgan" in *Outward Dreams* (*see* following entry), is a good source for what could be a focus on scientists' biographies from different regions of the United States.

1. Julian, Percy, (1898-1975) 2. Scientists 3. Blacks—Biography.

92 Julian, Percy

Haskins, James. "Health and Safety: Percy Julian and Garrett Morgan" in *Outward Dreams: Black Inventors and Their Inventions*. Walker (0-827-6993-4), 1991 pp. 72-79. (Interest level: 4-7).

Haskins gives a brief biographical background about this chemist from Alabama, then focuses on the scientist's life work of developing cortisone and many other synthetic medications and the significance of his discoveries. Though brief, the information is readable and clearly presented and fills a need for a biographical sketch of this important chemist, of whom so little has been written for children.

♦ Students can research (interview grandparents and others) about life before cortisone—how people coped with arthritis.

1. Julian, Percy, (1898-1975) 2. Scientists 3. Blacks—Biography.

92 Keller, Helen

Adler, David A. *A Picture Book of Helen Keller*. Illus. by John and Alexandra Wallner. Holiday House (0-8234-0881-3), 1990. 32p. Color illus. (Interest level: K-3).

The text supplies the essential points about Helen Keller's whole life, but the illustrations fill in the details that make her life real for the book's young readers. The illustrations provide the setting and show the warmth of the human touch as Helen goes through life giving and receiving love.

♦ Children can explore the five senses, then focus on touch, taste, and smell alone to discover what the world is like without the benefit of sight and hearing.

1. Keller, Helen, 1880-1968 2. Blind 3. Deaf 4. Physically handicapped.

92 Keller, Helen

Kudlinski, Kathleen. *Helen Keller: A Light for the Blind*. Illus. by Donna Diamond. Viking Kestrel (0-670-82460-7), 1989. (Women of Our Time). 58p. B/W illus. (Interest level: 3-6).

Helen Keller emerges as a real person through vivid descriptions of what she felt and how she expressed herself. This is a beautiful book to read or read aloud; details include how Keller imagined colors: green as young plants; purple as strong, deep feelings; and yellow as joy and sweet warm sunlight.

♦ Children can list and discuss the many ways and diverse people for whom Helen Keller brought hope, joy, and lasting help, and can write about ways in which they might contribute to make others' lives better now and contribute through future careers.

1. Keller, Helen, 1880-1968 2. Blind 3. Deaf 4. Physically handicapped.

92 Keller, Helen

Sabin, Francene. *The Courage of Helen Keller*. Illus. by Jean Meyer. Troll (0-89375-754-3 cloth; 0-89375-755-1 pbk), 1982. 48p. B/W illus. (Interest level: 1-3).

The author captures Keller's struggle to learn to communicate and portrays her as courageous and tireless in bringing hope and help to the blind everywhere. Though slightly fictionalized, with a few inaccuracies, this is a lively account of Keller's life, well suited to reading aloud.

♦ Students can discuss ways in which they can make it easier for other children with handicaps to participate in class and play.

1. Keller, Helen, 1880-1968 2. Blind 3. Deaf 4. Physically Handicapped.

92 Keller, Helen

Tames, Richard. *Helen Keller*. Watts (0-531-10764-7), 1989. (Lifetimes). 32p. B/W photos. (Interest level: 4-7).

Helen Keller is presented, through photographs, quotations, narratives, and informative inserts, as a productive member of twentieth-century society, who touched many lives and whose work resulted in lasting improvements for the blind, for instance in stimulating the creation of Social Security legislation aiding the blind.

♦ Taking a historical perspective, students can explore the events of the twentieth century through the experiences of diverse groups, including the disabled.

1. Keller, Helen, 1880-1968 2. Blind 3. Deaf 4. Physically handicapped.

92 Keller, Helen

Wepman, Dennis. *Helen Keller: Humanitarian*. Chelsea House (0-7910-0417-1), 1987. (American Women of Achievement). 111p. B/W photos. (Interest level: 5-8).

Among the plethora of books on Helen Keller, this stands out in its thoroughness and unsentimental, yet moving presentation of Keller's life. Frequent quotations from Keller, Annie Sullivan's letters, and the many supporters and admirers of both, along with numerous excellent photographs, provide a vivid, multifaceted portrait.

♦ To stimulate awareness, students can explore the building or classroom for the many obstacles and hazards it offers for the blind. Students can try reading and writing their names in Braille, based on the alphabet provided in the book.

1. Keller, Helen, 1880-1968 2. Blind 3. Deaf 4. Physically handicapped.

92 King, Coretta Scott

Henry, Sondra and **Taitz, Emily**. *Coretta Scott King: Keeper of the Dream*. Enslow (0-89490-334-9), 1992. (Contemporary Women Series). 128p. B/W photos. (Interest level: 5-8).

The authors present Coretta King as a strong and determined person, from her early childhood in Perry County, Alabama, through her life as partner of Martin Luther King, Jr., and mother to their four children, and finally in her work for peace and justice for all people. Appropriate photos highlight this honest presentation which shows Coretta King's strengths, but does not hide the problems in her life.

♦ Students should obtain literature about the Martin Luther King, Jr. Center for Non-Violent Change and

discuss ways that its teachings can be followed in everyday life.
1. King, Coretta Scott 1927- 2. Civil rights—history 3. Blacks—Civil rights.

92 King, Martin Luther, Jr.
Great Americans—Martin Luther King, Jr. (Motion picture). Encyclopedia Britannica Films (Order #3576), 1982. 16mm; VHS; B/W (17 min.). $615.00 for film; $300.00 for video. (Interest level: 6-8).

This film introduces young people to Martin Luther King, Jr., and the era between 1955 and 1968, with original footage showing Dr. King and civil rights actions in Montgomery, Birmingham, and Selma, Alabama, and Augusta, Georgia; interspersed with commentary by U.S. Ambassador to the U. N., Andrew Young, as well as by Coretta Scott King and President Emeritus of Moorhouse College, Benjamin E. Mays. The narration, the footage, and the commentary add up to a balanced picture with issues clearly defined; this is one of the best sources on this topic for young people.
♦ Students will find this film is excellent for preceding discussions of the Civil Rights Movement.
1. King, Martin Luther, Jr., 1929-1968 2. Civil rights—History 3. Blacks—Civil rights.

92 King, Martin Luther, Jr.
Martin Luther King: From Montgomery to Memphis. (Motion picture). Phoenix/BFA Films (Order #70314), 1969. 16mm; VHS; B/W (25 min.). $400.00 for 16mm; $190.00 for VHS. (Interest level: 7+).

Through original footage, this film follows the Civil Rights Movement from the bus boycott of 1956 in Montgomery and Martin Luther King's emergence as leader to his assasination in Memphis. King's philosophy of nonviolent resistance is shown through the many film clips of sit-ins, demonstrations, arrests, and speeches, including "I Have a Dream." These film clips show, as no dramatized reenactment can, the depth of commitment and high seriousness of the protestors.
♦ A discussion of the changes that have been brought about by the sacrifices of the people who protested in order to gain civil rights, as well as those areas that still need work, should follow viewing.
1. King, Martin Luther, Jr., 1929-1968 2. Civil rights—History 3. Blacks—Civil rights.

92 Louis, Joe
Jakoubek, Robert. *Joe Louis.* Chelsea House (1555-46-599-4; 07910-0244 pbk), 1990. 127p. B/W photos. (Interest level: 5-9).

This biography describes both Joe Louis (Barrow)'s career and the social milieu in which he lived, first as one of eight in a sharecropping family in Lafayette and Camp Hill, Alabama, then as a young man in Detroit. Besides learning about Louis, readers can gain insight into the migration of southern African Americans to the northern cities, the role Louis played in breaking the color barrier in professional sports, and the political events of the Depression and World War II that impinged on Louis' life.
♦ Students may discuss the lives of various great athletes comparing their achievements and sources

of success, or lack of it, beyond their years as athletes.
1. Louis, Joe 1914-1981 2. Boxers (Sports) 3. Black athletes.

92 Mays, Willie
Grabowski, John. *Willie Mays.* Chelsea House (0-7910-1183-6; 0-7910-1217-4 pbk), 1990. 64p. (Baseball Legends). B/W photos. (Interest level: 4-8).

A baseball lover's biography, this book briefly describes Willie Mays' background as a youngster in Birmingham, Alabama, where he started his baseball career on the mill team for which his father played. But the primary focuses is on Mays' adult career, and the many games in which he starred. Though much of the book is devoted to baseball statistics, Mays as a person does emerge through accounts of the reactions of others to him and through his own words.
♦ Students may compare biographies of Hank Aaron and Babe Ruth with this book for a study in what it takes to be a star.
1. Mays, Willie, 1931- 2. Baseball 3. Black athletes.

92 Mays, Willie
Sabin, Louis. *Willie Mays, Young Superstar.* Illus. by John R. Jones. Troll (0-8167-1775-3 lib bind; 0-8167-1776-1 pbk), 1990. 48p. B/W illus.(Interest level: 2-4).

This biography shows Mays' early life, emphasizing his father's role in his early training and showing a little of the conditions of work and play in Depression-era Alabama. The tone of this biography is warm, focusing on the human factors, such as family support, enthusiasm, and hard work, along with superior ability, that made it possible for Mays to be the great and popular baseball player he was.
♦ Children can write about a game or other activity at which they work hard to excel.
1. Mays, Willie, 1931- 2. Baseball 3. Black athletes.

92 Owens, Jesse
Gentry, Tony. *Jesse Owens.* Chelsea House (1-55546-603-6; 0-7910-0247-0 pbk), 1990. 110p. B/W photos. (Interest level: 5-8).

Owens' life is presented sympathetically, showing his meteoric climb from a sickly boy, newly arrived in Cleveland, to the world's fastest runner, through his uneven career trying to find meaningful work for the rest of his life. The author provides a balanced picture, showing both the glory and the pathos of Owens' life.
♦ Students may view *The Jesse Owens Story.* Discussion of the political issues affecting Owens, from the 1936 to the 1968 Olympics, would be useful in helping students understand how a hero can also be a victim of the political agendas of others.
1. Owens, Jesse, 1913-1980 2. Runners 3. Black athletes.

92 Parks, Rosa
Celsi, Teresa. *Rosa Parks and the Montgomery Bus Boycott.* The Millbrook Press (1-878841-14-9), 1991. Color and B/W photos. (Interest level: 4-6).

The focus is on Rosa Parks' life as a civil rights worker, from early childhood to the Democratic convention of 1988, with informative inserts that provide background on the Ku Klux Klan, the Freedom Train of the 1940s, segregation, and the concept of boycotts. The high-interest, easy-reading text is both informative and interesting, and the photographs provide good portraits of Parks and other civil rights workers.

♦ Students can write reports about Parks and others who, by taking a stand, have made a difference.

1. Parks, Rosa, 1913- 2. Civil rights—History 3. Blacks—Civil rights.

92 Parks, Rosa
Greenfield, Eloise. *Rosa Parks.* Illus. by Eric Marlow. Crowell (8-690-7120-3; 0-690-71211-7), 1973. 32p. B/W illus with a touch of color. (Interest level: 2-4).

Rosa Parks' childhood near Tuskegee and in Montgomery, Alabama, and the fears and indignities she suffered through segregation are shown, as are the specific circumstances of the Montgomery Bus Boycott. Accurate and readable, this biography gives enough background for young children to understand the historical events without overwhelming them with too many details.

♦ Children can select one incident from Rosa Parks' life and create a script for a short dramatized scene.

1. Parks, Rosa, 1913- 2. Civil rights—History 3. Blacks—Civil rights.

92 Parks, Rosa
Parks, Rosa, with Haskins, James. *Rosa Parks: My Story.* Dial (0-8037-0673-1), 1992. 192p. B/W Photos. (Interest level: 4-6).

Rosa Parks begins with her early childhood, interweaves family stories with descriptions of an African-American child's life in Alabama during the 1920s and 1930s, then describes her early activism as a young woman, the Montgomery boycott, and her subsequent move to Detroit. This is an engaging narrative; accounts of her fears and her defiance of racists as a child and of whites who treated her like a "regular" person help to make Parks real.

♦ Students can read other accounts of the Montgomery Bus Boycott and test them against Parks' self report, especially with respect to Parks' personal motivation.

1. Parks, Rosa, 1913- 2. Civil rights—History 3. Blacks—Civil rights.

92 Soto, Hernando de
Zadra, Dan. *De Soto: Explorer of the Southeast (1500-1542).* Illus. by Harold Henriksen. Creative Education (0-88682-185-1), 1988. 32p. Color illus. (Interest level: 2-4)

From his early conquests in Peru, the book traces de Soto's routes in search of gold, showing his quest from Florida to the Mississippi and the battle of Maubila in Alabama, where the Chocktaws and Chief Tuskaloosa nearly stopped him. De Soto is presented as ambitious, greedy, and ruthless in this bare-bones account that is aided by charcoal and watercolor illustrations.

♦ Students may trace de Soto's route on a world map, a United States map, and a map of the Southeast.

1. Soto, Hernando de, ca. 1500-1542 2. Explorers.

92 Tuskaloosa, Chocktaw Chief
Geist, Maggie. *Chief Tuskaloosa: The Dream of a Young Chief.* Illus. by Chris Ballard. Portals Press (0-916620-89-1), 1988. 31p. B/W illus. (Interest level: 2-4).

The life of Chief Tuskaloosa is described in a somewhat fictionalized manner, though the factual information closely follows other sources. The author's descriptions of customs and historic events make this a good resource for younger children.

♦ Students can trace de Soto's route and that of Tuskaloosa, as described in this book, for a geography lesson. They can also read Zadra's *De Soto: Explorer of the Southeast* (*see* preceding entry).

1. Tuskaloosa (Chief) 1500?-1540 2. Indians of North America—Alabama—Antiquities.

92 Tutwiler, Julia
Cooper, Richard. *Julia Tutwiler: Teacher, Leader.* Creative Productions (0-89136-069-7), 1987. (Famous Alabamians). 48p. Color illus.; B/W photos. (Interest level: 4-6).

A pioneer in educational and social reform, Julia Tutwiler is presented in eight easy, yet lively, chapters. Though brief, the narrative gives a good idea of Tutwiler's passion for improving education for women and prison conditions for all in post-Civil War Alabama. The book ends with her 1873 poem "Alabama," which was adopted as the state song in 1931.

♦ Students can compare Tutwiler's life with those of Jane Addams and Dorothea Dix.

1. Tutwiler, Julia, 1841-1962 2. Educators—Alabama 3. Reformers—Alabama.

92 Washington, Booker T.
Booker. (Motion picture). Walt Disney Educational Media Co., 1984. 16mm, Color; (40 min.). $250.00. (Interest level: 5-8).

A dramatized version of Booker T. Washington's early life, this film follows the incidents described in *Up from Slavery* (*see* following entry), Washington's autobiography, fairly closely. Though the film includes some purely fictional scenes, which stand out by their implausibility, its spirit is close to the facts and tone of the book, and the acting is convincing.

♦ Students may compare the film version with Booker T. Washington's own description of the events.

1. Washington, Booker T. 1858?-1915 2. Blacks—Biography.

92 Washington, Booker T.
Washington, Booker T. *Up from Slavery: An Autobiography.* Penguin, (0-141-039051-0 pbk), c1901, 1986. 181p. (Interest level: 7+).

Washington's highly readable autobiography continues to provide valuable insight into the lives of African Americans during the post-Civil War era, the early years of Tuskegee Institute, and life at the turn of the century in Alabama. His philosophy of advancement for African Americans is expounded throughout the book, giving students an opportunity to see how ideas on this subject have changed over the years.

♦ Students can compare Washington's and W.E.B. Du Bois' approaches to race relations and the improvement of conditions for African-Americans.
1. Washington, Booker T., 1858?-1915 2. Blacks—Biography.

Fiction

Brown, Mary Ward. *Tongues of Flame*. Washington Square Press (0-671-1064157-3 pbk), 1987. (Interest level: 7-8+; Professional).

A winner of the Hemingway Award for Best Fiction, Brown's short stories are more about character than place, and they are about people Alabamians recognize, from the revival preacher brought in to rekindle the spirit of a small country church, to the retired judge whose children have no time to share in his joy over an amaryllis he has grown. The stories have a homey, familiar feel and taken together, give a good picture of the hopes and hurts, the private and public lives of Alabamians from various walks of life.
♦ Several of the stories should be accessible to students in seventh and eighth grade.
1. Alabama—Fiction.

Brown, Virginia Pounds. *The Gold Disc of Coosa*. Illus. by Neil Wilson. Strode Publishers, 1975 (out of print). 121p. (Interest level: 4-7).

Utina, the 16-year-old son of a Native American chief at the time of de Soto's invasion, is captured by de Soto, but manages to join forces with Chief Tuscaloosa, in Maubila (in what is now Alabama) to try to thwart de Soto's plans. This suspenseful story is also historically accurate and attempts to look at the meeting between de Soto and the Indians from the Indians' point of view.
♦ Students may read about Chief Tuscaloosa and about de Soto from other sources (*see* Alabama "Biography," above).
1. Mounds and Mound builders—Fiction 2. Indians of North America—Fiction 3. Tuskaloosa (Chief).

Capote, Truman. *A Christmas Memory*. Illus. by Beth Peck. Knopf (0-679-80040-9), 1989. 48p. Book and Cassette (0-394-82500-4). (Interest level: 4+).

Though written for an adult audience, this reminiscence of a warm friendship and simple pleasures shared between the author and an elderly cousin could make a good read-aloud. Rural Alabama of the early 1930s is brought to life as the reader follows the young Capote's and his cousin's preparations for Christmas.
♦ Younger children can describe an adult friend or relative with whom they share a special relationship. Older children can read Marianne Moates' *A Bridge to Childhood: Truman Capote's Southern Years* (*see* page 11), in which the author describes how Capote's relatives reacted to the book.
1. Capote, Truman, 1924-1984—Fiction 2. Christmas—Alabama—Fiction.

Capote, Truman. *The Thanksgiving Visitor*. Random (0-394-44824), 1968. 63p. (Interest level: 4+).

Young Buddy, his shy elderly cousin, and the school bully are described in this novelette about one memorable Thanksgiving in Monroeville, Alabama, during the Depression. Though written for an adult audience, the conflict between Odd Henderson, the poor but proud bully, and Buddy is likely to involve young readers.
♦ Students may collect family recipes for Thanksgiving to share with the class and try them out during a fall harvest festival.
1. Capote, Truman 1824-1984—Fiction 2. Thanksgiving—Alabama—Fiction.

Carcache, Marian M. and **Greenleaf, Robert B**. *Under the Arbor*. (Video). Auburn Television, 1992. VHS, Color, (120 min.). Approx. $30.00. For exact price and ordering information inquire from Dr. Robert Greenleaf, Department of Music, Goodwin Music Hall, Auburn University, AL 36849. (Interest level: 8+; Professional).

Greenleaf's opera, based on Carcache's short story, is set in a small Alabama town on the Chattahoochee River in the 1940s, where 14-year-old Hallie Jernigen dreams of growing up to be a movie star and discovers that her distant cousin Bobby Lee, who too has dreams, is not a little boy. This is a delightful comic opera, painting a tableau of growing up in a small town, complete with scenes at Sunday School and dinner on the grounds, and a subplot about Annie and Duck, two African-American friends of Hallie.
♦ Scenes between Hallie and Bobby; Duck's play-acting at being Madam Queen, the local fortune teller; and the Sunday school and picnic should be especially appealing to students.
1. Opera—Alabama.

Childress, Mark. *Joshua and Bigtooth*. Illus. by Rick Meyerowitz. Little, Brown (0-316-14011-2), 1992. 32p. Color illus. (Interest level: Preschool-2).

Fishing one day on the Magnolia River in south Alabama, Joshua befriends a baby alligator with the sweetest smile. This lighthearted fantasy is a tall tale, which granny used to tell, come to life in modern bayou country, amid cypresses, log cabins, and a modern school house.
♦ Children can identify trees, birds, and flowers of the region from the illustrations; children can retell other stories told by grandparents, putting them in modern settings.
1. Alligators—Fiction 2. Alabama—Fiction.

Davis, Ossie. *Just Like Martin*. Simon & Schuster, (0-671-73202-1), 1992. 215p. (Interest level: 5+).

Set in Birmingham during the days of the 1963 bombing of the Sixteenth Street Baptist Church, this is both historical fiction and a rite-of-passage book. Davis focuses on one young boy, Isaac Stone, who must balance his love for his war veteran, anti-nonviolence movement father and the ideals of Dr. Martin Luther King, Jr. This is a fast-paced novel using lively, authentic dialogue with believable characterizations, such as that of idealistic but quick-tempered Reverend Cable.
♦ Newspaper and other accounts of the Sixteenth Street Church bombing will help students sort out fiction and fact. Listening to the "I Have a Dream" speech in Dr. King's own voice will help students understand both the content and the emotion of the

speech that helped Isaac begin and the community carry on after the bombings.
1. Civil rights—History—Fiction 2. Blacks—Civil rights—Fiction.

Flagg, Fannie. *Fried Green Tomatoes at the Whistlestop Cafe*. McGraw-Hill (0-07-021257-0 pbk), 1988. 403p. (Interest level: 8+; Professional).

Set at a whistle stop near Birmingham during the 1920s through 1940s, the adventures, loves, and sorrows of Idgie Threadgood and Ruth Jameson and their friends are depicted and contrasted with those of Evelyn Couch who in 1985 learns about the old times from Mrs. Threadgood and learns wisdom from her and her stories. A moving, happy-sad story, this is also a great way to gain a vivid impression of life in a small Alabama town and the Birmingham of the past.
♦ Teachers might want to assign the book to more mature students, or read aloud portions to their classes. The film version, though not as good, has excellent characterization and would be more appropriate for class.
1. Alabama—Fiction.

Gibbons, Faye. *King's Shoes and Clown Pockets*. Morrow (0-688-06592-9), 1989. 231p. (Interest level: 5-7).

When Raymond Brock and his family move to a trailer park in Alabama, Raymond feels lonely for his old home until he makes friends with another loner, tough-acting Bruce Manis, the neglected son of the local junk dealer. The themes of friendship and family ties, believable characters, adventurous plot, and vivid setting make this more than a regional book, although it provides a good picture of life in modern small-town Alabama.
♦ Students can project how Bruce will face the same problems he had been trying to run away from now that he is staying.
1. Friendship—Fiction 2. Alabama—Fiction.

Lee, Harper. *To Kill a Mockingbird*. Warner Books (0-446-31078-6), c1960, 1982. 284p. (Interest level: 8+).

Set in south Alabama of the 1930s, this is a story of prejudice and complacency born of narrowness of vision, and about the courage to stand alone. Atticus Finch, a small-town lawyer, defends Tom Robinson, the African-American man falsely accused of raping and beating Mayella Ewell, who herself is a victim of abuse by her father. Though the setting, speech, and manners depicted evoke a small southern town of the 1930s, the theme is universal and the characters recognizable.
♦ Students may view the film after reading the book and discuss in what ways the filmmakers conveyed some of the symbolism through visual images rather than words.
1. Prejudice—Fiction 2. Alabama—Fiction.

Milton, Hilary. *Mayday, Mayday*. Watts, 1979 (out of print). 152p. (Interest level: 4-7).

After two families crash in a small airplane on a mountainside with an abandoned iron mine near Birmingham, two of the children manage to clamber down the mountain in the January night to get help, fighting off wild dogs and crossing icy streams. This suspenseful story introduces children to the rugged hill country near Birmingham.
♦ Students can map the airplane's route and probable crash site. One caution: the author changed Shelby County to Shelton County; the rest of the names are accurate.
1. Aeronautics—Accidents—Fiction 2. Survival—Fiction.

Ready to be a Wise Man. (Motion Picture). Written and directed by Robert Clem. Dill Productions. Direct Cinema, distributor (1-55974-115-5), 1988. 16mm; VHS; Color, (30 min.). $535.00 for 16mm; $250.00 for VHS. (Interest level: 4-7).

David, the young son of a minister, stands up for his values, even against the influential members of the church who, in this small southern town in the 1950s, find the idea of a black Wise Man intolerable. Themes of courage, stereotyping, and the violent climate of the 1950s are developed in a sensitive and believable portrayal of David, his friend, an African-American janitor, and the "red neck" who comes to their aid.
♦ Students can look for other acts of courage, small and great, in literature and in the news.
1. Race relations.

Searcy, Margaret Zehmer. *The Charm of the Bear Claw Necklace*. Illus. by Hazel Bough. Pelican (0-88289-777-2), c1981, 1990. 67p. B/W illus. (Interest level: 3-6).

It is spring, and a small band of prehistoric Southeast Indians must find food, recover two of their hunters' souls from the bear they had mortally wounded, and resolve young Mink's conflict with her family over the man they chose for her husband versus the man she loves, an enemy of the tribe. The plot, which focuses on 12-year-old Redwolf's, his sister's, and his cousins' attempt to help the band survive, is exciting and carefully interweaves adventure and authentic details about prehistoric hunter-gatherer life in the Southeast.
♦ Students can reenact the story, as there are quite a few specific characters named. Students can identify, collect, and use as part of the scenery the various plants mentioned in the book..
1. Stone age—Fiction 2. Indians of North America—Antiquities—Fiction 3. Indians of North America—Southern states—Fiction.

Searcy, Margaret Zehmer. *Ikwa of the Mound Builder Indians*. Pelican, (088289-762-4; 0-88289-742-X pbk), 1989. 80p. B/W photos. (Interest level:3-5).

Ikwa, age 11, wavers between being a little girl and a responsible young woman, well versed in sacred, as well as domestic knowledge, about to be married to a young man from a neighboring village. Readers can learn much about the everyday lives and beliefs of the Mound Builder Indians through a believable plot, photographs of modern Cherokees at work, life-size tableaux of Mound Builders, and sketches made by de Soto's men.

♦ The story lends itself to dramatization and reconstruction of Mound Builder Indian homes, pottery, and baskets.

1. Mounds and Mound Builders—Fiction 2. Indians of North America—Antiquities—Fiction.

Searcy, Margaret Zehmer. *Wolf Dog of the Woodland Indians*. Illus. by Hazel Brough. Pelican (0-88289-778-0 pbk), 1991. 112p. B/W illus. (Interest level: 3-6).

Cub, a Copena Indian boy, tries to save his pet wolf dog who is too dangerous to keep in the village. Set in Alabama of 2000 years ago, this suspenseful story is based on archeological finds and the author's imagination, providing authentic details of Woodland culture.

♦ Children can develop a play or build a detailed Copena Indian village based on facts and incidents from the book.

1. Copena Indians—Fiction 2. Indians of North America—Antiquities—Fiction 3. Stone Age—Fiction.

Thacker, Nola. *Summer Stories*. Lippincott (0-396-32288-7 lib bind); Scholastic (0-590-42191-3 pbk), 1987. 150p. (Interest level: 3-7).

Ten-year-old Red visits her cousins on the Gulf Coast for the summer. Good characterizations and a well-crafted episodic plot allow readers to experience a typical Gulf Coast small-town setting, including family life and activities, such as fishing, attending church, picking blackberries, and listening to tall tales.

♦ Children can write about summer activities in other regions of the U.S., comparing and contrasting them with those described for southern Alabama.

1. Vacations—Fiction 2. Alabama—Social life and customs—Fiction.

Windham, Katherine T. *My Name is Julia*. Birmingham Public Library (0-942310-18-8), 1991. 39p. B/W photos. (Interest level: 6+).

Written as a monologue for an impersonator of the famous Alabama reformer and educator Julia Tutwiler, the script has Tutwiler reminiscing, at age 70, about her life and accomplishments. Windham creates a believable character, including such personal touches as having Ms. Tutwiler check that she has not lost yet another bonnet, and using language likely to have been used by her.

♦ Several students in the class might interpret different portions of the monologue. It can also be used as a model for creative writing based on other biographies.

1. Tutwiler, Julia, 1841-1962 2. Educators—Alabama 3. Reformers—Alabama.

Periodicals

508.761
Nature South: The Magazine of the Alabama Natural History Society. Alabama Museum of Natural History, University of Alabama. 1990- Quarterly. Color photos. $18.00/yr. (Interest level: 6+).

Each issue of this small (seven-page) magazine is devoted to a different topic, including topics, such as a

biographical sketch of Sequoia, who spent much of his adult life in what is now Alabama; Alabama archeological sites; dinosaurs in Alabama; and cave exploration in Alabama. Color photographs of good quality make this both an interesting and aesthetically pleasing magazine, and an excellent resource.

♦ Students may use this publication to explore specific Alabama nature topics.

1. Nature study—Periodicals 2. Archeology—Periodicals.

976.1
Alabama Heritage. Alabama Heritage, University of Alabama (0887-493-X), Quarterly. Color and B/W photos. $5.00/issue. (Interest level: 7+).

Topics included in this sumptuous magazine are history, biography, natural science, art, and architecture, with a recent issue featuring articles on the "Creek Prophetic Movement," the Cattle Egret, Tidewater-type cottages in Alabama, and a biographical sketch of Julia Tutwiler, the nineteenth/twentieth century educator and reformer from Alabama. Each article is lively and informative, illustrated lavishly with contemporary photographs, sketches, and documents.

♦ Because of the varied topics covered in depth by the journal, this is an excellent resource for students to gain greater insight into specific topics related to the Southeast.

1. Alabama—History—Periodicals 2. Alabama—Natural history—Periodicals.

Professional Materials

305.5
Flynt, J. Wayne. *Poor But Proud: Alabama's Poor Whites*. University of Alabama Press (0-8173-0424-x), 469p. B/W photos. (Interest level: Professional).

In this social and economic history of Alabama, the author presents the point of view of a large segment of the state's population, the striving working poor, whose culture and outlook on social and political issues have helped shape contemporary Alabama's politics. A highly readable book, this is a pleasure to read for any layperson, but a must for anyone trying to understand the Alabama of the past and of the present.

♦ A companion and contrasting reading might be *Let Us Now Praise Famous Men*, written by James Agee and photographed by Walker Evans (Houghton Mifflin, 1941).

1. Alabama—Rural conditions 2. Alabama—History 3. Alabama—Politics and government.

306.489
Martin, Stephen H., ed. *Alabama Folklife: Collected Essays*. Alabama Folklife Association, 1989. 70p. B/W photos. (Interest level: Professional).

Nine essays introduce the history of folklore research and collecting in Alabama, three forms of traditional crafts (quilt making, pottery, and basket making), and five forms of performing arts, including fiddling, Sacred Harp, and gospel quartet singing. The value of this work is in providing a historic context to each of these art forms, showing how each fits into the utilitarian, social, aesthetic, and spiritual lives of the people who created and used them, and in connecting the conditions peculiar to Alabama to American history in general.

♦ Older students can be introduced to the various folk crafts and productions, with field trips and other research planned to learn about the existence of similar activities locally.

1. Folk art—Alabama 2. Folk music—Alabama.

323.1

Eyes on the Prize: America's Civil Rights Years. Episode 1: Awakenings (1954-56) and Episode 5: Bridge to Freedom (1965). (Video). Public Broadcasting Service (1-55851-198-2; 1-55951-203-2), 1986. VHS, Color (60 min each). $59.95 each. (Interest level: Professional).

Interviews, discussions, and reenactments of scenes from the civil rights era alternate in presenting the sequence of events in the fight for social and political equality. The focus in these two emotion-laden episodes is on Alabama—Montgomery Boycott, 1955-56 and the March from Selma to Montgomery, 1965.

♦ Young teachers, who have not lived through the era, can gain a clearer picture of the movement, while all viewers can see the whole movement with greater clarity, and can select specific segments to use in class.

1. Blacks—Civil rights 2. Civil rights—History.

331.8

Work in Alabama. (Video). Produced by University of Alabama at Birmingham. Center for Labor Education and Research, 1980. VHS, B/W, (35 min.). Inquire directly for price. (Interest level: Professional).

Based on original photographs of workers in Alabama's mines, factories, and fields, this video traces the vicissitudes of the history of organized labor in Alabama from its weak beginnings in the 1830s through its highs during the New Deal era, its lows after the two world wars, to the 1970s. Told from the point of view of organized labor, this is a highly informative video about an important aspect of the state's history.

♦ Segments, though not the whole film, would be worth showing to classes studying Alabama and American history.

1. Labor—Alabama 2. Labor unions—Alabama.

363.61

Tennessee Valley Authority. *Catalog of Water Quality Educational Materials*. Tennessee Valley Authority, Water Quality Department, 1991. 40p. (Interest level: Professional).

This is an annotated list of free or low cost TVA and non-TVA pamphlets, brochures, curriculum materials, and posters, complete with ordering information. The value of this catalog is in the variety of materials listed, from the history of TVA to specific topics, such as "Protecting a Homeowner's Well Supply," "Wetlands Wildlife," "Homemade Sampling Equipment," "Teacher/Student Water Quality Monitoring Network," and "How Topographic Maps are Made."

♦ Students can select specific aspects of water quality monitoring and research.

1. Water supply—Catalogs 2. Water—Purification—Catalogs.

371

Where We Once Stood: The Lincoln School. (Video). Produced by Dwight Cameron and University of Alabama Center for Public Television, 1989. VHS, Color (58 min., 45 sec.). $25.00. (Interest level: Professional).

The history of Lincoln School in Perry County, Alabama, which produced a remarkable number of African Americans of high achievement, is retold by narrator Julian Bond and by its graduates and former teachers and ministers, including Coretta Scott King and Andrew Young. Informative and inspiring, this film reveals an aspect of African-American life that is little publicized today, the striving of many Alabama African Americans to gain an education for their children as a way to a better future.

♦ While too long for classroom use, teachers could use segments when teaching Alabama history and African-American history.

1. Blacks—History—Alabama 2. Blacks—Education—Alabama.

745

Outsider Artists in Alabama: Catalogue. Project of the Alabama State Council of the Arts, 1991. 56p. Color and B/W photos. (Interest level: Professional).

The works of visionary folk artists of Alabama are celebrated with two essays, one-page biographies of each artist, and photographs of their works. The book is an excellent introduction to one facet of Alabama culture; the essays, biographical sketches, and most of all the photographs of art works bring to life the spiritual and emotional lives of many varied people.

♦ Teachers, who are likely to become enthusiastic about the works, will want to share the art with their students and will want to encourage them in creative modes of self-expression.

1. Folk art—Alabama.

759.1761

New South, New Deal and Beyond: An Exhibition of New Deal Era Art, 1933-1943. Alabama Artists Gallery, 1990. 36p. Order from Alabama State Council on the Arts. Color and B/W photos. (Interest level: Professional).

An essay on the New Deal era in Alabama by historian Virginia Van der Veer Hamilton and an essay on the New South School and Gallery introduce this exhibition catalog, which features the art of five social realist artists whose works depicted the lives of the poor during the Depression. The catalog includes good reproductions and puts the work of these artists in the context of the social and cultural conditions of the times.

♦ The catalog can be used as a resource in both art history and social studies.

1. Art—Alabaman 2. Alabama—History—1933-1945.

976.1
Brown, Jerry Elijah, ed. *Clearings in the Thicket: An Alabama Humanities Reader: Essays and Stories from the 1983 Alabama History and Heritage Festival.* Mercer University Press (0-86554-144-2), 1983. B/W photos. (Interest level: Professional).

Well-known Alabama scholars contributed articles on the state's history and literature; articles are about the First Creek War, early travellers' accounts, a modern humorist's writings, the modern humanistic African-American heritage, and the legacy of being a Baptist minister. James Haskins, noted children's author, contributed an article that should be of special interest to teachers who are familiar with his many excellent biographies of African Americans.

1. Alabama—History 2. Alabama—Literature 3. Alabama—Fiction.

Arkansas

by Carolyn Brodie

Nonfiction

305.4

Jacoway, Elizabeth. *Behold, Our Works Were Good: A Handbook of Arkansas Women's History*. Arkansas Women's History Institute/August House (No ISBN), 1988. 98p. B/W photos. (Interest level: 6+).

This handbook provides an introduction to the history of Arkansas women, a bibliography on sources important in Arkansas women's history, and a guide to an exhibit of the same name. It includes important descriptions of the work of the Arkansas Women's History Institute; a documented historical overview of women of Arkansas; an interesting oral history of an older woman, Bethal May; and a valuable study guide for teachers and students.

♦ Students may interview women in their area who are perceived as leaders in their community or students may be interested in reading women's biographies.
1. Women—Arkansas—History 2. Women—Arkansas—Social conditions.

333.7

Arkansas Historical Association. *Arkansas Forests*. Rose Publishing, 1985. (12 min. each). $39.95 (Interest level: 5+).

This set (two filmstrips, one audiocassette) discusses the major forestry sections of the state and includes an overview of the environmental issues related to the preservation of forests.

♦ Students may locate books about trees for more information and write concrete poetry in the shape of trees or leaves.
1. Forests and forestry 2. Arkansas.

333.7

Arkansas Natural Heritage Commission. *Arkansas' Natural World*. Rose Publishing. (16 min. each). $39.95 (Interest level: 5+).

This set (two filmstrips, one audiocassette) explains the importance of preserving natural areas by using a collection of color photographs featuring Arkansas' natural resources. This source will prompt discussion of the Arkansas environment.

♦ Students may make a list of things they can do to help the environment, especially concentrating on ways to help preserve natural resources.
1. Natural areas 2. Arkansas.

398.2

Cumming, William, arranger. *The Arkansas Traveller and Rackinsac Waltz*. Arkansas Territorial Restoration Foundation (No ISBN), n.d. B/W illus. (Interest level: 3+).

This arrangement for the piano, from the music originally published in 1847, also includes an arrangement for the "Rackinsac Waltz." This reproduced version is published and for sale only by the Arkansas Territorial Restoration Foundation.

♦ After sharing Liz Smith Parkhurst's *The Arkansas Traveller: Adapted for Today's Readers* (see page 23), students may enjoy hearing "The Arkansas Traveller" played on the piano and possibly adding words to the music.
1. Piano music, Arranged 2. Waltzes (Piano).

398.2

Harris, Aurand. *The Arkansaw Bear*. Anchorage Press. (0-87602-226-3), 1980. 38p. (Interest level: 5+).

Somewhere in Arkansas, a young girl named Tish tries to cope with her grandfather's impending death with the help of a star and imaginary members of a circus. This serious yet sensitive play makes a reassuring statement about death.

♦ Parts may be assigned for the play and either read aloud in class or performed as a production.
1. Tall tales—Arkansas 2. Arkansas.

398.2

Lankford, George E. *Native American Legends, Southeastern Legends: Tales from the Natchez, Caddo, Biloxi, Chickasaw, and Other Nations*. (American Folklore Series). August House (0-87483-038-9), 1987. 265p. (Interest level: 7+).

Written by an eminent scholar of Native American culture, this collection includes some 131 legends, from creation myths to adventure sagas. The volume is enhanced by maps, illustrations, and discussions of the cultures that generated the legends.

◆ Students may be interested in selecting specific legends from this volume and learning more about the cultures that kept them alive through oral traditions.
1. Indians of North America—Southern States—Legends 2. Indians of North America—Legends.

398.2
Masterson, James R. *Arkansas Folklore: The Arkansas Traveler, Davy Crockett and Other Legends*. Rose Publishing (0-914546-04-X), 1974. 443p. (Interest level: 7+).
   Originally published in 1942 under the title *Tall Tales of Arkansas*, this is the most comprehensive collection of Arkansas legends in existence. As the best single volume on Arkansas folklore, it includes the original version of the "Arkansas Traveller," colorful stories of Davy Crockett's days in the state, a story explaining the original name of the state, and the big bear story.
◆ Students may select a story from the volume for retelling or for dramatization.
1. American wit and humor 2. Arkansas.

398.2
Parkhurst, Liz Smith. *The Arkansas Traveller: Adapted for Today's Readers*. Illus. by Carron Bain Hocut. August House (0-935394-43-6), 1982. 44p. B/W Illus. (Interest level: 3+).
   Set in the Ozark Mountains, this version of one of the most famous items of Arkansas folklore describes the encounter of a lost traveller from the east with a fiddler who repeatedly plays the beginning of a fiddle tune. This almost unwelcome encounter is sweetened when the traveller is able to provide the forgotten ending for the tune.
◆ Students may listen to fiddle music on tape, such as Gerald Milnes' "Granny Will Your Dog Bite, and Other Mountain Rhymes" (Knopf, 1990), or have a fiddler as a guest.
1. Arkansas—Authors 2. Arkansas—Music.

398.2
Steele, Phillip. *Ozark Tales and Superstitions*. Pelican Publishing (0-8828-9404-8), 1983. 96p. B/W illus. (Interest level: 6+).
   This collection of folklore was gathered by an authority long active in the Arkansas Folklore Society. The interesting assortment is suitable for reading aloud.
◆ After sharing selections from the book, students may be interested in collecting other tales and superstitions from the older members of their families or others.
1. Ozark Mountains Region.

398.2
Young, Richard and **Young, Judy Dockrey**. *Ozark Ghost Stories*. August House (0-87483-211-X), 1992. (45 min.). $9.95. (Interest level: 5+).
   These scary stories from the Ozark Mountains, including "The Vanishing Rider" and "Raw Head and Bloody Bones," are told by people everywhere. As professional storytellers, the Youngs offer inspired telling, enhanced with traditional music and interesting sound effects.

◆ After listening to a selection of stories from the audiotape, students may be interested in locating and comparing other ghost stories from other regions of the country or they may be interested in making audiotapes of ghost stories to share.
1. Tales—Arkansas 2. Ghost stories, American—Arkansas.

398.2
Young, Richard and **Young, Judy Dockrey**. *Ozark Tall Tales*. August House (0-87483-212-8), 1992. (60 min.). $9.95. (Interest level: 2+).
   This authentic collection of Ozark Mountain stories may be used in conjunction with the cassette of the same title (*see* following entry). Gathered by a pair of native Ozark tellers, the stories are appropriate for sharing and telling.
◆ Students may be interested in reading Alvin Schwartz's *Whoppers* (Harper, 1975) or students may be interested in learning about such tall tale heroes as Paul Bunyan, Mike Fink, John Henry, or Pecos Bill.
1. Tall tales—Ozark Mountains Region 2. Legends—Ozark Mountains Region 3. Ozark Mountains Region—Miscellanea 4. Folklore—Ozark Mountains Region.

398.2
Young, Richard and **Young, Judy Dockrey**. (Audiotape). *Ozark Tall Tales: Collected from Oral Tradition*. August House (0-87483-099-0), 1989. 215p. (Interest level: 5+).
   This collection gathered from the Ozark Mountains includes "The Bog's Tale," "The Meanest Man in the World," and "The Great Hog Meat Swindle." This rip-roaring collection is retold by native Ozark storytellers and enhanced by Ozark music using such traditional instruments as the banjo, hammered dulcimer, and fiddle. This tape may be used with the book by the same title (*see* preceding entry).
◆ Students may create their own tall tale story about some event in their own lives.
1. Tall tales—Ozark Mountains Region 2. Legends—Ozark Mountains Region 3. Ozark Mountains Region—Miscellanea 4. Folklore—Ozark Mountains Region.

409
Ladwig, Tom. *Granny Had a Word for It!* Rose Publishing (0-914546-75-9), 1988. 52p. B/W Illus. (Interest level: 3+).
   This collection of illustrated phrases gathered from southern history include such colorful expressions as "the only thing she got against singing is her voice" and "he moves slower than cold molasses."
◆ Students may collect descriptive phrases from older relatives, friends, or neighbors and compile a booklet similar to Ladwig's.
1. English Language—Provincialisms—United States 2. Americanisms.

508.7
Mills, William. *The Arkansas: An American River*. The University of Arkansas Press (1-55728-043-6), 1988. 241p. Color photos. (Interest level: 4+).

This is a photo essay of the 1460 miles of the Arkansas River, which begins in Colorado, flows southeast across Arkansas, and empties into the Mississippi River. This book extends the awareness of river ecology by emphasizing the importance of this river to the nation while also sharing the river's beauty.

♦ Students may be interested in studying about the other important rivers related to Arkansas: the Mississippi, Ouachita, St. Francis, Red, and White.

1. River ecology—Arkansas River 2. Arkansas River—Description and travel 3. Natural history—Arkansas River.

582.1

Hunter, Carl G. *Wildflowers of Arkansas*. Ozark Society Foundation (0-912456-00-7), 1988. 296p. Color photos. (Interest level: 6+).

This comprehensive collection of photographs and general descriptions of Arkansas wildflowers includes 484 color photographs, with 116 other wildflowers described, for a total coverage of 600 wildflowers. This book provides a thorough representation of all major wildflowers that grow in the state.

♦ Students may bring wildflowers for identification using Hunter's book.

1. Wild flowers—Arkansas—Identification 2. Wild flowers—Arkansas—Pictorial works.

582.1

Moore, Dwight. *Trees of Arkansas*. 4th revised ed. Arkansas Forestry Commission (No ISBN), 1950, 1991. 142p. B/W illus. (Interest level: 3+).

This is the definitive source for descriptions of species of trees in Arkansas. Illustrations provide additional information for identifying trees.

♦ Students may use the Moore book to assist in identifying the trees in their area or for help in selecting leaves for a collection.

1. Trees—Arkansas.

591.9

Morrison, Susan. *Arkansas Wildlife*. Rose Publishing (0-914546-32-5), 1980. 58p. B/W Illus. (Interest level: All ages).

This book includes text provided by the Arkansas Game and Fish Commission which describes the habitat and living patterns of 50 Arkansas birds and mammals. Morrison's collection of pen and ink drawings and selections of poetry add impressive dimensions to this informational source.

♦ As a special research project, students may each choose a bird or mammal described in the text.

1. Wilderness areas—Arkansas 2. Arkansas—Poetry.

598.2

James, Douglas A. and **Neal, Joseph C**. *Arkansas Birds: Their Distribution and Abundance*. University of Arkansas Press (0-938626-38-8), 1986. 416p. Color and B/W illus. (Interest level: 4+).

This comprehensive and detailed guide to the identification, habitats, and locations of birds within the state is the definitive source for such information, which it presents in an attractive format.

♦ Students may set up a bird feeder outside their classroom window, take a field trip to identify birds

in their area with the use of binoculars, or have an ornithologist visit their classroom.

1. Birds—Arkansas—Identification.

599

Sealander, John and **Heidt, Gary**. *A Guide to Arkansas Mammals*. University of Arkansas Press (1-55728-102-5), 1990. 308p. Color and B/W illus. and photos. (Interest level: 7+).

This book covers all 69 species of Arkansas mammals and provides their characteristics, specific locations, and life histories, along with maps of actual and reported sightings.Extensive appendices include animal tracking with track measurements. This comprehensive guide by the leading authority on Arkansas mammals also provides scientific names.

♦ Using Sealander as a reference source, students may investigate animal tracking further by using suggestions provided in Jim Arnosky's *Crinkleroot's Book of Animal Tracking* (Bradbury, 1989).

1. Mammals—Arkansas.

641.5

Ashley, Liza. *Thirty Years at the Mansion: Recipes and Recollections*. As told to Carolyn Huber. August House (0-87483-135-0), 1991. 176p. Color and B/W photos. (Interest level: 6+).

Liza Ashley was the cook at the Arkansas Governor's Mansion for 30 years. This cookbook shares the informal recollections of what life was like working with the different families who lived in the mansion and includes 150 favorite recipes.

♦ Select a recipe from the cookbook and share it with students while discussing the history of the governor with whom the recipe is associated.

1. Cookery, American—Arkansas 2. Arkansas—Governors—Miscellanea.

725.1

Smith, Hubert. *A Century of Pride: The Arkansas State Capitol*. Foreword by Paul Riviere. Arkansas State Capitol Association (No ISBN), 1983. 46p. Color photos. (Interest level: 4+).

The government of Arkansas had outgrown the Old State House built in 1836, so in 1899 the citizens of the state decided to build a new state capitol. This is a detailed pictorial history of the building designed by St. Louis architect, George A. Mann, which replicates on a smaller scale the United States Capitol in Washington, D.C.

♦ Students may write to the Arkansas State Capitol for information about the building or they may, if possible, plan a field trip to visit the building.

1. Arkansas—Capital and capitol 2. Historic buildings—Arkansas—Little Rock.

746.4

Arkansas Quilter's Guild, Inc. *Arkansas Quilts: Arkansas Warmth*. American Quilter's Society, 1987. 143p. Color photos. (Interest level: 4+).

This is a colorful photograph collection of Arkansas' rich heritage of antique quilts. The collection provides the available information on each quilt, including present owners, quilter, history, and if the quilt was made for a special event.

♦ Students may be interested in creating similar quilting squares using colored powdered sugar icings and graham cracker squares.
1. Quilts—History—Arkansas 2. Quiltmakers—Arkansas.

782.8
McNeil, W.K., editor and compiler. *Southern Folk Ballads: American Originals: A Heritage in Song.* (American Folklore Series). August House (0-87483-038-9), 1987. 219p. (Interest level: 8+).

This large selection of regional folk ballads maintained by oral tradition includes 10 ballads credited to Arkansas. This interesting collection contains ballads recorded since 1955. Some were widely popular, some were known only in a relatively small area, and some may not be unique to the South, though commonly known in particular states.
♦ Students may select one of the ballads credited to Arkansas and discuss its possible origins.
1. Folk music—Southern States 2. Ballads, English—Southern States.

796.3
Bradley, Matt, ed. *The Hogs: Moments Remembered.* Bradley Publishing (0-940716-00-3), 1981. 142p. B/W photos. (Interest level: 4+).

This chronological history of University of Arkansas Razorback sports programs is provided through a collection of photographs beginning with the football season of 1894. Moments are remembered through the numerous featured sports stars and coaches.
♦ Students may follow the University of Arkansas sports teams, write to the University of Arkansas for general information about the school, or display a poster of Razorback sporting events in the classroom.
1. University of Arkansas—Football 2. University of Arkansas—Basketball.

796.3
Kavanagh, Jack. *Dizzy Dean*. (Baseball Legends series). Introduction by Jim Murray. Chelsea House (0-7910-1173-9), 1991. 64p. B/W photos. (Interest level: 4+).

Baseball great Dizzy Dean was born and raised in the small southwestern Arkansas town of Lucas, where he lived until he joined the Army at age 16. This book carefully chronicles, with easy-to-read text, the life of a man who, in his prime, led major league baseball in wins, strikeouts, complete games, and innings pitched, and who moved into a broadcasting career after his retirement as a player.
♦ Students may be interested in reading other books in the Baseball Legends series or in having a baseball card swap.
1. Dean, Dizzy, 1911-1974 2. Baseball players.

796.3
Moncrief, Sidney. *Moncrief: My Journey to the NBA.* Edited by Myra McLarey. August House (0-87483-113-X), 1990. 95p. Color and B/W photos. (Interest level: 6+).

This is the account of the former Milwaukee Bucks basketball star whose humble beginnings were in the East End Housing Project in Little Rock, Arkansas. Described, are the influences on Moncreif's life of his iron-willed mother, a Boy Scout leader, his high school sweetheart, and University of Arkansas basketball coach, Eddie Sutton.
♦ Students may be interested in following the University of Arkansas basketball team for the season and keeping a chart that notes their wins and losses.
1. Moncrief, Sidney, 1957- 2. Basketball players—United States—Biography 3. Milwaukee Bucks (Basketball team).

811.5
Couch, Ruth. *This Land of Legend.* Illus. by Jerry Poole and Foy Lisenby. Rose Publishing (0-914546-88-0), 1992. 71p. B/W illus. (Interest level: 4+).

This collection of original poetry depicts Arkansas' most famous legends, including Carry A. Nation, Petit Jean, the Crossett Light, the vanishing hitchhiker, and War Eagle. These legends reflect history and humor in an entertaining and educational style.
♦ Using the poetry in the book as a model, students may select an Arkansas historic figure or place and write additional ballads and poems about their selection.
1. American poetry—20th century—Arkansas.

876.7
Bloom, Louise. *Victorian Arkansas: How They Lived, Played and Worked.* Compiled and edited by Mala Daggett. Arkansas Commemorative Commission, Old State House (0-686-30547-7), 1981. 207p. B/W illus. (Interest level: 5+).

This guide to the Victorian era (1865-1920) in Arkansas covers ethnic groups and immigration, architecture, social attitudes and customs, clothing, entertainment, education, and occupations. This excellent work gives an overview of this period in Arkansas history.
♦ Using *Victorian Arkansas* as a guide, students may set up a Victorian vaudeville show that might include acrobats, singers, skits, joke tellers, musicians, jugglers, and animal acts, or they might play Victorian card games, including Old Maid, Finch, Rook, or Pitch.
1. Arkansas—Social life and customs—Juvenile literature 2. Arkansas—History—Juvenile literature.

911.7
Hanson, Gerald T. and **Moneyhon, Carl**. *Historical Atlas of Arkansas.* University of Oklahoma Press (0-8061-1844-X), 1989. 142p. B/W illus. (Interest level: All ages).

This book uses historical maps to provide insights into the relationships among Arkansas geography, people, and technology and describes how Arkansans have transcended the limits of their state. The detailed, well-researched maps include prehistorical settlement patterns, routes of the explorers, Indian trails, military settlements, human migration patterns, railroads, and highway construction.
♦ Using a selection of the historical maps, students may investigate the history of a particular county or area in the state.
1. Arkansas—Historical geography—Maps.

912.7

Best, Michael. *The Roads of Arkansas*. Shearer Publishing (0-940672-53-7), 1990. 128p. Color illus. (Interest level: 4+).

This book includes detailed information about the roads of Arkansas, from the interstates to the backroads, based on county maps from the Arkansas State Highway and Transportation Department. It includes a comprehensive index of more that 2500 cities, towns, and communities with glimpses of Arkansas history, place names, famous people, roadside attractions, weather and road facts, Arkansas-based movies, annual attractions, and special events.
♦ Students may be given two cities or points of interest in the state and they may plan a route of travel between the two, listing the places they would see on the way.
1. Arkansas—Road Maps 2. Arkansas—Description and travel—Guidebooks.

912.7

Smith, Richard M. *The Atlas of Arkansas*. University of Arkansas Press (1-55728-048-7), 1989. 226p. Color maps. (Interest level: All ages).

This printed version of the *Electronic Atlas of Arkansas* is the first computer-based state atlas published in the United States that provides over 100 computer-generated maps and charts. It is a comprehensive, well-documented overview of locations, nature settings, weather and climate, population, socio-economic information, history, health, government and politics, economics, finance, transportation, communication, agriculture and agricultural products, minerals and energy, manufacturing, tourism, and recreation.
♦ Students may be interested in comparing the information in this atlas to other atlas information available about Arkansas or looking at particular products produced in different areas of the state.
1. Arkansas—Maps 2. Arkansas—Economic conditions 3. Arkansas—Social conditions—Maps.

917.6

Arkansas Almanac: A Colorful, Fact-filled Guide to Bill Clinton's Arkansas. (Videotape). Jones Productions, Inc. (No ISBN), 1992. Color, 1/2", (60 min.). (Interest level: All ages).

Beginning with Clinton's election night speech at the Old State House, this video provides an introduction to the state of Arkansas with coverage of 11 topics, including geography, brief facts, famous Arkansans, points of interest, historical notes, politics and government since 1957, natural heritage, vital statistics, cities and towns, and sports. This information is provided in an attractive and interesting fashion.
♦ Students may jot down Arkansas facts as they watch the video and then use their notes to study for a trivia question and answer game designed like a spelling bee.
1. Arkansas.

917.6

Christ, Mark. *Places in Time: A Guide to Arkansas Properties on the National Register of Historic Places*. Arkansas Historic Preservation Program (No ISBN), 1992. 106p. B/W photos. (Interest level: 6+).

Arkansas history is reflected in this National Register of Historic Places listing, includes Native American sites that pre-date European settlement, humble log cabins of the first pioneers, railroad depots, and Victorian homes. This guide provides the name, address, location, and the year built for these sites (many of which are private residences). These sites share a cultural heritage that makes the state and the people of Arkansas unique.
♦ Students may chart on a map the locations of the Arkansas National Register sites or, if possible, visit one of the sites.
1. Arkansas.

917.6

DeLano, Patti. *Arkansas: Off the Beaten Path*. Globe Pequot (1-56440-013-1), 1992. 157p. Illus. (Interest level: 6+).

This guide to the out-of-the-way places to visit in the state serves as an excellent resource for planning one-day trips and adventures.
♦ Using the book as a travel guide, students may plan a series of interesting one-day imaginary trips complete with picnic menus, or students may create travel brochures for some of the places mentioned.
1. Arkansas—Guidebooks.

917.6

Dillard, Tom W. (Filmstrip). *A Trip Through Arkansas of Yesterday*. Rose Publishing, 1980. (15 min.). $39.95. (Interest level: 5+).

This filmstrip tours important historical sites around the state by utilizing a pleasing blend of old and new photographs and illustrations. The filmstrip is accompanied by a manual and may serve as an interesting introduction to the study of the state or as a review to historic places.
♦ Students may assist with a bulletin board or display on the historic sites in Arkansas by combining photographs, postcards, brochures, newspaper clippings, and travel information.
1. Arkansas—History.

917.6

Earngey, Bill. *Arkansas Roadsides: A Guidebook for the State*. East Mountain Press/August House (0-9619592-0-7), 1987. 150p. B/W illus. (Interest level: 4+).

This book includes modern and historical maps, roadside information, city information, campgrounds, river parks, float streams, national parks, national wildlife refuges, state parks, hiking and backpacking trails, and wildlife management areas. This guide fosters the spirit of adventure and serves as a practical reference for Arkansas' attractions.
♦ Students may use the guide to plan an imaginary trip around the state; using an Arkansas map, they may calculate mileage from point to point.
1. Arkansas—Description and travel 2. Cities and towns—Arkansas.

917.6

Foti, Thomas and **Hanson, Gerald**. *Arkansas and the Land*. The University of Arkansas Press (1-55728-210-2), 1992. 113p. Color photos. (Interest level: 4+).

This book explores the place and people of Arkansas by presenting the state as a set of regions or "natural divisions" which have each contributed to a rich and wonderful diversity. The comparison of regions shows how the people and the land have interacted in specific ways to develop a distinctive lifestyle, economy, and history.

♦ Students may depict the six natural divisions on an Arkansas map and discuss how the land has affected the way people live in each of the regions.

1. Arkansas—Geography.

917.6
McDonough, Nancy. *Garden Sass: A Catalog of Arkansas Folkways*. Coward, McCann and Geoghegen (0-698-10640-7), 1975. 319p. (Interest level: 8+).

"Garden Sass" is a mountain term for a plate of fresh vegetables served straight from the garden without dressing. This source provides valuable information about old time customs, practical advice, and traditions in relation to old time games, house raisings, honey gathering, music making, water witching, food preserving, quilting, and generally making do.

♦ Students may be interested in a demonstration of or in trying some of the old ways of life, such as water witching, food preserving, or playing old time games (for more information, consult the "Foxfire" series (Anchor Press/Doubleday, 1972-1982), edited by Eliot Wiggington.

1. Folklore—Arkansas.

917.6
Rice, Maylon, ed. *The Best of the Arkansas Traveler, 1956-1986: As Seen in the Arkansas Gazette*. August House (0-87483-004-4), 1986. 173p. (Interest level: 7+).

Selected articles represent a 30-year span from the column that appeared in the *Arkansas Gazette* and was written by several different columnists. Always representing the human element, the column served to "reach and report about persons who are not necessarily newsmakers."

♦ After listening to several columns read aloud, students may choose to write their own "Arkansas Traveller" column about someone who is interesting, but not necessarily a newsmaker.

1. Arkansas—Social life and customs 2. Arkansas—Description and travel-1951-1980 3. Arkansas—Description and travel-1981.

917.6
Stroud, Hubert and **Hanson, Gerald**. *Arkansas Geography: The Physical Landscape and the Historical-Cultural Setting*. Rose Publishing (0-914546-34-1), 1981. 90p. B/W illus. (Interest level: 6+).

Divided into two parts, this work provides an overview of physical geography in one section and cultural geography (including Native American settlement) in the other. As Arkansas' first geography book, it provides detailed, yet easy-to-understand information.

♦ Students may use present-day Arkansas maps to discuss the geography of the state.

1. Arkansas—Description and travel 2. Arkansas—Maps 3. Arkansas—Economic conditions.

970.4
Schambach, Frank F. and **Newell, Leslie**. *Crossroads of the Past: 12,000 Years of Indian Life in Arkansas*. Arkansas Archeological Survey/Arkansas Endowment for the Humanities (1-56349-068-4), 1990. 59p. B/W illus. (Interest level: 7+).

This overview of the history and ways of life of the early peoples of Arkansas includes information about patterns of migration and settlement, elements of daily life, such as gathering and preparing food, and an explanation of the devastating impact of European exploration and settlement on indigenous populations.

♦ As a follow-up, the students may be interested in viewing one of the slide sets or videos suggested in the book or they may be interested in making a chronological time line that features the peoples mentioned.

1. Arkansas—History 2. Indians of North America—Arkansas.

973
Heinrichs, Ann. *Arkansas*. (America the Beautiful series). Childrens Press (0-516-00450-6), 1989. 144p. Color illus. (Interest level: 4+).

This informative source covers the geography, history, government, economy, and cultural and recreational aspects of the state. It also provides a useful yet comprehensive overview of state information and culminates with a section that includes maps, a chronology, people profiles, and state facts.

♦ Students may be interested to know that Arkansas' nickname is "the Land of Opportunity" and may wish to discuss why Arkansas was given this name, or students may be interested in learning the nicknames of other states.

1. Arkansas.

976.01
Dillard, Tom W. *Arkansas Indians*. (Filmstrio). Rose Publishing. (16 min.). $39.95. (Interest level: 6+).

This set (filmstrip and ausiocassette) is a descriptive history of the American Indians who were native to Arkansas. An accompanying teacher's manual, with a tape transcript, background material, and suggested questions for students, makes this a valuable and useable source.

♦ Students may make a diorama depicting the Native American groups from the state.

1. Indians of North America—Arkansas.

976.01
Sabo, George, III. *Paths of Our Children: A Brief Description of the Historic Indians of Arkansas*. (Popular Series, No. 3). Arkansas Archeological Survey (1-56349-073-0), 1992. 144p. B/W illus. (Interest level: 7+).

This work provides basic information on the way of life of the early peoples of the state that was irreversibly impacted by historical developments. This interesting source provides report information and will serve as a background teacher resource.

♦ Students may be interested in hearing a guest speaker who is knowledgeable about the early peoples of the state, or they may be interested in creating a diorama based on factual information.

1. Indians of North America—Arkansas—First Contact with Europeans 2. Indians of North America—Arkansas—History—Sources 3. Indians of North America—Arkansas—Social life and customs.

976.7
Anderson, Clay. *Ozarks*. Photographed by David Fitzgerald. Graphic Arts Center Publishing (0-912856-94-7), 1985. 158p. Color photos. (Interest level: 3+).

This photo essay of the land and the people of the Ozark Mountain region provides full color sections which share the beauty of the mountains at different times of day and during different seasons.
♦ Using an Arkansas map, students may make a list of the Arkansas counties in the Ozark Mountain region, or they may read about the people of other mountain regions in the United States.
1. Ozark Mountain Region.

976.7
Arkansas History. (Filmstrips and Audiotapes). Northwest Educational Systems, n.d. $115.00 (Interest level: 5+).

This series of filmstrips covers six topics of study: lands and first peoples of Arkansas, five major Indian groups, European explorers, immigrant settlement and statehood, Civil War and Reconstruction, and recent history and natural wonders. An excellent addition to teaching Arkansas history, these six colorful filmstrips and audiocassettes are accompanied by a large full-color map and a teacher's guide.
♦ As a culminating experience to studying Arkansas history, students may be interested in constructing a time line that includes pertinent events, people, and places.
1. Arkansas—History.

976.7
Ashmore, Harry. *Arkansas: A Bicentennial History*. (States and the Nation series). W.W. Norton (0-393-30177-X), 1984. 202p. B/W illus. (Interest level: 7+).

This guide to historical places in Arkansas, including Arkansas Post, Historic Little Rock, and Pea Ridge Battlefield, offers important insights into Arkansas' often misunderstood historical character.
♦ Young people may be interested in writing for more information about the historical sites included and plotting these sites on a present-day Arkansas map.
1. Arkansas—History.

976.7
Berry, Fred and **Novak, John**. *The History of Arkansas*. Rose Publishing (0-914546-61-9), 1987. 278p. (Interest level: 8+).

This comprehensive resource on historical developments in Arkansas is often cited as one of the most definite sources of information.
♦ Students may use this book as a reference source for background information on the history of Arkansas or use the information provided to write short articles for a historical newspaper.
1. Arkansas—History.

976.7
Bolsterli, Margaret Jones, ed. *Vinegar Pie and Chicken Bread: A Woman's Diary of Life in the Rural South, 1890-91*. University of Arkansas Press (No ISBN), 1982. 108p. (Interest level: 7+).

This is a transcription of Nannie Stillwell's small, pencil-written ledger which she kept from June 11, 1890 to April 15, 1891. Recorded are the best and most meaningful moments of her life on a small farm in Deshea County, Arkansas.
♦ Students may be interested in beginning to keep their own diaries or in reading other books in diary format.
1. Deshea County (Ark.)—Social life and customs
2. County life—Arkansas—Deshea County.

976.7
Bolton, Charles, Ledbetter, Cal, Jr., and **Hanson, Gerald**. *Arkansas Becomes a State*. Center for Arkansas Studies/University of Arkansas at Little Rock (no ISBN), 1985. 80p. (Interest level: 8+).

This book details the development of the area that became Arkansas, the twenty-sixth state in the nation in 1836. The chronological developments described are the emergence of a territory; frontier Arkansas, 1819-1840; frontier society; movement for statehood; writing a constitution; and statehood achieved.
♦ Arkansas students may be interested in looking over the copy of the 1836 Arkansas Constitution and discussing how this document affects their daily lives; student in other states may do the same with their state constitutions.
1. Arkansas—History 2. Arkansas Politics and Government—To 1850 3. Arkansas—Constitution.

976.7
Carpenter, John Allan. *Arkansas*. (The New Enchantment of America series). Childrens Press, 1978. 96p. Color and B/W illus. (Interest level: 4+).

This book presents the history, resources, and points of interest in the state nicknamed the "Land of Opportunity." Though dated, this source provides general information suitable for reports.
♦ Students may use the chapters in the book to create an illustrated overview of Arkansas.
1. Arkansas.

976.7
Deane, Ernie. *Arkansas Place Names*. The Ozarks Mountaineer (No ISBN), 1986. 201p. B/W photos. (Interest Level: 6+).

This book details the origins of Arkansas place names: 75 county names; 91 present or former county seat names; 153 ordinary place names, such as Bug Scuffle, Cow Faced Hill, Granny's Gap, and Toad Suck; and 232 additional name origins of general interest. Some of the origins are poetic and some are prosaic.
♦ This source may interest students in name origins, and they may wish to pursue the origin of place names in their area.
1. Ozarks Mountain Region—Collected works.

976.7
Dillard, Tom W. and **Thwing, Valerie**. *Researching Arkansas History: A Beginner's Guide*. Rose Publishing (0-91456-25-2), 1979 62p. B/W illus. (Interest level: 7+).

Though dated, this valuable resource provides information on a variety of sources which may be consulted when studying and researching Arkansas history. Included is information on Arkansas libraries, the Arkansas History Commission, municipal records, county records, University of Arkansas Special Collections, African-American history sources, oral history research, and genealogical research.
♦ Using Dillard and Thwing as a guide, students may select a topic or subject related to Arkansas history to research and then employ some of the methods suggested for gathering information.
1. Arkansas—History—Study and teaching 2. Arkansas—Civilization—Study and teaching 3. Arkansas—Bibliography 4. Arkansas—Handbooks, guides, etc.

976.7
Foti, Thomas L. *Natural Divisions of Arkansas*. (Filmstrip). Rose Publishing, n.d. (18 min.). $39.95. (Interest level: 4-8).

This film (with audiotape) describes the natural geographic divisions in the state from the mountainous regions in the northwest to the flatlands of the south and the delta region in the east. An accompanying 70-page booklet supplements this film and can provide a three-week unit.
♦ Using the materials provided, students may embark on an intensive study of the regions of the state.
1. Natural history—Arkansas.

976.7
Fradin, Dennis B. *Arkansas in Words and Pictures*. Childrens Press (0-516-03904-0), 1980. 48p. Color and B/W illus. (Interest level: 3-6).

This work provides a brief introduction to the land, history, cities, industries, and famous sites and citizens of the twenty-sixth state in the union. Though dated, this source provides some brief information about the state.
♦ Students may chronicle the developments in the state since 1980 and write an additional chapter that adds to this resource.
1. Arkansas.

976.7
Hendrix, Bobbie Lou. *Crater of Diamonds: Jewel of Arkansas*. B.L. Hendrix (No ISBN), 1989. 40p. B/W illus. (Interest level: 6+).

This source serves as a brief history and overview of the role Arkansas has played as the only diamond producing state in the United States, which is reflected in the design of the state flag. Documented information includes how diamonds were first found near Murfreesboro and a chronology of the various diamonds located since.
♦ Students might be interested in hearing a jeweler or gemologist discuss how diamonds are formed and why they are valuable.
1. Diamond mines and mining—Arkansas 2. Crater of Diamonds State Park (Ark.).

976.7
Jameson, W.C. *Buried Treasures of the Ozarks*. (Buried Treasure Series). August House (0-87483-106-7), 1990. 189p. B/W illus. (Interest level: 5+).

This book contains 43 legends from Arkansas, Missouri, and Oklahoma, including stories of famous mines abandoned by de Soto's soldiers, ingots carried partway across the Ozarks long ago, lodes of precious metals known only to Native Americans, and thieves' and murderers' plunder that still lies underground. Included among the collection are 15 suspenseful Arkansas stories, such as stories of the Civil War, the mystery of Turtle Rock, and the stories of lost mines.
♦ Students may work together in teams and discuss what might be important strategies for treasure hunting, or it might be interesting to request a demonstration of a Geiger counter.
1. Treasure trove—Ozark Mountains Region 2. Legends—Ozark Mountains Region 3. Ozark Mountains Region—Miscellanea.

976.7
Killion, John. *Arkansas Legislature*. (Videotape). Rose Publishing, n.d. (30 min.). $59.95. (Interest level: 5+).

This video shows the Arkansas General Assembly in action, describes its legislative process, and explains the composition of the House and Senate and apportionment. This informative video outlines the committee system and includes the steps to passage of an Arkansas law.
♦ After viewing the video, students may take the brief legislative quiz that follows the program, or they may work on an organizational chart that describes the roles of those involved in the Arkansas General Assembly.
1. Arkansas.

976.7
Killion, John. *Old State House*. (Videotape). Rose Publishing, n.d. $39.95. (Interest level: 5+).

This video provides a description of the Old State House, one of Arkansas' greatest landmarks and the seat of state government until the completion of the current capitol in 1911. The Old State House was the site of then Governor Bill Clinton's announcement of his intention to run for the presidency and also the site of his victory speech in November, 1992.
♦ Because the video does not describe the role of the Old State House in the campaign of President Bill Clinton, students might be interested in writing a description of how the building might have "felt" as the site for presidential victory in 1992.
1. Arkansas.

976.7
Life in Arkansas: The First One Hundred Years. Arkansas State Society, Daughters of the American Revolution (No ISBN), 1985. 183p. B/W photos. (Interest level: 5+).

As a contribution to the commemoration of the sesquicentennial of Arkansas statehood in 1986, members of the 56 Daughters of the American Revolution chapters were asked to furnish pictures taken in the state before 1936. The 330 pictures collected tell the story of the first 100 years of statehood, with every area of the state represented.

♦ Students may be interested in listening to a presentation from the Daughters of the American Revolution, looking at a collection of very old photographs, or writing imaginary historical accounts of people in old photographs purchased at a flea market.

1. Arkansas—Description and travel—Views 2. Arkansas—Social life and customs—Pictorial works.

976.7

Megna, Ralph. *More Than a Memory: Little Rock's Historic Quapaw Quarter.* Illustrated by Richard DeSpain. Rose Publishing (0-914546-37-6), 1981. 69p. B/W illus. (Interest level: 6+).

The preservation and restoration of the Quapaw Quarter is one of the great revitalization stories of the nation; a number of restored nineteenth-century homes give the area an appearance of a turn-of-the-century town. The text is complemented by DeSpains's detailed pen-and-ink drawings of the famous homes in this area.

♦ Students may compile their own "memory book" of present-day homes in their area, either by drawing or photographing their own homes or by drawing or photographing the notable buildings in their area.

1. Quapaw Quarter (Little Rock, Ark.).

976.7

Mitchell, Ruth. *Arkansas Heritage.* Rose Publishing (0-914546-62-7), 1986. 165p. Illus. (Interest level: 5+).

This work covers earliest Arkansas history, pioneer Arkansas, Civil War and Reconstruction, Gilded Age, Progressive Era, 1930-1960, and modern Arkansas. The information may be used for reports and as a background history resource for teachers.

♦ After studying Arkansas, the students may present an "Arkansas History Fair" with exhibits based on their studies and organized similar to a science fair.

1. Arkansas—History.

976.7

Shands, Alice. *Arkansas Heritage.* (Filmstrip and Audiotape). Rose Publishing, n.d. (30 min.) $39.95. (Interest level: 4+).

This visual overview of major events in Arkansas history begins with the Native Americans and de Soto and continues to the present area. The interesting narration is extended with simple, yet powerful images.

♦ After studying Arkansas history, students might be interested in suggesting pertinent items for a time capsule that would reflect the heritage of the state.

1. Arkansas—History—Juvenile films.

976.7

Smith, Diann Sutherlin. *The Arkansas Handbook: A Fascinating, Fact-Filled Guide to the Land of Opportunity.* Emerald City Press (0-932531-00-8), 1984. 480p. B/W illus and photos. (Interest level: 4+).

Though dated, this book is the nearest source to an almanac that there is; it includes Arkie expressions, historical events, a brief history of Arkansas, zip codes, strange place names, folk remedies, points of interest, and famous Arkansans. It is divided in 11 sections,

including Down-Home Arkansas; Facts at Your Fingertips; Points of Interest; Calendar of Annual Events; Cities and Towns; Arkansas, the Natural; Arkansas Government; Arkansas History; and Arkansas Sports.

♦ Students may select a section of the *Handbook* to update, or students may use the source as a guide to compiling a handbook about their own area or state.

1. Arkansas—Handbooks.

976.7

Steinmetz, Tucker. *Tell Me about Arkansas: A Commemorative Perspective on Arkansas After One Hundred and Fifty Years of Statehood.* Introduction by Bill Clinton. State of Arkansas, Office of the Governor, Arkansas Sesquicentennial Commission, and Department of Arkansas Heritage (0-944325-00-9), 1988. 133p. Color illus. (Interest level: 6+).

Published in honor of the 150th anniversary of Arkansas statehood, this booklet is divided into three parts: perspectives on the state, photographs published in honor of the sesquicentennial, and brief biographies and photographs of 21 leading Arkansas citizens. The interesting photographs and descriptive text offer a print visualization for "telling about Arkansas."

♦ Students may use the format of the booklet to design their own booklet about their own city or town and include photographs and biographies about leading citizens in their community.

1. Arkansas—Civilization 2. Arkansas—Description and travel—1981—Views 3. Arkansas—Biography.

976.7

Stewart, Judith C. *Life Threads: Clothing Fashions in Early Arkansas, 1810-1870.* Arkansas Territorial Restoration Foundation/Department of Arkansas Heritage (No ISBN), 1989. 40p. B/W photos. (Interest level: 4+).

This book is based on the "Life Threads" exhibit at the Arkansas Territorial Restoration; it was prepared by the exhibition curator. The exhibit features original examples of clothing and accessories typical of early Arkansas. Photographs of clothing made in the nineteenth century provide enhancement for the text that discusses clothing from the height of fashion to everyday wear to ceremonial dress and military clothing.

♦ Someone in the area may have vintage clothing that they could share with the students or students may be interested in researching other types of clothing worn in the past..

1. Costume—Arkansas—History 2. Clothing and dress—History—Exhibitions 3. Arkansas—History.

976.7

Thompson, J.J. *Arkansas: Her Beauty and Character.* Photographs by Kay Danielson. August House. (0-87483-092-3), 1989. 144p. Color photos. (Interest level: 4+).

This portrayal of life in Arkansas today provides full-color photographs of mountain geography, bayous, timber country, rocky bluffs, people, places of work, Arkansas heritage, recreation, artists, and scholars.

♦ Students may create a collage by using selected photographs or may cut out photographs from magazines to portray their own everyday life.

1. Arkansas—Description and travel 2. Arkansas—Social life and customs.

976.7

Thompson, Kathleen. *Arkansas*. (Portrait of America series). Raintree Publishers (0-86514-4494), 1987. 48p. Color and B/W illus. (Interest level: 3+).

This introduction to the state of Arkansas covers geography, history, government, economy, industry, agriculture, culture, historic sites, and famous people. It provides extensive general information about the state and its people suitable for reports.

◆ Students may use the information provided to design a travel poster featuring Arkansas.

1. Arkansas.

976.7

Williams, Fred C. *Arkansas, An Illustrated History of the Land of Opportunity*. Windsor Publications (0-89781-182-8), 1986. 383p. Color and B/W illus. (Interest level: 4+).

This history of Arkansas was published during the state's sesquicentennial year and is an overview of the state's accomplishments. Students will enjoy this illustrated history which details events from pre-statehood times to contemporary Arkansas.

◆ Students may choose a particular event in Arkansas history to illustrate in a cartoon format.

1. Arkansas—History 2. Arkansas—Description and travel 3. Arkansas—Industries.

977

Aylesworth, Thomas G. and **Aylesworth, Virginia L**. *South Central: Louisiana, Arkansas, Missouri, Kansas, Oklahoma*. (Let's Discover the States Series). Chelsea House. (0-7910-1047-3), 1992. 64p. Color illus. (Interest level: 3+).

The book is divided into sections on each of the states; each section includes basic information suitable for student reports. A carefully designed text incorporates contemporary photographs and historical engravings.

◆ Using the information provided, students may write an "infomercial" about the state and share it with others either as a live or videotaped presentation.

1. Southern States—Juvenile literature.

Biography

See also biographical entries in the Arkansas Nonfiction section, especially under 796.3 and 976.7.

920

McMath, Anne. *First Ladies of Arkansas: Women of Their Time*. August House (0-87483-0915), 1989. 264p. B/W photos. (Interest level: 4+).

This definitive work on the wives of Arkansas governors was written by a former first lady. It includes a detailed biographical section on each first lady and concludes with a section on Hillary Clinton.

◆ Students may follow the newspaper and collect information about the current Arkansas first lady.

1. Arkansas—Governors—Wives—Biography 2. Arkansas—Politics and government.

92 Clinton, Bill

Landau, Elaine. *Bill Clinton*. Franklin Watts (0-531-11143-1), 1993. 64p. Color and B/W photos. (Interest level: 1+).

This biography details the life of Bill Clinton, beginning with his childhood in Arkansas to his tenure as governor of the state and ultimately focuses on his 1992 presidential campaign concluding with his victory on election night. A useful format for reports and as a basic information source on the current President of the United States.

◆ Students may write to the President, 1600 Pennsylvania Avenue, Washington, D.C. 20500, or they may collect newspaper/magazine articles for a current events display of materials on President Bill Clinton.

1. Clinton, Bill, 1946- 2. Presidents.

92 Walton, Sam

Canadeo, Anne. *Sam Walton: The Giant of Wal-Mart*. (Wizards of Business) Garrett Educational Corporation (1-56071-025-6), 1992. 64p. B/W photos. (Interest level: 3+).

This book describes the life of the late Samuel M. Walton (though written prior to his death on April 5, 1992) a Springdale, Arkansas native, whose ingenuity and persistence contributed to his becoming one of the wealthiest men in the United States. Provides useful information for reports on the life of an interesting individual who built a billion dollar corporation.

◆ Students may be interested in locating other biographies about important business people in history or studying retail merchandising by setting up a small school supplies store in their building.

1. Walton, Sam, 1918-1992 2. Businesspeople 3. Wal-Mart (Firm)—History.

Fiction

Branscum, Robbie. *The Adventures of Johnny May*. Illustrated by Deborah Howland. Harper & Row (0-06-020615-2), 1984. 87p. B/W illus. (Interest level: 4-6).

Eleven-year-old Johnny May of the Arkansas hills struggles to care for and feed her grandparents, have Christmas in spite of the family's poverty, and deal with Homer, whom she saw shoot a man. Told in regional dialect, this sensitive story depicts Johnny May's struggle against great odds and is a sequel to *Johnny May* (1975).

◆ Students may compile a list of some of the regional dialect included in this book and talk about the meanings and pronunciations of some of the words and phrases.

1. Arkansas—Fiction 2. Family life—Fiction 3. Grandparents—Fiction 4. Mountain Life—Fiction 5. Christmas—Fiction.

Branscum, Robbie. *Cameo Rose*. Harper & Row (0-06-020558-X), 1989. 84p. (Interest level: 6-9).

Fourteen-year-old Cameo Rose is cursed with an insatiable curiosity that gets her into trouble when she is interested in a murder that takes place in the Arkansas hills. In this intriguing story, Cameo Rose must suffer the consequences of her curiosity.

♦ Students may make a list of things they are curious about or for which they need more information.

1. Arkansas—Fiction.

Branscum, Robbie. *The Girl*. Harper & Row (0-06-020702-7), 1986. 113p. (Interest level: 4-8).

An 11-year-old girl struggles for survival in a poor Arkansas hill community, where she is left with her four brothers and sisters under the care of an ambivalent grandmother. The girl's poignant story will provide many insights into personal stamina and the struggle to survive.

♦ Students may write a brief passage that tells the story from the grandmother's perspective and explains her reactions to particular passages in the book.

1. Arkansas—Fiction.

Branscum, Robbie. *Johnny May Grows Up*. Illustrated by Bob Marstall. Harper & Collins (0-06-020606-3), 1987. 88p. B/W illus. (Interest level: 5-8).

Johnny May comes of age at 13, when she finally realizes that her attempts at self-improvement are for her own gratification, not just to please her boyfriend. Johnny May's desire to lose weight and to learn about the world outside the isolated Arkansas hills is a sympathetic portrayal of a determined and courageous young woman who learns to make the most of her situation.

♦ Students may make a list of goals they have for their own future, some they may wish to share with others and some they may wish to keep privately.

1. Mountain life—Fiction 2. Arkansas—Fiction.

Branscum, Robbie. *The Murder of Hound Dog Bates*. Penguin (0-670-49521-2), 1982. 90p. (Interest level: 5-8)

When spunky 13-year-old Sassafras Bates finds his favorite dog dead, he suspects that one of his three spinster aunts—Faith, Hope, and Velda—is the murderer. This well-written, Arkansas story centers on Sassafras' attempts to make the guilty party confess.

♦ The book may be read aloud in chapters and students may serve as detectives along with Sassafras as he collects evidence.

1. Mystery and detective stories 2. Dogs—Fiction 3. Aunts—Fiction 4. Mountain life—Fiction 5. Arkansas—Fiction.

Branscum, Robbie. *Old Blue Tilley*. Macmillan (0-02-711931-9), 1991. 90p. (Interest level: 4-8).

Hambone, a 14-year-old orphan, accompanies a circuit riding preacher known as Old Blue Tilley on his rounds in the Ozark Mountains. This stirring novel full of memorable characters and conflicts details Hambone's journey to manhood on the eve of World War II.

♦ Students may make a list of things they look forward to being able to do when they become adults.

1. Ozark Mountains—Fiction 2. Mountain Life—Fiction.

Branscum, Robbie. *Spud Tackett and the Angel of Doom*. Viking (0-670-66582-7), 1983. 124p. (Interest level: 4-8).

An evil preacher makes life difficult in the Arkansas hills farm community of 15-year-old Spud, his grandmother, and cousin Leroy who has come to live with them from the city. This story of loyalty and deception takes place during World War II.

♦ Students may make a list of important characteristics for friends to have.

1. Farm life—Fiction 2. Evangelists—Fiction.

Dragonwagon, Crescent. *The Itch Book*. Macmillan (0-02-733121-0), 1990. 32p. Color illus. (Interest level: K-3).

This book relates what happens on a hot summer day in the Ozarks when heat makes everyone itch and head toward the creek for a nighttime picnic. It is a lively, humorously illustrated story of what happens when the weather is too hot.

♦ Students may talk about what to do in the summer when they are too hot or they may plan the menu for a picnic.

1. Heat—Fiction 2. Mountain life—Fiction 3. Stories in rhyme.

Greene, Bette. *Get On Out of Here, Philip Hall*. Dial (0-8037-2871-9), 1981. 150p. (Interest level: 4-7).

In the rural African-American southern community of Pocohontas, Arkansas, Beth Lambert competes with Philip Hall and tries to win the Abner Jerome Brady Leadership Award given out in their church each year. This story shares Beth's learning of an important but painful lesson about leadership and is a sequel to the 1975 Newbery Honor book, *Philip Hall Likes Me, I Reckon Maybe* (*see* following entry).

♦ Students may make a list of what qualities might be most important in someone receiving a leadership award.

1. Friendship—Fiction 2. Blacks—Fiction 3. Arkansas—Fiction 4. Leadership—Fiction.

Greene, Bette. *Philip Hall Likes Me, I Reckon Maybe*. Dial (0-8037-6098-1), 1974. 135p. (Interest level: 4-6).

This book looks at one year in the life of Beth Lambert, a young African-American girl whose biggest problem is her infatuation with Philip Hall, the boy from the next farm near Pocohontas, Arkansas. This sensitively told story of the progression of an intelligent and vivacious 11-year old's first crush was a 1975 Newbery Honor book.

♦ Students may be interested in reading a selection of Newbery Honor Books and in discussing them and the award.

1. Friendship—Fiction 2. Blacks—Fiction 3. Arkansas—Fiction.

Greene, Bette. *The Summer of My German Soldier*. Dial (0-8037-8321-3), 1973. 230p. (Interest level: 6+).

Anton Reiker is a German prisoner of war in a camp outside of Jenkinsville, Arkansas, and when he escapes, a young girl named Patty helps him. A complex story is further complicated because Patty's family is Jewish.

♦ Students may be interested in reading other books of the time period or in conducting a discussion about the true meaning of friendship.

1. World War II, 1939-1945—Fiction 2. Prisoners of war—Fiction 3. Arkansas—Fiction.

Lenski, Lois. *Cotton in My Sack*. Lippincott, 1949. (Interest level: 3-7).

Lenski shares the simple yet very prideful life of Joanda, the daughter in a poor Arkansas cotton family of the 1940s. Each of the very descriptive chapters in the book makes an excellent read aloud.
♦ Students may look into the history of cotton or have a cotton farmer visit the classroom.
1. Farm life—Fiction 2. Cotton—Fiction 3. Arkansas—Fiction.

Ludwig, Warren. *Good Morning Granny Rose: An Arkansas Folktale*. Putnam (0-399-21950-1), 1990. 32p. Color illus. (Interest level: Preschool-3).

Living in the foothills of the Ozark Mountains, Granny Rose and her old dog Henry get lost in a sudden blizzard and happen to share a cave with a hibernating bear. This warmly written folktale is portrayed with colorful, humorous illustrations.
♦ Students may make a list of animals that hibernate and investigate why they sleep during winter.
1. Folklore—Arkansas.

Medearis, Mary. *Big Doc's Girl*. Lippincott (0-87483-105-9), 1942; reissued by August House, 1985/1989. 141p. (Interest level: 6+).

When misfortune comes, Mary Clayborne, piano teacher and teenage daughter of a doctor in rural Arkansas, becomes head of the household and sets aside her romantic dreams of going to the conservatory and becoming a concert pianist. This story is warmly written and filled with good humor and good dialogue.
♦ Students may be interested in interviewing and documenting family members and others about life experiences that have not always turned out as the individual had hoped.
1. Arkansas—Fiction.

Simon, Charlie Mae. *The Arkansas Stories of Charlie Mae Simon*. Collected, edited, and introduced by Lyman B. Hagen. Illus. by Susan O'Reilly. August House (0-935304-47-9), 1981. 84p. Ilusl. (Interest level: 1-7).

This is a collection of six short stories set in Arkansas by a renowned Arkansas author. Change is the focus of these brief tales, with Simon's narration providing vivid characterization and happy endings.

♦ Students may write an autobiography that focuses on the major changes that have taken place in their own lives.
1. Arkansas—Fiction 2. Children's stories—America.

Professional Materials

976.7
Dillard, Tom W. and **Dougan, Michael B**. Arkansas History: A Selected Research Bibliography. Department of Arkansas Natural and Cultural Heritage (No ISBN), 1984. 378p. (Interest level: Professional).

This research bibliography of 5,121 sources of information included, as of the time of publication, every book, thesis, dissertation, and large pamphlet of significance on Arkansas history. This extensive bibliography represents a wide range of subjects.
♦ This comprehensive bibliography may be used by professionals to plan activities within Arkansas units of study.
1. Arkansas—History—Bibliography.

976.7
A Handbook for Teachers of Arkansas Studies. rev. ed. General Education Division/Department of Education (no ISBN), 1991. 59p. (Interest level: 4; Professional).

This guide was developed to provide basic information about a variety of historical resources, including museums, parks, and historic sites; libraries and archives; federal, state, and local organizations; and bibliographies. A well-organized and timely resource, this book provides an invaluable source of information for schools and Arkansas reference collections and may be customized to a particular area of the state by placing it in a three-ring binder and adding information.
♦ Using the sources provided, students may assist a teacher or librarian in letter writing for materials to add to their collection of information on the state, or, if in Arkansas, they may add to the section on local information sources by providing organizations and materials from their own area of the state.
1. Arkansas—History—Study and teaching 2. Arkansas—Civilization—Study and teaching 3. Arkansas—Bibliography.

Florida

by Henrietta M. Smith

Nonfiction

310 (Reference)
Sherymen, Anne H., ed. *1992 Florida Statistical Abstracts*. University of Florida Press (0-8130-1146-9), 1992. 752p. (Interest level: 6-8).

This is a compact, vital reference source for studies related to the state's economic, demographic, political, and other statistical concepts. Tables are clear and well indexed to facilitate use.

♦ Students may design graphs to demonstrate statistical information related to an area of study in which they are presently engaged. Have the students check newspapers for reports of changes in Florida in economic growth, population, political activity, etc.

1. Florida—Statistics.

331.88
McKissack, Patricia and **McKissack, Fredrick**. *A Long Hard Journey: The Story of the Pullman Porters*. Walker (0-8027-6884-9), 1989. 144p. B&W photos. (Interest level: 6-8).

This is a readable, indepth study of the life of African-American porters who served the trains that crossed this country in the late nineteenth and early twentieth centuries. The authors have painted poignant pictures of hardships, difficult working conditions, lack of job security, and other factors that led to the establishment of the first African-American controlled labor union—the Brotherhood of Sleeping Car Porters, led by A. Philip Randolph.

♦ Have the students interview an elderly African-American to see how working conditions have changed over the years.

1. Porters—United States—History—Juvenile literature. 2. Brotherhood of Sleeping Car Porters—History—Juvenile literature.

398.2
Belpre, Pura. *The Tiger and the Rabbit and Other Tales*. Illus. by Kay Peterson Parker. Houghton Mifflin, 1944 (out of print). 119p. (Interest level: 3-6).

Readers will enjoy this useful collection of Spanish tales, adapted by a master storyteller. The book is now out of print but copies are sometimes available in larger libraries and in special collections.

♦ Students may compare the themes in some of these tales with similar tales in other cultures.
Folktales—Spanish.

398.2
Cohen, Amy L., ed. *From Sea to Shining Sea*. Illus. by various children's book illustrators. Scholastic (0-590-4286-83), 1994. (Interest level: 3-6).

This compilation of folktales reflects the ethnic history of the United States. Included are folktales of Spanish origin, e.g., *Juan Bobo and the Bunuelos* from Puerto Rico and *El Gallo de Bodas* from Cuba.

♦ Students may make a mobile depicting characters from their favorite stories.

1. Folklore.

398.2
Gonzalez, Lucia. *El Gallo de Bodas (The Rooster's Wedding)*. Illus. by Lulu Delacre. Scholastic (0-590-46-843X), 1994. Unpaginated. (Interest level: K-3).

This Cuban version of a traditional Spanish cumulative tale tells of a little rooster who almost misses a wedding because he could not get the grass and the goat could not get the water, to help him clean his (pico) beak. The Spanish-English text makes the story accessible to a wide audience.

♦ The nature of this story lends itself easily to group participation "response" and spontaneous creative dramatics.

1. Folklore 2. Cuba—Folklore.

398.2
Jumper, Betty Mae. *The Corn Lady: Seminole Indian Legends*. (Videotape). Produced by Seminole Tribe of Florida, 1991. $ 19.95. (Interest level: 3-6).

This video collection of Seminole animal stories quietly recalls stories the narrator heard from her grandfather. A few watercolor sketches illustrate the selections.

♦ Students may read tales from other Native American cultures, looking for differences and similarities in theme, characters, etc. They may also write some animal "why" stories from their imagination or lis-

ten to tales from an elder in their family or community.
1. Seminole Indians—Folklore. 2. Florida—Folklore.

500.5′03
Simon, Seymour. *Space Words: A Dictionary*. Ilus. by Randy Chewning. HarperCollins (0-06-022533-5), 1991. 48p. (Interest level: 3-6).

In this dictionary, a well-known science writer provides beginning students with contemporary and historical words related to space. Added information includes brief biographical notes on such science pioneers as Kepler and Newton, and current information about zero gravity, space stations, etc.
♦ Students may make a mobile from some of the figures identified in the text or research more in-depth information on concepts introduced in the book.
1. Outer space—Dictionaries.

525
Lauber, Patricia. *Seeing Earth from Space*. Orchard Books (0-531-05902-2), 1990. 80p. Color photos. (Interest level: 4-8).

Exciting photographs and a lively text record the story of earth as seen by astronauts whose flights began at Kennedy Space Center, Cape Canaveral, Florida.
♦ Students may read biographical material on some of the astronauts and design their own spacecraft.
1. Earth—Juvenile literature. 2. Earth sciences—Juvenile literature.

574.5′2636
Bendick, Jeanne. *Exploring an Ocean Tide Pool*. Illus.by Todd Telander. Henry Holt (0-8050-2043-8), 1992. 56p.(Interest level: 3-6).

This is a useful introduction to plants and animals living in tide pools, which are common along the Florida coast. Clear writing and a compact index will appeal to intended audience.
♦ If an ocean is nearby, have students observe some of the tide pool creatures described in the text and draw their own concept of some of their observations. Students not living near an ocean may further research a particular tide pool plant or animal.
1. Tide pool ecology. 2. Ecology.

591.5′25325
Guiberson, Brenda. *Spoonbill Swamps*. Illus. by Megan Lloyd. Henry Holt (0-8050-1583-3), 1992. Unpaginated. (Interest level: K-3).

This colorfully illustrated story introduces young readers to birds of the wetlands, including those from Florida.
♦ Students may draw their own birds and make a class collage.
1. Swamp animals. 2. Spoonbills. 3. Alligators.

597.98
George, Jean Craighead. *Moon of the Alligator*. Illus., by Michael Rothman. Harpercollins (0-022427-4), 1991. 48p. (Interest level: 3-6).

Poetic prose describes the life cycle of the alligator, its search for food, and its struggle for survival in the Everglades, particularly during the dry season. Skill-

fully interwoven in the alligator's story is that of the other animals that inhabit this special area of Florida.
♦ Students may try to find poetry featuring the alligator.
1. Alligators—Florida. 2. The Everglades. 3. Florida—Everglades.

598
Arnosky, Jim. *Crinkleroot's Guide to Knowing the Birds*. Bradbury Press (0-02-705857-3), 1992. 32p. (Interest level: K-6).

This book is designed to awaken young readers to the joy of observing birds that frequent their local areas. In addition to its colorful illustrations, the volume is enriched with fascinating bird lore.
♦ Students can plan to do some birdwatching and start a sketchbook of birds seen in their area.
1. Birds. 2. Birds—Identification.

598.29
Audubon Society's Video Guide to Birds of North America. (Videotapes). Godfrey-Stadin Productions. Master Visions (01-55919-079-5), l988. Five volumes. $29.95 each. (Interest level: 3-8).

These highly rated videos depict the sight and sounds of North American birds, many of which migrate to Florida in the winter season. The productions are expertly done.
♦ Students can become birdwatchers for species in their own geographical area, noting observations and making sketches in a birdwatch notebook.
1.Birds 2. Birds—Identification.

598.29′24
Brown, Mary Barrett. *Wings Along the Waterway*. Illus. by author. Orchard Books (0-531-05981-2), 1992. 80p. Color illus. (Interest level: 4-8).

This book describes the habitat, life cycle, and physical appearance of birds, several of which inhabit Florida. The author includes concerns for survival of these water fowl. Double spread illustrations in full color expand the well-written text.
♦ Students may design their own water birds scrapbook.
1. Water birds—Juvenile literature. 2. Birds.

598.2′973 (Reference)
Peterson, Roger Tory and **Peterson, Virginia Marie.** *Audubon's Birds of America*.Audubon Society Elephant Folio, (Harrison House) Crown (0-517-47975-3), Unpaginated. (Interest level: 5-8).

This volume is composed of double-spread color reproductions of birds, many of which are found in Florida. The visual experience is enhanced by factual information and some direct quotations from Audubon's notes.
♦ In art classes students may draw, paint, or develop in multi-dimension design birds of their own choosing. They may also develop a notebook on birds in their area.
1. Birds. 2. Florida—Birds.

598.2′9759 (Reference)
Proby, Kathryn. *Audubon in Florida.* University of Miami Press (0-87024-241-5), 1974. 384p. (Interest level: 6-8).

Proby's research and selections from Audubon's writings open vistas on the life and interest of the man who spent much time in Florida studying and drawing birdlife from Key West to Jacksonville.
♦ History buffs may research what was going on in Florida while Audubon was studying and painting. Students may visit the Audubon home and museum in Key West or send off for information from this center.
1. Audubon, John James, 1785-1851. 2. Birds—Florida.

629.4
Markle, Sandra. *Pioneering Space.* Atheneum (0-689-31748-4), 1992. 40p. Illus., with full color photographs. (Interest level: 3-6).

The text describes how spacecraft work, how space stations function, and "how people live in these unusual environments." The book provides current information for students who live in Florida, a major center of space activity.
♦ Students in the area may visit the space center; students from other areas may write for information and plan an imaginary tour of the center.
1.Outer space—Exploration.

629.45′4
Gold, Susan Dudley. *Countdown to the Moon.* Crestwood House (0-89686-689-0), 1992. 48p. (Interest level: 4-6).

This book may be described as a historical review of human efforts to reach the moon. The text, designed to attract the "reluctant" reader, is extended with a useful glossary of terms.
♦ Students may write to a space center for information about their favorite astronaut.
1. Moon—Exploration. 2. Space flight to the moon.

641.5
Rawlings, Marjorie Kinnan. *Cross Creek Cookery.* Scribner's (0-684-71876-6), 1942. 264p. (Interest level: 6-8).

This anecdotal cookbook is based on meals prepared with foodstuffs garnered from the natural environment in which the naturalist author lived. The book's format results in a high quality blend of history, nature, and personal narrative.
♦ Students can try some of these really different food preparations and determine whether their initial impressions were lasting.
1.Cookery. 2. Florida—Cookery.

641.5′9759
Nickerson, Jane. *Jane Nickerson's Florida Cookbook.* University of Florida Presses (0-8130-0443-8), 1973. 204p. (Interest level: 6-8).

Culinary traditions indigenous to geographical locations from Key West to Pensacola reflect the diverse backgrounds of Florida settlers. Informative notes precede each recipe and make this a fun book for browsing or experimenting.

♦ Students may begin personal scrapbooks of recipes from their own and other areas. Some students may want to try recipes from the author's collection.
1. Cookery. 2. Florida—cookery.

746.46 (Reference)
Williams, Charlotte Allen. *Florida Quilts.* University of Florida Press (0-8130-1163-9), 1992. 256p. Color and B/W photos. (Interest level: 7-8).

Illustrated with color and black-and-white photographs, this book gives the history of quilts and quiltmaking in Florida from 1845 to the present. The text includes quilt-related anecdotal records and social history with a focus on women's roles in the historical accounts.
♦ Some students may want to try their hand at simple quilt making. Students may interview quilt makers in their areas and perhaps take pictures of the persons at work.
1. Quiltmaking—Florida.

770
Weber, William J. *Florida Nature Photography.* University of Florida Press (0-8130-1161-2), 1992. 176p. Color photos. (Interest level: 6-8).

A noted wildlife photographer has compiled a book of hundreds of pictures taken in Florida wildlife areas. In addition to the photographs, the author gives information on sites to visit and hints on how to achieve quality photographs.
♦ Amateur photographers may try taking outdoor pictures following some of Weber's suggestions.
1. Photography. 2. Florida Wildlife—Photography. 3. Nature photography.

783.675
Johnson, James Weldon and **Johnson, Rosamond.** *The Books of American Negro Spirituals.* DaCapo Paperback (0-306-80074-8), 1977. (Two volumes in one). 187p., each volume. (Interest level:4-8).

James and Rosamond Johnson, natives of Jacksonville, Florida, capture the dignity of the music of African-Americans in this reissue of a 1925 publication that speaks of survival and hope for life in a better world. James Weldon Johnson wrote the words to "Lift Every Voice and Sing," now called the Negro National Anthem; brother Rosamond wrote the music.
♦ Involve students in learning some of the spirituals. Older students may be interested in studying the meaning and significance of some of the titles.
1. Spirituals.

784
Delacre, Lulu. *Arroz con Leche: Popular Songs and Rhymes from Latin America.* Illus. by the author. Scholastic (0-590-4188-74), 1989. 329p. (Interest level: 3-6).

Popular songs with musical notations and English translations introduce English-speaking children to the songs of another country and provide familiar music and rhymes to Spanish-speaking children.
♦ Students can learn the songs and present them to other classes or to parents at a school function.
1. Folksongs—Spanish. 2. Children's songs—Spanish.

784.49 (Reference)
Morris, Allen. *Folksongs of Florida*. University Press of Florida (0-8130-0983-9), 1990. 488p. (Interest level: 5-8).

Commentaries on political, social, and economic culture of a people are expressed through song, and this material is enriched by the historical notations that precede each song section. The single line notation system provides tunes for entries that cover work songs, war songs, nursery songs, etc.
♦ As a class project, students may learn a medley of songs to present at a parents program or school assembly.
1. Florida—Folksongs. 2. Folksongs—Florida.

790.06′80975924 (Reference)
Beard, Richard R. *Walt Disney's Epcot*. Henry Abrams (0-8109-0819-0), 1982. 238p. Color photos. (Interest level:6-8).

Photographs and fluid text describe Epcot, the Disney Corporation's dream of the world of tomorrow. Quality writing and exciting perspectives invite readers to move from browsing to indepth reading.
♦ Influenced by new knowledge, students may try to "create" their own tomorrow's world with three-dimensional figures.
1. EPCOT (Florida). I. Disney, Walt, 1901-1966.

796.5′1
Arnosky, Jim. *Crinkleroot's Guide to Walking in Wild Places*. Bradbury Press (0-02-705842-5), 1990. 37p. (Interest level: 3-6).

This is an informative guide to safely exploring and finding the unexpected sights of your neighborhood. The author's approach adds fun to the learning process.
♦ Students may walk in the woods or parks of their area and either photograph or make notes on *new* discoveries.
1. Walking. 2. Walking—Safety measures.

808.1
Jumper, Moses, Jr. *Echoes in the Wind: Seminole Indian Poetry*. Illus. by Susan Hartline. Boca Raton Printing, 1990. 48p. (Interest level: 5-8).

This small volume captures the Native American love for the land and respect for tradition, and offers a sharing of cultures. The book may be ordered directly from the Seminole Reservation—Stirling Road, Hollywood, FL 33024.
♦ Students can compare some of the nature themes with nature themes in the poetry of other cultures. They can also try writing poetry based on some of their own nature observations.
1. Seminole Indians—Poetry.

813.52
Lyons, Mary. *Sorrow's Kitchen*. Scribner's (0-684-19198), 1990. 144p. B/W photos. (Interest level: 6-8).

This is a record of the life and work of Zora Neale Hurston, the prolific African-American author from the all black town of Eatonville, Florida. Hurston was a folklorist who was a part of the Harlem Renaissance and whose work is now enjoying a revival. A useful bibliography is included.

♦ Have students share some of Hurston's tales and then locate tales of similar themes to compare and contrast.
1. Hurston, Zora Neale—Juvenile literature. 2. African-Americans—Folklore.

909.09823
Fichter, George S. *Floridians All*. Pelican Publishing Company (0-88239-804-3), 1991. 88p. B/W illus. (Interest level: 4-6).

This collection of biographical sketches introduces readers to the diverse personalities responsible for the growth and development of Florida. Brief chapters may have special appeal for reluctant readers.
♦ Students may want to find more detailed pictures than the black-and-white line drawings used to identify the personalities included.
1.Florida—Biography—Juvenile literature.

912.759 (Reference)
Fernald, Edward and **Purdum, Elizabeth**. *Atlas of Florida*. University Press of Florida (0-8130-1131-0), 1992. 280p. (Interest level: 6-8).

Maps in this collection cover Florida's natural environment, history, social development, and demographics. The wide expanse of information covered and clarity of the visual projections make this a useful reference in many subject disciplines.
♦ Students may be assigned to write a news report relating to one of the areas on which a map in the collection focuses.
1. Florida—maps.

917.5
George, Jean Craighead. *Everglades Wildguide: Natural History of Everglades National Park*. USGO (0-16-003420-5), 1988. 103p. (Interest level: 4-8).

Florida collections should include this classic, well-documented story of the Everglades—a unique nature area.
♦ Students can plan an imaginary trip to the Everglades and write of their survival techniques or draw a map of the directions they took during their trip.
1. Everglades—Florida. 2. Florida—Wildlife.

917.5
Vizcaya. (Videotape). United Video, 1987. $ 19.95. (Interest level: 4-8).

The video gives a 60-minute narrated tour of the James Deering mansion and sculptured gardens in Coral Gables, Florida. The mansion, now a museum, is an exquisite example of European decorative art in the furniture, furnishings, and accouterments of gracious living.
♦ Students who cannot visit the mansion can research aspects of the countries from which Deering imported materials mentioned in the video.
1. Florida—Vizcaya. 2. Museums—Florida.

917.59
Florida Department of Natural Resources. *Travel Florida: State and National Parks*. (Videotape). International Video Projects, 1990. $19.95. (Interest level: 3-6).

This video provides a 30-minute color-filled "trip" through Florida parks and waterways. Knowledgeable rangers point out flora and fauna and wildlife in local areas.

♦ Students may visit national parks in home areas and take photographs of flora and fauna indigenous to a particular area.

1. Florida—Recreation centers. 2. Florida—Wildlife. 3. Florida—Natural resources.

917.59 (Reference)
Morris, Allen, comp. *The Florida Handbook 1991-1992*. Peninsular Publishing Company, 1983-continuous. 720p. (Interest level: 6-8).

This comprehensive handbook covers Florida history and governmental structure, and gives biographical notes on selected Florida personalities, past and present. In a volume that is constantly updated, the editor adds visual representations of the various state symbols: bird, flag, seal, etc.

♦ Students may select topics for more indepth research: e.g., habitats of state bird; history behind the various flags that flew over Florida; life of some individual included in the text.

1. Florida—History 2. Florida—Travel.

917.59 (Reference)
Morris, Allen. *Florida Place Names* . University Press (0-87024-256-3), 1974. 160p. (Interest level: 5-8).

This volume is an alphabetical listing of place names around the state. The entries vary in length and significance but provide interesting browsing material.

♦ Students may research and report an anecdote about a place name not included in the text.

1. Florida—History. 2. Names—Geographical—Florida.

917.59'0463
Gleasner, Bill and **Gleasner, Diane**. *Florida Off the Beaten Path*. 2nd ed. Globe Pequot (0-87106-481-2), 1990. 160p. (Interest level: 4-8).

This book is filled with frank, insightful nature-oriented descriptions of places to visit for both fun-filled and thought-provoking experiences in the out of doors. The guide is a pocket-sized traveling companion.

♦ Students can discover some of the off-the-beaten-path sites in their own areas.

1. Florida—description and travel. 2. Florida—guidebooks.

917.59'39
Carr, Archie. *The Everglades* (American Wilderness Series). Time-Life Books (0-910923-38-8), 1973, 1988 (out of print). 488p. Color photos. (Interest level: 6-8).

Color photographs and informative poetic text provide insight into a "unique watery wilderness." Vivid descriptions bring to life mangrove swamps, the life of spiny lobsters, and a tale of hurricane-ravaged Cape Sable. The book, considered a classic, is out of print, but available in special Florida collections.

♦ Students may take an imaginary trip through some of the places cited in the text and send a report to the local newspaper.

1. The Everglades. 2. Florida—Everglades.

919.9'04
Dudley, Mark. *An Eye to the Sky*. Crestwood House (0-896-691-2), 1992. 48p. Color photos. (Interest level: 4-6).

The text provides introductory descriptions of the telescope, rockets, satellites, and other scientific inventions used for unmanned probes of outer space. Simple definitions and illustrative photographs help to clarify some complex concepts.

♦ Students may visit a museum in the area that exhibits some of the items described in the text.

1. Space probes. 2. Travel—Outer Space. 3. Artificial satellites. 4. Rockets. I. Title.

970.01'6'092
Carson, Robert. *Hernando DeSoto*. (World's Great Explorers Series). Children's Press (0-516-03065-5), 1991. 128p. (Interest level: 3-6).

Carson introduces young readers to one of the early explorers of northern Florida. The text includes limited information about de Soto, the man, and useful map drawings tracing his travels.

♦ Students may use a map to follow deSoto's path.

1. Explorers. 2. America —Exploration.

970.1 (Reference)
Faber, Harold. *The Discoverers of America*. Scribner's (0-684-19217-9), 1992. 290p. (Interest level: 7-8).

Geographical perspective on the discovery of America includes sections on those explorers who sought to add these territories to their native land's possessions. Florida is included under the activities of explorers from Spain, France, and England.

♦ Students may use the brief passages as a catalyst for more indepth study of individual explorers or in map studies to trace the explorers' routes on various trips. Students can also imagine themselves members of an expedition and keep a diary.

1. America—Discovery and exploration. 2. Explorers.

975
[Clark, Bill]. *Florida Black Heritage Trail*. Florida State Historical Museum, 1992. Unpaginated. (Interest level: 4-8).

This attractive booklet records the location of historical sites focusing on African-American contributions to Florida history. This compact and colorful pamphlet provides factual information often overlooked in guides.

♦ Students may investigate ethnic minority sites and monuments in their area.

1. Florida—History. 2. African-Americans—Florida—History.

975
Fischer, Maylyn. *Miami*. Macmillan (0-87518-428-6), 1990. 60p. (Interest level: 3-6).

This is a beginner's introduction to the history and culture of one of Florida's most ethnically diverse cities. The author's choice of language paints a clear and balanced picture of the mosaic that is Miami.

♦ Students in the area may visit historical sites or participate in any of the many ethnic festivals; stu-

dents outside the area may visit vicariously through newspaper reports.
1. Miami. 2. Florida—cities.

975.00497
Lepthien, Emilie. *The Seminoles*. (New True Book Series). Children's Press (0-516-01941-1), 1985. 45p. Color photos. (Interest level: 2-4).

Written for primary level readers, this book is an introduction to the past and present history of the Seminoles now living in South Florida. Simple but accurate concepts are enlivened with color photographs of the area and the people.
♦ Students may listen to native tales as told by Betty Mae Jumper on the *Corn Lady: Seminole Indian Legends* videotapes (*see* page 34).
1. Seminole Indians.

975.9
Boone, Floyd Edward, comp. *Florida Historical Markers and Sites*. Rainbow Books (0-935834-62-1), 1988. 371p. (Interest level: 6-8).

This book contains descriptions, legends and some photographs of the "295 state approved markers" located in the 67 Florida counties. The author visited each of the sites.
♦ Students can check with local chambers of commerce to learn if additional markers have been established since the publication of this book.
1. Florida—History.

975.9
Harter, Walter. *Four Flags Over Florida*. Illus. by Russell Hoover. Julian Messner/Simon & Schuster (0-671-32399-7), 1971. 96p. (Interest level: 4-6).

This is a simplified introduction to Florida's early history, when European nations vied for superiority in this new land. The author provides a time line of changes in the "power structure."
♦ Students may draw a flag and note things of interest about the nation at the time the chosen flag was flying over Florida.
1. Florida—History.

975.9'00497
Costabel, Eva Deutsch. *The Early People of Florida*. Atheneum (0-689-31500-7), 1993. 54p. (Interest level: 3-6).

The author shares with young readers the unique history of Florida and the people who lived in the land long before the advent of the European explorers. In words and pictures students see the everyday life of the earliest people and then are moved into the story of the first explorers and settlers, up until the beginning of statehood.
♦ Students may keep an imaginary diary of their activities as dwellers in this early civilization.
1. Indians of North America—Florida—History.
2. Florida—Discovery and Exploration. 3. Indians of North America—Florida—Antiquities.

Biography

See also biographical entries in the Florida Nonfiction section, especially under 970.01 and 970.1.

920
Katz, William Loren and **Franklin, Paula A**. *Proudly Red and Black: Stories of African and Native Americans*. Atheneum (0-689-31801-4), 1993. 88p. (Interest level: 3-5).

This slight volume relates the achievements of selected individuals overcoming barriers caused by the fact that they were of mixed Native-American and African blood. This book contains a wide range of personalities, although it is somewhat weakened by too many generalities.
♦ Using other sources, students may locate information and/or pictures of one of the individuals discussed in this book.
1. African-Americans—Biography. 2. Native-Americans—Biography. 3. Florida—Biographies.

92 Bethune, Mary McLeod
Greenfield, Eloise. *Mary McLeod Bethune*. Illus. by Jerry Pinkney. HarperCollins (0-690-01129-6), 1977. 40p. (Interest level: 3-6).

Of interest to young readers, this book tells the story of the daughter of a former slave with an unquenchable thirst for knowledge, who learned to read, earned college scholarships, founded a college in Daytona Beach, Florida, and served as advisor to President Franklin D. Roosevelt.
♦ Area children may visit Bethune Cookman College; students in other areas may research the history of the college.
1. Bethune, Mary McLeod. 2. Florida—Education.

92 Bethune, Mary McLeod
McKissack, Patricia and **McKissack, Fred**. *Mary McLeod Bethune*. Children's Press (0-516-06658-7), n.d. 32p. (Corner Stones of Freedom Series). Color and B/W photos. (Interest level: 3-5).

Using simple yet informative language, the authors have captured the essence of the life of a courageous and dauntless educator whose early efforts to educate negro boys and girls evolved into a life of working for youth of all ages, advising presidents, and breaking barriers for civil rights in many areas.
♦ Children may write to Bethune-Cookman College for information on the history of the school and its status in contemporary times.
1. Bethune, Mary McLeod—Biography. 2. Florida—Education. 3. African-Americans—Education.

92 Crews, Donald
Crews, Donald. *Bigmama's*. Illus. by author. Greenwillow (0-688-09950-5), 1991. Unpaginated. (Interest level: K-3).

A noted illustrator takes young readers on a warm and friendly visit to his childhood home in Cottondale, Florida. Uncluttered pictures extend the text.
♦ Children may write of "adventures" on a visit to their own grandparents' home.
1. Crews, Donald—Biography. 2. Florida—Juvenile literature 3. Family life. 4. Illustrators.

92 Douglas, Marjory Stoneham
Bryant, Jennifer. *Marjory Stoneham Douglas: Voice of the Everglades*. Illus. by Larry Raymond. Twenty-First Century Books-Henry Holt and Co. (0-8050-2113-2), 1992. 72p. (Interest level: 4-6).

A simple but well-written test introduces young readers to the life and work of the matriarch of Florida environmental concerns, with particular focus on the Everglades. In addition to biographical information, the reader is helped to understand Douglas's awareness of the widespread importance of the Everglades as a vital part of the entire ecosystem.

♦ Using magazine pictures or their own drawings, students can create a picture of some of the flora and fauna of the Everglades.

1. Douglas, Marjory Stoneham—Biography. 2. Florida—The Everglades. 3. Conservationists.

92 Edison, Thomas Alva
Adler, David. *Thomas Alva Edison, Great Inventor*. Illus. by Lyle Miller. Holiday House (0-8234-0820-5), 1990. 47p. (Interest level: 3-5)

The author introduces young readers to the life and creative inventions of Thomas Edison, a man once thought to be a "bumbler" who came up with 300 theories on the electric light! The black-and-white illustrations show sketches of some inventions like the mimeograph machine.

♦ Students can use their imaginations to invent some useful item. Area students may visit Edison's Florida home in Ft. Myers and observe his lab and some of his inventions.

1. Edison, Thomas Alva, 1847-1931—Biography. 2. Ft. Myers—Florida—Historic Sites. 3. Inventors, U.S.—Biography.

92 Estefan, Gloria
Stefoff, Rebecca.*Gloria Estefan*. Chelsea House (0-7910-1244-1). 1991. 103p. (Hispanics of Achievement Series). (Interest level: 7-8).

This is the personal story of the popular and talented Havana-born singer who not only performs for the public, but spends much time and energy in humanitarian causes. In a text extended with black-and-white photographs, young readers will learn not only of Gloria the pop star and the survivor of a near fatal automobile accident, but also the family person who respects her parents and believes in a stable family life for herself in a show biz world that too often overlooks this facet of living.

♦ Students can listen to some of Estafan's records in both English and Spanish, and discuss some of the difficulties a famous person may encounter in his or her personal life because of that fame.

1. Estefan, Gloria, 1957—Biography. 2. Cubans—Florida.

92 Flagler, Henry
Chandler, David Leon. *Henry Flagler: The Astonishing Life and Time of the Visionary Robber Baron Who Founded Florida*. Macmillan (0-02-523690-3), 1986. (Interest level: 8).

This is a sophisticated, candid study of an ambitious businessman. Through land development, investments in transportation, and creative business ventures, Flagler is described as having "carved the state of Florida out of the wilderness." Landmarks to his ingenuity survive throughout the state today.

♦ Students can discuss what the term "Robber Baron" in the title means, and how such persons might be viewed differently today from the way they were viewed in their own time. Florida students might visit a site in their area that is a memorial to Flagler.

1. Flagler, Henry Morrison 1830-1913—Biography. 2. Pioneers—Florida. 3. Florida—History, 1865.

92 Hemingway, Ernest
Lyttle, Richard B. *Ernest Hemingway, The Life and Legend*. Atheneum (0-689-31670-4), 1992. 212p. Illus, with photos. (Interest level: 8).

This is a fast-paced, objective study of Ernest Hemingway, the complex personality who made an indelible impact on American literature. Of particular interest to students in Florida might be those sections discussing Hemingway's time spent in Key West, where he is still revered as a type of folk hero.

♦ Students can read and research Hemingway's life and writings and then discuss how his life experiences shaped what he wrote.

1. Hemingway, Ernest—Biography. 2. Key West, Florida.

92 Jackson, Andrew
Osinski, Alice. *Andrew Jackson*. Children's Press (0-516-01387-4), 1987. 98p. (Encyclopedia of Presidents Series). (Interest level: 6-8).

This comprehensive text includes information on Jackson's activities in Florida, his ongoing confrontations with the Seminole Indians, and political moves that finally resulted in Florida receiving statehood in 1845. Black-and-white photographs and sketches and a chronological table of events are an added dimension in this biography.

♦ Students can research activities in other parts of the country and the world during a chosen year of Jackson's presidency (1829-37).

1. Jackson, Andrew, 1767-1845—Biography. 2. Florida—Seminole Indians—History. 3. Presidents—United States—History.

92 James, Daniel, Jr.
Phelps, J. Alfred. *Chappie: America's First Black Four-Star General*. Presidio Press (0-89141-396-0), 1991. 366p. (Interest level: 8).

A challenging book for older students, this fast-paced biography describes a man of action whose courage was demonstrated on the battlefield and in the struggle against racial prejudice. James serves well as a role model; he went from being a student in a one-room school house in Pensacola, Florida, to being a fighter pilot in Korea and Vietnam, and a four-star general.

♦ Students can research the history of aviation in the United States from the perspective of African-American pilots.

1. James, Daniel, Jr—Biography. 2. Pilots—African-American. 3. Florida-African-Americans—Biography.

92 Johnson, James Weldon

Egypt, Ophelia Settle. *James Weldon Johnson*. Illus. by Moneta Barnett. Crowell, (0-690-00214-9), 1974. 41 p. (Interest level: 2-4).

The conversational tone of this book introduces early elementary students to the life of Jacksonville-born Johnson who was a musician, a poet, an educator, a lawyer, and a public speaker. A sense of strong family relationships is clearly shown as the activities of James Weldon and his brother Rosamond are discussed. The artist used pencil sketches with touches of green and sepia to illustrate the story.

♦ Students may locate and read some of Johnson's poety and listen to the words and music of "Lift Every Voice and Sing."

1. Johnson, James Weldon, 1871-1938—Biography.
2. Authors—American. 3. African-Americans—Biography.

92 Lloyd, Chris Evert

Lloyd, Chris Evert, with **Admur, Neil**. *Chrissie: My Own Story*. Simon & Schuster (0-671-44376-3), 1982. 237p. (Interest level: 8)

Much more than a recital of triumphs and defeats on tennis courts around the world, this book gives interesting insights into Chris Evert Lloyd the person. In a text that is sometimes "preachy," Chris emerges as fun-loving, family oriented, often insecure, and earnestly concerned with young tennis players who enter the pro circuit too soon.

♦ Students can discuss the impact of fame and wealth on young tennis stars—male and female—who turn pro too soon.

1. Evert, Chris—Biography. 2. Tennis.

92 Osceola

Blassingame, Wyatt. *Osceola: Seminole War Chief*. Garrard (No ISBN), 1967. 80p. (Interest level: 2-4).

This is a dated but factual introduction to the life of a courageous Native American who fought against signing the white man's too-often broken treaties regarding Indian land. Simple but forceful writing will appeal to young readers and make them aware of the Seminoles, many of whom continue to live independently in South Florida on part of the land defended by Osceola.

♦ Students may write for brochures that describe the availability of tours of Seminole Village in South Florida. Area students may visit the reservation and see the Native Americans working their crafts.

1. Osceola—Biography. 2. The Seminoles. 3. Florida—The Seminoles

92 Parker, Idella

Parker, Idella, with **Keating, Mary**. *Idella: Marjorie Rawlings' "Perfect Maid."* University of Florida Press (0-8130-1143-4), (0-8130-1144-2 pbk), 1992. 166p. (Interest level: 8).

This book is a multi-faceted record of Idella Parker's life as Marjorie Kinnan Rawlings' maid. Insights are provided about Rawlings, *the person*, for whom "it was not always easy to work."

♦ Students can discuss Parker's perspective of her employer's character, and how and why it might differ from other people's views of Rawlings.

1. Parker, Idella—Biography. 2. Rawlings, Marjorie Kinnan—Biography. 3. Florida—History.

92 Ringling Brothers

Cone, Molly. *The Ringling Brothers*. Illus. by James and Ruth McCrea. Crowell (0-690-70287-6), 1971. 40 p. (Interest level: 2-4).

For beginning readers, this is an adequate introduction to the family whose name is synonymous with circuses around the world. The short text also covers a bit of circus history. The legacy of the circus is emblazoned in the Circus Hall of Fame in Sarasota, Florida. Humorous illustrations extend the text.

♦ Students can research what it would take to become part of a circus act: a clown, a trapeze artist, a costume designer, etc.

1. Ringling, John—Biography. 2. Circus—History.
3. Sarasota—Florida—Museums.

Fiction

Caras, Roger. *Panther!* Illus. by Charles Frace.University of Nebraska Press (0-8032-6338-4), 1989. 185p. (Interest level:6-8).

Caras has written a dramatic adventure story in which the endangered panther is pitted against nature and its worst enemy—Man! Recently reissued, this classic is replete with descriptions of all manner of life in the Everglades.

♦ Students may research the present status of the Florida panther and compare their findings with the life of panthers in other geographical areas.

1. Panthers—Fiction. 2. Everglades—Fiction.

Cavanagh, Helen. *Panther Glade*. Simon & Schuster (0-671-75617-6), 1993. 144p. (Interest level: 5-7).

When Bill Craven's parents send him to spend the summer with his Aunt Cait in Florida, he is totally unprepared for the series of adventures that follows, including narrowly escaping the bite of a rattle snake, an encounter with a dolphin, and a test of his survival skills when caught in a storm in the area close to Marco Key. Mixed with touches of humor and thought provoking concepts, this book weaves into Bill's Everglades adventures legends of the Calusa tribes, nature stories, and the importance of digs in connecting the past with the present.

♦ As a class project, students can make an illustrated scrapbook of Calusa legends.

1. Florida—Fiction. 2. Calusa Indians-Antiquities—Fiction. 3. Self-Confidence—Fiction.

Cleaver, Vera and **Cleaver, William J**. *Hazel Rye*. Lippincott (0-397-31951-7), 1983. 178p. (Interest level: 5-7).

Hazel Rye, acting older than her eleven years, has mapped out her future. She calls her father Millard, rather than Dad, and faces the world with feisty independence, until she meets Felder Poole. Felder shows her how to really make her way in the world by teaching her how to care for her own orange grove. The moods in the story provide readers with a real slice of life in a small southern town.

♦ Students can plant and nurture some seedlings of their choice.

1. Florida—Fiction. 2. Oranges—Fiction.

Crews, Donald. *Shortcut*. Illus. by the author. Greenwillow (0-688-06436-1), 1992. Unpaginated. (Interest level: K-3).

While on a summer visit to his grandmother's home, the author and his cousins take a shortcut home by way of the railroad track and narrowly escape an oncoming train! A suspenseful and little bit "scary" continuation of the author's happy recollections of childhood days in Cottondale, Florida (*see* preceding entry). Graphic illustrations take the reader right up to the path of the train!

♦ Student may write or dictate a personal "scary" adventure.

1. Florida—Fiction. 2. Railroads—Fiction. 3. African-Americans—Fiction.

Curtin, Margaretta. *Cubanitos in a New Land: Cuban Children in Miami*. Mazon Press (No ISBN), 1975. 73p. (Interest level: 3-4).

Although dated, this collection of vignettes recalls the early days of the Cuban migration as seen through the eyes of the children who endured the 90-mile trek across open waters.

♦ Students can compare information in the stories with records of life of Cubans in Miami today. Florida students can interview someone who has come to the U.S. from Cuba.

1. Miami—Fiction. 2. Florida—Fiction. 3. Cubans—Fiction.

Flipper. (Videotape). Home Video, 1963. $ 24.95.(Interest level: 3-6).

This video portrays a heartwarming story of the relationship between a Florida family and a dolphin wounded during a hurricane. The film, based on an earlier popular TV series, features the fine acting of Chuck Connors and Lucas Halpin.

♦ Students may enjoy reading a nonfiction book about dolphins and comparing it with information extrapolated from the film. If near a seaquarium, students may visit the dolphin show.

1. Florida—Fiction. 2. Dolphins—Fiction.

George, Jean Craighead. *The Cry of the Crow*. Harper & Row (0-06-021956-4), 1980. 147p. (Interest level: 4-6).

In the strawberry growing region of Florida, crows are unwelcome intruders and usually destroyed by the berry growers. In this setting, Mandy adopts and nurtures an orphaned crow. But Mandy's refusal to let the bird join other crows brings about its demise. Interwoven into this nature tale is George's factual knowledge of the ways and language of crows.

♦ Students can listen to crows in their area to see if they can distinguish some of the sounds described in the text. Students may also draw a picture of Nina Terrance, the crow, as they imagine her.

1. Florida—Fiction. 2. Crows—Fiction.

George, Jean Craighead. *The Missing Alligator of Gumbo Limbo; an Ecological Mystery*. HarperCollins (0-06-020397-8), 1992. 148p. (Interest level: 5-8).

Set in the Florida Everglades, this slow-paced mystery is the story of Dajun, an oversized alligator, and a ranger who is out to destroy him. Through his own skill and the aid of a diverse collection of homeless hammock residents, Dajun survives—to the benefit of the Everglades. Mystery and reality are skillfully interwoven into this story.

♦ Students may compare information in George's book with that in a nonfiction book on the Everglades.

1. Alligators—Fiction. 2. Wildlife conservation—Fiction. 3. Florida—Fiction. 4. The Homeless—Fiction.

George, Jean Craighead. *The Talking Earth*. HarperCollins (0-06-021975-0), 1983. 160p. (Interest level: 4-6).

Billie Wind, contemporary Seminole Indian girl, questions the legends and stories of her people, until, in a "rites of passage" experience in the Everglades, she learns and appreciates the "talk" of the animals and the survival value of the native plants. The author's first-hand knowledge about the natural habitat of the Everglades and the traditions of the Seminoles give credibility to this story's plot.

♦ Students should research information on wilderness survival and catalog a list of edible plants, with pictures of as many as can be found.

1. Seminole Indian—Fiction. 2. Everglades—Fiction.

Harvey, Dean. *The Secret Elephant of Harlan Kooter*. Illus. by Mark Richardson. Houghton Mifflin (0395-62523-8), 1992. 130p. (Interest level: 3-5).

In this humorous fantasy, an oft beleaguered Harlan Kooter befriends and *hides!* a runaway elephant who is tired of performing in the circus. In a predictable conclusion, Harlan and Hannibal rescue the family of Harlan's tormentor in the midst of a ravaging flood. Hannibal is returned to his home in Africa, Harlan becomes a hero, and all's well that ends well. A fun-filled tale for young readers.

♦ Students can make a collage of circus activities and draw a map of Hannibal's homeland in Africa.

1. Florida—Fiction. 2. Elephants—Fiction. 3. Friendship—Fiction.

Hest, Amy. *Travel Tips from Harry: A Guide to Family Vacations in the Sun*. Illus. by Sue Truesdell. Morrow (0-688-07972-5), 1989. 53p. (Interest level: 3-5).

There is tongue-in-cheek-humor in the text that offers suggestions for making the most of a visit with grandparents who live in a Miami condominium. Many of the suggestions would serve well in other situations: take a "good" report card, be polite to grandparents' older friends, don't fuss about carrying food home in a doggy bag. Truesdell's black-and-white cartoon-like illustrations extend the text.

♦ Students can make their own list of things to do to make a visit with older relatives pleasant for all.

1. Miami—Fiction. 2. Florida—Fiction. 3. Grandparents—Fiction.

Hurston, Zora Neale. *Their Eyes Were Watching God.* HarperCollins (0-06-091650-8), 1990. 286p. (Interest level: 8).

This literary classic uses the picturesque language of a small Florida town to relate a 1930s African-American woman's quest for self-identity—a quest that seems surprisingly contemporary.
1. Eatonville, Florida—Fiction. 2. Florida—Fiction. 3. African-Americans—Fiction. 4. Women—Fiction.

Lenski, Lois. *Strawberry Girl.* Lippincott, Harper (0-397-30109-X), 1945. 208p. (Interest level: 4-6).

Feisty and independent Birdie Boyer helps her family cope with "shiftless" neighbors while earning a living picking strawberries. This early picture of regional migrant life is a Newbery Award classic.
♦ Students may read other "migrant" stories and compare information.
1. Florida—Fiction. 2. Migrant workers—Fiction.

Ney, John. *Ox: The Story of the Kid at the Top.* Little Brown (No ISBN), 1970. 140p. (Interest level: 5-7).

With a mixture of humor and pathos, Ney shows the world of some of the wealthy, but dysfunctional residents of Palm Beach. Ox, oversized, insecure, and misunderstood, travels with his alcoholic father from Palm Beach to Mexico so that Ox can see a cow first hand. This trek is symbolic of the money-can-buy-it lifestyle, the folly of which is not lost on Ox, who works to survive and find his own personal self. Ox's quest for self-esteem continues in the sequel: *Ox Goes North* (Harper & Row, 1973).
♦ Students can read more about and discuss families and alcoholism.
1. Florida—Fiction. 2. Alcholism—Fiction. I. Title.

O'Dell, Scott. *Alexandra.* Houghton, Mifflin (0-395-35571-0), 1984. 146p. (Interest level: 6-8).

When her sponge-diving father dies of the bends, Alexandra, along with her crippled grandfather, takes on the business and finds herself unwittingly involved in a drug smuggling scheme. This fast-paced story, set in the sponge-diving area of Tarpon Springs, provides factual information on this unique industry.
♦ Students can research differences between the many varieties of sponges.
1. Florida—Fiction. 2. Sponge fisheries—Fiction. 3. Greek-Americans—Fiction.

Peck, Robert Newton. *Arly.* Walker (0-8027-6856-3), 1989. 151p. (Interest level: 5-7).

Writing in the dialect of the unschooled migrant worker, Peck paints a vivid picture of the life of the "pickers" in Roscoe Broda's camp—the torment, degradation, and the "enslavement." Protagonist Arly Poole looks forward to going to Moore Haven to attend school. The "in the air" conclusion leads to the sequel, *Arly's Run* (*see* following entry).

♦ Students can read and compare other stories about migrant camps, discussing the reasons for the hardships in this kind of life and what can be done to change conditions.
1. Florida—Fiction. 2. Migrant labor—Fiction. 3. Teachers—Fiction.

Peck, Robert Newton. *Arly's Run.* Walker (0-8027-8120-9), 1991. 160p. (Interest level: 5-7).

After a tortuous trip across Okechobee, destruction of the boat in which he was traveling, and what he thought was the loss of his friend, Brother Smith, Arly arrives near Moore Haven only to learn that the town of Moore Haven and most of its inhabitants have been destroyed by a hurricane. With dashed hopes, and after a few exciting experiences, Arly returns to Jailtown, once again escapes Broda's cruelty, and sees a chance for an education through the undaunted persistence of a teacher, Miss Hoe. Fortunately, the sequel stands fairly independent of the first book.
♦ As a class project, students can collect school supplies for distribution in a migrant school area.
1. Florida—Fiction. 2. Orphans—Fiction. 3. Hurricanes—Fiction. 4. Education—Fiction.

Peck, Robert Newton. *The Horse Hunters.* Random House (0-394-56980-6), 1988, 214p. (Interest level: 6-8).

Ranch dweller Ladd Bodeen, living under the constant barbed criticism of his much older brother, strikes off alone to round up a herd of wild horses. With decisive and exciting writing, Peck packs into this rite-of-passage story moments of danger and death in Florida swampland, graphic information about the habits of wild horses, and a non-didactic message about the power that comes of believing in one's self.
♦ Students can read other books that tell of the nature of wild horses and watch the action of a rodeo either in person or on TV or video.
1. Florida—Fiction. 2. Horses—Fiction. 3. Brothers—Fiction.

Prather, Ray. *Fish and Bones.* HarperCollins (0-06-025121-2), 1992, 225p. (Interest level: 7-8).

The unlikely combination of a mystifying bank robbery, a racial incident centered around a who-has-the-longest-rattle-snake contest, and a botched wedding are deftly woven into a rousing tale. Fast-changing scenes keep the reader alert in this challenging and not always funny story of personal relationships between teenagers.
♦ Using clues scattered in the text, studnets can create their solutions to the bank robbery mystery.
1. Florida—Fiction. 2. African-American—Fiction. 3. Race Relations—Fiction. 4. Mystery and Detective Stories—Fiction.

Pratt, Theodore. *Seminole.* Duell, Sloan and Pearce, 1954 (out of print). 180p. (Interest level: 8).

This novel is based on the life of Chief Osceola, who relentlessly waged war against white settlers in defense of his home territory. The book is no longer in print but Florida collections hold many Pratt titles.
1. Osceola—Fiction. 2. Seminole Indians—Fiction.

Rawlings, Marjorie Kinnan. *The Yearling*. Illus, by Andrew Wyeth. Scribner's (0-684-18461-3), 1985. 416p. (Illustrated classics); Macmillan (0-02-0449431-3 pbk), 1988. 448p. (Interest level: 5-8).

Rawlings has written a warm and moving story about a young boy and an orphaned deer that becomes a pet and then tragically must be destroyed. As Jody grows from boy to man, both he and the reader learn that animals of the wild cannot "make it in domesticated settings"
♦ Students may compare the novel with the film interpretation.
1. Florida—Fiction. 2. Deer—Fiction.

Smith, Patrick. *Angel City*. Valkyrie Press (0-912760-71-0), 1978. 190p. (Interest level: 8).

A West Virginia family's search for a better life ends in riots, death, and destruction before they decide to leave Florida. This haunting classic novel is based on research into the degrading conditions of migrant work in Homestead, Florida.
♦ Have students compare the novel with the film interpretation, which changed the original ending.
1. Migrant workers—Florida. 2. Florida—Fiction.

Smith, Patrick. *Forever Island and Allapattah: A Patrick Smith Reader*. Pineapple Press (0-910-923-42-6), 1987. 186p. (Interest level: 8).

Forever Island and *Allapattah* are novels about the Seminole Indians in South Florida and the life of Charlie Jumper and Toby Tiger, both of whom try to fight the "establishment" in a fruitless effort to protect their home territory *and* their culture against the invasion of ever encroaching developers. This book offers fast-paced, thought-provoking reading.
1. Seminoles—Fiction. 2. Florida Everglades—Fiction.

Stolz, Mary. *Go and Catch a Flying Fish*. HarperKeypoint (0-06-447090-3), 1992, 1979. 213p. (Interest level: 6-8).

The protagonists find their most stable support in a rather strict but loving grandmother who cares for them as their family slowly falls apart. This is a fast-paced intergenerational novel.
♦ Students can read and compare the role of the elders in other cross-generational novels with the grandmother's role in this book.
1. Family life—Fiction. 2. Florida—Fiction.

Stolz, Mary. *Go Fish!*. Illus. by Pat Cummings. Harper (0-06-25822-5), 1991. 74p. (Interest level: 3-6).

This book is a continuation of the pleasant life of Thomas, Ringo, and Grandfather, the characters in Stolz's *Storm in the Night* (*see* page 44). The book is full of tales that might be told on a fishing expedition and ends with the Thomas and his Grandfather's favorite card game—Go Fish.
♦ Each student can share one of his or her favorite tales from the book.
1. Grandfathers—Fiction. 2. Gulf of Mexico—Fiction.

Stolz, Mary. *Stealing Home*. HarperCollins (0-06-021154-7), 1992. 154p. (Interest level: 4-6).

The third title in this intergenerational "series" shows a major change in the household when Thomas'

great aunt comes to stay "for a while." Young readers will delight in Thomas' slow and often humorous growth into the acceptance of a new life experience as Aunt Linzy almost literally "steals" their home.
♦ Students may write an imaginary episode of a "stranger" coming into a family's settled home life.
1. Grandfathers—Fiction. 2. Baseball—Fiction. 3. Old Age—Fiction.

Stolz, Mary. *Storm in the Night*. Illus. by Pat Cummings. (Harper (0-06-025912-4), 1988. Unpaginated. (Interest level: K-4).

This is a warm intergenerational story about a grandfather who comforts his young grandson and his cat, Ringo, during a Florida thunderstorm. The book is a Coretta Scott King Honor Winner for the illustrations.
♦ Students can research information on thunderstorms, hurricanes, and other weather conditions.
1. Thunderstorms—Fiction 2. Grandparents—Fiction. 3. Fear—Fiction.

Temple, Frances. *Taste of Salt: A Story of Modern Haiti*. Orchard Books (0-531-05459-4), 1992. 179p. (Interest level: 8).

Jeremie, a young journalist, is recording the traumatic story of Djo, hospitalized in a thwarted attempt to escape the island of Haiti. This very powerful and contemporary narrative has implications for Florida residents of all ages because of the influx of the Haitian population into the state.
♦ Students can collect newspaper articles recounting stories of escapes or attempted escapes from Haiti and discuss what the situation means for Florida residents and the U.S.
1. Haiti—Fiction. 2. Florida—Fiction. 3. Aritstide, Jean-Bertrand—Fiction.

Waldron, Ann. *The Luckie Star*. E.P. Dutton (0-525-34270-2), 1977. 266p. (Interest level: 6+).

Twelve year old Quincy Luckie, a science buff, is considered an "anomaly" in her music and art oriented family. All of this changes after a hurricane, when Quincy's scientific methods lead to the discovery of a sunken Spanish galleon off the West Coast of Florida—with some of its treasure still aboard! Without intrusion, the author includes historical events relevant to pirates, shipwrecks, etc.
♦ In a more than one-day project, students can hide an object in the classroom and draw a "pirate's map" for fellow students to use in locating the "treasure."
1. Florida—Fiction. 2. Hurricanes—Fiction. 3. Buried Treasure—Fiction.

Whittaker, Dorothy Raymond. *Angels of the Swamp*. Walker and Company (0-8027-8129-2), 1992. 209p. (Interest level: 7-8).

Set in the Depression years, this is the story of three runaways, orphaned Taffy, age 15; Jody, 12, escaping an alcoholic uncle; and Jeff, who has been unable to find and keep a decent job. The three make a life together in a swamp off the West Coast of Florida, and, with problems that seem a little too easily solved, life becomes good for all of them.
♦ Students can find out some of the things one would need to know to survive in a swampy area for even a week.

1. Florida—Fiction. 2. Depressions—Fiction. 3. Orphans—Fiction.

Professional Materials

332.5'44
Wilkinson, Alec. *Big Sugar: Seasons in the Cane Fields of Florida*. Knopf (0-394-57312-9), 1989. 263p. (Interest level: Professional).

Flowing prose provides graphic descriptions of the dangerous job, the exploitation, the degradation, the life-threatening conditions under which male workers from the West Indies struggle in the cane fields of Florida. The author calls Belle Glade and Clewiston, the main centers of the cane crop, "a little piece of the third world."
1. Sugar workers—Florida. 2. Migrant agricultural laborers—Florida.

381.439
Kersey, Harry. *Pelts, Plumes and Hides: White Traders Among the Seminole Indians,1870-1930*. University Presses of Florida (0-8130-0680-5), 1975. 158p. (Interest level: Professional).

This scholarly and readable presentation of the changing relationships between the Seminole Indians and the white traders in South Florida during the late nineteenth and early twentieth centuries provides excellent background preparation for teaching aspects of Seminole history.
1. Seminole Indians.

387.1
McCarthy, Kevin M. *Florida Lighthouses*. Illus. with paintings by William L. Trotter. University of Florida Press (LC 89-29035), 1990. 134p. (Interest level: Professional).

This historical survey of lighthouses along Florida's coastlines is a fascinating piece of history. With the current move to computerize lighthouses, this well-documented volume provides useful historical information. The text is enriched with paintings and maps of lighthouses—some better known than others.
1. Lighthouses—Florida. 2. Navigation—Florida.

808
Oppel, Frank and **Meisel, Tony**, ed. *Tales of Old Florida*. Castle (1-55521-225-5), 1987. 477p. B/W photos. (Interest level: Professional).

This collection of short tales recounts events, real and imaginary, that trace Florida history from 1894 to the early 1920s. Black-and-white vintage photographs add to the historical perspective of the text.
1. Short stories—Florida 2. Florida—short stories.

813.54
McCarthy, Kevin M., ed. *Nine Florida Stories by Marjory Stoneham Douglas*. University of North Florida Press (LC89-29037), paper, 1990. 198p. (Interest level: Professional).

This collection of short stories is set in Florida in the early 1900s. Each story conveys an aspect of Douglas's lifelong concern for human dignity, civil rights, and preservation of the environment. The writing is fluidly poetic, sparse, and powerful.
1. Florida—short stories. I. Douglas, Marjory Stoneham.

973
Wheeler, Mary Bray, ed. *Directory of Historical Organizations in the United States and Canada*. American Association for State and Local History (0-942063-05-8),1990. 1190p. (Interest level: Professional).

Brief annotations give purpose, location, types of collections, and contact information. The Florida section is on pages 112-128.
1 Directories—United States.

975.9'1
Bennett, Charles E., ed. *Twelve on the River St. Johns*. University of North Florida Press (0-8130-0913-8), 1989. 166p. (Interest level: Professional).

This is a scholarly but readable collection of biographical sketches of historical figures whose activities are centered around the St. Johns River in North Florida "from times remote to the present."
1. Saint Johns River region— Biography 2. Florida—Biography.

Georgia

by Priscilla Bennett

Nonfiction

303.482
Dolphin, Laurie. *Georgia to Georgia: Making Friends in the U.S.S.R.* Tambourine (0-688-09896-7), 1991. 32p. Color photos. (Interest level: 3-6).

This is the story of an Atlanta boy's visit to Tbilisi, U.S.S.R., before the breakup of the Soviet Union. The photographs show modern Russia and give students a realistic look at another country.
♦ Students could chart the comparisons between life in the two Georgias and think about the changes in Tbilisi since the Soviet breakup.
1. Georgian U.S.S.R.—Social life and customs 2. Soviet Union—Social life and customs.

333.952
Underwater Oases: Georgia's Artificial Reefs. (Videotape). Georgia Department of Natural Resources, 1989. VHS, (28 min.). (Interest level: 6+).

Since 1972, Georgia has introduced artificial reefs along the coast to provide a habitat for sea life. Students interested in fishing will enjoy this production.
♦ Students might brainstorm other materials that could be used for the artificial reefs.
1. Marine Resources.

345.08
What's Going to Happen to Me? A Look at the Juvenile Court in Georgia. (Videotape). Carl Vinson Institute of Government, The University of Georgia, 1989. VHS, (37 min.). (Interest level: 8+).

The story follows the fate of three Georgia teenagers who are caught attempting to steal from a parked car. The workings of the court system in the three different circumstances are clearly shown and should give teens a healthy respect for the law.
♦ Students might invite representatives from their local court system to talk to their group or they might plan a field trip to the court room.
1. Juvenile Courts.

363.19
Patterns of Change. (Videotape). Georgia Department of Natural Resources, 1988. VHS, (28 min.). (Interest level: 6+).

Examples of historical preservation projects in Georgia are shown, and reasons for preservation are given. This is a good beginning to a subject not often explored with students.
♦ Students could find out if there is a historical preservation project in their area and visit the site if possible. If there is none, students could brainstorm buildings that should be preserved and why.
1. Historic buildings—Georgia.

363.7392
Air: The Vital Resource. (Videotape). Georgia Department of Natural Resources, 1981. VHS, (14 min.). (Interest level: 8+).

The causes of air pollution and the ways Georgia is fighting it are clearly explained in this production. The problems of balancing progress and quality of life are raised and would encourage discussion.
♦ Students could research the sources of air pollutants in their area and how they are regulated.
1. Air—Pollution.

363.7394
Clean Water: Georgia's Treasure. (Videotape). Georgia Department of Natural Resources, 1983. VHS, (26 min.). (Interest level: 5+).

The sources, treatment, usage, and monitoring of Georgia's water supply are shown in this video. The water cycle is also discussed.
♦ Students could write a paragraph of what would happen if they got up one morning and there was no water supply.
1. Water—Pollution.

398.2
Jaquith, Priscilla. *Bo Rabbit Smart for True.* Illus. by Ed Young. Phimolel (0-399-20793-7), 1981. 55p. B/W Illus. (Interest level: 3-8).

The author's foreword discusses the origin of these Bo Rabbit tales in the Gullah language of the Georgia sea islands. The stories are set in an interesting format

with four panels of pictures down the side of each page alongside the text.
♦ Students could use this format to illustrate other folktales commonly told in Georgia.
1. Folklore—Afrrican-American 2. Folklore—Georgia.

398.2089975
Arneach, Lloyd Teller. *The Animal's Ballgame.* Illus. by Lynda Halverson. Children's Press (0-516-05139-3), 1992. Unpaginated. Color illus. (Interest level: K-4).

This Cherokee tale is told in pictures with the text included at the end. Lloyd Arneach telling the story is available on audiotape.
♦ Students could collect other folktales that explain how animals got certain characteristics.
1. Cherokee Indians—Legends 2. Indians of North American—Legends.

398.20975
Burrison, John. *Storytellers: Folktales and Legends from the South.* University of Georgia (0-8203-1099-9), 1989. 261p. B/W photos. (Interest level: 4+).

In the three sections of the book—Storytelling Communities, Individual Storytellers, and Individual Tales—two Georgia communities are featured, as well as two Georgia storytellers and a third storyteller of Cherokee myths and legends. This book is a result of the academic study of folklore, but it offers students an appreciation of folklore as a discipline in a very understandable format.
♦ There are many short stories included that would be ideal for students to learn in a beginning storytelling unit.
1. Tales—Southern States 2. Legends—Southern States 3. Storytelling—Southern States.

398.209758
Killion, Ronald and **Waller, Charles.** *A Treasury of Georgia Folklore.* Cherokee (L.C. 72-88901), 1972. (out of stock but will be reprinted). 267p. B/W line drawings. (Interest level: 6+).

Many facets of Georgia folklore collected by the W.P.A. are included in this collection. The children's lore, folk songs, superstitions, and beliefs will interest the young reader.
♦ Students could examine one area, such as superstitions or songs, and try to discover items that are still active in the culture.
1. Folklore—Georgia 2. Georgia—Social life and customs.

398.209758
Thompson, Rose, collector, and **Beaumont, Charles,** ed. *Hush Child! Can't You Hear the Music?* University of Georgia (0-8203-0588-X), 1982. 93p. B/W photos. (Interest level: 6+).

This book includes African-American folktales collected in middle Georgia in the 1930s and 1940s accompanied by photographs of the tellers. The author's introductions to the tellers and their stories give an authentic flavor to the tales and introduce students to folklore as more than just stories.

♦ After the teacher reads aloud selected stories, the students could identify themes and motifs they recognize from other folk literature.
1. African-Americans—Georgia folklore 2. Georgia—Social life and customs.

398.2509758
Windham, Kathryn Tucker. *Thirteen Georgia Ghosts and Jeffrey.* Illus. by Frances Lanier. University of Alabama, 1987. 154p. Photos. (Interest level: 4-8).

Windham has collected 13 authentic ghost stories from Georgia locations. Photographs taken at the site of each story lend a verisimilitude to these tales that live in the folklore of Georgia.
♦ Students could be introduced to storytelling and try telling one of these stories, other ghost stories from books, or stories passed down in their family or neighborhood.
1. Ghost stories—Georgia.

574.526
A Swamp Ecosystem. (Videotape). National Geographic, 1983. VHS, (23 min.). (Interest level: 5+).

The stages in the formation of the Okefenokee Swamp, the wildlife living there, and the role of fire in the swamp's development are covered.
♦ Students could chart the development of a maturing swamp, using words and pictures. They might also make reports on some of the myriad animals that live in the Okefenokee.
1. Okefenokee swamp.

582.16 (Reference)
Duncan, Wilbur and **Duncan, Marion.** *Trees of the Southeastern United States.* University of Georgia (0-8203-0954-0), 1988. 322p. Color photos. (Interest level: 5+).

This field guide describes trees in the Southeast, including Georgia. Included are maps and a center section of color plates to help identify trees.
♦ Students could assemble a display of tree leaves from their area and identify them using this guide.
1. Trees—Southern States—Identification.

590.744
Johnston, Ginny and **Cutchins, Judy.** *Windows on Wildlife.* Morrow (0-688-07872-9), 1990. 48p. Color photos. (Interest level: 3-8).

The first chapter in this book, describing various wildlife exhibits in zoos, features the gorilla habitat at Zoo Atlanta. The book is beautifully formatted and includes information that is not commonly known.
♦ Students could investigate what other animals would be happy in the environment created for the gorillas.
1. Zoos 2. Aquariums, Public 3. Captive wild animals.

591
Our Georgia Wildlife. (Sound Filmstrip). Beckley Films, 1975. (Our Georgia Series). 60 frames, 1 cassette, (17 min.). Includes teacher's guide. (Interest level: 3-6).

The marvelous variety of wildlife found in Georgia is shown in this strip. This program may require some updating but it has the advantage of allowing the instructor to stop for study of a single frame.

♦ Georgia students could chart the animals that are found in their part of the state. Students in other states could do further research on a Georgia animal of their choice.

1. Animals—Georgia.

597.92

Creatures of the Night: Georgia's Sea Turtles. (Videotape). Georgia Department of Natural Resources, 1980. VHS, (10 min.). (Interest level: 4+).

This production examines the problems of the loggerhead turtle along Georgia's coast and includes a sequence of egg laying and hatching. An updated version of this video will soon be available, and it promises to be even more interesting.

♦ Students could identify the barrier islands and research which ones provide safe haven for the turtles.

1. Loggerhead turtles.

597.98

Realm of the Alligator. (Videotape). National Geographic (0-8051-0441-0), 1986. VHS, (59 min.). (Interest level: 4+).

The alligator is shown in the Okefenokee Swamp on the Georgia-Florida border. The alligator nests and hatching of young alligators will particularly interest students.

♦ Students may research the diet of alligators and discover how the Okefenokee provides for their needs.

1. Alligators 2. Okefenokee Swamp.

597.98

Rulers of the Swamp. (Videotape). Georgia Department of Natural Resources, 1980. VHS, (10 min.). (Interest level: 3+).

Georgia's management of the increased number of alligators since passage of the Endangered Species Act is stressed in this production. Information about the life of alligators along with video sequences will attract learners no matter how reluctant.

♦ Younger students might chart the life cycle of the alligator. Older ones might research the activities of the Georgia Department of Natural Resources in protecting people and animals from each other.

1. Alligators—Georgia.

598.72

Woodpeckers: Birds in Trouble. (Videotape). Georgia Department of Natural Resources, 1980. VHS, (10 min.). (Interest level: 4+).

Georgia's efforts to save the endangered ivory bill and red cockatiel woodpeckers are discussed. Live sequences of the cockatiel make this video interesting to students.

♦ Students might do a bird survey of the various woodpeckers they can see in their own neighborhoods.

1. Woodpeckers.

599.7357

Whitetails: Creatures of the Woods. (Videotape). Georgia Department of Natural Resources, 1986. VHS, (28 min.). (Interest level: 4+).

The life cycle of Georgia's white-tailed deer and the herds near demise and resurgence are shown. The appeal of deer will ensure interest in this nature video.

♦ Students could survey family and friends about sightings of deer.

1. Deer.

630.9758

Georgia Agriculture. Artwork by Georgia students and teachers. Georgia Department of Agriculture, n.d. 44p. B/W drawings, photos, and maps. (Interest level: 3-8).

A full page is given to each agricultural product and includes a picture, map, basic statistics, and several paragraphs of information. This paperback is full of readily accessible information in an interesting format.

♦ Georgia students can study the maps and determine the prevalent products in their area. Students in other states can identify and discuss the major agricultural products of their state. Older students can discuss why certain products are grown in particular parts of Georgia.

1. Agriculture—Georgia.

630.9758

Our Georgia Agriculture. (Sound Filmstrip). Beckley Films, 1975. (Our Georgia Series). 60 frames, 1 cassette, (14 min.). Includes teacher's guide. (Interest level: 3-6).

Peanuts, peaches, and pecans lead the list of agricultural products, followed by lumber and animal husbandry. Although this strip is old, it concentrates on one often neglected aspect of Georgia, and changes that have taken place since 1975 can easily be corrected by the teacher.

♦ Students could plan nutritious meals using only Georgia products.

1. Agriculture—Georgia.

639.9

Give Wildlife a Chance. (Videotape). Georgia Department of Natural Resources, 1989. VHS, (22 min.). (Interest level: 8+).

Nongame wildlife management in Georgia is explained, and the need for such programs is stressed. Although this video is designed to promote fundraising, it gives the rationale for the existence of such programs.

♦ Students might like to document wildlife that is on the increase because of habitat protection programs.

1. Wildlife refuges 2. Wildlife conservation.

639.9

The Road to Extinction: Will We Save the Plants? (Videotape). Georgia Department of Natural Resources, 1991. VHS, (28 min.). (Interest level: 6+).

Plants threatened with extinction in Georgia are shown, and programs designed to save them are discussed. This video is a consciousness-raising effort on behalf of saving plants.

♦ Students could discuss why plants are important to people.

1. Rare plants 2. Wildlife conservation.

639.9

A Time for Choice. (Videotape). Georgia Department of Natural Resources, 1979. VHS, (27 min.). (Interest level: 6+).

The plight of wildlife in Georgia on the brink of extinction is discussed. This is a comprehensive look at endangered animals in Georgia.

♦ Students could list additional animals that they would want protected and give the reasons why.

1. Endangered species—Georgia 2. Wildlife conservation.

641.509758

Godby, Marty. *Dining in Historic Georgia: A Restaurant Guide with Recipes.* McClanahan (0-913383-25-2), 1993. 208p. B/W illus. (Interest level: 7+).

The restaurants in this book were chosen on the basis of historic, architectural, and culinary interest, and each entry is preceded by several paragraphs on the historical background of the area and the building. Line drawings of the restaurants and a map showing the locations will help students use the book to add knowledge about a particular part of Georgia.

♦ Students could prepare some of the less elaborate recipes given in the book to highlight their topic of study.

1. Cookery—Georgia 2. Historic buildings—Georgia.

658.408

The Disposal Dilemma. (Videotape). Georgia Department of Natural Resources, 1982. VHS, (26 min.). (Interest level: 8+).

The problem of hazardous waste disposal in Georgia is discussed using several industries as examples. Research and environmental viewpoints are represented in the presentation.

♦ Students could research the various ways hazardous waste could affect their environment and their lives.

1. Hazardous wastes—Georgia.

745.092 (Reference)

Siporin, Steve. *American Folk Masters: The National Heritage Fellows.* Photos by Michael Monteaux. Abrams (0-8109-1917-6), 1992. 255p. Color and B/W photos. (Interest level: 8+).

Beneficiaries of the American Heritage Fellowship Program for folk artists, including several Georgia winners, are spotlighted in this volume. The book includes excellent photographs of the winners and their work, a directory of all the winners up to 1990, and a good index to enable the user to locate local artists.

♦ Through the excellent directory and bibliography, the teacher could introduce students to outstanding Georgia folk artists. Students could identify local artists who work in similar media.

1. Folk artist—United States—Biography.

759.13

O'Kelley, Mattie Lou. *From the Hills of Georgia.* Illus. by author. Little Brown (0-316-63800-5), 1983. 32p. Color illus. (Interest level: 1+).

Twenty-eight paintings make up this visual autobiography of O'Kelley's life in Maysville, Georgia. Each painting is full of life and detail.

♦ Students could write or talk about the things they would do if they were "in" one of the paintings.

1. O'Kelley, Mattie Lou 2. Painters—Georgia 3. Primitivism—Georgia.

812

Griffith, Benjamin. *The Murder of Chief McIntosh.* (Unpublished play; contact author, 330 Kramer St., Carrollton, GA 30117). Performed 1992. (Interest level: 7-8).

The story of McIntosh is told through characters' conversations on the last two days of McIntosh's life. Flashbacks emanating from the conversations add historical background to this unique way to learn history.

♦ This play would lend itself well to a reader's theater production by the students.

1. McIntosh, Chief William—Drama 2. Georgia—History—Drama.

912.758

Georgia. (Jigsaw puzzle). Puzzles and Such. 1 Puzzle, 16" x 20", Color. (Interest level: 4-8).

This colorful puzzle includes pictures of the state bird, butterfly, fossil, tree, and flower. Students can learn geography in a fun context by assembling this puzzle.

♦ Teams of students could record the time it takes to complete the puzzle and challenge other groups to better their time.

1. Georgia.

917.00497

Stuart, George. "Etowah" in *National Geographic.* Vol. 180, No. 4, Oct. 1991, pp. 54-56. National Geographic Society (0027-9358), Monthly. 146p. (Interest level: 5+).

The author tells of the excavation of Native American mounds at Etowah and speculates on the life of these people in 1492. Color photographs and paintings, showing how the village might have looked, give students an opportunity for visual learning.

♦ Students could gain practice using a periodicals index by developing a bibliography using Etowah as a subject.

1. Indians of North America 2. Archaeology—Georgia.

917.58

Brown, Fred and Jones, Nell, eds. *The Georgia Conservancy's Guide to the North Georgia Mountains.* 2nd ed. Longstreet (0-929264-46-0), 1991. 251p. Two color maps and drawings. (Interest level: 6+).

Careful descriptions and directions and maps for hiking, camping, bicycling, and canoeing in the mountains of Georgia are interspersed with maps and drawings of wildlife. Although designed for adults, interested students could read this book and help plan outings.

♦ Students could read about several trips and choose the one they would most like to do and give reasons why.

1. Outdoor recreation—Georgia—Guidebooks 2. Georgia—Description and travel.

917.58
Conniff, Richard. "Blackwater Country" in *National Geographic*. Vol. 181, No. 4, April 1992, pp. 34-36. National Geographic Society (0027-9358), Monthly. 136p. (Interest level: 5+).

In this article on the Okefenokee Swamp, the author stresses the issues brought on by development. Wonderful photographs make any area that *National Geographic* features better understood.

◆ Students could list the developments that are threatening the environment and give the pros and cons for each.
1. Okefenokee Swamp.

917.58
De Vorsey, Louis and **Rice, Marion**. *The Plantation South*. Rutgers University Press (0-8135-1873-3), 1992. 193p. B/W photos. (Interest level: 8+).

Set up as an 11-day itinerary for travelers, the book includes strong historical and geographical background information about each of the sites visited. This publication is packed with information and is indexed so that the facts can be found.

◆ A class could research and plan a trip of their own, following the model of this publication.
1. Georgia—Description and travel—Guidebooks.

917.58
Doster, Gary L. *From Abbyville to Zebulon: Early Postcard Views of Georgia*. University of Georgia (0-8203-1334-3), 1991. 222p. B/W photos. (Interest level: 3-8).

More than 850 photo postcards of Georgia from 1900 to 1920 are sorted into categories and labeled for the viewer to enjoy. In addition to the chapter divisions, such as churches, schools and colleges, and public buildings, there is also an index to towns and counties.

◆ Students might bring in modern postcards of Georgia locations to compare to those in the book.
1. Georgia—Description and travel—Views 2. Postcards—Georgia.

917.58
Experiencing Georgia. (Audiotape). Experience America, Inc., 1991. 1 cassette tape, (40 min.). (Interest level: 6+).

The main points of the history and geography of Georgia are given on this tape. Although this is not an exciting production, it will serve as a source of information or reinforcement for students who have reading problems.

◆ Students could write scripts and produce short tapes about the historical or geographical features of their area.
1. Georgia.

917.58
A Guide to Georgia State Parks and Historic Sites. Georgia Department of Natural Resources, n.d. 52p. Color photos. (Interest level: 5+).

A paragraph about each site is given, in addition to the basics concerning the facilities and costs. Color photographs and a state map generate interest in the sites.

◆ Students could gain practice understanding charts and improving math skills by reading the charts and compiling information on cottages, trails, fishing, or boating.
1. Georgia—Description and travel.

917.58
A Guide to the Georgia Coast. The Georgia Conservancy (0-9614284-0-6), 1984. 199p. B/W illus. (Interest level: 6+).

Cemeteries, parks, wildlife refuges, and museums are all found in this guide written by Conservancy volunteers. The guide contains valuable information on the wildlife of the area and, of course, has a conservation slant that makes it more than just a guidebook.

◆ Students might discuss what they can do on vacations to help conserve the environment.
1. Georgia—Description and travel—Guidebooks 2. Outdoor recreation—Georgia—Guidebooks.

917.58
Harman, Jeanne and **Harman, Harry**. *Georgia at Its Best*. Rutledge Hill Press (1-55853-032-0), 1989. 384p. (Interest level: 7+).

This guidebook divides Georgia into 10 geographical areas and discusses cities and towns, where to stay, where to eat, what to see, where to shop, and the sports for each area. A mileage chart and lists of state parks, historical sites, airports, festivals, and national landmarks add to the usability of this guide for trip planning.

◆ Students could plan trips and include such tasks as planning the mileage and budget.
1. Georgia—Description and travel—Guidebooks.

917.58
Homan, Tim. *The Hiking Trails of North Georgia*. Peachtree (0-931948-11-8), 1981. 216p. (Interest level: 8+).

Down-to-earth information on hiking trails, such as length, location, difficulty, and starting and ending points, is given in this conventional-sized paperback. This is a fine book for a beginner or a newcomer to Georgia who wants to hike.

◆ After reading the descriptions of several trails, students could write a description of a route they know well for another student to follow.
1. Hiking—Georgia—Guidebooks 2. Georgia—Description and travel—Guidebooks.

917.58
Martin, Van Jones, photographer, with text by **Reiter, Beth**. *Coastal Georgia*. Golden Coast Publishing (0-932958-02-8), 1985. 120p. Color photos. (Interest level: 8+).

This coffee table type book is primarily a collection of photographs of coastal Georgia with some original text and a few quotations from other sources. Because the photographs are excellent and are accessible by area, this book could be used with other less showy materials.

◆ Students could key the photographs by page number to reports or material from other sources. For exam-

ple, if rice production were being studied, the appropriate photographs could be found in this book.
1. Georgia—Description and travel.

917.58
Our Georgia. (Sound Filmstrip). Beckley Films, 1975. (Our Georgia Series). 60 frames, 1 cassette, (12 min.). Includes teacher's guide. (Interest level: 3-6).

This overview of Georgia includes historical, recreational, and cultural sites along with the state flag, seal, flower, and other miscellaneous information. This strip would be useful for review.
♦ Students could brainstorm a list that would update this production and compose a letter to the producer with their ideas.
1. Georgia.

917.58
Randklev, James, photographer. *Georgia—Images of Wildness*. Westcliffe (092-9969-75-8), 1992. 128p. Color photos. (Interest level: 3+).

Each chapter details one of Georgia's physiographic regions with color photographs and brief commentaries by naturalists. Each region is superbly portrayed in large color photographs that can be appreciated by any age.
♦ Young Georgia students could find pictures that most closely resemble their own area of the state and point out the details that led them to that conclusion; non-Georgia students could do the same for their local areas.
1. Georgia—Description and travel—Illustrated works.

917.58231
Loewen, Nance. *Atlanta*. Rourke (0-86592-543-7), 1989. 47p. Color photos. (Interest level: 4-8).

This up-to-date overview of Atlanta includes everything from history to Six Flags Over Georgia. This colorful attractive volume is from the series "Great Cities of the USA" and will attract readers of all ages who want a quick feel for Atlanta.
♦ Students might plan tours of the places that interest them in Atlanta and try to "sell" their tours to other students.
1. Atlanta (GA)—Description—Guide.

917.60443
Logan, Williams Bryan and **Muse, Vance**. *The Smithsonian Guide to Historical America: The Deep South*. Stewart, Tabori & Chang. (1-55670-068-7 pbk), 1989. 464p. Color photos. (Interest level: 6+).

Three chapters cover historical sites in Georgia: "Savannah and the Coastal Plain," "Atlanta and Northern Georgia," and "Heart of the Piedmont." The impeccable research, clear writing, and superb photography can be appreciated by students studying history or planning trips.
♦ The students might use the information to plan a field trip to a Georgia site.
1. Southern States—Description and travel—Guidebooks 2. Historic sites—Southern States—Guidebooks.

970.497
The Next Americans. (Sound Filmstrip). Gateway Productions, 1984. (Indians of Georgia Series). 89 frames, 1 cassette, (15 min.). Includes teacher's guide. (Interest level: 5-8).

The advances of Georgia's Native American culture through the Mississippian period until the "Trail of Tears" is covered in this strip. The fine craft work of the Indians is stressed.
♦ The teacher and students might try to identify a local museum or individual with Indian weaving and pottery for the students to view first hand.
1. Indians of North America.

973
Aylesworth, Thomas and **Aylesworth, Virginia**. *The Southeast: Georgia, Kentucky, Tennessee*. Chelsea House (1-55546-557-9), 1988. 64p. Color illus. (Interest level: 3-6).

One-third of this book is devoted to Georgia and includes chapters on land, history, people, and special interests. There is a short bibliography for each state and especially good captions under the pictures.
♦ Students could collect pictures from Georgia brochures and practice writing captions following the models given in this book.
1. Southern states 2. Georgia 3. Kentucky 4. Tennessee.

975.00497
Bealer, Alex. *Only the Names Remain: The Cherokees and the Trail of Tears*. Illus. by William Bock. Little Brown (L.C. 71-169008), 1972. 88p. B/W illus. (Interest level: 4-8).

The history of the Cherokee from the coming of the whites to this tribe's removal is chronicled in this easy-to-read history. Lots of pictures, large print, and enough detail to be interesting make this a good choice for introducing this chapter of Georgia's history.
♦ Students could map the removal routes and research the weather for each one.
1. Cherokee Indians 2. Indians of North America.

975.00497
Brown, Virginia Pounds and **Owens, Laurella**. *The World of the Southern Indians*. Illus. by Nathan Glick. Beechwood (0-912221-00-3), 1983. 176p. B/W illus. (Interest level: 6+).

A history of the southern Native American tribes followed by a section, "Seeing the South's Indian Heritage: A Guide by States," helps the reader see the overall picture and then identify local sites. The format draws readers into the book and the interesting style and helpful illustrations keep their attention.
♦ Students would be interested to learn the meanings of the Native American place names in their locality and perhaps research additional Native American names.
1. Indians of North America—Southern States.

975.00497
The Eastern Indians. (Sound Filmstrip). National Geographic Society (L.C. 73-733090), 1973. (Indians of North America Series). 60 frames, 1 cassette, (14 min.). Includes teacher's guide. (Interest level: 4-8).

The second half of this strip deals with southeastern tribes, including the Cherokees of Georgia. This strip and the series from which it comes, enable students to put the Georgia Indians into the total context of Native American life.

♦ Students would enjoy researching and playing the games mentioned in the program.

1. Indians of North America.

975.00497

The First Georgians. (Sound Filmstrip). Gateway Productions, 1984. (Indians of Georgia Series). 67 frames, 1 cassette, (14 min.). Includes teacher's guide. (Interest level: 5-8).

The Paleo-Indians' presence in Georgia is discussed and illustrated through the use of drawings and museum displays. Although the visuals are not always top quality, the information about this early period makes the strip useful.

♦ Students could design a time line showing the parallel cultural development in China, Egypt, and Europe at the time of the Paleo-Indians.

1. Indians of North America.

975.00497

Marching Toward Civilization. (Sound Filmstrip). Gateway Productions, 1984. (Indians of Georgia Series). 73 frames, 1 cassette, (15 min.). Includes teacher's guide. (Interest level: 5-8).

The Native American culture of the Woodland tribes is traced from its center in Louisiana to Georgia. Marginal visuals, often photographs of museum displays, result in a strip that is useful for its content but technically weak.

♦ Students could research and place on a map the Native American mounds found in Georgia.

1. Indians of North America.

975.00497

Stein, R. Conrad. *The Story of the Trail of Tears.* Illus. by David Catrow III. Children's Press (0-516-04683-7), 1985. 31p. Two color illus. (Interest level: 4-6).

The Cherokees of Georgia are a major part of this story of the Indian Removal Act. Large print makes some fairly sophisticated information accessible to young or reluctant readers.

♦ Students might act out how a Cherokee family might have reacted when they heard the news that they had to leave their homes.

1. Cherokee Removal—1838 2. Cherokee Indians—History 3. Indians of North America—Southern States.

975.8

The Battle of Pickett's Mill. (Videotape). Georgia Department of Natural Resources, 1990. VHS, (16 min.). (Interest level: 5+).

The Confederate victory at the Battle of Pickett's Mill near New Hope, Georgia, is recounted. The battle is shown in the context of Sherman's Atlanta campaign.

♦ Students might examine the roles of chance and planning in the outcome of this battle.

1. Georgia—History.

975.8

Carpenter, Allan. *Georgia.* Children's Press (0-516-04110-X), 1979. (The New Enchantment of America). 96p. Color photos. (Interest level: 4-8).

All facets of Georgia's history are included in this typical volume from "The New Enchantment of America" series. Since the focus is primarily historical and the illustrations are in color, the datedness of the book does not effect the usefulness of the volume.

♦ Students might choose the time in Georgia's history that interests them most and write a letter to an imaginary cousin describing the events of the time.

1. Georgia.

975.8 (Reference)

Clements, John. *Georgia Facts: A Comprehensive Look at Georgia Today County by County.* Clements Research II, Inc. (ISSN 1044-9086), 1989. (Flying the Colors). 518p. Color and B/W photos. (Interest level: 5+).

This volume gives facts on the land, people, economy, transportation, community services, recreation, and communities in each Georgia county. Details about each county will be useful to students doing local projects.

♦ Students could choose two counties and write a paper comparing and contrasting the two.

1. Georgia.

975.8

Couch, Jill. *Georgia Trivia.* Rutledge Hill (0-934935-21-7), 1986. 191p. (Interest level: 6+).

Questions and answers about Georgia are presented in the categories of geography, entertainment, history, arts and literature, sports and leisure, and science and nature. The format encourages students to read.

♦ Students could easily use a TV game show as a model to design a Georgia game show.

1. Georgia—Miscellaneous 2. Questions and answers.

975.8

Fort McAllister: Guardian of the Ogeechee. (Videotape). Georgia Department of Natural Resources, 1987. VHS,. (11 min.). (Interest level: 5+).

The history of Fort McAllister and its role in the Civil War are shown. Descriptions and illustrations of how earthwork fortifications were built give students an understanding of this kind of defense.

♦ Students could write how life might have been for the men in the fort during the six attacks by the British.

1. Georgia—History.

975.8

Fradin, Dennis. *Georgia.* Children's Press (0516-03810-9), 1991. (Sea to Shining Sea). 64p. Color photos. (Interest level: 2-4).

This large print overview of Georgia is arranged in chapter format and has more information than many primary titles.

♦ Because of the wealth of information, this would be a good book for practicing the use of an index and producing a web of Georgia facts.

1. Georgia.

975.8
Fradin, Dennis. *The Georgia Colony.* Children's Press (0-516-00392-5), 1990. 143p. B/W illus. (Interest level: 4+).

Beginning with the Indians and ending with statehood, this book gives a straightforward account of colonial Georgia interspersed with six biographical sketches. Large print and simple sentences make this information accessible, if not exciting, to younger students or less able readers.
♦ Students could imagine themselves colonists and write letters back home to England to describe their lives.
1. Georgia—History—Colonial period, ca. 1600-1775.

975.8
Georgia Illustrated, 1513-1793. (Videotape). National Society of the Colonial Dames of America in the State of Georgia, 1992, VHS, (30 min.). (Interest level: 8+).

In 1931, the Georgia Colonial Dames produced lantern slides from photographs, paintings, etc., to be used for programs around the country. This tape is produced from those slides and is interesting because of its uniqueness even though it moves slowly for today's youth.
♦ Students could choose the sites in their community they would want to have preserved in today's technology for future generations to see and perhaps transfer to their newest technology. They might also discuss what that technology might be like.
1. Georgia—History.

975.8
Gleason, David King. *Antebellum Homes of Georgia.* Louisiana State University Press (0-8071-1432-4), 1987. 136p. Color photos. (Interest level: 4-8).

This oversized book includes homes by geographical area and gives a paragraph concerning the history of each site. Spectacular oversize photographs show architectural detail and the text gives enough information to pique students' curiosity.
♦ After marking the locations on a Georgia map, students could research and discuss why the homes were built in each particular area.
1. Plantations—Georgia—Pictorial works 2. Georgia—Description and travel.

975.8
Gold Fever. (Videotape). Georgia Department of Natural Resources, 1985. VHS, (27 min.). (Interest level: 4+).

Interesting interviews with old-timers who were involved in gold mining lead into the story of the gold rush in Dahlonega in 1828. In order for students to understand the "Trail of Tears," they must understand the importance of the gold rush.
♦ Students could compare the dates and activities of the Georgia gold rush with other gold rushes in history.
1. Gold mines and mining—Georgia 2. Dahlonega (GA)—History.

975.8
Kent, Zachary. *Georgia*. Children's Press (0-516-00456-5), 1988. 144p. Color photos. (Interest level: 4-8).

Georgia history, geography, government, culture, and recreation are covered in this colorful book. The appendix, "Facts at a Glance," includes a chronology, important people, a list of governors, and maps to give reference value to this nonfiction title.
♦ Students could choose some facet of Georgia that interests them and design a book jacket for this book.
1. Georgia.

975.8
LaDoux, Rita. *Georgia*. Learner (0-8225-2703-0), 1991. (Hello U.S.A.). 72p. Color and B/W photos. (Interest level: 3-6).

This up-to-date overview of Georgia offers color photographs, an attractive format, and a "Did you Know" first chapter that will entice readers.
♦ Students can research "Did you Know" questions on their own and put them in a class book.
1. Georgia.

975.8
Our Georgia History. (Sound Filmstrip). Beckley Films, 1975. (Our Georgia Series). 60 frames, 1 cassette, (14 min.). Includes teacher's guide. (Interest level: 4-8).

This quick overview would serve well as an introduction to Georgia history.
♦ Students could be assigned to write down place names as the strip is viewed and place them on a map for further study.
1. Georgia—History.

975.8
Scruggs, Carroll Proctor. *Georgia During the Revolution.* Cherokee (0-87797-095-5), 1975. 176p. Color photos and maps. (Interest level: 8+).

This history reviews, in an orderly way, Georgia's role in the Revolutionary War. Color photographs of sites, maps, an index, and a bibliography will help students locate information that might otherwise be difficult to find.
♦ Students might research daily life in Georgia during the Revolutionary War.
1. Georgia—History—Revolution, 1775-1783.

957.8
Spirit of Sapelo. (Videotape). Georgia Department of Natural Resources, 1983. VHS, (28 min.). (Interest level: 8+).

The nature and history of Georgia's Sapelo Island are shown and described in this production. The relaxed pace of the video, designed in keeping with the mood of nature on the island, will require preparation by an adult before some students will appreciate it.
♦ Students could be given lists in different categories (such as birds, plants, buildings, etc.) to watch for in the video.
1. Sapelo Island (GA)—History 2. Sapelo Island (GA)—Description and travel.

975.8
Whitson, Skip. *Georgia 100 Years Ago*. Sun Books (0-89540-025-1), 1976. 40p. B/W illus. (Interest level: 8+).

Articles are assembled from *Harper's* 1879 and 1888, and *Century* 1882. The illustrations give students an idea of how places and people were depicted in magazines in the late nineteenth century.
♦ Students could assemble copies of contemporary articles about Georgia and put together a compilation for future generations.
1. Georgia—History.

975.8
Wigginton, Eliott, ed. *Foxfire*. Anchor Press/Doubleday (0-385-07353-4), 1974. 384p. B/W photos. (Interest level: 7-8).

Life in the Appalachians is chronicled by the students in Rabun Gap-Nacoochee School in North Georgia. The students interviewed long-time residents for information about their lives. Of the nine volumes in print, Georgia is emphasized most in the earlier editions. Volume one includes skills, such as slaughtering, churning, hunting, and moonshining. The contents of the books are anthologies based primarily on the *Foxfire* magazine.
♦ Students can look for community members to demonstrate some of the crafts and skills discussed in the book for an "old-timey" day.
1. Georgia—Social life and customs 2. Country life—Georgia.

975.8004975
The Cherokee Nation: The Story of New Echota. (Video tape). Georgia Department of Natural Resources, 1990. VHS. (15 minutes) (Interest level: 4+).

The history of New Echota, Georgia, from its founding in 1825 to 1838 when the Indians were driven out, is presented with visuals of old materials and present-day shots of the reconstruction. Explanations are provided of the Cherokee courts, newspaper, homes, and city life.
♦ Students might write to New Echota and request a facsimile of the newspaper from the rebuilt printing office.
1. Cherokee—History 2. Indians of North America.

975.800497
Landau, Elaine. *The Cherokees* Franklin Watts (0-531-20066-3), 1992. 61p. Color Illus. (Interest level: 4-8).

Sequoyah is featured in this overview of the Cherokees. The present day situation of the Cherokee is included along with excellent full-page color photographs.
♦ Students might research Cherokee dress throughout history.
1. Cherokee Indians 2. Indians of North America.

975.8004975
Lepthien, Emilie. *The Cherokee*. Children's Press (0-516-01938-4), 1985. (New True Books). 45p. Color photos. (Interest level: 1-3).

In the typical large print, simple sentence format of this series, this account of the Cherokee includes the founding of New Echota. Accurate information, a glossary, and an index make this a fine beginning book.
♦ After reading the book, students could write several sentences about what interests them most about the Cherokee.
1. Cherokee Indians 2. Indians of North America—Southern States.

975.8004975
McCall, Barbara. *The Cherokee*. Illus. by Luciano Lazzarino. Rouke (0-86625-376-9), 1989. (Indian Tribes of America). 31p. Color illus. (Interest level: 5+).

This book tells the story of the Cherokee in one- or two-page chapters with illustrations on every page. An index and important dates are appended to make this book useful as a reference tool for readers who might not be motivated to read the entire text.
♦ The important dates in Cherokee history could be inserted into a Georgia or American history time line.
1. Cherokee Indians 2. Indians of North America.

975.8231
Atlanta: Yankees Invade the Deep South. (Videotape). Classic Images (0-929265-14-9), 1989. (The Civil War Series). VHS, (60 min.). (Interest level: 8+).

Historical photographs, charts, maps, and live action reenactment cover Sherman's campaign to capture Atlanta. The video is divided into two parts, which make it more usable in normal class periods. Civil war buffs younger than eighth grade may also be interested in the content.
♦ The importance of Atlanta as a railroad center is stressed in this production. Students could research what was important about each of the rail links.
1. Georgia—History 2. American History—Civil War.

975.8231
Garrison, Webb. *The Legacy of Atlanta*. Peachtree Publishers (0-934601-14-3), 173p. B/W photos. (Interest level: 7-8).

Thirty-five short chapters investigate topics of interest in the development of Atlanta. The stories of the founding of many of Atlanta's biggest businesses along with tales of *Gone with the Wind* and other miscellaneous topics are covered in newspaper article format.
♦ Students could compare the information and writing style of these articles to ones on the same topics in encyclopedias or other reference books.
1. Atlanta—History.

975.8231
Shavin, Norman. *Whatever Became of Atlanta*. Photos by Bob Phillips. Capricorn Corporation (0-910719-09-8), 1984. 84p. B/W photos. (Interest level: 5-8).

Included are nostalgic vignettes and 175 then-and-now photographs of Atlanta. The changes in Atlanta and society in a relatively short period of time have a dramatic impact through the comparison of photographs.
♦ Students could gather old photographs of their community and take current pictures of the same location for a display in the style of this book.
1. Atlanta (GA).

975.8231

Snow, Pegeen. *Atlanta*. Dillon Press (0-87518-389-1), 1989. (Downtown America). 60p. Color photos. (Interest level: 2-6).

The history, neighborhoods, cultural opportunities, business, education, and other aspects of Atlanta are reviewed in this book. Attractive illustrations, fast facts, places to visit, and a time line make this book useful to students.

♦ Students could update the information given on such items as sports teams, olympic bids, and tallest building.

1. Atlanta (GA).

975.8231

Under Georgia's Gold Dome. (Sound Filmstrip). 2nd ed. Carl Vinson Institute of Government, 1987. 79 frames, 1 cassette, (18 min.). (Interest level: 6-8).

This strip traces the five locations of Georgia's capital city and gives the history and description of the present capitol building. Students will be surprised to discover all the things there are to see at the capitol complex.

♦ Georgia students could review the names of legislators from their district who are also "Under Georgia's Gold Dome." Students in other states could learn the names of their own state legislators.

1. Atlanta (GA) 2. Georgia—History.

Biography

920

Dictionary of Georgia Biography. 2 vols. University of Georgia (0-8203-0662-2), 1983. 1108p. (Interest level: adult).

In order to be included in this work the subject must have done something of statewide significance while a resident of Georgia and be deceased. The entries average two columns in length and are of a scholarly nature.

♦ Teachers could use this book for background information as they teach about the history of Georgia.

1. Georgia—Biography.

920

Miller, Zell. *Great Georgians*. Cherokee Press (L.C. 82-084745), 1983. 215p. B/W photos. (Interest level: 8+).

A biographical essay of three or four pages and a small black-and-white photograph are included for each person. The choices are Miller's favorite Georgians and range across time and occupation from Tomochichi to Jimmy Carter and Margaret Mitchell to Dean Rusk.

♦ Students might chart the included Georgians by various categories, such as occupations or eras when they lived.

1. Georgia—Biography.

92 Berry, Martha

Blackburn, Joyce. *Martha Berry: Little Woman with a Big Dream*. Lippincott, 1968 (out of print, but widely available in libraries). 158p. (Interest level: 4-8).

This story covers Martha Berry's life and the founding and nurturing of The Berry Schools and Berry College. Although written in 1968, the story of Martha Berry's vision and determination will still be interesting to students.

♦ A time line that compares the events in the lives of Martha Berry and Juliette Low might be designed.

1. Berry, Martha—Biography.

92 Carter, Jimmy

Smith, Betsy Covington. *Jimmy Carter, President*. Walker (0-8027-6650-1), 1986. 124p. B/W photos. (Interest level: 8+).

This biography of Jimmy Carter of Plains, Georgia, begins with him as president and continues as flashbacks.

♦ Students could research what Carter is doing now that he is no longer president. Is he still in the news?

1. Carter, Jimmy 2. Presidents.

92 Deedy, Carmen

Deedy, Carmen. *Growing Up Cuban in Atlanta*. (Audiotape) Peachtree, 1993. 1 cassette, (45 min.). (Interest level: 6+).

Deedy tells of her own experiences trying to juggle her Cuban family's expectations and those of the Atlanta society in which she lived. These funny and poignant stories speak to students struggling toward maturity.

♦ Students could learn and tell a story from their own or their family's experiences.

1. Deedy, Carmen 2. Cuban Americans.

92 King, Coretta Scott

Henry, Sondra and **Taitz, Emily**. *Coretta Scott King: Keeper of the Dream*. Enslow (0-89490-334-9), 1992. 128p. B/W illus. (Interest level: 6-8).

This biography begins with Coretta's humble beginnings and ends with her extensive work to keep Dr. Martin Luther King's ideas alive. Looking at the King legend from a different point of view will add to readers' understanding of it.

♦ Students could research other civil rights workers who are mentioned in the text.

1. King, Coretta Scott 2. Civil rights workers 3. African-Americans—Biography 4. King, Martin Luther, Jr.

92 King, Matin Luther, Jr.

Adler, David A. *Martin Luther King, Jr.: Free at Last*. Illus. by Robert Casilla. Holiday House (0-8234-0618-0), 1986. 48p. B/W illus. (Interest level: 3-8).

This book covers the basics in the life of Martin Luther King, Jr. Although short, neither the text nor the illustrations are condescending, making this book suitable for older reluctant readers.

♦ After identifying key events in the life of Martin Luther King, Jr., from reading the book, students could research the actual text of speeches or primary sources reporting the events.

1. King, Martin Luther 2. Civil rights workers. 3. Clergy 4. African-Americans—Biography.

92 King, Martin Luther, Jr.
Greene, Carol. *Martin Luther King, Jr.: A Man Who Changed Things*. Children's Press (0-516-04205-X), 1989. (Rookie Biography). 45p. Color and B/W photos. (Interest level: 1-2).

This biography includes an overview of King's life and includes many pictures of Atlanta landmarks. The basics are given in an attractive format for beginning readers with large type and lots of photographs.
♦ Young children could discuss the incidents in the book with older family members and compile a class record of memories of the times.
1. King, Martin Luther 2. Civil rights workers 3. Clergy 4. African-Americans—Biography.

92 King, Martin Luther, Jr.
MacMillan, Diane. *Martin Luther King, Jr. Day*. Enslow (0-89490-382-9), 1992. 48p. Color and B/W illus. (Interest level: 3-5).

King's life, including his Atlanta days, is told as the basis of the founding of King Day. Coverage of the struggle to establish the holiday is given at a simple level.
♦ Students could enlarge on the suggestions for appropriate ways to celebrate M.L.K. Day.
1. King, Martin Luther, Jr. 2. Civil Rights Workers 3. Clergy 4. African-Americans—Biography.

92 King, Martin Luther, Jr.
Marzollo, Jean. *Happy Birthday, Martin Luther King*. Scholastic (0-590-44065-9), 1993. Unpaginated. Color illus. (Interest level: K-2).

This biography of Martin Luther King, Jr., is designed as an introduction to King for young children. Pinkney's illustrations make the book a strong read-aloud.
♦ Children could write a simple biography of their own lives, including such things as birth date, parent names, and birth place. They could also illustrate with a drawing or two.
1. King, Martin Luther, Jr. 2. Civil rights workers 3. African-American—Biography.

92 King, Martin Luther, Jr.
McKissack, Patricia. *Martin Luther King, Jr.: A Man to Remember*. Children's Press (0-516-03206-2), 1984. 128p. B/W photos. (Interest level: 4-8).

This solid account of the life of Martin Luther King, including his years in Atlanta, incorporates enough detail for students to gain an understanding of the man and the civil rights movement of the time.
♦ Students could look up the complete text of the quotations that begin each chapter and perhaps discuss why the author chose them.
1. King, Martin Luther 2. Civil rights workers 3. Clergy 4. African-Americans—Biography.

92 King, Martin Luther, Jr.
Patrick, Diane. *Martin Luther King, Jr*. Franklin Watts (0-531-10892-9), 1990. 64p. B/W and Color photos. (Interest level: 5-8).

King's life is telescoped into six chapters that focus on one phase of his activities. The attractive format and large number of photographs will attract readers.

♦ Students could research and list the civil rights laws that have been enacted since King was active in political life.
1. King, Martin Luther 2. Civil rights workers 3. African-American—Biography.

92 Low, Juliette Gordon
Kudlinski, Kathleen V. *Juliette Gordon Low: America's First Girl Scout*. Viking (0-670-82208-6), 1988. (Women of Our Time). 55p. B/W illus. (Interest level: 4-6).

This biography of Low recounts her life from her birth in Savannah through all her travels to her final burial in that same city. The author includes colorful and interesting stories about Low's life, not all of which put her in a favorable light.
♦ Students could compare the *Girl Scout Handbook* of 1912 with the current ones.
1. Low, Juliette Gordon 2. Girl Scouts of the United States of America—Biography.

92 Oglethorpe, James Edward
Blackburn, Joyce. *James Edward Oglethorpe*. Dodd, Mead (0-369-08158-4), 1979. (out of print, but widely available in libraries). 144p. (Interest level: 8+).

This well-researched biography of the English founder and first governor of Georgia is suitable for good readers. The well-written text is enlivened with dialogue that makes interesting portions for the teacher to read aloud.
♦ Readers could list the many Georgia place names that had their origins in Oglethorpe's time.
1. Oglethorpe, James Edward 2. Governors.

92 Roosevelt, Franklin D.
Osinski, Alice. *Franklin D. Roosevelt*. Children's Press (0-516-01395-5), 1987. 98p. B/W photos. (Interest level: 4-8).

This life story of Roosevelt includes his development of Warm Springs, Georgia, as a therapeutic center. The photographs on almost every page provide an attractive format to draw in readers.
♦ Students might explore what has happened to Warm Springs since the polio vaccine has almost eliminated the disease.
1. Roosevelt, Franklin D. 2. Presidents.

92 Sequoyah
Petersen, David. *Sequoyah: Father of the Cherokee Alphabet*. Children's Press (0-516-04180-0), 1991. 329p. B/W illus. (Interest level: 3-6).

Sequoyah's work with the Cherokee alphabet in the New Echota area is included in this biography. Overcoming obstacles to reach one's goal is stressed.
♦ Students could divide their own names into syllables and compare this with the alphabetic spelling to illustrate the difference between an alphabet and a syllabary.
1. Sequoyah 2. Cherokee Indians—Biography 3. Indians of North America—Biography.

92 Thomas, Clarence
Halliburton, Warren. *Clarence Thomas: Supreme Court Justice*. Enslow (0-89490-414-0), 1993. (People to Know). 104p. B/W illus. (Interest level: 5-8).

Thomas's childhood in Georgia is included in this story of his life. The author has attempted to represent both sides of the issues surrounding the controversy in Thomas' life.

♦ Students could research the other justices on the Supreme Court as to their birthplace and education.

1. Thomas, Clarence 2. Judges 3. African-Americans—Biography 4. United States Supreme Court—Biography.

92 Toombs, Robert
Robert Toombs: 1810-1885 (Videotape). Georgia Department of Natural Resources, 1983. VHS, (25 min.). (Interest level: 6+).

The highlights of Toombs' life are revealed by a reenactment of a reporter interviewing Toombs late in his life. Some of the colorful personality of the man is brought out by this "you are there" treatment.

♦ Students could create a web of the famous people with whom Toombs had contact and try to discover some of their opinions of him.

1. Toombs, Robert.

92 Walker, Herschell
Burchard, S.H. *Herschell Walker*. Harcourt (0-15-278052-1), 1984. (Sports Star). 63p. B/W photos. (Interest level: 4-6)

Walker's life is covered from his birth in Wrightsville, Georgia, through his first year in the USFL. Walker's name and the highly pictorial format should attract readers who might not otherwise be interested in reading.

♦ Students could research other prominent sports figures from Georgia.

1. Walker, Herschell—Biography 2. Football.

92 Whitney, Eli
Alter, Judith. *Eli Whitney*. Franklin Watts (0-531-10875-9), 1990. 63p. Color illus. (Interest level: 4-8).

This biography of Eli Whitney includes his years in Georgia during which he invented the cotton gin. An index, glossary, and accessible format make this book useful to students.

♦ Students might investigate the patent law and its importance in the industrial and information ages.

1. Whitney, Eli 2. Inventors.

92 Whitney, Eli
Latham, Jean Lee. *Eli Whitney: Great Inventor*. Chelsea House (0-7910-1453-3), 1991. 80p. Color illus. (Interest level: 1-3).

This simple life story of Whitney, his days in Georgia, and the invention of the cotton gin is a reprint of the 1963 book published by Gerrard. Although old, this large print beginning biography is appropriate for young students who wish to know about Whitney.

♦ Students could begin a simple database on famous Georgians, including such things as the time they lived, accomplishments and the part of Georgia with which they were associated.

1. Whitney, Eli—Biography 2. Inventors—United States—Biography.

Fiction

Armstrong, William. *Sounder*. Illus. by James Barkley. Harper (L.C. 70-85030), 1969. 116p. B/W illus. (Interest level: 6-8).

This coming of age story tells of a Georgia boy maturing while his father is serving an unjust jail sentence. The man's injured dog, Sounder, waits for his return in this moving story.

♦ Students might compile a bibliography of other books in which a relationship between a human and a dog is important.

1. Georgia—fiction.

Beatty, Patricia. *Be Ever Hopeful, Hannalee*. (0-688-07502-9), 1988. 216p. (Interest level: 5-8).

Hannalee, a poor mill worker, and her family are trying to make their way in Atlanta immediately after the Civil War. The author's notes help readers sort historical facts from the fiction of the story.

♦ Students could identify on a modern map of Atlanta the locations in the book.

1. Georgia—History—Fiction.

Blackburn, Joyce. *The Bloody Summer of 1742: A Colonial Boy's Journal*. (0-930803-00-0), 1984. 63p. B/W illus. (Interest level: 3-5).

The purpose of this fictional journal is to bring alive the history of Fort Frederica. Through one young boy's eyes, the reader sees the historical events and characters in a way they can understand.

♦ Individuals or groups could write journals as if they were present at other historical events.

1. Georgia—History—Fiction.

Burch, Robert. *Queenie Peavy*. Illus. by Jerry Lazare. Viking, 1966. 159p. B/W drawings. (Interest level: 5-8).

Queenie, a 13-year-old tomboy with a father in jail, has a tough time growing up in a small Georgia town during the Depression. It's easy to identify with Queenie and cheer for her successes.

♦ Students could compare the tomboy behaviors that gave Queenie a bad name with what would be acceptable behavior for a girl today.

1. Georgia—Fiction.

Gibbons, Faye. *Mighty Close to Heaven*. Morrow (0-688-04147-7), 1985. 183p. (Interest level: 5-7).

Dave is lonesome for his father, who works in town, and feels unloved by his grandparents, especially his stern, hymn-singing grandfather. The vivid descriptions of the North Georgia mountains and of an old timey woodcrafter who helps Dave discover where he belongs make this a story about rootedness in both family and place.

♦ Ask students to draw or find pictures that look like they imagine the mountain settings of this book.

1. Georgia—Fiction 2. Family—Fiction 3. Grandparents—Fiction.

Gibbons, Faye. *Some Glad Morning*. Morrow (0-688-01068-7), 1982. 237p. (Interest level: 5-7).

Maude, her mother, and two siblings are on their own when her daddy disappears, but they have plenty of family to turn to, or, as Maude might put it, contend with. The rural northern Georgia setting of a generation ago and the prickly, tough characters, especially Maude's step-grandfather, whose true worth Maude comes to slowly discover, are unforgettable.

♦ Students could select a section of rich dialogue and edit it for a readers' theater presentation.

1. Georgia—Fiction 2. Family—Fiction.

Griffith, Helen. *Georgia Music*. Illus. by James Stevenson. Greenwillow (0-688-06071-4), 1986. Unpaginated. Color illus. (Interest level: 1-4).

A little girl spends an idyllic summer with her grandfather enjoying Georgia and music, only to return the following summer to find the grandfather too ill to stay alone. Illustrations and text portray the simple joys of life in a small cabin.

♦ Students could survey parents, grandparents, and peers and chart the songs each group remembers from their childhood.

1. Georgia—Fiction 2. Grandfathers—Fiction 3. Music—Fiction.

Smith, Doris Buchanan. *Kelly's Creek*. Illus. by Alan Tiegreen. Thomas Y. Crowell (0-690-00731-0), 1975. B/W illus. (Interest level: 4-6).

Nine-year-old learning disabled Kelly lives in Brunswick, Georgia, and makes steps toward maturity by explaining to his class what he has learned in the marsh near his home. The frustration of a learning disability to both the disabled child and his family is shown.

♦ Students could identify a natural site near their school or home and make a study of it.

1. Physically handicapped—Fiction 2. Marshes—Fiction.

Smith, Doris Buchanan. *A Taste of Blackberries*. Illus. by Charles Robinson. Thomas Y. Crowell (0-690-80511X), 1973. 58p. B/W illus. (Interest level: 4-6).

This easy chapter book, set in Georgia, tells of the death of a young boy from a bee sting and how his friend copes with the tragedy.

♦ Students might list other environmental hazards and how to guard against them.

1. Death and dying—Fiction.

Wilkinson, Brenda. *Ludelle & Willie*. Harper (0-06-026488-8), 1977. 181p. (Interest level: 7-8).

Ludelle, a high school senior in Waycross, Georgia, in the fifties, copes with her boyfriend, Willie, her aging grandmother, and the social unrest brewing at the time. The dialogue is written in African-American dialect and illustrates positive moral values.

♦ Students could document Ludelle's grandmother's deteriorating health and investigate the social services that would be available today to help Ludelle with her grandmother.

1. African-American—Fiction 2. School Stories 3. Georgia—Fiction.

Periodicals

630.5
Farmers and Consumers Market Bulletin. Carlton Moore, editor. Georgia Department of Agriculture (USPS 187620), Weekly. 12p. (Interest level: 6+).

This newspaper, devoted primarily to classified advertisements, is of interest to Georgia farmers and consumers who wish to purchase directly from farmers. The "for sale" and "wanted" advertisements give a living picture of small farms in rural Georgia.

♦ Students could graph or chart, over a period of several months, the frequency of products or livestock for sale and draw conclusions from their data.

1. Agriculture—Georgia.

917
Georgia Journal. Grimes Publication (ISSN 0746-5963), Quarterly. 76p. Color photos. (Interest level: 6+).

A wide range of articles and photographic essays about Georgia and Georgians is included in this magazine. There is something for everyone here, including an extensive listing of upcoming events called "Travelogue and Fun Calendar."

♦ Students could choose an event that interests them from the listings, locate it on a map, research it, and give a short oral presentation advertising it to classmates.

1. Georgia—Description and travel.

917
North Georgia Journal. Legacy Communications (8756-9256), Quarterly. 64p. B/W illus. (Interest level: 6+).

This magazine's masthead proclaims travel tips, history, lifestyles, and real estate. Although the focus is a bit heavy on luring tourists, the easy style of the articles should interest and inform students.

♦ Students could design advertisements for imaginary places or products suitable for the magazine.

1. Georgia—Description and travel.

975.8
Foxfire. Foxfire Fund, Inc. (0015-9220), Quarterly. 64p. B/W illus. (Interest level: 6+).

Published by the students of Rabun County High School in Clayton, Georgia, this journal reports on interviews with older (usually) residents of the mountains. There is always something to interest readers in the journal's wide variety of topics.

♦ Students could do interviews in their own area and produce a newsletter reporting their findings.

1. Georgia—Social life and customs 2. Country life—Georgia.

Professional Materials

372.3
Hamilton, Nancy. *Great Science Outings: A Guide to Science and Nature Centers in Georgia*. APPLE Corps, 1989. 78p. B/W illus. (Interest level: Professional).

This publication gives basic information about science field trips throughout Georgia: addresses, phone numbers, description, hours, ages, fees, contact persons, and special services or materials. Access to this booklet would be invaluable to teachers in Georgia, especially since there will be an updated edition in 1993. Also included is a list of contact information for agencies, organizations, and companies that provide outreach services to groups.
♦ Field trips or speakers can be efficiently planned using this guide.
1. Field trips.

796.1

Jones, Bessie and **Hawes, Bess Lomax**. *Step It Down: Games, Plays, Songs, and Stories from the Afro-American Heritage*. University of Georgia (0-8203-0960-5), 1987. 233p. (Interest level: 8 or Professional).

These games and songs are from Bessie Jones' experience growing up in Dawson, Georgia. Ring dances, singing plays, chants, and riddles emphasize cooperation and sharing, and teach children how to have fun with no expenditure.
♦ Since most are simple and all are designed to be accompanied only by clapping and singing, children can easily learn to play many of the games. A recording *Step It Down* (Rounder 8004) is out of production but may be available in some schools or libraries.
1. Play—party 2. African-Americans—Music.

811

Lanier, Sidney. *Poems of Sidney Lanier*. University of Georgia (L.C. 80-29576), 1981. 314p. (Interest level: Adult)

This is a facsimile of the 1916 edition published by Scribners. Although few of these poems will be of interest to students, it seems necessary to have this volume for "Song of the Chattahoochee."
♦ The teacher should arrange for a storyteller to present this poem to maximize student's appreciation.
1. Georgia—Poetry.

917.58

English, John, ed. *Brown's Guide to the Georgia Outdoors: Biking, Hiking, and Canoeing Trips*. Cherokee (0-87797-128-5 pbk), 1986. 272p. Maps; B/W photos. (Interest level: Professional).

This is a collection of articles from *Brown's Guide* and is divided by type and then by area. Since each article is an essay on an individual trip rather than a how-to, they are of limited use to students but provide good background for adults.
♦ Adults will find human interest items to enrich the study of many natural areas of Georgia.
1. Outdoor recreation—Georgia—Guidebooks.

975.00497

Ehle, John. *Trail of Tears: The Rise and Fall of the Cherokee Nation*. Doubleday (0-385-23954-8), 1988. 424p. (Interest level: Adult)

This story of the Cherokee is scholarly but interesting. It will give teachers a stronger background to enrich their teaching.
♦ Parents or teachers could tell stories to the students based on incidents from the book.
1. Cherokee Indians—History 2. Cherokee Indians—Removal 3. Indians of North America—Southern States—History.

Kentucky

by Vandelia VanMeter and Linda Esser

Nonfiction

289.8
Byrd, William S. *Letters from a Young Shaker at Pleasant Hill*. University Press of Kentucky (0-8131-1542-6), 1985. 165p. (Interest level: 7+).

During the early 1800s, a young male member of the prominent Byrd family of Virginia came to Kentucky and joined the Shaker community at Pleasant Hill. Through the lively, personal letters he wrote home to his family, this book offers the reader an experience of Shaker life.
♦ Students can assume they are members of the Shaker community at Pleasant Hill and write letters to family members describing a day in their life.
1. Shakers, Kentucky—Pleasant Hill 2. Pleasant Hill (Ky.) 3. Kentucky—History

289.8
Clark, Thomas Dionysius and **Ham, F. Gerald**. *Pleasant Hill and Its Shakers*. Pleasant Hill Press. 1993. 104p. Illus. (Interest level: 6+).

The Shakers who settled Pleasant Hill, Kentucky, developed a thriving, competitive agrarian community whose handicrafts and products were frequently the blue-ribbon winners at the county fairs. Using the excellent written records and journals kept by those who lived at Pleasant Hill, the authors provide lively accounts of the day-to-day life and spiritual practices of the society.
♦ Students may build a model of "Shakertown" (Pleasant Hill).
1. Pleasant Hill (Ky.)—History 2. Shakers—Kentucky—Pleasant Hill

289.8
Neal, Julia. *The Kentucky Shakers*. University Press of Kentucky (0-8131-0236-7), 1982. 102p. B/W photos. (Interest level: 6+).

This book relates the fascinating history of the followers of a unique religion who established three communities in Kentucky in 1805. Through selected excerpts from personal journals and illustrative photographs, their heritage of simplicity, beauty, and service within these communities is vividly brought to life.

♦ Students may explore other religious denominations living simple, self-sufficient lifestyles in communities.
1. Shakers—Kentucky 2. Kentucky—Church history

289.8
Sprigg, June and **Larkin, David**. *Shaker: Life, Work, and Art*. Photos by Michael Freeman. Stewart, Tabori & Chang (1-55670-011-3), 1987. 272p. Color photos. (Interest level: 5+).

During the nineteenth century, the Shakers established 18 thriving communities scattered from Maine to Kentucky. Using more than 200 magnificent, full-color photographs, this book presents the simplicity of Shaker design characteristics for the reader's visual pleasure. A brief explanatory text accompanies this exceptional work.
♦ Students may visit furniture stores in their area and observe the styles of beds and chairs; they should note any made in the Shaker style as seen in the book.
1. Shakers

301.41
Irvin, Helen Deiss. *Women in Kentucky*. University Press of Kentucky (0-8131-0239-1), 1979. 134p. B/W illus. (Interest level: 7+).

The contributions women have made to the heritage and history of Kentucky are examined in illustration and text for browsers, as well as serious students. This volume provides specific information on an aspect of the state's history that is not widely available in other resources.
♦ Students can make a chart of the categories used in the book and list under each heading the appropriate names and a significant accomplishment of each woman.
1. Women—Kentucky—History

305.4
Crowe-Carraco, Carol. *Women Who Made a Difference*. University Press of Kentucky (0-8131-0901-9), 1989. 63p. B/W photos. (Interest level: 4-8).

This book consists of inspiring, short biographies of nine of Kentucky's unsung heroes—women who contributed to the history and cultural heritage of the state. The small black and white photos provide a focus for the reader and add interest to the brief, concise chapters.

♦ Students can investigate other women who have had an impact on the history of Kentucky.

1. Women—Kentucky—Biography

331.8928
Wooly, Bryan. *We Be Here When the Morning Comes*. Photos by Ford Reid. University Press of Kentucky (0-8131-1337-7), 1975. 168p. B/W photos. (Interest level: 7+).

The history of Appalachian coal miners and their bitter relationship with the coal industry are documented in this story of a 13-month strike against the Brookside and High Splint coal mines in Harlan County, Kentucky in 1974. This poignant account vividly tells, in words and pictures, the story of a community divided by economic needs and realities.

♦ Students might investigate the use of coal as an energy source in the United States, or the current working conditions, benefits, and wages of coal miners in the Harlan County region.

1. Coal mines and mining—Kentucky

371.01
Hartford, Ellis Ford. *The Little White Schoolhouse*. University Press of Kentucky (0-8131-0231-6), 1977. 107p. (Interest level: 6+).

A Kentucky institution, the Little White Schoolhouse, saw students of all ages sit side by side in the same room, often with little or no heat and few materials, being instructed by a teacher who had more dedication than training. Lively vignettes of "books time" and the ever-present recess lighten this history and capture reader interest.

♦ Students can compare the "Little White Schoolhouse" to schools of the present day and note similarities and differences.

1. Schools—Kentucky 2. Kentucky—History

378.769
Dutton, William Sherman. *Stay On, Stranger! An Extraordinary Story of the Kentucky Mountains*. Farrar, Straus, and Young, 1954 (out of print). 79p. (Interest level: 7+).

When Alice Lloyd came to Knott County, Kentucky, she met resistance from the community when she tried to convince citizens of the need for an elementary school. This readable account of Lloyd's indomitable spirit and determination is a hero tale at its finest.

♦ Students can research the "Miracle on Caney Creek" and dramatize the events.

1. Lloyd, Alice 2. Caney Junior College 3. Kentucky—History

386.22436
Memories of Steamboats. PCR Publications, 1991. 64p. B/W photos. (Interest level: 4+).

This is a pictorial history of the steamboat era in Louisville, Kentucky, during the "Golden Age" of steamboats, 1820-1850, in magazine format. Filled with photographs of the great boats that traveled up and down the Ohio, this booklet will spark the interest of any would-be riverboat captain.

♦ Students may research the term, "mark twain" and determine which famous author used this term as his pen name and why.

1. River steamers—Kentucky—History 2. Steamboats—Kentucky—History

398.2
Alvey, R. Gerald. *Kentucky Folklore*. University Press of Kentucky (0-8131-00902-7), 1989. 61p. (Interest level: 5-8).

The traditional folk culture and folklore of Kentucky are presented in riddles, rhymes, proverbs, and songs. Alvey emphasizes folklore as an oral tradition of a people who share common beliefs and customs, and encourages readers to take ownership of this unique part of their heritage.

♦ The class can hold a storytelling festival, using this work and other works that provide samples of readily learned folklore.

1. Folklore—Kentucky 2. Kentucky—Social life and customs

398.2
Chase, Richard. *Grandfather Tales: American-English Folk Tales*. Illus. by Berkeley Williams, Jr. Houghton Mifflin Company (0-395-06692-1), 1943, 1976. 239p. B/W illus. (Interest level: 4+).

These wonderful stories, some of which can be traced to Kentucky, were meant to entertain young and old alike, make work go faster, and bring families together. This book is an excellent resource for teachers who wish to introduce students to the joys of folklore and storytelling, or for intermediate readers with an interest in storytelling.

♦ After listening to "Ashpet" or "The Old Sow and the Three Shoats," students will discuss other stories with which they are familiar that seem to be related to the two tales mentioned. This can be repeated with many of the stories, thus emphasizing the universality of the story and its oral tradition.

1. Folklore

398.2
Chase, Richard. *The Jack Tales*. Illus. by Berkeley Williams, Jr. Houghton Mifflin Company (0-395-06694-8), 1943. 202p. B/W illus. (Interest level: 4+).

These "handed-down tales" from the southeastern Appalachian Mountains relate the timeless adventures of a boy named Jack who jumps from one difficulty to another. Wiley Jack should find devoted followers of his exploits among intermediate school students.

♦ Students can trace one of the Jack Tales to its country of origin.

1. Folklore

398.2
Eastman, Mary and **Bolte, Mary**. *Dark and Bloodied Ground*. Photos by Mary Eastman. Chatham Press, 1973 (out of print). 128p. B/W photos. (Interest level: 4+).

Peopled with the ghosts of Kentucky's past, this volume describes scoundrels, witches, pirates, and others who, some say, still haunt the dark hollows and shadowed woodlands of the region. Eerie photographs, taken at the exact site of the old legends, will intrigue upper elementary and intermediate school browsers.

♦ Students may wish to investigate "ghost stories" of other regions of the United States. Compare the "ghost stories" with those from Kentucky.
1. Ghosts—Kentucky 2. Southern States—History—Miscellanea 3. Kentucky—History—Miscellanea

398.2
Galdone, Joanna. *The Tailypo: A Ghost Story*. Illus. by Paul Galdone. Houghton Mifflin (0-395-28809-6), 1977. Unpaginated. Color illus. (Interest level: 1-4).

The old man was hungry that evening, as he sat in his cabin in the southeastern Appalachians, and his hunger drove him to eat the tail of the odd, furry creature that crept through a crack in the cabin wall. Shivers of fear and delight are sure to run up and down the reader's spine, as the creature comes back and demands the return of its "Tailypo" in this memorable, delightfully illustrated folktale.

♦ This would be a marvelous tale for a readers' theater. The children can create a script from the book, and practice and perform their script complete with appropriate sound effects.
1. Folkore—Appalachian region

398.2
Haley, Gail E. *Jack and the Bean Tree*. Crown Publishers (0-517-55717-7), 1986. Unpaginated. Color illus. (Interest level: 1-4).

The traditional southeastern Appalachian folktale of Jack and his magic beans is retold in the soft cadences of the region and richly colored illustrations painted on wood. Haley turns Jack's tale into an heroic adventure just right for reading aloud.

♦ As a reading follow-up, students may plant beans and monitor the growth process from seed to plant.
1. Folklore—Appalachian region

398.2
Haley, Gail E. *Jack and the Fire Dragon*. Crown Publishers (0-517-56814-4), 1988. Unpaginated. Color illus. (Interest level: 3-5).

In this Jack Tale from the southeastern Appalachian region, Jack tackles a fire-breathing dragon and rescues three lovely maidens from its evil clutches. The folk art illustrations in bold, primary colors add richness and interest to the story.

♦ Students can research other Jack Tales from the Appalachian region of the United States.
1. Folklore—Appalachian region

398.2
Roberts, Leonard W. *South from Hell fer Sartin: Kentucky Mountain Folktales*. University Press of Kentucky (0-831-0175-1 pbk), 1955. 287p. (Interest level: 4+).

This is a collection of folktales from one of the most isolated sections of the Kentucky hills; it includes 200 jokes, anecdotes, myths, legends, animal tales, and ordinary tales—many short and easily learned. The intriguing title of this folktale collection should readily attract browsers.

♦ Students may draw or paint an illustration of a scene from their favorite tale after reading or hearing several of the stories from the book.
1. Folklore—Kentucky—Leslie County 2. Folklore—Kentucky—Perry County

398.6
Still, James. *Rusties and Riddles & Gee-Haw Whimmy-Diddles*. Illus. by Janet McCaffrey. University Press of Kentucky (0-8131-1686- 4), 1989. Unpaginated. B/W illus. (Interest level: 3-5).

This collection of witticisms, riddles, and rusties (pranks) from the Appalachians of Kentucky offers a glimpse into the humor and folklore of the region. This engaging book will entice the casual browser to take a closer look at its text and supporting illustrations.

♦ After reading some of the riddles in the book, students can try imitating the style and write two or three original riddles.
1. Folklore—Kentucky

582.16
Lyon, George Ella. *A B Cedar: An Alphabet of Trees*. Illus. by Tom Parker. Orchard Books (0-531-05795-X), 1989. Unpaginated. Color illus. (Interest level: K-1).

Kentucky native George Ella Lyon presents a unique look at the alphabet, accompanied by 26 trees from Aspen to Zebrawood. The soft earth tones of the illustrations, with their precise depiction of different species, allow for easy matching of common leaves and trees when used as a reference on a nature walk.

♦ After enjoying the book, young students can take a nature walk, gather leaves for identification, and use the book's illustrations as a guide.
1. Trees—Identification 2. Leaves—Identification 3. Alphabet

598.2
Barbour, Roger W., Peterson, Clell T., Rust, Delbert, Shadowen, Herbert E., and Whitt, A.L., Jr. *Birds of Kentucky*. University Press of Kentucky (0-8131-1281-8), 1973. 306p. Color photos. (Interest level: 4+).

This guide contains a description of the 321 bird species that have been reliably recorded in Kentucky. Precise, nontechnical terms and color photos give the novice watcher an easy-to-understand guide.

♦ Using the guide, students may keep a log of birds seen on the school grounds. At the end of the period being tracked, the number of different species can be tallied.
1. Birds—Kentucky

599.09769
Barbour, Roger W. and **Davis, Wayne H**. *Mammals of Kentucky*. University Press of Kentucky (0-8031-1314-8), 1974. 320p. Color and B/W photos. (Interest level: 5+).

This book examines 63 mammal species that claim Kentucky as their natural habitat. It includes maps that denote the range of specific species and over 300 photographs, many in color, of the animals discussed in the accompanying text.

◆ Students may visit a nature preserve or protected forest and observe animal behavior in a natural habitat, recording the species observed.
1. Mammals—Kentucky

633.31
Arnow, Jan. *Hay from Feed to Seed*. Knopf (0-394-96508-6), 1986. 39p. B/W photos. (Interest level: 3-7).
Through easy-to-read text and black-and-white photographs, the author takes readers to a Kentucky farm where the processes of planting and harvesting alfalfa are described. The importance of hay as a cash crop and its use as fodder for livestock are stressed, giving city dwellers an insight into farm life.
◆ Students may investigate the principle cash crops grown in Kentucky and make a chart illustrating their uses in manufacturing or other industries.
1. Alfalfa—Kentucky 2. Hay—Kentucky 3. Farms and farming—Kentucky

641.5
Anderson, Janet Alm. *A Taste of Kentucky*. University Press of Kentucky (0-8131-1580-9), 1986. 98p. B/W photos. (Interest level: 5+).
Providing much more than recipes, this book of favorite foods from Kentucky also gives readers anecdotes and bits of local wisdom from bygone days. Readers will delight in folk remedies for aches and ills, such as rheumatism, which include application of raccoon grease, and eating a lemon each day.
◆ Students can puree apples or other fruit with a food grinder and spread in a thin layer on a cookie sheet to dry in the sun for fruit leathers.
1. Cookery—Kentucky 2. Kentucky—Social life and customs

688.76357
Arnow, Jan. *Louisville Slugger: The Making of a Baseball Bat*. Pantheon Books (0-394-96297-4), 1984. 39p. B/W photos. (Interest level: 3-7).
In a season, a professional baseball player will use an average of 70 bats, most of which bear the "Louisville Slugger" trademark. In this informative photo-essay for elementary-age sports enthusiasts, Jan Arnow takes the reader through the production process for making these bats at the Hillerich & Bradsby plant in Louisville, Kentucky.
◆ Kentucky students might tour the Hillerich & Bradsby plant in Louisville, Kentucky, and report on their experiences. Students in other states might tour a local manufacturing plant and compare their experiences to the book.
1. Baseball bats 2. Baseball

709.769
Coleman, J. Winston. *Three Kentucky Artists—Hart, Price, Troye*. University Press of Kentucky (0-8131-0202-2), 1974. 76p. B/W photos. (Interest level: 7+).
Biographical portraits of three Kentucky artists who enjoyed significant distinction in their own day are presented in this volume. Essays on the lives of sculptor Joel Tanner Hart, portrait artist Samuel Woodson Price, and American sports painter Edward Troye provide the reader with information not readily accessible elsewhere.

◆ Using pictorial works from the Kentucky collection, students may search for statues and paintings by the three artists.
1. Hart, Joel Tanner, 1810-1877 2. Price, Samuel Woodson, 1828-1918 3. Troye, Edward, 1808-1874 4. Artists—Kentucky—Biography

745
Brown, Phyllis George. *Kentucky Crafts: Handmade and Heartfelt in Kentucky*. Crown Publishers (0-517-57327-X), 1989. 203p. Color photos. (Interest level: 6+).
Brown displays the work of over 200 Kentucky artisans from Appalachia to the Bluegrass region, documents the tradition of arts and crafts in the state, and describes the skill of the people who create them. More than 400 superb color photographs accompany the narrative, making this an eye-catching volume for browsers.
◆ Students may visit an arts and crafts exhibit in their area and interview one of the artisans about his or her work.
1. Handicraft—Kentucky

745
Parish, Peggy. *Let's Be Early Settlers with Daniel Boone*. Illus. by Arnold Lobel. Harper & Row (06-024648-0), 1967. 96p. B/W illus. (Interest level: 1-5).
Students of Kentucky history will delight in selecting a project from the many that Peggy Parish has collected to underscore the study of pioneer life. Simple, complete instructions for fresh, creative ideas will assist teacher and student alike in making a study of the life of the early settlers a multi-faceted learning experience.
◆ Students may select a project of interest from the book, or from teacher-designed learning centers to extend their study of the early settlers.
1. Frontier and pioneer life 2. Handicraft

750.2
Jones, Arthur Frederick. *The Art of Paul Sawyier*. University Press of Kentucky (0-8131-1340-7), 1976 (out of print). 120p. Color illus. (Interest level: 6+).
This book is a thorough study of the work of Kentucky artist Paul Sawyier by an art historian who regards Sawyier as a minor master of American impressionism. A wealth of illustrations and photographs trace Sawyier's growth as an artist.
◆ Students can research "American impressionism" and describe the characteristics of the style in relation to Sawyier's works.
1. Sawyier, Paul, 1865-1917 2. Painters—United States—Biography 3. Kentucky—Biography

779
A Kentucky Album: Farm Security Administration Photographs, 1933-1943. University Press of Kentucky (0-8131-1563-9), 1986. 148p. B/W photos. (Interest level: 6+).
This photographic essay on Kentucky visually details life in the state from 1935 to 1943, presenting a moving social history of the time period. Although the photographs are in black and white, their exceptional clarity and distinction make this a title worth exploring.

♦ Each student can select one photograph and create a biographical sketch for one of the people in the photograph.
1. Kentucky—Social life and customs—Pictorial works 2. Kentucky—Description and travel 3. Kentucky—History—Pictorial works

796.357
Golenbock, Peter. *Teammates.* Illus. by Paul Bacon. Harcourt Brace Jovanovich (0-15-200603-6), 1990. Unpaginated. Color photos; illus. (Interest level: 1-4).

This book describes the strength of Kentuckian Pee Wee Reese and African-American Jackie Robinson, who together challenged racial prejudice in major league baseball. The story is enriched by a unique combination of photographs and illustrations, making it an ideal read-aloud for younger elementary students.
♦ Students may wish to discover the names of other Kentucky athletes who have contributed to organized professional sports.
1. Robinson, Jackie, 1919-1972 2. Reese, Pee Wee, 1919- 3. Baseball players 4. Blacks—Biography 5. Race relations

798.43
Hirsch, Joe and **Bolus, Jim.** *Kentucky Derby: The Chance of a Lifetime.* McGraw-Hill (0-07-029069-5), 1988 (out of print). 150p. Color and B/W photos. (Interest level: 5+).

Defined as "the greatest two minutes in sports," the Kentucky Derby is documented in pictures and text by some of racing's most notable writers and photographers, providing a colorful, fascinating portrait of the Derby's past and present. Although out of print, the photographs and narrative in this volume make it a book well worth pursuing.
♦ Each student can design a poster for the Kentucky Derby Festival.
1. Kentucky Derby, Louisville, Ky.—Pictorial works 2. Louisville (Ky.)—Description and travel

798.43
May, Julian. *The Kentucky Derby.* Creative Education (0-87191-442-5), 1975. 47p. Illus. (Interest level: 2-4).

This book details the history and horses of "the greatest two minutes in sports," the Kentucky Derby. Although this book is outdated, the illustrations and narrative are an excellent introduction to the Kentucky Derby for younger readers.
♦ The class can organize a "Kentucky Derby" and write to the Kentucky Derby Museum for information on the Derby and Churchill Downs.
1. Kentucky Derby 2. Horse racing

811.54
Milnes, Gerald. *Granny Will Your Dog Bite and Other Mountain Rhymes.* Illus. by Kimberley Bulcken Root. Alred A. Knopf (0-394-94749-5), 1990. (Interest level: 1-4)

This collection of rhymes and poetry, filled with humor and whimsy, is from the mountain regions of the United States, including Kentucky. Droll, comical illustrations will intrigue young readers and enhance the sense of the ridiculous present in many of the selections.

♦ Each child may choose one of the poems and set it to a simple melody.
1. Mountain life—Poetry 2. American poetry

817
Hudson, Virginia Cary. *O Ye Jigs & Juleps!* Illus. by Karla Kuskin. Macmillan, 1962. 50p. B/W illus. (Interest level: 3-6).

Discovered in an attic trunk, these essays written by a lively 10-year-old Kentuckian who was confined to an Episcopal boarding school have a distinct, early 1900s flavor. The observations of the mischievous sprite who penned this collection are timeless in nature and as rib-tickling today as they must have been for the understanding teacher who gave the assignment to the precocious young author.
♦ After reading the book, children can describe their impressions of the boarding school and discuss how a boarding school differs from their school.
1. Humorous stories 2. School stories 3. Children's writings, American

917.69 (Reference)
Atlas of Kentucky. University Press of Kentucky (0-8131-1348-2), 1977. 163p. Illus. (Interest level: 4+).

This geographic and thematic atlas of Kentucky focuses on the land, social and economic patterns, transportation, distribution of minerals, and other aspects of the state. Well organized into easily digested chapters with uncluttered maps and illustrations, this would make an excellent addition to a Kentucky collection and be useful to both teachers and students.
♦ The class can make a topographic map of Kentucky showing the rivers and six natural regions.
1. Kentucky—Atlases 2. Kentucky—Geography 3. Kentucky

917.69
Berry, Wendell. *The Unforseen Wilderness: An Essay on Kentucky's Red River Gorge.* Photos. by Gene Meatyard. University Press of Kentucky, 1971. 140p. B/W photos. (Interest level: 6+).

Kentucky author Wendell Berry takes the reader on an excursion to the rocky dells of Red River Gorge in richly poetic prose that lyrically describes the natural wonders of the region. The black-and-white photographs of Gene Meatyard are exquisite studies in the landscape and character of the region.
♦ Students may pretend they are early Kentucky settlers who have just sighted the Red River Gorge. They can write a description of observations for the their journals.
1. Red River Gorge (Ky.) 2. Kentucky—Description and travel

917.69
Davis, H. Harold. *This Place Kentucky.* Louisville, Kentucky: DataCourier, 1975. 79p. Color photos. (Interest level: 4+).

Wade Hall selects poetry and prose to enhance a magnificent collection of color photographs that define the character and beauty of Kentucky. This volume combines both information for the serious student of Kentucky history with visual pleasure for the casual browser.

♦ Using a camera or sketchbook, students may collect scenes from their neighborhoods and city. They should select appropriate prose or poetry to accompany their choices.
1. Kentucky—Description and travel

917.69
Radlauer, Ruth. *Mammoth Cave National Park*. Photos. by Ed Radlauer. Children's Press (0-516-07496-2), 1978. 48p. Color photos. (Interest level: 3-5).

Mammoth Cave, located in south-central Kentucky, invites visitors to gasp in wonder at its spectacular geological formations and breathtaking scenery through the pages of this book. Intriguing animal and insect life unique to caves are also introduced to the young reader in concise, descriptive prose supported by quality photographs.
♦ Pretending they are spelunkers, students can write a story about their adventure in Mammoth Cave.
1. Mammoth Cave National Park 2. Caves—Kentucky

917.6904
Kentucky, a Picture Book to Remember Her By. Crescent Books, (0-517-47803), 1992. 64p. Color photos. (Interest level: 1-5).

This title lets the lush photographs of natural and historical sites in Kentucky tell their own unique stories. Very eye-appealing, this book would provide browsing younger students with an excellent introduction to Kentucky.
♦ Students can pretend they are on a trip through Kentucky. Using a large piece of construction paper, they can make a postcard with their favorite scene on one side and a note to their families on the other, including the address.
1. Kentucky—Description and travel

917.6904
Powell, Robert A. *This Is Kentucky*. Kentucky Images, 1975. 148p. B/W illus. (Interest level: 5+).

In this collection of pen-and-ink sketches, Kentucky Heritage Artist, Robert A. Powell, portrays many historical landmarks that chronicle the history of the state. Brief narratives that describe the importance of the site enhance each drawing.
♦ Pretending they are members of the State Tourism Commission, students may design a poster showing visitors things to see and do in Kentucky.
1. Kentucky—History 2. Kentucky—Description and travel 3. Historic sites—Kentucky

917.6944
Karem, Kenny. *Discover Louisville: An Illustrated Guidebook for Exploring City and County Neighborhoods*. Louisville Historical League, 1988. B/W illus. 131p. (Interest level: 6+).

This guide to the diverse neighborhoods and cultures that comprise the city of Louisville, Kentucky, takes the reader on tour in words and pictures. The brief, informative text describes the history and unique characteristics of each neighborhood in the city, providing the reader with information not readily available elsewhere.

♦ Each student can create a neighborhood history or time line for her or his neighborhood.
1. Louisville (Ky.)—History

923.1
Hamilton, Holman. *Three Kentucky Presidents: Lincoln, Taylor, and Davis*. University Press of Kentucky (0-8131-0246-4), 1978. 69p. 4 leaves of plates. (Interest level: 6+).

Three native Kentuckians advanced to the presidency of their respective nations. Zachary Taylor and Abraham Lincoln became presidents of the United States, and Jefferson Davis led the confederacy during the Civil War. This book offers a brief look at these three presidents, noting parallels and contrasts that will intrigue intermediate students engaged in research activities.
♦ Students may choose one of the three presidents and create a chronology of the major events in his life, being sure to include those incidents which marked his presidency and made it distinctive.
1. Lincoln, Abraham, 1809-1865 2. Davis, Jefferson, 1808-1889 3. Taylor, Zachary, 1784-1850 4. Kentucky—History—Biography 5. Presidents—United States—Biography

923.2769 (Reference)
Kentucky's Governors, 1792-1985. The University Press of Kentucky (0-8131-1539-6), 1985. 217p. (Interest level: 6+).

This book provides brief biographical sketches of the governors of Kentucky, stressing the administrative activities of each chief executive officer during his or her term. Although lacking illustrations, the effective descriptions of the often controversial personalities would be useful to advanced elementary or middle school students involved in research.
♦ Students may select a governor who interests them and discover the events occurring in the United States during the governor's term of office.
1. Kentucky—Governors—Biography 2. Kentucky—Politics and government

970.3
Bealer, Alex. *Only the Names Remain: The Cherokees and the Trail of Tears*. Illus. by William Sauts Book. Little, Brown (0-316-08520-0), 1972. 88p. B/W illus. (Interest level: 4-6).

This is the poignant story of the proud Cherokee people who lived in the southeastern Appalachian mountain region. They were gathered together, deprived of their land and rights, and forced into exile along what became known as the "Trail of Tears." The information available to students in this work deals objectively with the darker side of American westward expansion.
♦ To dramatize the meetings between the chiefs of the Cherokee nation and President Andrew Jackson, students may need to do additional research on this subject.
1. Cherokee Indians 2. Indians of North America 3. Kentucky—History

973.2
McCall, Edith S. *Cumberland Gap and Trails West*. Illus. by Carol Rogers. Children's Press, 1961. 126p. B/W illus. (Interest level: 4-5).

This book details the adventures of six explorers of Kentucky and the Cumberland Gap region, including George Washington and Daniel Boone, who pushed westward through the Appalachian Mountains in the eighteenth and nineteenth centuries. Pen-and-ink sketches extend the text for the late elementary reader.
♦ The class can create a model of the mountains and the Cumberland Gap.
1. Frontier and pioneer life 2. Appalachian Region—History 3. Kentucky—History 4. Explorers

973.7
Hale, Duane K. and **Gibson, Arrell M**. *The Chickasaw*. Chelsea House (1-55546-697-4), 1990. 111p. Color and B/W illus. (Interest level: 5-9).

Using traditional stories, artifacts, and journals kept by European visitors, the history of the Chickasaw nation, who lived in the southeastern United States, is condensed for middle schoolers. The text is supported by extensive illustrations.
♦ Students may draw a map of Kentucky and place the Cherokee, Chickasaw, and Shawnee tribes into their appropriate regions.
1. Chickasaw Indians 2. Indians of North America

973.7
Harrison, Lowell H. *The Civil War in Kentucky*. University Press of Kentucky (0-8131-0209-X), 1975. 115p. (Interest level: 6+).

Kentucky, with many of its families and institutions painfully divided during the Civil War, became a battle ground for ideas and ideals. Using selected quotations, the story of those who fought in the Civil War is related in readable, personal accounts.
♦ Students may choose to support the cause of the North or South and write a letter to a family member who supports the opposite side in the conflict.
1. Kentucky—History—Civil War, 1861-1865

975
Rylant, Cynthia. *Appalachia: The Voices of Sleeping Birds*. Illus. by Barry Moser. Harcourt Brace Jovanovich (0-15-201605-8), 1991. 23p. Color illus. (Interest level: 2-5).

The southeastern Appalachian region is described with love and warmth by author Cynthia Rylant. Barry Moser adds portraits of the people and way of life to enrich Rylant's heartfelt narration in this beautiful book.
♦ Students can research some of the musical instruments traditionally used in the Appalachian region and listen to music performed on these instruments.
1. Appalachian region—Description and travel 2. Appalachian region—Social life and customs

976.9
Brown, Dottie. *Kentucky*. Lerner Publications Company, 1992. 72p. Color photos. (Interest level: 2-4).

A treat of a book for young Kentuckians and others interested in the state, this compact volume offers beautiful color photographs, interesting facts and tid-bits, along with geography, history, economics, and culture. Appended charts, lists of famous authors, entertainers, journalists, and "Facts-at-a-Glance" provide for easy access to essential information.
♦ Students can prepare a picture map of the state, showing major tourist attractions, crops, etc.
1. Kentucky

976.9
Clark, Thomas D. *A History of Kentucky*. Jesse Stuart Foundation (0-945084-30-7), 1988. 531p. Illus. (Interest level: 6+).

This definitive history of the state of Kentucky from its earliest settlements to the 1970s is extensively indexed and provides a useful, detailed state history for the student involved in extensive research.
♦ Skimming and scanning are important research skills. Students should choose a subject from the index and skim the suggested pages for information, then choose a section of the book to scan for another subject of their choosing.
1. Kentucky—History

976.9 (Reference)
Encyclopedia of Kentucky. Somerset Publishers (0-403-09981-1), 1987. 529p. Illus. (Interest level: 5+).

This definitive volume on Kentucky covers a wide-range of subjects, such as history, geography, major cities, places, governors, and government. The all-inclusive subject coverage, enhanced by the extensive use of graphs, maps, and charts, makes this an essential item for the Kentucky reference collection.
♦ the class can create a mural depicting significant events in Kentucky's history.
1. Kentucky—Dictionaries and encyclopedias

976.9
Fradin, Dennis B. *Kentucky in Words and Pictures*. Children's Press (0-516-03917-2), 1981. 48p. Color illus. (Interest level: 2-4).

This is a brief introduction to the history, geography, industry, cities, economy, and people of Kentucky, the "Bluegrass State." Colorful photographs of historic places, natural wonders, and individuals who influenced the history of the state add to the information easily available to early elementary readers.
♦ Students will create a "Kentucky Fact Book," illustrating the state flag, bird, flower, fish, and other topics of interest.
1. Kentucky

976.9
Kentucky: A Pictorial History. University Press of Kentucky (0-8131-0092-5), 1971 (out of print). 256p. Color and B/W photos. (Interest level: 4+).

A panorama of two centuries of Kentucky history is given visual expression in 625 photographs, paintings, and drawings. The distinctive character of Kentucky's people and culture is presented in attractive, well-conceived, concisely organized chapters.
♦ Students may select a prominent figure from Kentucky history after reading the book, and present a brief dramatization of an event from that individual's life.
1. Kentucky—History—Pictorial works

976.9 (Reference)
Kentucky Encyclopedia. University Press of Kentucky (0-8131-1772-0), 1992. 1045p. (Interest level: 5+).

Published in August 1992, this comprehensive reference work presents broad coverage of information about Kentucky. Organized alphabetically by subject, as well as extensively indexed, this is an ideal source for students engaged in research, as well as a ready reference for curriculum support.
♦ Students may browse through the index, selecting a subject of interest, and use the index to find the information in the book. Students should be encouraged to compare the amount of information retrieved when only the alphabetical organization of the book is used to access data.
1. Kentucky—Dictionaries and encyclopedias

976.9 (Reference)
Kentucky Facts. Clements Research II, Inc., 1990. 454p. B/W illus. (Interest level: 6+).

This is a comprehensive look at Kentucky, county by county, including geography, people, transportation, economy, recreation/entertainment, and employment. Comparative charts provide students with research information not readily available in similar reference tools.
♦ Students may select five counties and prepare a chart comparing three of the topics covered in the book.
1. Kentucky

976.9
McNair, Sylvia. *America the Beautiful, Kentucky.* Children's Press (0-516-00463-8), 1988. 144p. Color and B/W photos. (Interest level: 3-6).

This book is an introduction to Kentucky, including history, geography, economy, and government, as well as a brief tour of sites of historical significance and cultural importance. Well-designed chapters, a section of "Facts at a Glance," and a detailed index make this an accessible book for students engaged in research.
♦ Students will develop a "living" time line of Kentucky's history, with each student in the class choosing an event to represent and discuss.
1. Kentucky

976.9
Powell, Robert A. *Frontier Kentucky.* Kentucky Images, 1985. 144p. Illus. (Interest level: 3-5).

This book provides an overview of Kentucky history and geography, including an extensive chapter on Kentucky's counties. The index and glossary assist in making this book an excellent choice for late elementary and middle school research assignments.
♦ Students may choose to construct a time line of Kentucky's movement toward statehood, or a map illustrating early settlements in Kentucky.
1. Kentucky—History 2. Kentucky—Geography

976.9
Powell, Robert A. *Kentucky Tidbits: Vital Statistics and Interesting Information about Kentucky's Past.* Kentucky Images, 1989. 64p. Sepia illus. (Interest level: 4+).

Filled with bits and pieces about the history, geography, and personalities of Kentucky, this book is a trivia buff's best friend. Illustrations and photographs add interest to the many facts found in print.
♦ This book begs for a trivia game to be designed from the information sandwiched between its covers.
1. Kentucky—History 2. Kentucky—Description and travel—Miscellanea

976.944
Munro-Leighton, Judy. *Changes at the Falls: Witnesses and Workers, Louisville and Portland, 1830-1860.* Portland Museum, 1982. 111p. Illus. (Interest level: 4-6).

This book traces the development of the community of Portland in the city of Louisville, Kentucky, from 1830 to 1860, prior to the Civil War. Produced by the Portland Museum, this book is designed to attract and hold the interest of middle school readers with its topically organized chapters and strategically placed illustrations.
♦ Students may investigate "Big Jim Porter" and write a physical description or draw a picture based on what they have discovered.
1. Louisville (Ky.)—History 2. Kentucky—History 3. Falls of the Ohio

976.944
Munro-Leighton, Judy and **Munro-Leighton, Bill.** *The Falls, a Stopping Place, a Starting Point.* Illus. by Billie Burrus Shulhafer. Portland Museum, 1987. 81p. B/W illus. (Interest level: 3-5).

This book serves as a history of the Falls of the Ohio at Louisville, Kentucky, for middle elementary readers, relating the story of the early settlers who came to the region and used the Ohio River for transportation to the west. Each chapter includes fact boxes and a glossary of unusual terms and places to assist the student doing research or casually browsing.
♦ Students can imagine they are one of the early settlers traveling down the Ohio River on a flat boat and write a story about an exciting experience that has occurred.
1. Louisville (Ky.)—History 2. Kentucky—History 3. Falls of the Ohio

976.944
Powell, Robert A. *Louisville/Jefferson County Sketchbook.* Kentucky Images, 1985. 72p. B/W illus. (Interest level: 6+).

This book presents detailed black-and-white sketches of historical sites and buildings of architectural significance from Louisville, Kentucky, and Jefferson County. Concise, descriptive narratives, conveniently placed on the facing page, elucidate the importance of each structure for the reader.
♦ Students may extend their knowledge of architecture by comparing columns from the sketches in the book to the classic columns from Greek architecture.
1. Louisville (Ky.)—Description and travel 2. Louisville (Ky.)—History

976.94709
Kerr, Bettie L. *Lexington: A Century in Photographs.* Lexington-Fayette County Historic Commission (0-912839-07-04), 1984. 246p. B/W photos. (Interest level: 6+).

This book provides a visual history of Lexington, Kentucky, captured through photographs dating from the Civil War through the early 1950s. Brief descriptions inform the reader of the importance of each photograph, making this book ideal for the browsing history student.

♦ Students can discuss the ways in which photographs document change and history, using examples from the book. They can also make a poster documenting their history using photographs of themselves.

1. Lexington (Ky.)—Description and travel 2. Kentucky—History—Pictorial works

976.991
Yater, George. *Two Hundred Years at the Falls of the Ohio: A History of Louisville and Jefferson County*. Filson Club, 1987. 261p. Color and B/W photos. (Interest level: 6+).

An exhaustive search of letters, journals, and historical documents culminated in this history of the city of Louisville, Kentucky. Hundreds of photographs, many in color, are described in the style of a seasoned newspaper reporter documenting events and personalities.

♦ Students can pretend they are a newspaper reporter for the *Courier Journal* and can choose an event described in the book and write an article about it for the newspaper.

1. Louisville (Ky.)—History 2. Kentucky—History

977
Pearce, John Ed. *The Ohio River*. University Press of Kentucky (0-8131-1693-7), 1989. 187p. Color photos. (Interest level: 6+).

Lush color photographs grace the pages of this history of the Ohio River by Kentucky author John Ed Pearce. The story of the people and places along its shores is wonderfully presented for the casual browser or serious reader, making it a useful addition to the Kentucky collection despite its lack of an index.

♦ Students may choose a community discussed in the book and research its history more extensively.

1. Ohio River—History 2. Ohio River—Description and travel 3. Ohio River Valley—History 4. Kentucky—History

977.2
Baird, Clay Patterson. *A Journey to the Falls*. Pinaire Lithographing Corp., 1976. 88p. B/W illus. (Interest level: 5-9).

Located on the Ohio River near Louisville, Kentucky, the Falls of the Ohio acted as a magnet for explorers and settlers alike. Line drawings of fossilized ancient sea life and photographs of artifacts left by early explorers, some as early as 1170, catch the reader's interest.

♦ Students will make "fossils" using shells and plaster of paris.

1. Kentucky—History 2. Falls of the Ohio

Biography

920.0769
Reed, Billy. *Famous Kentuckians*. Data Courier, Inc., 1977. 119p. Photos. (Interest level: 7+).

This book presents profiles of 52 famous Kentuckians that appeared in *The Courier-Journal* newspaper in Louisville during 1976. Billy Reed's brief biographies are written with warmth and humor, leaving the reader chuckling at the antics of some of Kentucky's most famous sons and daughters.

♦ After browsing through the book, students may select a personality who has acquired legendary status, such as Casey Jones, and compare the factual information contained in the biography with the legend.

1. Kentucky—Biography

92 Audubon, John J.
Keating, L. Clark. *Audubon: The Kentucky Years*. University Press of Kentucky (0-8131-0215-4), 1976. 92p. (Interest level: 7+).

This book provides a delightful account of naturalist John J. Audubon's sojourn in Kentucky from 1807 to his departure in 1819 when the collapse of his business ventures compelled him to attempt to earn his living as an artist. The easily read text invites the reader to explore this critical time in Audubon's life.

♦ The class can explore the Audubon Society, reporting on its founding, activities, and goals.

1. Audubon, John James, 1785-1851 2. Kentucky—Biography

92 Boone, Daniel
Brandt, Keith. *Daniel Boone: Frontier Adventures*. Illus. by John Lawn. Troll Associates (0-89375-843-4), 1983. 48p. B/W illus. (Interest level: 3-5).

This book details the early life of frontier hero, Daniel Boone, from his boyhood in Pennsylvania to his first sight of Kentucky in 1765. The black-and-white illustrations add interest and support the text, making this a good choice for younger readers.

♦ Students may create pioneer costumes or vests from paper bags or other materials.

1. Boone, Daniel, 1734-1820 2. Pioneers 3. Frontier and pioneer life 4. Kentucky—History—Biography

92 Boone, Daniel
Cavan, Seamus. *Daniel Boone and the Opening of the Ohio Country*. Chelsea House (0-7910-1309-X), 1991. 111p. Illus. (Interest level: 3-6).

This book chronicles the life of adventurer and explorer Daniel Boone, who helped open the land now known as Kentucky and the vast expanses beyond. Combining text and illustrations in an attractive format, this book offers the reader an extensive index, chronology, and bibliography.

♦ Students may choose a scene from Daniel Boone's life and write a dramatization of the event for presentation to a group of students or adults.

1. Boone, Daniel, 1734-1820 2. Pioneers 3. Kentucky—History—Biography 4. Frontier and pioneer life

92 Boone, Daniel
Daugherty, James. *Daniel Boone.* Viking Press, 1939. 95p. Color illus. (Interest level: 4+).

A Newbery Award winning book, this classic biography of Kentucky's Daniel Boone presents a comprehensive look at the events and people who shaped the life and legend of one of history's most interesting characters. Although this book was written decades ago, the illustrations and text have withstood the test of time and still offer upper elementary readers one of the best biographies available on the subject.
♦ Students can choose one of the incidents described in the biography and create a character web around the event.
1. Boone, Daniel, 1734-1820 2. Kentucky—History 3. Frontier and pioneer life—Kentucky

92 Boone, Daniel
Greene, Carol. *Daniel Boone, Man of the Forests.* Children's Press (0-516-04210-6), 1990. (Rookie Biography). 47p. Color illus. (Interest level: 2-4).

This biography gives young readers an excellent introduction to the life and adventures of Kentuckian, Daniel Boone. Ideal for curriculum support and early elementary report writers, this book includes an index, list of important dates, and many color illustrations to assist in comprehension of the readable text.
♦ Students may create a time line of Daniel Boone's life, highlighting those incidents pertinent to Kentucky history.
1. Boone, Daniel, 1734-1820 2. Kentucky—History 3. Frontier and pioneer life—Kentucky

92 Boone, Daniel
Hargrove, Jim. *Daniel Boone: Pioneer Trailblazer.* Children's Press (0-516-03215-1), 1985. 124p. B/W illus. (Interest level: 4-6).

This biography presents the life of American frontiersman, Daniel Boone, from his early life to his adventures in the wilderness of Kentucky and neighboring regions. Black-and-white illustrations depict some of the highlights of Boone's colorful life.
♦ Students may make dioramas of Boonesborough, or another scene from Daniel Boone's life.
1. Boone, Daniel, 1734-1820 2. Pioneers 3. Frontier and pioneer life 4. Kentucky—History—Biography

92 Boone, Daniel
Lawlor, Laurie. *Daniel Boone.* Illus. by Bert Dodson. Albert Whitman & Company (0-8075-1462-4), 1989. 160p. B/W illus. (Interest level: 5-8).

Kentucky's legendary Daniel Boone is described in this biographical account as a compassionate man of simple tastes and quiet ways, with a habit of whistling between his teeth or singing softly to himself. A chronology of Boone's life adds a useful appendix to this treatment which endeavors to present the personal side of the man who was always ready to explore the land beyond the next mountain.
♦ The class can discuss how biographies differ in their approach to a subject and in what they emphasize.
1. Boone, Daniel, 1734-1820 2. Pioneers 3. Frontier and pioneer life 4. Kentucky—History—Biography

92 Boone, Rebecca Bryan
Degering, Etta. *Wilderness Wife: The Story of Rebecca Bryan Boone.* Illus. by Ursula Koering. D. McKay Co., 1966 (out of print). 138p. B/W illus. (Interest level: 5-8).

Willowy, tall, black-haired and black-eyed, Rebecca Bryan Boone displayed the same tenacity as her husband Daniel, standing by his side as he pushed westward into Kentucky. Writing from information gathered from journals, letters, and personal interviews with remaining members of the Boone family, the author paints a highly readable portrait of a couple united in determination and personal integrity.
♦ By imagining they are Rebecca Boone, students can write a letter to Daniel telling him about their daily activities at home.
1. Boone, Rebecca 2. Boone, Daniel, 1734-1820. 3. Kentucky—History 4. Pioneers 5. Frontier and pioneer life

92 Clark, George Rogers
Nolan, Jeanette Covert. *George Rogers Clark, Soldier and Hero.* Illus. by Lee Amos. Julian Messner, Inc., 1954. 190p. B/W illus. (Interest level: 5-8).

This is a classic account of pioneer and hero of the American Revolution, George Rogers Clark, who helped form the first government of Kentucky. Accounts of the hardships of pioneer life, acts of heroism, and tribal raids draw the reader into the story of Clark's role in the forging of a new nation.
♦ Students will assume the identity of George Rogers Clark and write letters home to other members of the Clark family, including William Rogers Clark, who became co-leader of the Lewis and Clark expedition.
1. Kentucky—Biography 2. Kentucky—History

92 Davis, Jefferson
King, Perry Scott. *Jefferson Davis.* Chelsea House (1-55546-806-3), 1990. 112p. B/W photos. (Interest level: 6+).

Born in a log cabin in Kentucky in 1808, Jefferson Davis became the South's leading advocate of states' rights and the institution of slavery, culminating in his election as the first and only president of the Confederate States of America. Numerous black-and-white photographs, clearly and interestingly captioned, invite the reader to pursue the text of this biography more closely.
♦ Students should read a biography of Abraham Lincoln and make a chart comparing Lincoln and Davis.
1. Davis, Jefferson, 1808-1889 2. Confederate States of America—History 3. Kentucky—History—Biography

92 Lincoln, Abraham
Abraham Lincoln. (Videorecording). Encyclopedia Britannica Educational Corporation, 1982. VHS, 1 videocassette, (23 min.). Color. Includes teacher's guide. (Interest level: 5+).

This piece provides a dramatic account of Lincoln's early political life in Kentucky and Illinois, as well as scenes from his personal life. This video is an excellent introduction to the person of Abraham Lincoln for middle grade students and above.

♦ Students may draw a political cartoon depicting an incident in Lincoln's life.

1. Lincoln, Abraham, 1809-1865 2. Presidents—United States—Biography 3. Kentucky—History—Biography

92 Lincoln, Abraham

Abraham Lincoln. (Videorecording). Spoken Arts, 1987. VHS, 1 videocassette, (30 min.). Color. Includes teacher's guide. (Interest level: 3-5).

Based on *Abraham Lincoln* (*see* following entry) by Ingri and Edgar Parin D'Aulaire, this film visually presents the story of Kentucky native Abraham Lincoln from his early childhood on the frontier through the difficult period of the Civil War. The film shows the human side of Lincoln, focusing on his wit, wisdom, and courage.

♦ The class can make a diorama of the cabin Lincoln lived in as a boy.

1. Lincoln, Abraham, 1809-1865 2. Presidents—United States—Biography 3. Kentucky—History

92 Lincoln, Abraham

D'Aulaire, Ingri and **D'Aulaire, Edgar Parin**. *Abraham Lincoln.* Doubleday & Company, Inc. (0-385-07674-6), 1939, 1957. Unpaginated. Color illus. (Interest level: 1-3).

This classic biography of Kentuckian Abraham Lincoln has been reissued to take advantage of modern printing methods, with the D'Aulaires redrawing the illustrations to maximize the benefits. From his wilderness beginnings to his evolution into "Honest Abe," the D'Aulaires have visually chronicled the life and, in some cases, legend of Abraham Lincoln.

♦ Students may discuss the events from Lincoln's life described in the book, judging whether the incident is likely to have happened, or whether it was imagined by the author to demonstrate a quality of Lincoln's personality the author wished to emphasize.

1. Lincoln, Abraham, 1809-1865 2. Presidents—United States—Biography 3. Kentucky—History—Biography

92 Lincoln, Abraham

Freedman, Russell. *Lincoln: A Photobiography.* Clarion Books (0-89919-380-3), 1987. 150p. B/W photos. (Interest level: 4+).

This photobiography of Kentucky-born Abraham Lincoln touches on his boyhood and young adult years, but focuses on the years Lincoln served as president of the United States. The soft cream paper, sepia-toned photographs, and accounts of Lincoln's personal joys and tragedies portray the humanity of the craggy-faced "Honest Abe."

♦ Using the photographs in the book, students can discuss how Lincoln's face changed during the years of his presidency.

1. Lincoln, Abraham, 1809-1865 2. Presidents—United States—Biography 3. Kentucky—History—Biography

92 Lincoln, Abraham

Hargrove, Jim. *Abraham Lincoln: Sixteenth President of the United States.* Children's Press (0-516-01359-9), 1988. 97p. B/W illus. and photos. (Interest level: 4-8).

This work traces the major events in the life of native Kentuckian, Abraham Lincoln, from his boyhood in Hodgenville, to his rise to the presidency of the United States. A careful selection of photographs accompanies and enhances the story of Lincoln's life, along with several appendices that assist the reader with research.

♦ The class can investigate the Lincoln-Douglas debates and stage a re-enactment as it might occur today.

1. Lincoln, Abraham, 1809-1865 2. Presidents—United States—Biography 3. Kentucky—History—Biography

92 Stuart, Jesse

Stuart, Jesse. *The Thread That Runs So True.* Scribner, 1963. 313p. (Interest level: 7+).

Kentuckian Jesse Stuart describes his experiences as a teacher, first in a one-room schoolhouse and then in a high school. A tribute to both education and educators, Stuart's book also provides insight into the changes that have taken place in education over the past several decades.

♦ Imagining themselves students in Jesse Stuart's class, the children should write an essay describing their teacher, Mr. Stuart.

1. Stuart, Jesse, 1907—Biography 2. Kentucky—Biography 3. Authors, American—Biography

92 Taylor, Zachary

Kent, Zachary. *Zachary Taylor.* Children's Press (0-516-01352-1), 1988. 100p. B/W illus. (Interest level: 4-8).

A native of Kentucky, Zachary Taylor, "Old Rough and Ready," served his nation first as a soldier and ultimately as the twelfth president of the United States. Generously illustrated with black-and-white sketches and photographs, this biography of Taylor gives an accurate portrayal of the man and his place in history.

♦ Students may develop a chronology of the major events in Zachary Taylor's life.

1. Taylor, Zachary, 1784-1850 2. Presidents—United States—Biography 3. Kentucky—History—Biography

92 Tecumseh, Shawnee Chief

Shorto, Russell. *Tecumseh and the Dream of an American Indian Nation.* Illus. by Tim Sisco. Silver Burdett (0-382-09569-3), 1989. B/W illus. 123p. (Interest level: 5-9).

Tecumseh, chief of the Shawnee, was a man with a vision of greatness for the scattered tribes who inhabited the territory of Kentucky and surrounding regions. While lacking an index, this biography effectively relates his extraordinary efforts to unite the Native American tribes into one vital nation.

♦ Students can write an essay describing how the United States would be different if Tecumseh had succeeded in uniting the Native American nations.

1. Tecumseh, Shawnee Chief, 1768-1813 2. Shawnee Indians—History 3. Indians of North America

Fiction

Cannon, Bettie Waddell. *A Bellsong for Sarah Raines*. Orchard Books (0-89490-859-5), 1987. 184p. (Interest level: 7+).

After Sarah's father commits suicide, she and her mother move to a small Kentucky town where they are surrounded by the support and warmth of relatives and friends as they try to come to terms with the change in their lives. Sarah learns to accept her father's death and celebrate his life in this seemingly effortless and exciting account.

♦ The class can research the psychological effects of the Great Depression on people in the United States.
1. Fathers and daughters—Fiction 2. Suicide—Fiction 3. Kentucky—Fiction 4. Depressions—1929—Fiction

Caudill, Rebecca. *A Certain Small Shepherd*. Illus. by William Pene Du Bois. Henry Holt and Company (0-8050-1323-7), 1965. 48p. Color illus. (Interest level: 1-4).

Kentucky author Rebecca Caudill shares the story of a mute boy who is made painfully aware of his disability when he can not join his classmates in song during the school Christmas pageant. The soft, yet richly hued illustrations translate winter in the Appalachians to the printed page in this charming tale.

♦ Students may extend the book by discussing other kinds of physical disabilities and the limitations these impose on the individuals who have them.
1. Christmas—Fiction 2. Kentucky—Fiction 3. Handicapped—Fiction

Caudill, Rebecca. *Did You Carry the Flag Today, Charley?* Illus. by Nancy Grossman. Henry Holt and Company (0-8050-1201-X), 1966. 95p. B/W illus. (Interest level: 1-3).

Harlan County, Kentucky, is the setting for this school story of a young Appalachian Mountain boy, Charley Cornett, whose mischievous tendencies get in the way of his receiving the award for being the most helpful child in school—carrying the flag. The distinctive black-and-white illustrations and soft cadences of the mountain region of Kentucky make this story an excellent read-aloud.

♦ After reading Charlie's story, children can "parade" around the school carrying the flag in imitation of Charlie and his classmates.
1. School stories 2. Kentucky—Fiction

Caudill, Rebecca. *A Pocketful of Cricket*. Illus. by Evaline Ness. Henry Holt and Company, Inc. (0-8050-1200-1), 1964. Unpaginated. Color illus. (Interest level: 1-3).

Young Jay finds a cricket on his way home and puts it in his pocket, lavishing care and attention on his newly acquired friend in this story set in Kentucky. The simple, childlike illustrations offer visual insight into Jay's feelings as he moves through the pages of the story.

♦ Children can decide which insect they might choose for a pet and discuss its care and feeding.
1. Crickets—Fiction 2. Insects—Fiction 3. Kentucky—Fiction

Caudill, Rebecca. *Schoolhouse in the Woods*. Illus. by Decie Merwin. Dell Publishing (0-440-40170-4), 1949, 1989. 120p. B/W illus. (Interest level: 2-3).

In the one-room schoolhouse attended by the Fairchild children who live in Harlan County, Kentucky, Miss Cora teaches her students about nature and the principles of living, as well as the three R's. Black-and-white line drawings extend the story of the Fairchild children and invite readers to share their daily activities.

♦ After reading the story, students will write a letter to one of the Fairchilds, discussing the differences between present-day school settings and the one-room schoolhouse.
1. School stories 2. Kentucky—Fiction

Caudill, Rebecca. *Tree of Freedom*. Illus. by Dorothy Bayley Morse. Puffin Books (0-14-032908-0) 1947, 1977. 279p. (Interest level: 4-6).

Stephanie Venable carries an apple seed with her when her family moves from Carolina to Kentucky, a symbol of the new way of life her pioneering family will build—a "tree of freedom." This Newbery Honor Book will transport middle school readers back in time to share Stephanie's exciting adventures.

♦ Students can imagine that they have moved from Carolina to Kentucky and can write a letter to a friend describing their journey and new home.
1. Kentucky—Fiction 2. Frontier and pioneer life—Fiction 3. Families and family life—Fiction

Chaffin, Lillie D. *Freeman*. Macmillan, 1972 (out of print). 152p. (Interest level: 4-6).

Set in the coal-mining region of eastern Kentucky, 12-year-old Freeman, who has lived with his grandparents all of his life, learns that he must go to live with his parents now that his father is out of prison. A sensitive story of a pre-adolescent's anger, frustration, and fear as he struggles to determine who he is and attempts to reconstruct his image of family.

♦ The class can construct a model of a coal mining operation.
1. Families and family life 2. Kentucky—Fiction

Chaffin, Lillie D. *We Be Warm Till Springtime Comes*. Illus. by Lloyd Bloom. Macmillan Publishing Company (0-02-717910-9), 1980 (out of print). Unpaginated. B/W illus. (Interest level: 1-3).

In a coal mining town in the southeastern Appalachian region, a young boy feels it is his responsibility to find the means to keep his mother and baby sister warm during the harsh winter. This picture book radiates the warmth and caring of family love.

♦ Each student should write a poem based on the characters in the story.
1. Fuel 2. Winter—Fiction 3. Appalachian region—Fiction

Chambers, Catherine E. *Flatboats on the Ohio: Westward Bound*. Illus. by John Lawn. Troll Associates (0-8167-0049-4), 1984. 32p. B/W illus. (Interest level: 2-4).

The Sawyer family decides to move from Pennsylvania and travel to the Ohio River Valley, navigating the treacherous Falls of the Ohio near Louisville, Ken-

tucky, on their way. This story of their fortitude and adventures makes an exciting tale for young readers.
♦ Students may construct a model of a flatboat.
1. Frontier and pioneer life—Fiction 2. Flatboats—Fiction 3. Ohio River Valley—History—Fiction

Cole, Norma. *The Final Tide*. Margaret K. McElderry Books (0-689-50510-8), 1990. 153p. (Interest level: 5+).

Fourteen-year-old Geneva goes to Eastern Kentucky to spend the summer with her obstreperous grandmother who refuses to vacate her home as the Wolf Creek Dam nears completion. Geneva's discovery of her own strength of will and her close family ties is told with feeling and humor in this readable novel for middle and upper elementary students.
♦ Students can research the Wolf Creek Dam and its effects on communities in eastern Kentucky.
1. Kentucky—Fiction 2. Families and family life—Fiction 3. Grandmothers—Fiction

Davis, Jenny. *Good-bye and Keep Cold*. Orchard Books (0-531-08315-2), 1987. 210p. (Interest level: 7+).

Henry John Fitzpatrick is welcomed into Edda's home after he causes an accident in a Kentucky strip mine that takes her father's life. Edda's confusion and sorting through of her feelings toward John Henry are handled with great sensitivity and understanding by this outstanding Young Adult author.
♦ Pretending they are friends of Edda and frequently write letters to her, the students can respond to one she has written to them describing her feelings about John Henry.
1. Family life—Fiction 2. Kentucky—Fiction

Gaines, Edith M. *Freedom Light*. New Day Press (0-913678-20-1), 1991. Illus. by Cliff Clay. 36p. B/W illus. (Interest level: 6-8).

This narrative is a fictionalized account of the activities of the Underground Railroad in Kentucky and elsewhere, based on eyewitness accounts of two leaders who were involved, John Rankin and John Parker. It serves as a valuable resource for multicultural aspects of a Kentucky collection.
♦ Students can research other heroes of the Underground Railroad, select one, and design a biography box for their choice.
1. Underground railroad—Fiction 2. Blacks—Fiction

Hay, John. *Rover and Coo Coo*. Illus. by Tim Solliday. Green Tiger Press (0-88138-078-4), 1986. Unpaginated. Color and B/W illus. (Interest level: 3-6).

Kentucky author John Hay captures the pioneer spirit as he relates the story of two faithful dogs who rescue their master from wolves and certain death. Based on an adventure lived by one of Hay's ancestors, this stirring story presents a true life experience of early American frontier life.
♦ Students can interview a family member, preferably a grandparent, and record a family story to share with classmates.
1. Dogs—Fiction 2. Kentucky—Fiction 3. Frontier and pioneer life—Fiction

Hendershot, Judith. *In Coal Country*. Illus. by Thomas B. Allen. Alfred A. Knopf (0-394-88190-7), 1987. Unpaginated. Color illus. (Interest level: 1-4).

Life in a coal mining community is described through the eyes of a child who watches her father go off to work every night with his silver lunch bucket and a miner's lighted hat. The story is strengthened by Allen's sensitive portrayal of the family and his rich hued renderings of the changing seasons.
♦ Students can choose an illustration and write a paragraph describing the picture.
1. Coal mines and mining—Fiction

Hiser, Berniece T. *The Adventures of Charlie and His Wheat-Straw Hat: A Memorat*. Illus. by Mary Szilagyi. Dodd, Mead & Company (0-396-08772-8), 1986. Unpaginated. (Interest level: 1-3)

In this story set in eastern Kentucky in the Appalachians, a loving grandmother comes to the rescue of young Charlie who desperately wants a new hat to start the school year. Vividly colored illustrations enrich the narrative and tell of Charlie's relationship with his grandmother.
♦ Each student can bring a favorite hat to school and share stories about the hats.
1. Hats—Fiction 2. Grandmothers—Fiction 3. Mountain life—Fiction 4. United States—History—Civil War, 1861-1865—Fiction 5. Kentucky—Fiction

Jamison, Andrew J. *Kentucky Boy*. Winston-Derek Publishers (1-55523-034-2), 1987. 123p. (Interest level: 6-8).

The adventures of a young boy growing up on a small farm in western Kentucky during the early 1900s are based on events from the author's childhood. Close, caring family relationships that have lasted throughout the years give the reader a sense of timelessness and tradition.
♦ The class can discuss how family life has changed since the early 1900s and make a chart comparing the 1990s and 1900s.
1. Farm life—Kentucky—Fiction 2. Families and family life—Kentucky—Fiction 3. Kentucky—Fiction

Langstaff, John. *Frog Went A-Courtin'*. Illus. by Feodor Rojankovsky. Harcourt Brace Jovanovich (0-15-230214), 1955. Unpaginated. Color illus. (Interest level: K-3).

Children of the southeastern Appalachian region sing their version of this traditional folktale using the melody presented by Langstaff. The rib-tickling story of the frog's wedding is played out in comical illustrations that are sure to leave early readers chuckling.
♦ The students can draw a story map, charting the events that occur at frog's wedding.
1. Folklore—Appalachian region

Love, Sandra. *But What about Me?* Illus. by Joan Sandin. Harcourt Brace Jovanovich (0-15-249900-8), 1976. 152p. B/W illus. (Interest level: 4-5).

Lucy Hoffman's resentment of her mother's decision to go back to work hurls the family into a crisis of misadventures and minor tragedies in this novel by Kentucky author, Sandra Love. Assisted by black-and-white line drawings, Love presents a contemporary issue to late elementary readers in a caring, humorous fashion.

♦ Students may create a diary for Lucy, writing about her activities and her feelings regarding her mother's decision to work outside the home.

1. Families and family life—Fiction 2. Mothers—Fiction

Lyon, George Ella. *Basket*. Illus. by Mary Szilagyi. Orchard Books (0-531-08486), 1990. Unpaginated. Color illus. (Interest level: K-3).

From family stories, native Kentuckian, George Ella Lyon, remembers her grandmother's special basket and the many treasures kept in it. Soft, evocative illustrations capture the mood of looking back into the warm, loving days of childhood in this story of a grandparent-grandchild relationship.

♦ Students should be encouraged to remember special moments in their childhood spent with a grandparent or other family member. Relating the incident to the class becomes the sharing of a family story for the child.

1. Kentucky—Fiction 2. Families and family life—Fiction 3. Grandmothers—Fiction

Lyon, George Ella. *Borrowed Children*. Orchard Books (0-531-05751-8), 1988. 154p. (Interest level: 5-7).

Twelve-year-old Amanda is given the opportunity to visit family in Memphis, experiencing a place and lifestyle far different from that of her Kentucky mountain home. This novel richly articulates the difficulties and joys of family life in a rural mountain community during the Depression era.

♦ George Ella Lyon draws wonderful word pictures with her writing. After reading this book, students might wish to choose a scene from the book to illustrate.

1. Depression—1929—Fiction 2. Mountain life—Fiction 3. Family life—Fiction 4. Kentucky—Fiction

Lyon, George Ella. *Cecil's Story*. Illus. by Peter Catalanotto. Orchard Books (0-531-08512-0), 1991. Unpaginated. Color illus. (Interest level: 1-3).

Kentucky author George Ella Lyon plays out the possible scenarios of what might happen to the father of a family if he were to go to war. Set in the Civil War period, the story does not choose North or South, but speaks of the universality of human feelings of those who go to fight the war and of those who wait at home.

♦ Pretending they are Cecil, the students can write a letter to their father who is fighting in the Civil War.

1. War—Fiction 2. United States—History—Civil War, 1861-1865—Fiction

Lyon, George Ella. *Come a Tide*. Illus. by Stephen Gammell. Orchard Books (0-531-08454-X), 1990. Unpaginated. Color illus. (Interest level: K-3).

George Ella Lyon writes of the residents of Harlan County, Kentucky, and their experiences with one of nature's fiercest creations—a flood. Stephen Gammell's pencil color illustrations capture the excitement, fear, and courage of the people who weather the storm and prepare to pick up the threads of their lives once more.

♦ Children should be encouraged to study and discuss the many "stories" taking place in Gammell's illustrations.

1. Floods—Fiction 2. Country life—Fiction

Lyon, George Ella. *The Outside Inn*. Illus. by Vera Rosenberry. Orchard Books (0-531-05936-7), 1991. Unpaginated. Color illus. (Interest level: K-2).

Kentucky author George Ella Lyon presents "taste treats" in verse for children to chuckle over, such as snacks of "caterpillar feet." The squiggly, squirmy suggestions are faithfully captured in watercolor illustrations that creep and crawl across the pages.

♦ Students can imagine their own "taste treat" and illustrate it for classmates.

1. Stories in rhyme 2. Humorous stories

Lyon, George Ella. *Red Rover, Red Rover*. Orchard Books (0-531-08432-9), 1989. 131p. (Interest level: 6-8).

In this story set in Kentucky, 12-year-old Sumi Mitchell must deal with a series of losses as her older brother goes off to prep school, her grandfather dies, her mother retreats into a world of grief, and her best friend moves away. Sumi's struggle to reach out and find healing in the midst of an autumn "too filled with absence," enables the reader to grow with Sumi and share her triumph.

♦ After reading the book, students can discuss the importance of setting, including the time of year.

1. Families and family life—Fiction 2. Kentucky—Fiction

Lyon, George Ella. *A Regular Rolling Noah*. Illus. by Stephen Gammell. Bradbury Press (0-02-761330-5), 1986. Unpaginated. Color illus. (Interest level: 1-3).

A young lad travels from Pathfork, Kentucky, to Canada with a family who has decided to move all of their household goods and animals. In charge of the boxcar of animals, he's dubbed a "Regular Rolling Noah" by one of the characters he meets on the train as the story rollicks along, aided by Stephen Gammell's illustrations.

♦ Students can illustrate their favorite scene from this humorous book.

1. Voyages and travel—Fiction 2. Domestic animals—Fiction 3. Railroads—Trains—Fiction 4. Kentucky—Fiction

Mills, Lauren A. *The Rag Coat*. Little, Brown & Company (0-316-57407-4), 1992. 32p. Color illus. (Interest level: 3-5).

Minna, a child of the southeastern Appalachian region, needs a new coat before she can begin school, so the Quilting Mothers stitch together the scraps of fabric Minna carefully selects, each with a story attached. The rich tradition of family stories is emphasized in this sensitively illustrated book for late elementary readers.

♦ The class can design a quilt using crayons or create a class quilt with the help of parent volunteers.

1. Coats—Fiction 2. Appalachian region—Fiction 3. Families and family life—Fiction

Monjo, F.N. *Indian Summer*. Illus. by Anita Lobel. Harper & Row, 1968. (I Can Read History Book). 62p. Illus. (Interest level: 1-3).

Set on the Kentucky frontier, this book offers the exciting story of three children and their mother caught in the terror of a tribal raid. The expressive, lifelike illustrations extend and enhance the drama of the narrative.

♦ Students may discuss how young children might feel when they think their parents are in danger.
1. Kentucky—History—Fiction 2. Frontier and pioneer life—Fiction

Moser, Barry. *Polly Vaughn*. Little, Brown & Company (0-316-58541-6), 1992. 28p. Color illus. (Interest level: 6-8).

In this traditional ballad from the southeastern Appalachian region, two childhood sweethearts are destined for tragedy caused by a hunting accident. Barry Moser's distinctive paintings are as haunting as the ghost of Polly Vaughn who loves her "Jimmer" in life and in death.

♦ There are other traditional folk ballads that deal with star-crossed love. Children may investigate as many of these ballads as they can find.
1. Appalachian region—Fiction 2. Ballads, English—South (U.S.)

Rice, Alice Hegan. *Mrs. Wiggs of the Cabbage Patch*. University Press of Kentucky (0-8131-1391-1), 1901, 1979. 153p. (Interest level: 2-4).

Mrs. Wiggs and her children live in a tumble-down house called "The Cabbage Patch" in this story of the struggle to survive set in Louisville, Kentucky. The realities presented are harsh, but are an accurate portrayal of life at the turn of the century.

♦ Students should investigate "Cabbage Patch Settlement House," which exists in Louisville today, and determine whether or not they believe its roots might lie in this story.
1. Families and family life 2. Louisville (Ky.)—Fiction 3. Mothers—Fiction

Shelby, Anne. *We Keep a Store*. Illus. by John Ward. Orchard Books (0-531-08456-6), 1990. Unpaginated. Color illus. (Interest level: 1-2).

A young girl describes her life and activities as the child of storekeepers in a small rural community in this book by Kentucky author Anne Shelby. Color illustrations in soft, muted tones suit the mood of the story.

♦ The class can set up a "store" like that in the story in the classroom where children may "shop."
1. Stores, Retail—Fiction 2. Families and family life—Fiction 3. Country life—Fiction

Smith, Doris Buchanan. *Return to Bitter Creek*. Viking Kestrel (0-670-80783-4), 1986. 174p. (Interest level: 6+).

Lacy returns to the southern Appalachian home of her birth and to a large extended family. When tragedy strikes, Lacy discovers the security of family strength and love in this powerful family story.

♦ The class can discuss the ways in which families come together to support each other in times of hardship and difficulty.
1. Families and family life—Fiction 2. Southern States—Fiction 3. Appalachian region—Fiction

Stuart, Jesse. *The Beatinest Boy*. Illus. by Robert Henneberger. The Jesse Stuart Foundation, 1952, 1989. 73p. B/W illus. (Interest level: 3-6).

Grandma Beverley takes in the orphaned David and creates a family and home for him in this novel set in the Appalachian region of Kentucky. The characters of Stuart's book are rich and warm, the sights and sounds worth the reader's time to listen to and look at as the mountains and the people who inhabit them come to life.

♦ Students may investigate the customs and culture of the Appalachian Mountain region of Kentucky and share their most interesting discovery with classmates.
1. Kentucky—Fiction 2. Families and family life—Fiction

Stuart, Jesse. *Old Ben*. Illus. by Richard Cuffari. McGraw-Hill, 1970. 92p. B/W illus. (Interest level: 3-4).

Shan's Kentucky mountain family learns snakes have a place in nature when Shan befriends a large, black bull snake and makes a pet of him. This novel does not minimize the danger of certain species of snakes but does much to dispel the unreasoning fear of these often helpful creatures.

♦ Students may investigate bull snakes and make a poster illustrating facts they discover.
1. Snakes—Fiction 2. Kentucky—Fiction

Stuart, Jesse. *A Penny's Worth of Character*. Illus. by Robert G. Henneberger. McGraw-Hill, 1954. 61p. B/W illus. (Interest level: 3-5).

In this timeless story set in Kentucky, young Shan takes paper sacks back to the store keeper to earn money but slips one over on the storekeeper by putting a sack with a hole in it in the middle of the stack. Shan's battle with his conscience and his mother's caring compassion will linger with the reader long after the covers of the book are closed.

♦ The children should apply the saying, "Honesty is the best policy," to this story.
1. Families and family life—Fiction 2. Kentucky—Fiction

Winter, Jeanette. *Follow the Drinking Gourd*. Illus by author. Knopf (0-394-99694-1), 1988. Unpaginated. Color illus. (Interest level: 1-4).

An old sailor named Peg Leg Joe teaches runaway slaves in the South the words to a song, "The Drinking Gourd," which secretly gives them the directions for the journey along the Underground Railroad to the North and freedom. Vividly colored illustrations depict the pilgrimage of these people to Canada as the lyrics of the song are explained to the reader.

♦ The class can design a chart illustrating the true meaning of the lyrics of "The Drinking Gourd."
1. Slavery—Fiction 2. Underground railroad—Fiction

Periodicals

976.9

Jefferson County Gazette. Ron Puckett, Quarterly. $7.50/year. (Interest level: 6+).

This periodical is designed to assist readers in learning the history of Jefferson County and Louisville, Kentucky. It contains articles accompanied by reproductions of black-and-white photographs that will intrigue middle school readers.

♦ The class may create a school "Gazette" with articles and drawings similar to those in the *Jefferson County Gazette.*

1. Kentucky—Periodicals

976.9

The Kentucky Explorer. Kentucky Explorer, 10/year. $15.00/year. (Interest level: 3+).

Eighty pages of articles and anecdotes about Kentucky are presented in this magazine featuring "things old and new" about the state. Black-and-white photographs enhance biographies, history, geography, folklore, and a host of other subjects.

♦ The class can begin a "Kentucky Book of Facts" using information from *The Kentucky Explorer.*

1. Kentucky—Periodicals

976.9

Kentucky Images. Kentucky Images, 5/year. (Interest level: 7+).

This illustrated magazine focuses on Kentucky's culture, geography, and history. It contains maps and charts, as well as black-and-white line drawings.

♦ Students can reproduce and color one of the maps, mounting it on poster board and cutting it into parts to create a "Kentucky Puzzle."

1. Kentucky—Periodicals

976.9

Louisville. Louisville Chamber of Commerce, Monthly. (Interest level: 7+).

A publication by the Louisville, Kentucky, Chamber of Commerce, this magazine highlights events taking place in the city and the state. Illustrated with color and black-and-white photographs, *Louisville* is an attractive, eye-catching publication.

♦ Pretending to be members of the Chamber of Commerce, students can write a radio commercial about an event taking place in Louisville.

1. Louisville (Ky.)—Periodicals 2. Kentucky—Periodicals

976.9

Pondering Kentucky the Magazine. (Audiocassette). Kentucky Sound, 1990-. (60 min. each). (Interest level: 7+).

This series of cassette tapes is produced monthly and defined as an "audio magazine" with wide-ranging vignettes of Kentucky, including folklore, descriptions of historical sites, festivals and events, and personalities. A complete listing of the contents for each back issue is available from the publisher, permitting teachers to select those tapes that would support the Kentucky unit most effectively.

♦ After listening to one or more of the tapes, students may script and produce their own version of *Pondering Kentucky.*

1. Kentucky—Periodicals 2. Kentucky—Audio-visual aids—Periodicals

Professional Materials

372.89043

Kentucky Department for Libraries and Archives. *Rediscover Kentucky: A Children's Services Manual.* Kentucky Department of Libraries and Archives, 1992. 372p. B/W illus. (Interest level: Adult).

Based on the state's bicentennial theme, "Rediscover Kentucky," this wealth of information on resources, activities, history, folklife, and environment will be invaluable to those searching for materials to enhance the study of Kentucky. Intended primarily for public service librarians, this would nonetheless be a valuable resource for any professional collection on the subject.

1. Kentucky—Study and teaching (Elementary)

911.769

Clark, Thomas Dionysius. *Historic Maps of Kentucky.* University Press of Kentucky (0-8131-0097-6), 1979. 89p. Color illus. (Interest level: Adult).

The 10 maps in this set provide teachers with information on the westward settlement of Kentucky, accompanied by an 88-page history. Printed on heavy cream stock with softly faded colors and lettering reminiscent of bygone days, each map presents a story of the state's expansion and development.

1. Kentucky—Maps 2. Kentucky—History 3. Kentucky—Geography

917.69

Kentucky's Natural Heritage. (Videorecording). Kentucky Educational Television. VHS, 1 videocassete (8-15 min. segments), Color. Includes teacher's guide. $25.00. (Interest level: 6-12).

This series of programs explores the unique environments in Kentucky, including biological and geological characteristics of the Red River Gorge area, Cumberland Falls, and Murphy's Pond. Viewers will experience the distinctive natural features of each region through this exceptional series.

1. Kentucky—Geography

976.9

Collins, Eleanor S., Driscoll, Martha, and Ford, Jane. *Learn about Kentucky: A Thematic Unit.* Illus. by Marion McMreevy. Bookabeast Series, 1992. Unpaginated. B/W illus. (Interest level: Adult)

A thematic unit for primary students based on the valued outcomes designed as part of the Kentucky Education Reform Act, this teacher resource provides an integrated approach to the study of Kentucky. Content areas of language arts, math, science, social studies, art, music, and physical education are woven into this study of Kentucky's history, geography, and people.

1. Kentucky

976.9

Kentucky, a Geographical and Historical Perspective: Teacher Resource Guide, Fourth Grade. Kentucky Educational Foundation, 1989. 105p. Illus. (Interest level: Adult).

A cooperative effort of the National Geographic Society, Kentucky Educational Foundation, Kentucky Department of Education, and Kentucky Geographic Alliance, this first of its kind resource seeks to provide a comprehensive integration of geography into Kentucky studies. Basing integrated instruction on five themes—Location, Place, Relationships within Places, Movement, and Regions—this highly useful guide presents sample lesson plans, teaching strategies, and suggestions for activities.
1. Kentucky—History—Study and teaching

976.9

Kentucky in the Classroom: A Resource Guide. Kentucky Department of Education, 1986. 207p. (Interest level: Adult).

A selected compilation of resources on the state of Kentucky for curriculum support, this guide covers such widely diverse topics as museums, field trip sites, organizations, maps, profiles of organizations, games, competitions, audio-visual sources, and listings of print materials, including books and periodicals. It is a comprehensive, well-organized resource guide for the professional collection.
1. Kentucky—Bibliography 2. Kentucky—Directories 3. Kentucky—Study and teaching

976.9

Kentucky Is My Land. (Videorecording). Kentucky Educational Television. VHS, 1 videocassette (12-20 min. segments), sd. Color. $50.00. (Interest level: 6).

This colorful video series relates the heritage of Kentucky, including its history, geography, government, politics, and statesmen; and it describes the six natural regions of the state and documents their exploration with visits to historical sites and dramatizations.

This is an excellent choice for teacher resource collections needing additional audio-visual materials.
1. Kentucky—Study and teaching

976.9

Kentucky's Story: Early History of Kentucky. (Videorecording). Kentucky Educational Television. VHS, 1 videocassette (9-15 min. segments), sd. Color. Includes teacher's guide. $50.00. (Interest level: 4-5).

Each brief segment documents the progressive incursion of white settlers into Native American lands of Kentucky, lending itself to use in chronological order over a period of time or as a complete instructional unit. Told from the viewpoint of a 10-year-old child, this series is not intended to convey facts or detailed information but, rather, an impression of the problems and feelings experienced by both groups.
1. Kentucky—History 2. Pioneers and pioneer life—Kentucky

976.9

Know Kentucky. (Videorecording NIMCO, Inc., 1988. VHS, 1 videocassette (4-10 min. segments), sd. Color. Includes teacher's guide. $149.00. (Interest level: 4-8).

This is a four-part video designed to give the viewer a look at Kentucky as a whole, then as three separate and unique regions: Eastern, Central, and Western Kentucky. Formerly four filmstrips, the video edition is of adequate quality and includes still photographs with voice-over narration and music.
1. Kentucky—Study and teaching

976.9

Know Kentucky Government. (Videorecording). NIMCO, Inc., 1988. VHS, 1 videocassette (4-10 min. segments), sd. Color. $149.00. (Interest level: 4-8).

This video provides students with an overview of state government—its organization and essential functions. The four-part series has been translated from filmstrip to video with visuals occasionally appearing faded or overly bright.
1. Kentucky—Politics and government

Louisiana

by Gayle E. Salvatore

Nonfiction

317.63 (Reference)
Calhoun, Milburn. *Louisiana Almanac 1992-1993*.
Pelican (0-88289-797-7), 1992. 622p. Charts, graphs,
tables, etc. (Interest level: 4+).

Anything and everthing about Louisiana is included in this statistical report, which is re-issued every
two years. It is an indispensable resource for studying
Louisiana in all areas.
♦ Pretending the editor of the *Louisiana Almanac* is
  planning to include a new section in the next printing
  entitled, "Dreams for Louisiana That Came True,"
  students can describe what they think should be
  included in this new section.
1. Almanacs, American—Louisiana.

338.2
Franks, Kenny Arthur. *Early Louisiana and Arkansas Oil*. Texas A. and M. University Press (0-89096-
134-4) 1982. 243p. B/W photos. (Interest level: 6+).

Louisiana's economy has always been affected by
the oil drilling industry. This title provides an overview
of the history of the industry with numerous photos.
♦ The class can describe the problems oil drillers may
  have experienced when exploring for oil in Louisiana.
1. Petroleum industry and trade—Louisiana—History—20th century 2. Petroleum industry and trade—
Arkansas—20th century.

353.9763
Reeves, Miriam G. *Governors of Louisiana*. 4th ed.
Pelican (0-911116-71-0), 1985. 128p. B/W photos.
(Interest level: 5+).

This indispensable reference for the school and
public library is easy to use and understand, and is
popular with students.
♦ Students may write a political platform using the
  features they think a good governor should include.
1. Louisiana—Governors.

355.709763
Parkerson, Codman. *New Orleans, America's Most
Fortified City*. Quest, 1990. 115p. B/W photos. (Inter-
est level: 4+).

Due to strategic location, New Orleans has, for the
first 200 years of its existence, been well protected with
forts, fortifications, etc. This fascinating book explores
numerous forts in Louisiana with a history and current
status of each and with many interesting photos.
♦ Students can discuss, in a brief paper, which forts in
  Louisiana played important roles in wars and why.
1. Fortification—New Orleans (Louisiana)—History
2. New Orleans (Louisiana)—History, Military.

370.9763 (Reference)
Cline, Rodney. *Education in Louisiana—History and
Development*. Claitors (0-87511-019-3), 1974. 215p.
B/W illus. (Interest level: 7+).

This title chronicles Louisiana education and its
many contributions to the people of Louisiana. Teachers and students will find this work to be an asset to the
study of Louisiana history.
♦ The class can describe what they would like to see
  as the next innovation or development in Louisiana's education system.
1. Education—Louisiana—History.

394.2
Hardy, Arthur, ed. *Arthur Hardy's Mardi Gras Guide*.
Arthur Hardy Enterprises, Inc. (ISBN 0-930892-17-8)
(ISSN 0195-3605), Annual. (Interest level: All ages).

This ultimate Mardi Gras guide, for pleasure or
research, provides all the information needed to celebrate this event, plus many detailed articles concerning
anything and everything connected with the carnival,
along with fabulous pictures. Included are histories of
each carnival krewe, a map of each parade route, a
picture of the krewe's official doubloon, what the
throws will be, celebrities who will ride on the floats,
and other information of all kinds.
♦ Students can design a costume for the King of Rex,
  or the Queen of Rex.
1. Carnival—New Orleans (La.) 2. New Orleans—
History 3. New Orleans—Social life and customs.

394.2 (Reference)
Kinser, Sam. *Carnival, American Style: Mardi Gras at New Orleans and Mobile*. University of Chicago Press (0-226-43729-9) 1990. 415p. B/W illus. (Interest level: 7+).

This definitive, historic worldwide study of carnivals with emphasis on New Orleans and Mobile, Alabama, may serve as a reference for teachers, students, and those interested in the history of carnivals and the New Orleans Mardi Gras.
♦ A new Mardi Gras Krewe is being organized. As a group project, the class can select a theme, number of floats, and name, and provide a brief design for the parade and each float; they can do the same for the ball to follow the parade.
1. Carnival—Louisiana—New Orleans 2. Carnival—Alabama—Mobile 3. New Orleans (La.)—Social life and customs 4. Mobile (Ala.)—Social life and customs.

394.25
Huber, Leonard Victor. *Mardi Gras: A Pictorial History of Carnival in New Orleans*. 2nd ed. Pelican (0-88289-160-X), 1989. 96p. B/W illus. (Interest level: 5+).

Mardi Gras has always been an important part of Louisiana, with numerous customs, traditions, and anecdotes. The photos in this title provide an excellent overview of the many facets of this popular carnival.
♦ Young people may design and sketch a costume that they would like to wear on Mardi Gras day.
1. Carnival—New Orleans—Louisiana—Pictorial works 2. New Orleans—Social life and customs—Pictorial works.

398.2
Carruth, Thomas J. *Tales of Old Louisiana*. Center for Louisiana Studies, University of Southwestern Louisiana (0-88289-822-1), 1979. 161p. B/W sketches. (Interest level: 4-12).

These are fascinating tales concerning famous men and historic events in Louisiana history. While well adapted to middle school and older students, this book could also provide a listening and learning experience for very young children.
♦ Students may select a favorite character from this title, pretend they are that person, and write a brief incident, similar to those found in these stories, that may have happened to them.
1. Louisiana—History—Anecdotes, facetiae, satire, etc. 2. Louisiana—History.

398.2
Saucier, Corinne L. *Folktales from French Louisiana*. Claitors (0-87511-100-9), 1962. 138p. (Interest Level: 3-10).

These folktales were recorded from oral storytelling and thus provide a rich source of Louisiana French heritage. This title is valuable as a learning, listening, and reading resource.
♦ Students may ask an older relative or friend to tell them an old folktale from their childhood to record and present to the class.
1. Folklore—Louisiana.

398.2
Saxon, Lyle. *Gumbo Ya-Ya*. Pelican (0-88289-645-8), 1987. 600p. B/W illus. (Interest level: 6+).

This title contains another wide variety of customs, traditions, and legends found in Louisiana, some real, and some not. It's easy reading for those wanting to know more than just the necessary history of Louisiana.
♦ Saint Joseph altars are discussed in this title. Students can read about the altars and then describe what they are and the customs they portray.
1. Plantation life 2. Louisiana—Social life and customs 3. Louisiana—Description and travel.

447
Rice, James. *Cajun Alphabet*. Pelican (0-88289-822-1), 1991. Unpaginated. Color illus. (Interest level: All ages).

With unusual rhymes and delightful art, James Rice takes Gaston, the green-nosed alligator, through the alphabet. This title is a fun way to learn the French language, culture, and customs found in Louisiana.
♦ After reading this alphabet, students may select several letters of the alphabet and create rhymes about them, perhaps using some French words.
1. Cajun French dialect 2. Cajuns 3. Alphabet rhymes.

551.5
Branley, Franklyn Mansfield. *Hurricane Watch*. Crowell (0-690-04470-4), 1985. (Let's Read and Find Out Book). 32p. Color illus. (Interest level: 2-4).

Illustrations and text depict the development of a storm into a hurricane in a clear and easily understood format. Since Louisiana is prone to hurricanes, the safety precautions are an excellent feature.
♦ After reading *Hurricane Watch*, the children can draw the four stages of a storm becoming a hurricane as depicted in the text.
1. Hurricanes—Juvenile literature.

574.52632
Dennis, John V. *The Great Cypress Swamps*. Louisiana State University Press (0-8071-1501-0), 1988. 142p. B/W photos. (Interest level: 4+).

Among the great cypress swamps in Louisiana are several described in detail in this work. The author includes much factual information about the swamp and its inhabitants, with many interesting photos.
♦ The class could debate this issue: Should the swamps be preserved? Each child could write brief arguments for and against this question.
1. Cypress swamp ecology—United States.

574.52632
Thomas, Bill. *The Swamp*. Norton (0-393-08747-6), 1976. 222p. Color photos. (Interest level: 4+).

This title will be used for reference and recreational reading. The text is easy to read and interesting, with excellent photos of Louisiana swamps.
♦ Students should read the last chapter concerning the building of a swamp and write a brief description of what they would do to build a swamp.
1. Swamps—United States.

581.9763
Stone, Margaret. *Flora of Louisiana*. Louisiana State University Press (0-807-1664-5), 1991. 220p. Watercolor drawings; B/W illus. (Interest level: 4+).

This volume contains exquisite botanical drawings of Louisiana flora with detailed text descriptions and an extensive directory of habitat, growing conditions, etc. While the text is suitable for middle grade to adult readers, the pictures may be enjoyed and recognized by younger children.
♦ By pretending Louisiana is sponsoring a contest to change the state flower, the students can write an entry with their selection, why they chose it, and include a simple sketch.
1. Botany—Louisiana 2. Drawings—Louisiana.

585.2
Brown, Clair A. *Baldcypress, the Tree Unique, the Wood Eternal*. Claitors (0-87511-780-5), 1986. 139p. B/W illus. (Interest level: 5+).

Bald cypress is plentiful in Louisiana and is widely used for construction, furniture, and in decorative items. This definitive text covers a wide spectrum of information about the bald cypress and its ecology.
♦ The bald cypress has many different shapes defined by the growing conditions. Children may sketch the different shapes the bald cypress may develop.
1. Cypress—Louisiana.

595.3
Coldrey, Jennifer. *The World of Crabs*. Gareth Stevens (1-55532-088-0), 1986. 32p. Color photos. (Interest level: 2-3).

Sea life is an important and crucial segment of Louisiana life and culture, as a source of sport, entertainment, and food. Excellent and clear color photos add much to the easily understood text that will be enjoyed by the young child.
♦ Students can pretend they are going on a fishing trip to catch crabs. They should ask a fisher friend how to catch crabs then discuss the different ways to do this with the class.
1. Crabs.

597.0929
Douglas, Neil H. *Freshwater Fishes of Louisiana*. Claitors (0-87511-028-2), 1974. 443p. B/W and Color photos. (Interest level: 5+).

Illustrated and described in this title are the histories of every known freshwater fish in Louisiana. This classic work in the field is frequently used by fishers and students.
♦ Students may illustrate and briefly describe which one of the fishes in the book they would choose for their pretend aquariums.
1. Fishes, Freshwater—Louisiana.

597.6
Hirschi, Ron. *Who Lives in...Alligator Swamp?* Dodd, Mead (0-396-09123-7), 1987. (A Where Animals Live Book). Unpaginated. Color photos. (Interest level: Preschool-2).

Louisiana swamps, where alligators live, may also be inhabited by many other animals, birds, and insects. The excellent color photos provide a vivid introduction to swamp life for the young child.
♦ Young children may pretend they are one of the alligators in the Louisiana swamp and demonstrate how an alligator looks, walks, and swims.
1. Swamp animals.

597.98
Bare, Colleen Stanley. *Never Kiss an Alligator*. Dutton (0-525-65003-2), 1989. Unpaginated. Color photos. (Interest level: Preschool-3).

Color photos add much to the appeal of this simple description of alligators for the young child. This book will provide material for group discussions about the alligators and other animals that live in the same environment.
♦ Baby alligators need protection to grow. children may discuss ways to help the young 'gators survive.
1. Alligators—Juvenile literature.

598.2
Lowery, Geroge Hines. *Louisiana Birds*. 3rd ed. Louisiana State University (0-8071-0087-0), 1974. 651p. Color and B/W illus. (Interest level: 6+).

Louisiana is listed in the top five states as an excellent place to observe birds. This definitive work, with maps, graphs, tables, etc. is scientific but easily usuable and understandable.
♦ Students may write a brief paper on the purpose of a bird sanctuary in Louisiana, including the reasons birds are important to the state and its residents.
1. Birds—Louisiana.

634.9
Kerr, Ed. *Tales of the Louisiana Forests*. Claitors (0-87511-519-5) 185p., 1980. (Interest level: 4-10).

Tales of the Louisiana Forests is the story of the great forests of Louisiana, their fall, and eventual return. Louisiana is a leading pulp and softwood plywood producer, thus this industry is important to the state economy.
♦ The class can discuss several ways to insure that Louisiana will have forests in the future.
1. Forests and forestry—Louisiana.

635.909763
Brown, Clair A. *Wildflowers of Louisiana*. Louisiana State University Press (0-8071-0232-8), 1972. 247p. Color photos. (Interest level: 4+).

This extensive work describes Louisiana wildflowers as those plants native to the state that can grow without cultivation. The scientific but easily understood descriptions will be of importance to several areas of study for students, gardeners, teachers, and laypersons.
♦ Students should obtain permission from their school, parents, or some civic organization to plant wildflowers as a class project.
1. Wild flowers—Louisiana.

639.209763
Gowanlock, James Nelson. *Fishes and Fishing in Louisiana, Including Recipes for the Preparation of Seafoods, with Addenda, Corrections, etc., by Claude*

"Grits" Gresham. Claitors (0-875-11680-9), 1965. 701p. B/W illus. (Interest level: 4+).

Long a favorite with fishers of all ages, this is the classic work for fishing enthusiasts in Louisiana. Besides the sport aspects, the identification of the native fishes is an important consideration for the study of Louisiana.

♦ Students should speak to a fisher and discuss if fishing in their local area has changed since his or her childhood. Students can prepare an oral report on this topic for the class.

1. Fishing—Louisiana 2. Cookery (Seafood) 3. Fishes—Louisiana 4. Seafood 5. Gresham, Claude "Grits."

676
Mitgutsch, Ali. *From Wood to Paper.* Carolrhoda (0-876142-96-X), 1982. (A Start to Finish Book). 24p. Color illus. (Interest level: 2-3).

This title describes the process of making paper from wood, one of Louisiana's industries. The simple text introduces new words, and the illustrations will be understood and enjoyed by the young child.

♦ Young children may be guided by a leader in a discussion about the importance of wood and paper in daily living.

1.Paper—Juvenile literature 2. Wood—Juvenile literature 3. Papermaking.

704.94
Huber, Leonard Victor. *Clasped Hands, Symbolism in New Orleans Cemeteries.* Center for Louisiana Studies, University of Southwestern Louisiana (0-940984-04-0), 1982. 154p. B/W illus. (Interest level: 4+).

Louisiana cemeteries, unique in their above ground burials, reflect an important part of Louisiana history through the numerous symbols that adorn many tombs. The excellent pictures and text offer an insight to the importance placed on these symbols, burial customs, and traditions.

♦ Students may interview members of their family about their ancestors, begin a family tree, and continue to research their ancestry.

1. Architecture—Louisiana—New Orleans 2. Cemeteries—Louisiana.

720.9763
Huber, Leonard Victor. *The Cemeteries.* Pelican (0-88-289-020-4), 1974. 198p. B/W and Color photos. (Interest level: 5+).

Cemeteries are an important part of Louisiana culture and history; this book describes their unique tombs in detail. Numerous black-and-white and color photos create an extensive pictorial history.

♦ Students may select a period of history and sketch a typical tomb of that time perhaps using a family tomb as a guide.

1. Architecture—Louisiana—New Orleans 2. Cemeteries—Louisiana.

781.65
Smith, Michael Proctor. *New Orleans Jazz Fest, a Pictorial History.* (0-88289-810-8), 1991. 207p. B/W illus. (Interest level: 5+).

Louisiana's unique heritage in music, culture, and crafts is presented in many unusual photographs. Louisianians and others will enjoy this visual history of one of Louisiana's most widely attended festivals.

♦ A contest has been announced to find a Jazz Fest poster for the next festival. Students can create a poster showing their interpretation of this festival.

1. New Orleans Jazz and Heritage Festival—Pictorial works 2. Jazz festivals—Louisiana—New Orleans—Pictorial works.

784.4
Gilmore, Jeanne. *Chantez Encore, Folksongs of French South Louisiana.* Pelican (0-88289-425-0), 1977. 63p. Piano music; B/W sketches. (Interest level: All ages).

The French culture, heritage, and music is deeply intertwined in Louisiana history. Teachers, scout leaders, etc., will find the simple piano, guitar, and voice music in this book easy to follow and delightful to share with students. All ages will enjoy singing these charming French songs.

♦ Students may select a French song from this collection that they particularly enjoy, learn the song, and invite their class and friends to join in a sing-a-long.

1. Folk songs, French—Louisiana 2. Folk music—Louisiana.

785.42
Case, Brian. *The Harmony Illustrated Encyclopedia of Jazz.* 3rd ed. Harmony Books (0-517-56442-4), 1986. 208p. Color and B/W photos. (Interest level: 4+).

This encyclopedia is profusely illustrated with photos and definitive entries. Extensive entries include New Orleans musicians.

♦ Children may design an album cover for a New Orleans Jazz recording.

1. Jazz music—Bio-bibliography.

796.332
Mack, Wayne. *The Saga of the Saints: An Illustrated History of the First Twenty-five Seasons.* Arthur Hardy Enterprises (0-930892-18-6), 1992. 176p. B/W and Color photos. (Interest level: All ages).

This book will provide many hours of enjoyable reading and promote countless discussions among Saints fans of all ages. Reading this title will be instructive and also very enjoyable.

♦ Students could write a brief paper explaining why they think the Saints football team is good for Louisiana or why the local football team is good for their state.

1. New Orleans Saints (Football team)—History.

811
Trosclair. *The Cajun Night Before Christmas.* Pelican (0-88289-002-6), 1973. Unpaginated. B/W and Color illus. (Interest level: All ages).

Christmas celebrated in the Louisiana bayous is like no other. This familiar Christmas poem is retold with Cajun words, phrases, traditions, and customs; the wonderful illustrations make it a truly Cajun celebration to be enjoyed by all.

♦ Students can create a Christmas card using a Louisiana bayou scene and including a Cajun-type greeting inside the card.

1. Christmas poetry.

912.763 (Reference)
Newton, Milton Birchard. *Atlas of Louisiana.* School of Geoscience, Louisiana State University (0-938-909-258), 1972. Miscellaneous Publication #72-1. 196p. B/W illus; Maps, graphs, tables. (Interest level: 4+).

Even though this atlas was published in 1972, it contains useful information for teachers and students. Since no comparable work has been recently published, this atlas is a usable reference.

♦ The class can discuss the advantages and disadvantages of the Mississippi River to Louisiana.

1. Geography 2. Louisiana—Maps.

917.306 (Reference)
Blassingame, John W. *The Slave Community, Plantation Life in the Antebellum South.* 2nd ed. Oxford (0-19-502563-6), 1979. 262p. (Interest level: 7+).

This study of the life of the African-American slave in the antebellum South provides an important aspect of Louisiana heritage and culture.

♦ After reading this title, students can describe a typical day in the life of a slave during antebellum times.

1. Slavery—Southern states 2. Plantation Life—Southern states.

917.63 (Reference)
Blassingame, John W. *Black New Orleans, 1860-1880.* University of Chicago Press (0-226-05708-9), 1976. 302p. (Interest level: 7+).

During Reconstruction, the life of the African American was different in New Orleans than in the rest of the United States. This title explores the economic and social life of the time.

♦ After reading about the plight of the African American during these years, students may describe what qualifications a African Americans needed when searching for a job following the abolition of slavery, and discuss what opportunities were then available.

1. African-Americans—Louisiana—New Orleans 2. New Orleans (Louisiana)—History.

917.63
Desmond, John. *Louisiana's Antebellum Architecture.* Claitors (0-87511-023-1), 1970. 97p. B/W illus. (Interest level: 4+).

Louisiana's plantations are unique as depictions of a former way of life that has had a decided influence on the state and its history. Brief paragraphs describe the types and kinds of Louisiana's antebellum architecture along with descriptions and sketches of famous homes and plantations.

♦ Students can describe what they think their days would have been if they had lived during the antebellum period of Louisiana history in one of the famous plantations included in this book.

1. Architecture—Louisiana 2. Architecture, Colonial—Louisiana 3. Architecture, Modern—19th century—Louisiana 4. Historic buildings—Louisiana.

917.63
Gulledge, Jo. *Red Pepper Paradise.* Audubon Park Press (0-9616452-0-2), 1986. 118p. Color illus. (Interest level: 5+).

Two centuries ago, the McIlhenny family began a red pepper industry and maintained a wildlife preserve on Avery Island in Louisiana. The vivid pictures and text will make learning about this Louisiana industry very enjoyable.

♦ The class should conduct an informal survey among family and friends to determine who loves hot sauce and what brand. After compiling the results of this survey, the class can write a letter to the winning manufacturer describing the survey and results and requesting information on the industry and samples!

1. Peppers.

917.63
Hanks, Amanda Sagrera. *Louisiana Paradise: The Chenieres and Wetlands of Southwestern Louisiana.* Center for Louisiana Studies, University of Southwestern Louisiana (0-940984-38-5), 1988. 129p. Color and B/W illus. (Interest level: 5+).

Louisiana's Gulf Coast chenieres have a unique history and culture. The photographs and text introduce these unusual people, customs, and traditions as a unique way of life still existing in southern Louisiana today.

♦ Students may sketch the Louisiana coastline and identify the chenieres.

1. Wetlands—Louisiana 2. Wildlife conservation—Louisiana 3. Louisiana—Description and travel.

917.63
Lockwood, C.C. *Atchafalaya, America's Largest River Basin Swamp.* Claitors (0-87511-695-7), 1982. 105p. Color photos. (Interest level: 4+).

All ages will find this title to be a spellbinding look at Louisiana. The text is excellent and the photos are superb.

♦ After reading *Atchafalaya*, students may draw a map of Louisiana and the Atchafalaya Basin, including cities and other important geographical features.

1. Natural history—Louisiana—Atchafalaya Swamp—Pictorial works 2. Atchafalaya Swamp (La.)—Description and travel.

917.63
Lockwood, C.C. *Discovering Louisiana.* Louisiana State University (0-8071-1335-2), 1986. 150p. Color photos. (Interest level: 4+).

This book is devoted to the natural history and geography of Louisiana. The photos are breathtaking, and the text is entertaining and informative.

♦ After reading about the natural history of Louisiana, the students can write a brief paper explaining reasons why it should be preserved for future generations and how they, as citizens, may accomplish it.

1. Louisiana—Description and travel 2. Natural history—Louisiana.

917.63 (Reference)
Stoddard, Amos. *Sketches, Historical and Descriptive of Louisiana.* Originally published M. Carey, 1812.

Claitors (0-87511-117-3), 1974. 488p. B/W illus. (Interest level: 7+).

This narrative history of Louisiana is best suited to teachers and advanced students. The text is very definitive and informative.

♦ Students should pretend they are grandparents writing to a grandchild about their youth in early Louisiana, including events that they might have witnessed.

1. Louisiana Purchase.

917.6302

Kniffen, Fred B. *Louisiana, Its Land and People*. Louisiana State University (0-807113-697), 1988. 213p. B/W illus. (Interest level: 4+).

While Louisiana geography is the main focus of this title, much additional and useful information is included. Maps, photos, and drawings will be helpful to students, teachers, scout leaders, etc.

♦ Students can use a poster board to draw a map of Louisiana showing important geographical features with color coding and legends.

1. Louisiana—Description and travel.

921

Pitre, Verne. *Grandma Was a Sailmaker, Tales of the Cajun Wetlands*. Blue Heron Press (0-9621724-5-6), 1991, 135p. B/W illus. (Interest level: 3-7).

The author describes in rich detail his Cajun life in the midst of a large, loving, and interesting family. Young children would enjoy listening to these tales while older children and adults would consider it enjoyable reading.

♦ With the class as audience, children can retell a tale their parents, grandparents, or other relatives may have told them.

1. Pitre, Verne. 2. Pitre family.

921

Tanenhaus, Sam. *Louis Armstrong*. Chelsea House Publishers (1-55546-571-4), 1989. 127p. B/W photos. (Interest level: 4-8).

Louis Armstrong was and is a part of Louisiana history and Louisiana music. This lavishly illustrated biography chronicles Armstrong's climb to fame.

♦ Armstrong displayed remarkable courage in achieving his goals. Students can describe acts of courage they have observed in family and friends.

1. Armstrong, Louis, 1900-1971. 2. Musicians. 3. Jazz Music. 4. Afro-American—Biography.

921

Wolfe, Charles. *Mahalia Jackson*. Chelsea House Publishers (1-55546-661-3), 1990. 103p. B/W photos. (Interest level: 4-8).

New Orleanian Mahalia Jackson's biography is filled with photographs taken during her life that add much to the enjoyment of the work. Jackson's achievements in bringing gospel music to her fans are admirable and her life is certainly a role model for youngsters.

♦ After reading this biography, what advice would students give to someone trying to achieve stardom?

1. Jackson, Mahalia, 1911-1972. 2. Gospel musicians—United States—Biography. 3. Singers. 4. African-Americans—Biography.

970.763

Dorman, Caroline. *Southern Indian Boy*. Claitors (0-87511-027-4), 1967. 52p. B/W and Color illus. (Interest level:4-7).

This chronicle of Louisiana Native Americans provides fascinating reading for all ages. These stories of the Chitimacha and Caddo tribes are well suited for independent, recreational, and informational reading.

♦ The children may draw pictures of Red Boot, Deer Runner, and Hi Chah.

1. Chitimacha Indians—Legends 2. Caddo Indians—Legends.

976.3 (Reference)

Ancelet, Barry Jean. *Cajun Country*. University Press of Mississippi, (0-87805-466-9), 1991. (Folklife in the South). 256p. (Interest level: 8+).

Cajun Country provides a broad overview of Cajun history, social life, customs, and culture. This story offers an up-to-date panorama of the Cajuns for the teacher and advanced student.

♦ Students may sketch maps to trace the path the Cajuns took from Nova Scotia to Louisiana, indicating where they have settled in Louisiana.

1. Cajuns—Social life and customs 2. Louisiana—Social life and customs.

976.3 (Reference)

Fortier, Alyce. *History of Louisiana*. Originally published 1904. 5vols. 2nd ed. by Jo Ann Carrigan. Claitors (0-875-11139-4), 1966. (Interest level: 8+).

Fortier wrote in the vernacular of his day, describing in detail the domination of Louisiana by different nations. This history is suitable for teachers and older, advanced students interested in specific aspects of Louisiana history.

♦ Students should describe what they think the first explorers saw when they came to Louisiana.

1. Louisiana—History 2. Carrigan, Jo Ann.

976.3

Gleason, David King. *Over New Orleans*. David King Gleason (0-9612038-0-3), 1983. 134p. Color photos. (Interest level: All ages).

The views from the air in this book explain much of Louisiana's history, such as the important role the Mississippi River has as the historic highway of the state. The text and the accompanying color photos are a delight for readers of all ages.

♦ Children can describe which photo they found to be the most unusual and why.

1. Historic buildings—New Orleans (La)—Pictorial works 2. New Orleans (La)—Pictorial works 3. Louisiana—Description and travel.

976.3

Kent, Deborah. *America the Beautiful, Louisiana*. Childrens (0-516-00464-6), 1988. 144p. Color photos. (Interest level:4-8).

Widely diversified information on Louisiana is found in this work, beginning with the earliest history to contemporary times. The color photographs, lists, tables, maps, glossary, etc. will be helpful to teachers and students.

♦ Students may submit a sketch for a new state flag and explain the meaning of the design and symbols.
1. Louisiana—Juvenile literature.

976.3
Kniffen, Fred B. *Historic Indian Tribes of Louisiana, from 1542 to the Present*. Louisiana State University Press (0-8071-1295-X), 1987. 324p. B/W photos; Maps. (Interest level: 4+).

Beginning with 1542 and coming to contemporary times, the author traces the history of Louisiana Native Americans. This work describes catastrophic events affecting the tribes, plus economic and political aspects of their history, in addition to informative maps, graphs, and tables.
♦ After studying about the Louisian Indians, the class may research and describe what the status of the different tribes is today.
1. Indians of North America—Louisiana.

976.3
Louisiana Pen Women. *Vignettes of Louisiana History*. Claitors (0-87511-0681), 1976. 174p. B/W illus. (Interest level 5+).

Many obscure but important sites are included in this collection of Louisiana anecdotes. The descriptions and text offer an added dimension to Louisiana's past.
♦ Students may ask older members of their community to share some experiences from their youth, record this oral history, and share it with classmates and friends.
1. Louisiana—History 2. Historic buildings—Louisiana.

976.3
Malone, Paul. *Louisiana Plantation Homes, a Return to Splendor*. Pelican (0-88289-403-X), 1986. 160p. Color photos. (Interest level:4+).

The lovely photos of Louisiana plantation homes and the informative history will delight readers of all ages. Additional information on the history of plantations is portrayed.
♦ Louisiana students might take a field trip to a plantation home in their area, carefully evaluating the trip afterwards. Students in other states might research the layout and workings of antebellum southern plantations.
1. Historic buildings—Louisiana—Pictorial works 2. Louisiana—Description and travel.

976.3
Perez, August. *The Last Line, a Streetcar Named Saint Charles*. Pelican (0-88289-007-7), 1973. 96p. B/W illus. (Interest level:4+).

New Orleans streetcars are another symbol of the past; the only one still in existence is the Saint Charles line. The pictures are unusual and the commentary on the history of transportation in New Orleans is very informative.
♦ Did the streetcars create pollution? The class can divide in half and present a debate on the topic, "Are streetcars or automobiles more effective in reducing pollution?"

1. Electric railroads—Pictorial works—Louisiana—New Orleans 2. Street railroads—Pictorial works—Louisiana—New Orleans 3. New Orleans (La.)—History.

976.3
Rushton, William Faulkner. *The Cajuns*. Farrar, Straus, Firoux (0-374-11817-5), 1979. 342p. Color illus. (Interest level: 5+).

No study of Louisiana would be complete without this work by Rushton. The book includes Acadian history; Cajun crafts, cooking, and sketches reflecting the Cajuns' perserverance against enormous odds; and their availability to "laisses les bons temps rouler" (let the good times roll).
♦ Students may interview family, friends, and neighbors to inquire if their ancestors might have come from another country. These experiences should be recorded and shared with the class, comparing these experiences with that of the Acadians.
1. Cajuns—History 2. Cajuns—Social life and customs 3. Acadians—History.

976.3
Saxon, Lyle. *Fabulous New Orleans*. Pelican. (0-88289-706-3), 1988. 338p. B/W illus. (Interest level: 6+).

This title includes a variety of events unique to New Orleans, such as the Mardi Gras, Mississippi River floods, the great plagues, duels, voodoo, and many more topics. The text chronicles New Orleans' development under the French, the Spanish, and the Americans.
♦ New Orleans courtyards are world famous. Students should describe the activities that might have taken place in these courtyards at the time of their inception.
1. Louisiana—Social life and customs 2. Louisiana—Description and travel.

976.3
Saxon, Lyle. *Old Louisiana*. Pelican (0-88289-705-5), 1988. 388p. B/W illus. (Interest level: 6+).

Saxon writes a chronicle of the two centuries of Louisiana plantation life that is such a large part of Louisiana history. Much of the text is previously unpublished and is taken from diaries and letters written by the people of Louisiana during the plantation period.
♦ Students might write an account of a day in the life of a plantation owner.
1. Louisiana—Social life and customs 2. Louisiana—Description and travel 3. Plantation life—Louisiana.

976.3
Smith, Andy. *Louisiana Proud*. Louisiana Proud Press (0-9618-5640-8), 1987. 175p. B/W illus. (Interest level: 4+).

Maps, sketches, and histories make this book a rich overview of Louisiana cities. This work will be valuable for students, teachers, and others interested in the history of Louisiana towns and cities.
♦ After selecting their favorite building or site in their city, students may draw a simple sketch, write a brief history, or describe why they selected it.

1. Historic buildings—Louisiana—Pictorial works 2. Cities and towns—Louisiana—History 3. Louisiana in art 4. Louisiana—History, Local.

976.3 (Reference)
Stacey, Truman. *Louisiana's French Heritage.* Acadian House (0-925-417-02-5), 1990. 190p. B/W illus. (Interest level: 5-10).

This thorough history of the French in Louisiana includes the passenger lists from seven ships that brought some Acadians to Louisiana. This book will be an important resource for students, teachers, etc.
♦ Students can select a name from the passenger lists and pretend to be that person, describing what the voyage was like and how they felt when stepping ashore in Louisiana.
1. Cajuns—History 2. Acadians—History 3. French—History.

976.3
Stall, Gaspar J. *Buddy Stall's Louisiana Potpourri.* Pelican (0-88289-913-9), 1991. 268p. Maps; B/W illus. (Interest level: 4+).

Louisiana Potpourri is a collection of interesting stories about Louisiana that cover plantations, the Civil War, weather, deltas, etc. This title will be valuable as a source of reports and talks for students, teachers, scout leaders, etc.
♦ The students can pretend they have been selected to pick a site and name for a new city to be built in Louisiana. They should explain why they made these selections.
1. Louisiana—History—Anecdotes 2. Louisiana—Folklore 3. Louisiana—Climate 4. Louisiana—History—Civil War, 1861-1865 5. Plantations—Louisiana.

976.3
Taylor, Joe Gray. *Louisiana, a Bicentennial History.* Norton (0-393-05602-3), 1976. 194p. B/W illus. (Interest level: 5+).

Taylor has written a definitive history of Louisiana for the national Bicentennial of the American Revolution. His special style will be enjoyed by students and teachers.
♦ How many flags have flown over Louisiana? Students can list the nations and their years of occupation with a sketch of each flag.
1. Louisiana—History.

976.335
Nichols, Joan Kane. *New Orleans.* Dillon (0-87518-403-0), 1989. (A Downtown America Book). 58p. Color illus. (Interest level: 4-8).

Written for children, this overview of New Orleans is easy to understand, has good photos, and presents much information about the city that children would find interesting. The maps, glossary, and details on places to visit would be especially interesting to the young child.
♦ Children can answer the question: If you could spend one day in New Orleans, what would you want to see and why?
1. New Orleans (La.).

976.335
Reeves, Sally K. Evans. *Historic City Park, New Orleans.* Friends of City Park (0-9610062-0-X), 1982. 234p. (Interest level: 5+).

This title provides a tremendous pictorial history of City Park with numerous black-and-white photos accompanied by extensive commentary. It describes the park's many features available for recreation, education, sports, etc.
♦ The class may form committees to plan a field trip to a nearby park. The committees will request permission from the school administration and the park administration, will plan the transportation, organize the food, develop a day's itinerary, and devise an evaluation form.
1. New Orleans—Parks.

976.335
Stall, Gaspar J. *Proud, Peculiar New Orleans; the Inside Story.* Claitors (0-87511-679-5), 1984. 184p. B/W illus. (Interest level: 4+).

Buddy Stall explains those features that may make New Orleans peculiar to non-residents but which instill pride in the heart of the natives. The easy-to-read, enjoyable text is a treasure chest of information about New Orleans that will be read and discussed for a long time to come.
♦ Students may create a new symbol (other than the fleur-de-lis) for New Orleans. They should sketch their idea and explain its meaning and why they selected it.
1. New Orleans (Louisiana)—History 2. New Orleans (Louisiana)—Social life and customs.

977
McCall, Edith S. *Biography of a River: The Mississippi.* Walker (0-8027-6915-2), 1990. 162p. B/W illus. (Interest level: 6+).

Louisiana's history, past and present, is interwoven with the Mississippi River, which controls the lives of many residents. This is a chronicle of human attempts to manipulate the river and the results.
♦ The class can discuss what might happen if the Mississippi River was not manipulated.
1. Mississippi River—History—Juvenile literature 2. Mississippi River Valley—History—Juvenile literature.

Biography

See also biographical entries in Louisiana Nonfiction section, especially under 353.9763 and 921.

920
Leavitt, Mel. *Great Characters of New Orleans.* Lixikos (0-938530-31-3), 1984. 89p. B/W illus. (Interest level: 4+).

Mel Leavitt includes brief biographies of historical and contemporary persons. This is a good reference not only for students and teachers but for anyone who wants to enjoy reading about New Orleans and learning about it at the same time.
♦ Students might write a brief biography of someone they think might be included in the book and explain

why they might be included (need not be a famous personality, but someone they know and admire).
1. New Orleans (La.)—Biography 2. New Orleans (La.)—History.

920
Louisiana Pen Women. *Louisiana Leaders*. Claitors (0-87511-067-3), 1970. 168p. B/W illus. (Interest level: 4+).

Brief biographies chronicle the lives of famous and obscure Louisiana leaders. A favorite reference for students and teachers.

♦ Students may pretend they lived during their favorite period of Louisiana history and create a brief biography of themselves as a famous or infamous Louisianian.
1. Louisiana—Biography 2. Louisiana—History.

920.075
Rand, Clayton. *Sons of the South*. Pelican (0-911116-76-1), 1961. 212p. B/W illus. (Interest level: 4+).

Numerous biographies of famous people important to Louisiana history are included in this work. It is a popular and useful reference.

♦ Students can describe what they hope to accomplish in their lifetimes and write adult biographies of themselves based on their hopes.
1. Southern states—Biography 2. Southern states—Biography—Portraits.

92 Lafitte, Jean
Gonzalez, Catherine Troxell. *Lafitte, the Terror of the Gulf*. Eakin (0-89015-284-5), 1981. 69p. B/W illus. (Interest level: 4-8).

Jean Lafitte and his men changed the course of Louisiana history and that of the United States. This biography is easy to read and will be enjoyed by students.

♦ The class can debate the question: Was Jean Lafitte a patriot or a pirate?
1. Lafitte, Jean.

92 Long, Huey
Williams, T. Harry. *Huey Long*. Knopf (0-394-74790-9), 1969. 884p. B/W illus. (Interest level: 5+).

The history of Louisiana was affected by the reign and assassination of Huey Pierce Long, one of Louisiana's most colorful and influential politicians. One of this state's most eminent historians and authors has written the classical, definitive biography of Huey Long, which will serve as a reference for everyone studying Louisiana.

♦ After reading about Huey Long's life and administration, the students can write a description of the advantages and disadvantages that the state derived from his tenure as governor.
1. Long, Huey Pierce, 1893-1935.

Fiction

Amoss, Berthe. *The Loup Garou*. Pelican (0-88289-189-8), 1979. Unpaginated. B/W illus. (Interest level: 4-6).

The young child will delight in this story of the Cajun expulsion. Beginning in Nova Scotia, the tale uses language that is easy to read and understand to depict the plight of the French Acadians and how they came to Louisiana.

♦ The children can draw a picture of the Loup Garou.
1. Nova Scotia—History—1713-1763 2. Cajuns—Fiction.

Bannister, Helen Mott. *A Coat of Blue and a Coat of Grey*. Chelsea House Publishers (1-55546-571-4), n.d. 66p. B/W illus. (Interest level: 4-7).

Set in the Louisiana countryside, this novel chronicles the adventures of two young boys and a young girl during the Civil War. Readers will derive insights into the agonies and lives of everyone, no matter what side they fought on.

♦ Students can pretend they are a Confederate soldier and their best friend is a Union solder and describe their feelings.
United States—History—Civil War, 1861-1865—Fiction.

Couvillon, Alice. *Mimi's First Mardi Gras*. Pelican (0-88289-840-X), 1992. Unpaginated. Color illus. (Interest level: Preschool-3).

The young child will enjoy the simple explanations of Mardi Gras and its customs and traditions found in this text. The illustrations are not only vivid but informative.

♦ The class can discuss some of the famous traditions of Mardi Gras, such as, the King Cake, etc.
1. Carnival—Fiction 2. New Orleans (Louisiana)—Fiction 3. Mardi Gras—Fiction.

Covington, Dennis. *Lizard*. Delacorte (0-385-30307-6), 1991. 198p. (Interest level: 4-8).

A disabled young boy's search for his identity and heritage while living in a school for retarded boys is the theme of this award-winning work of fiction. The Louisiana setting provies a background many readers will enjoy.

♦ Students can describe what they think Lizard might look like and how he might feel about being disabled.
1. Physically handicapped—Fiction. 2. Theatre—Fiction. 3. Louisiana—Fiction

Dartez, Cecilia Casrill. *Jenny Giraffe Discovers the French Quarter*. Pelican (0-88289-819-1), 1991. Unpaginated. Color illus. (Interest level: Preschool-3).

This fanciful tale of a giraffe, turned artist, explores the great diversity of the cultural and ethnic community known as the French Quarter in New Orleans. The text provides easy-to-understand concepts, and the art work is visually educational.

♦ The children can pretend they are a French Quarter artist and draw Jenny's portrait.
1. French Quarter (New Orleans, Louisiana)—Fiction 2. New Orleans (Louisiana)—Fiction 3. Artists—Fiction 4. Giraffes—Fiction.

Durio, Alice. *Cajun Columbus*. Pelican (0-88289-074-3), 1975. Unpaginated. Color illus. (Interest level: All ages).

This Louisiana folktale, with a decided Cajun influence, provides a good story-telling session.
♦ Children might practice reading this Louisiana folktale with a Cajun accent to community groups, such as scout groups, retirement homes, etc.
1. Columbus, Christopher—Fiction.

Fontenot, Mary Alice. *Clovis Crawfish and Bertile's Bon Voyage.* Pelican (0-88289-825-6), 1991. Unpaginated. B/W and color illus. (Interest level: Preschool-3).

Clovis Crawfish devises a plan to save Bertile Butterfly's injured wing so she can fly. The text develops the theme of working together and provides information on Louisiana wildlife.
♦ The class can try to explain why the butterflies fly South.
1. Crayfish—Fiction 2. Butterflies—Fiction 3. Animals—Fiction 4. Bayous—Fiction 5. Louisiana—Fiction.

Fontenot, Mary Alice. *Clovis Crawfish and His Friends.* Pelican (0-88289-479-X), 1985. Unpaginated. B/W and Color illus. (Interest level: Preschool-3).

This first book in the Clovis Crawfish series uses beautiful illustrations to introduce many creatures that live in Louisiana bayous. The story line provides many opportunities for instruction on bayou life.
♦ Children can use clay, PlayDough, or a similar material to fashion a mud house similar to the one Clovis Crawfish made in this story.
1. Crayfish—Fiction 2. Bayous—Fiction 3. Louisiana—Fiction.

Fontenot, Mary Alice. *Clovis Crawfish and Michelle Mantis.* Pelican (0-88289-730-6), 1989. Unpaginated. B/W and Color illus. (Interest level: Preschool-3).

Clovis Crawfish teaches Michelle Mantis not to eat her friends because there comes a time when everyone needs friends. An excellent example of the responsibilities of friendship taught in a Louisiana bayou.
♦ Students may describe what a praying mantis looks like and discuss their habits.
1. Crayfish—Fiction 2. Praying mantis—Fiction 3. Bayous—Fiction 4. Animals—Fiction 5. Louisiana—Fiction.

Fontenot, Mary Alice. *Clovis Crawfish and Petit Papillon.* Pelican (0-88289-448-X), 1984. Unpaginated. B/W and Color illus. (Interest level: Preschool-3).

This delightful story of the development of a butterfly is told with charm while providing much information about insects and other Louisiana creatures, including Clovis Crawfish. This title will also serve as a learning and listening tool for beginning French words and phrases.
♦ Children might describe how a caterpillar becomes a butterfly.
1. Butterflies—Fiction 2. Animals—Fiction 3. Bayous—Fiction.

Fontenot, Mary Alice. *Clovis Crawfish and Simeon Suce-Fleur.* Pelican (0-88289-751-9), 1990. Unpaginated. B/W and Color illus. (Interest level: Preschool-3).

Clovis Crawfish rescues a hummingbird from the cold by calling on his animal friends to help. Louisiana has many varieties of birds as described in this title.
♦ Children might draw a picture of a hummingbird as described and pictured in this story.
1. Crayfish—Fiction 2. Hummingbirds—Fiction 3. Animals—Fiction 4. Bayous—Fiction 5. Louisiana—Fiction.

Fontenot, Mary Alice. *Clovis Crawfish and the Big Betail.* Pelican (0-88289-689-X), 1988. Unpaginated. B/W and Color illus. (Interest level: Preschool-3).

Clovis Crawfish learns the meaning of Big Betail and solves the mystery of his wrecked house. Readers of all ages will enjoy the wonderful pictures, while the young child will learn about many animals found in Louisiana.
♦ Children can describe what they think the Big Betail looks like.
1. Armadillos—Fiction 2. Crayfish—Fiction 3. Bayous—Fiction 4. Louisiana—Fiction.

Fontenot, Mary Alice. *Clovis Crawfish and the Curious Crapaud.* Pelican (0-88289), 1986. Unpaginated. B/W and Color illus. (Interest level: Preschool-3).

Clovis Crawfish teaches the lesson that beauty is in the eye of the beholder while also giving a nature lesson. Beautiful color illustrations depicting Louisiana are a delight.
♦ Children can talk about the different kinds of frogs in the story, describe what they look like, and mention their habits.
1. Bayous—Fiction 2. Animals—Fiction.

Fontenot, Mary Alice. *Clovis Crawfish and the Orphan Zo-Zo.* Pelican (0-88289-312-2), 1983. Unpaginated. B/W and Color illus. (Interest level: Preschool-3).

The animals and Clovis Crawfish work together to save an orphaned bird and learn a lesson in the process. The Louisiana countryside is vividly portrayed in the illustrations.
♦ The class can learn to sing "Go to Sleep."
1. Animals—Fiction 2. Cajuns—Fiction.

Fontenot, Mary Alice. *Clovis Crawfish and the Singing Cigales.* Pelican (0-88289-270-3), 1981. Unpaginated. B/W and Color illus. (Interest level: Preschool-3).

Clovis Crawfish and his friends outsmart a blue jay and save a new friend. The fascinating colorful pictures of Louisiana bayou life will delight readers of all ages.
♦ Children might demonstrate how cigale sheds its skin.
1. Bayous—Fiction 2. Animals—Fiction.

Fontenot, Mary Alice. *Clovis Crawfish and the Spinning Spider.* Pelican (0-88289-644-X), 1987. Unpaginated. B/W and Color illus. (Interest level: Preschool-3).

This title explains how spiders spin webs to trap insects. Clovis Crawfish saves his friends from an unfriendly spider. The illustrations depict Louisiana insects in natural settings.

♦ Children can lay thin twine or similar material on a sheet of paper in the shape of a web and use drops of glue to secure the twine. They can then draw a spider to place on the web.
1. Animals—Fiction 2. Bayous—Fiction.

Karr, Kathleen. *Gideon and the Mummy Professor.* Farrar Straus Giroux (0-55546-661-3), 1993. 137p. B/W illus. (Interest level: 4-8).

This fiction work describes a young boy's adventures down the Mississippi River and into Louisiana with his mummy professor father. The mystery of voodoo, Marie Laveau, and Louisiana magic will make this book an enjoyable reading experience.
♦ After reading about Gideon, students can describe what they think Maria Laveau looks like and what she did to practice her voodoo.
1. Voodooism—Fiction. 2. Louisiana—Fiction.

Kovacs, Deborah. *Brewster's Courage.* Simon and Schuster Publishers (0-671-74016-4), 1992. 104p. B/W illus. (Interest level: 2-5).

Brewster, a ferret, leaves his home and travels to the Louisiana bayous in search of music. Young children will delight in the animal antics described in prose and in illustrations.
♦ After reading *Brewster's Courage*, students can draw a picture of the band with Brewster.
1. Ferrets—Fiction. 2. Animals—Fiction. 3. Bayous—Fiction. 4. Louisiana—Fiction. 5. Musicians—Fiction.

Rice, James. *Gaston Goes to Mardi Gras.* Pelican (0-88289-158-8), 1977. Unpaginated. B/W and Color illus. (Interest level: All ages).

Gaston, the green-nosed alligator, travels to the Mardi Gras in New Orleans and visits with his cousin, Alphonse. Mardi Gras customs and traditions are well explained in the text and art.
♦ Children can use a small rectangular box, about the size of a shoe box, as a base to create their own Mardi Gras float.
1. Alligators-Fiction 2. Mardi Gras—Fiction 3. New Orleans—Fiction.

Wilson, Justin. *Justin Wilson's Cajun Fables.* Pelican (0-88289-362-9), 1982. 32p. Color illus. (Interest level: All ages).

Justin Wilson has rewritten 24 traditional nursery rhymes and fairy tales with a Cajun twist. These will be enjoyed by all ages while providing a different view of Louisiana life.
♦ The class might act out one of these Cajun fables for another class, scout troop, or local retirement home.
1. Children's literature, American 2. Cajuns—Literature collections 3. Louisiana—Literary collections.

Periodicals

976.3

Louisiana Conservationist. Louisiana Department of Wildlife and Fisheries, Bimonthly. (Interest level: 4+).

Originating in the 1920s, this periodical focuses on the activities of the department and the many recreational and commercial uses of Louisiana's natural re-

sources. The issues are much used by sports enthusiasts and those interested in the preservation and ecology of the state's natural resources.
♦ Students might write a letter to *Louisiana Conservationist* citing their ideas for new ways the citizens of the state can assist in the ecology and preservation of natural resources.
1. Louisiana—Description and travel 2. Wildlife conservation—Louisiana 3. Wildlife—Louisiana.

976.3

Louisiana Life. Louisiana Magazine Corporation (ISSN 1042-9980), 6/year. (Interest level: 4+).

Articles of interest include Louisiana at large, art, music, sports, bayou life, food, calendar of events, etc. This is a good source of materials for residents, visitors, students, and teachers.
♦ Students can answer the question: Who would you include in a special issue on Louisiana politicians, and why?
1. Louisiana—Description and travel 2. Louisiana—Social life and customs 3. Louisiana—History.

976.3

Preservation in Print. Preservation Resource Center and the Louisiana State Historic Preservation Office, Monthly. (Interest level: 5+).

In a recent issue of this publication, the topics were: the renovation of the Tad Gormley stadium, Louisiana plantation homes, gambling, unusual neighborhoods, maps of ancient trails, etc. This is a good source for information not readily found elsewhere.
♦ Students can write an application for a loan to restore a house that has been in the family for generations, giving their reasoning for wanting to do the restoration.
1. Louisiana—Historic houses 2. Louisiana—History 3. Louisiana—Description and travel 4. Louisiana—Social life and customs.

976.335

New Orleans. New Orleans Publishing Group (ISSN 0897-8174), Monthly. (Interest level: 4+).

This is a periodical devoted to all the things that make New Orleans America's most interesting city: food, fun, fashions, news, etc. The history of New Orleans is well covered in the many articles of interest to students, teachers, etc.
♦ Students may investigate to determine if this periodical has recently covered a hobby, craft, or particular interest they may have. If not, they can write a letter to the magazine suggesting that it include an article on their suggested topic.
1. New Orleans—History 2. New Orleans—Social life and customs.

976.335

New Orleans Vignette, the Guide to New Orleans. Vignette Publications, Inc., Twice annually. (Interest level: 5+).

While the subtitle cites this periodical as a guide, it is more than that, since it contains many excellent articles on topics of interest to visitors, students, and teachers studying Louisiana history.

♦ The Vieux Carre is one of New Orleans' most famous attractions, but it is also important historically. Students may design a brief sketch of the French Quarter showing its streets and placement in the city of New Orleans.

1. New Orleans—History 2. New Orleans—Social life and customs.

Mississippi

by Charjean Laughlin-Graves and Sid F. Graves

Nonfiction

133.1
Hubbard, Sylvia Booth. *Ghosts: Personal Accounts of Modern Mississippi Hauntings*. Illus. by Robert Hubbard. Quail Ridge Press (0-937552-46-1), 1992. B/W photos. (Interest level: 5-8).

These 25 contemporary ghost stories, set in Mississippi, are based on interviews with living people and illustrated with haunting black-and-white photographs. From antebellum houses to modern suburbs, these are intriguing stories with roots to the past.
♦ As a follow-up activity, students may desire to research their own local ghost stories.
1. Ghosts—Mississippi.

133.1
Windham, Kathryn Tucker. *Thirteen Mississippi Ghosts and Jeffrey*. Illus. by H.R. Russell. Strode (0-87397-047- 0), 1974. 147p (Interest level: 4-6).

The 13 Mississippi ghost stories contained in this collection have been told for many years and are perennial favorites throughout the Magnolia State. Illustrated with drawings and photographs, this spooky book entertains children, as well as adults.
♦ Students may enjoy researching the area in which one of the stories is set.
1. Ghosts—Mississippi.

305.896
Meltzer, Milton. *Freedom Comes to Mississippi: The Story of Reconstruction*. Modern Curriculum (0-8136-7206-6), 1970, 1991. 141p. B/W photos. (Interest level: 7+).

This history of the post-Civil War years in Mississippi portrays the post-slavery decades when 4 million people were freed. This work chronicles the achievements that led to post-war Mississippi having the highest number of African Americans elected to public office.
♦ As a follow-up to this story, students may wish to research one of the ex-slaves who was elected to Congress.
1. African-Americans—Civil rights—Mississippi.

305.896
Walter, Mildred Pitts. *Mississippi Challenge*. Bradbury (0-02-792301-0), 1992. 205p. B/W photos. (Interest level: 6+).

This is an account of African-American struggles for civil rights in Mississippi from slavery to the Voting Rights Act of 1965. This work documents violence, Civil War, Reconstruction, the Student Nonviolent Coordinating Committee, leaders and others in this political history.
♦ Students may extend the book by researching civil rights leaders who worked in Mississippi.
1. African-Americans—Civil rights—Mississippi
2. Civil rights movements—Mississippi—History
3. Race relations.

364.152
Callon, Sim C. *The Goat Castle Murder: A True Natchez Story that Shocked the World*. Plantation Publishing (No ISBN), 1985. B/W photos. (Interest level: 6+).

This is an intriguing nonfiction account of the history and legend of the antebellum homes, Glenburnie and Glenwood, the latter known as "Goat Castle" and home to the alleged murderers of "Miss Jennie" Merrill. The many black-and-white photos depict the people connected with the death who were well known to much of the world.
♦ Students may investigate notorious crimes from their own area.
1. Murder—Mississippi—Natchez 2. Natchez (Miss.)—History.

386
The Delta Queen: Last of the Paddlewheel Palaces. Pelican (0-88289-008-5), 1981. 96p. B/W photos. (Interest level: 5+).

The historic and current black-and-white photographs depict the past and the present of the Mississippi River paddlewheel ships. An account of a contemporary trip up the river on the Delta Queen enlivens the photographs.
♦ Students might plan a day's itinerary on an imaginary trip.
1. Delta Queen (Steamboat).

386
Zeck, Pam. *Mississippi Sternwheelers*. Illus. by George Overlie. Carolrhoda (0-87614-180-7), 1982. Unpaginated. B/W photos. (Interest level: 2-4).

Photographs and text describe the origins of the sternwheel paddleboats that once dominated the Mississippi River. Along with the history of the sternwheeler and its importance in the settling of the interior of the United States, there is also a look at today's sternwheelers.
◆ Children may wish to construct or draw a model of a sternwheeler.
1. Mississippi River—Navigation—History 2. Paddle steamers—History.

398.2
Bang, Molly. *Wiley and the Hairy Man*. Macmillan (0-02-708370-5 lib bind), 1976. 64p. B/W illus. (Interest level: K-3).

This delightful children's book is set in the swamp of the Tombigbee River of eastern Mississippi. Excellent drawings and narrative language heighten the pleasures of this popular book based on the African folktale of the hairy creature.
◆ To extend the story, students may want to decide how they would trick the hairy man.
1. Folklore—United States.

398.2
Jagendorf, Moritz Adolf. *Folk Stories of the South*. Illus. By Michael Parks. Vanguard (0-8149-0716-4), 1972. 355p. B/W illus. (Interest level: 4-8).

Mississippi and 10 other states are the settings of the stories of animals, people, old times, and tall tales. This delightful collection includes ghost stories, legends, lores, and other entertainment of earlier days.
◆ Students may enjoy reading and comparing several versions of the Tar Baby tales.
1. Folklore—Southern States.

572.973
Herda, D.J. *Ethnic America: The South Central States*. Millbrook (1-56294-017-1), 1991. 64p. Color photos. (Interest level: 4-6).

This book explains the history and current social and cultural life of the diverse ethnic groups that shaped and continue to make up this region of the United States. Clearly written with a glossary, photos, and bibliography, it introduces the important race relations background and issues.
◆ Students may study a particular ethnic group and its evolution in Mississippi.
1. United States—Social life and custom 2. Gulf States 3. Ethnology—United States 4. Race relations.

582 (Reference)
Brown, Clair A. *Mississippi Trees*. Mississippi Forestry Commission (No ISBN), 1984. 96p. B/W photos. (Interest level: 4+).

This is a handbook for identification of the common trees of Mississippi. While not a complete account of all woody flora, it usefully presents black-and-white photos with common and scientific names and locations.

◆ Students may wish to compare two or three types of trees found in Mississippi.
1. Trees—Mississippi.

582.13
Parker, Lucile. *Mississippi Wildflowers*. Pelican (0-88289-165-0), 1982. Unpaginated. Color illus. (Interest level: 3-8).

Many of the native wildflowers of Mississippi are found in this botanical guide and art book with 117 full color reproductions of paintings. In this beautifully illustrated and easy-to-use book, common and scientific names and descriptions of plants and their habitats and related information are given. Most of the wildflowers included are also found in Alabama, Georgia, and Louisiana.
◆ Students can research the wildflowers from Mississippi that can be found in their own state or compare the wildflowers of the two states.
1. Wild flowers—Mississippi—Pictorial works 2. Fruit—Mississippi—Pictorial works 3. Watercolor painting, American.

582.13 (Reference)
Timme, S. Lee. *Wildflowers of Mississippi*. Illus. by Sam Minor. University Press of Mississippi (0-87805-484- 7), 1989. 278p. Color photos. (Interest level: 6+).

This beautiful guide to the many wildflowers of the diverse regions of the Magnolia State is an excellent reference work. It contains scientific names, descriptions, habitats, distribution, and other information.
◆ Students may wish to compare the flowers of Mississippi with those of their own states.
1. Wildflowers—Mississippi—Identification.

597
Crawford, Linda. *The Catfish Book*. University Press of Mississippi (0-87805-502-9 pbk), 1991. 137p. (Interest level: 5+).

This is the definitive work on the life and lore of the catfish, which is growing in popularity in the U. S. and abroad as a healthy and tasty food source, and which frequently appears in songs and literature. This clean and accessible book covers the fish itself, the sport of fishing, the agribusiness of its growth and harvest, and many recipes.
◆ Students might enjoy writing a story about fishing for catfish.
1. Catfishes 2. Catfishes—Folklore 3. Cookery (Catfish).

633.5
Gregory, Olive Barnes. *Cotton*. Illus. by Elsie Wrigley. Rourke (0-86625-162-6), 1981. 24p. Color illus. (Interest level: K-3).

The simple text describes how cotton, a major crop in Mississippi, is grown, harvested, then made into cloth. The glossary and color illustrations enhance the value of this book in the early grades.
◆ Students could plant a cotton seed to watch it grow.
1. Cotton.

633.5
Selsam, Millicent Ellis. *Cotton*. Illus. by Jerome Wexler. William Morrow (0-688-01499-2), 1982. B/W and Color illus. (Interest level: 2-5).

Cotton, which is becoming increasingly important to the state's economy, is explored in this well-illustrated introduction to the history, botany, production, and use of the fiber plant from which half of all textiles are made.

♦ Students may wish to study the production of another fiber and then compare the two.
1. Cotton.

677
Mitgutsch, Ali. *From Cotton to Pants*. Illus. by Sellier Verlag GmbH. Carolrhoda (0-87614-150-5), 1981. Unpaginated. Color illus. (Interest level: K-3).

The journey of cotton from plant to clothing factory is traced through this modest text. The simple, bold illustrations supplement the story of this important southern industry.

♦ As a reading follow-up, children may study different types of cotton fabrics.
1. Cotton.

782.1
Price, Leontyne. *Aida*. Illus. by Leo and Diane Dillon. Harcourt Brace Jovanovich (0-15-200405-X), 1990. Unpaginated. Color illus. (Interest level: 2-6).

The Royal Princess Aida's love story is told by opera diva and Laurel, Mississippi, native Leontyne Price in this memorable account. Lovely and enchanting paintings by Leo and Diane Dillon are fantastic accomplishments, enhancing Verdi's story of Aida, one of the world's most popular operas.

♦ Research Leontyne Price and list some of the operas in which she has starred.
1. Verdi, Guiseppe, 1813-1901 2. Operas—Stories, plots, etc.

784
Ferris, William. *Blues from the Delta*. Anchor Books (0-385-09920-7), 1978. 226p B/W photos. (Interest level: 7+).

The roots of American music are explained in this study of Mississippi Delta Blues. Interviews, lyrics, and photographs document the African-American people and places where American's original music began.

♦ Students may wish to compose original blues lyrics about today.
1. Blues (Songs, etc.)—Mississippi—History and criticism 2. Negro musicians—Mississippi 3. Mississippi—Musicians.

784
Good Morning Blues. (Videocassette). Mississippi Authority for Educational Television, 1978. VHS, (60 min.). $29.95. (Available from the Delta Blues Museum). (Interest level: 6+).

The videocassette offers an excellent introduction to the history, music, and artists of the Mississippi Delta blues heritage. Narrated by Mississippi artist B. B. King, this popular video presents a well-researched and narrated account of the African-American music from the poorest region of the nation.

♦ Students may want to listen to recordings of lesser-known blues artists.
1. Blues (Songs, etc.)—Mississippi 2. Negro musicians—Mississippi 3. Mississippi—Musicians.

791.5
The Art of the Muppets. Bantam (0-533-01313-0), 1980. Unpaginated. Color and B/W photos. (Interest level: 2-6).

Jim Henson, a Leland, Mississippi, native, created the extremely popular Muppets. This beautiful book with superb photography gives an intriguing and rewarding look behind the scenes at the Muppets' creation and history.

♦ Children may enjoy making a puppet and producing their own puppet show.
1. Henson, Jim 2. Puppets.

796.924
Anderson, Walter Inglis. *An Alphabet*. University Press of Mississippi (0-87805-224-0), 1984. Unpaginated. Color illus. (Interest level: K+).

Mississippi Gulf Coast artist, Walter Anderson, made this imaginative alphabet book for his own children with wonderful letters and pictures of butterflies, rabbits, birds, cats, and natural forms. His block prints are beautifully reproduced, with a delightful eccentric creativity that rewards children and adults with their attention to details and design.

♦ Young students may want to create their own alphabet book while the older student could research this interesting Mississippi artist.
1. Alphabet.

799
Neill, Robert Hitt. *The Jakes!*. Illus. by Sam Beibers, Mickey Kyzar, and Beau Neill. Mississippi River Publishing Company (0-9617591-4-3), 1990. 331p. B/W illus. (Interest level: 5+).

"Jakes" are young immature male turkeys, but these stories are about the adventures and teenage years of six Mississippi boys (and important adults in their lives) who hunt, camp, fish, and get into mischief. Through their comic adventures and misadventures, the reader (especially teenage boys) enjoys the trials and tribulations of characters ages 13 to 18.

♦ Students may wish to write about one of their own real or imagined outdoor adventures.
1. Fishing 2. Hunting.

917.9
Sorden, L. G. *I Am the Mississippi*. Wisconsin House (No ISBN), 1974. (Interest level: 6+).

This entertaining and educational history of the Mississippi River, or "Father of the Waters," contains much history and lore. An extensive glossary of "riverman's lingo" increases the book's value.

♦ As a reading follow-up, students may choose to create an original adventure on the Mississippi River.
1. Mississippi River.

970.3
Bounds, Thelma V. *Children of the Nanih Waiya.* Naylor (No ISBN), 1964. 64p. B/W illus. (Interest level: 6-8).

When whites made their first appearance in the Mississippi region, the most important tribes were the Natchez, the Choctaws, and the Chickasaws. This fact-filled book describes the Choctaws before white explorers, their relationship with the Europeans, the decline of native traditions, and the acceptance of the English-speaking people.
♦ Young people may research and compare the Choctaw with other Native Americans.
1. Choctaw Indians—History 2. Mississippi—Indians 3. Indians of North America.

970.3
Conklin, Paul. *Choctaw Boy.* Dodd, Mead (0-396-07067-1), 1975. 64p. B/W photos. (Interest level: 4-6).

An excellent introduction to contemporary Choctaw Indian life in Mississippi, this book tells the story of 11-year-old Clifton Henry who learns of his Choctaw ancestors and of the challenges of growing up in his home of Bogue Chitto, Mississippi, and the world beyond. This book is illustrated with black-and-white photographs that realistically depict the setting, customs, and cultures of the Mississippi Choctaw Indians.
♦ Students may want to decide how their own life is similar to Clifton's.
1. Choctaw Indians 2. Indians of North America.

973
Brain, Jeffrey. *The Tunica-Biloxi.* Chelsea House (1-55546-731-8), 1990. (Indians of North America Series). 104p. B/W and Color illus. (Interest level: 4-8).

Based on contemporary archaeological and historical research, this is a readable account of the Native Americans who lived on the fertile lands along the Mississippi River. The book, containing a glossary and many illustrations, includes accounts of European explorers and the gradual near-extinction of the tribes.
♦ Students may research other extinct Native American tribes.
1. Tunica Indians—History 2. Biloxi Indians—History 3. Indians of North America.

973
Hale, Duane K. and **Gibson, Arrell M**. *The Chickasaw.* Chelsea House (1-55546-697-4), 1990. (Indians of North America Series). 111p. B/W and Color illus. (Interest level: 4-8).

The Chickasaw were farmers and hunters in an area that included parts of Mississippi, Alabama, and Tennessee. With excellent color photographs, maps, and illustrations, this book accurately covers the "prehistory," archaeology, and life of Chickasaw from pre-European to contemporary times in the eastern and western United States.
♦ Students may wish to compare the Chickasaw religion to their own religion.
1. Chickasaw Indians 2. Indians of North America.

973
McKee, Jesse O. *The Choctaw.* Chelsea House (1-55546-699-0), 1989. (Indians of North America Series). 103p. B/W and Color illus. (Interest level: 4-8).

The Choctaw lived peacefully along the Mississippi River floodplains until Hernando de Soto and his men invaded their land and massacred 1,500 tribespeople. This book and the others in the series discuss the relationship of the tribal groups to the federal government and other forces that dramatically altered their cultures.
♦ Students may wish to pretend that they are Choctaws being removed to the west and describe how their last evening before the journey is spent.
1. Choctaw Indians 2. Indians of North America.

973.73
Jones, Virgil Carrington. *U.S.S. Cairo: The Story of a Civil War Gunboat.* U.S. Department of the Interior, National Park Service (No ISBN), 1971. 56p. B/W photos. (Interest level: 4+).

The U.S.S. *Cairo*, a federal gunboat, was sunk in the Yazoo River near Vicksburg by a confederate torpedo in 1862 after an important role in the Civil War. A century later, it was raised, salvaged, and reconstructed for display at Vicksburg National Military Park. This historical work interprets the boat, its artifacts, and Civil War naval battles through text, drawings, and photographs.
♦ As a follow-up to this publication, students may write for more information from the Vicksburg National Military Park.
1. United States—History—Civil War, 1861-1865—Naval operations.

973.91
McCafferty, Jim. *Holt and the Teddy Bear* . Illus. by Florence S. Davis. Pelican (0-88289-823-X), 1991. 40p. Color illus. (Interest level: 1-4).

Based on the true story of the origin of the teddy bear, this tale relates President Teddy Roosevelt's Mississippi hunting trip led by woodsman Holt Collier and his little dog Jocko. Colorful illustrations enhance the story of the African-American guide and the president who refused to kill "an old, tired, worn-out bear that was tied to a tree."
♦ As a reading follow-up, students may choose to research other game animals in Mississippi.
1. Roosevelt, Theodore, 1858-1919 2. Collier, Holt 3. Hunting—Mississippi—History—20th Century 4. Teddy bears—History.

976
Aylesworth, Thomas G. *The South: Alabama, Florida, and Mississippi.* Chelsea House (1-55546-558-7), 1988. 64p. Color photos. (Interest level: 2-6).

This book discusses the geographical, historical, and cultural aspects of three southern states. Using maps, illustrated fact sheets, and other illustrated materials in full-color, the land, history, and people of each state are highlighted.
♦ Compare some common aspect of the three states.
1. Alabama 2. Florida 3. Mississippi.

976.2
Akin, Edward N. *Mississippi, an Illustrated History.*
Windsor (0-89781-255-5), 1987. 168p. B/W and Color
illus. (Interest level: 6+).

This book examines the colorful events and personalities that have shaped the life and character of the
Magnolia State from the expedition of Hernando de
Soto to the challenges of today. These biographies of
leaders and artists, vintage photographs and other illustrations, and the information about business and
industry form an unequalled portrait of this fascinating
state.
◆ Students may wish to study an industry located in
their own state.
1. Mississippi—History 2. Mississippi—Description
and travel 3. Mississippi—Industries.

976.2
Black, Patti Carr, ed. *Documentary Portrait of Mississippi: The Thirties.* Photos by Arthur Rothstein, Ben
Shahn, Walker Evans, Dorothea Lange, Russell Lee,
and Marion Post Wolcott. University Press of Mississippi, (0-87805-166-X), 1982. 128p. B/W photos. (Interest level: 6+).

Photojournalism came of age as Farm Security
Administration photographers travelled throughout the
country to record the need for federal assistance during
the Depression. This remarkable photographic essay
documents the Depression in Mississippi when cotton
was king in this predominantly rural state.
◆ Students may wish to create a story around one or
two of the photographs included in this book.
1. Mississippi—Description and travel—Views 2. Depressions—1929—Mississippi—Pictorial works
3. Mississippi—Social conditions—Pictorial works.

976.2
Carson, Robert. *America the Beautiful, Mississippi.*
Childrens Press (0-516-00470-0), 1989. 144p. Color
illus. (Interest level: 4-7).

This introductory guide to the geography and history of the state includes many photographs, facts, and
statistics. This is an excellent beginner's guide to the
twentieth state with emphasis on the ethnic and cultural
diversity of its people and places.
◆ Students may enjoy researching one of the many
celebrities or writers listed in the text.
1. Mississippi.

976.2 (Reference)
*Mississippi Official and Statistical Register, 1988-
1992.* Dick Molpus, Secretary of State (No ISBN),
1989. 595p. Color and B/W illus. (Interest level: 5+).

This collection of information about Mississippi,
including census data, state and local agencies, elected
officials with photos, addresses, and lists of prominent
people, is published by the Secretary of State's office
every four years. It is a reference work that will find
value in every library.
◆ Students may want to compare data on counties.
1. Mississippi.

976.2
Sansing, David. *Natchez: An Illustrated History.* Plantation (0-9631823-1-5), 1992. 192p. B/W illus. (Interest level: 5+).

Natchez, named for the Natchez Indian tribe from
the area, was a wealthy Mississippi River city at the
outbreak of the Civil War. This engaging history of this
interesting, historical, and beautiful small city is illustrated with numerous black-and-white photographs,
drawings, and maps.
◆ Students could research one of the antebellum
homes for its history and occupants.
1. Natchez (Miss.)—History.

976.213
Cory, George. *Head-on with Hurricane Camille.* Illus.
by Tony Baldini. Raintree (0-8172-1565-4), 1980. 45p.
B/W illus. (Interest level: 3+).

In August, 1969, Hurricane Camille devastated the
Mississippi coast area. This fast-paced story narrates
the harrowing events that followed a family's decision
not to vacate their home in the path of the storm.
◆ Students may research another hurricane's effects,
such as Hurricane Andrew in 1992.
1. Gulf States—Hurricane, 1969 2. Hurricanes.

977
Crisman, Ruth. *The Mississippi.* Franklin Watts (0-
531-04826-8), 1984. 64p. B/W photos. (Interest level:
4-8).

The Mississippi River has had a profound effect on
the geography, history, economy, and people of the
region through which it flows. Black-and-white photos, drawings, and maps illustrate the history, special
problems, and future prospects of this waterway.
◆ Students may research some of the lakes that have
been formed in Mississippi by the river.
1. Mississippi River 2. Mississippi River Valley
3. Rivers.

Biography

920
Sewell, George A. and **Dwight, Margaret L**. *Mississippi Black History Makers.* University Press of Mississippi (0-87805-207-0), 1984. 468p. B/W photos.
(Interest level: 5+).

This excellent collection of 166 biographical articles on notable African Americans from Mississippi
includes opera star Leontyne Price, actor James Earl
Jones, writers Richard Wright and Margaret Walter
Alexander, musicians Charley Pride and B. B. King,
and others in sports, politics, civil rights, business,
education, literature, arts, science, religion, and the
military. The book is divided into 10 thematic sections,
and each section is introduced with a historical overview of the field.
◆ Students may wish to research in depth one of the
persons included in the collection.
1. African-Americans—Mississippi—Biography
2. Mississippi—Biography.

920
Wells, Dean Faulkner and **Cole, Hunter**, eds. *Mississippi Heroes*. University Press of Mississippi (0-87805-128-7, v.1), 1980. 230p. B/W photos. (Interest level: 7+).

The biographies of 10 important Mississippians are juxtaposed so that their lives spread across the history of Mississippi from the territorial period to the recent past. Included in this collection are a president, a governor, a chieftain, a civil rights leader (Medgar Evers), a musician, and two jurists.
♦ Students may want to complete a time line with the subjects of this book and list important events occurring in the state during their times.
1. Mississippi—Biography.

92 Davis, Jefferson
Green, Margaret. *President of the Confederacy: Jefferson Davis*. Julian Messner (No ISBN), 1963. 191p. (Interest level: 5-8).

This engaging biography of the president of the Confederacy describes his life from childhood to his retirement on the Mississippi Gulf Coast where he wrote his autobiography. This is a sympathetic story of his lost wealth, reputation, and citizenship.
♦ Students may want to write to his home, Beauvoir.
1. Davis, Jefferson, 1808-1889 2. Mississippi—Biography.

92 Hamer, Fannie Lou
Jordan, June. *Fannie Lou Hamer*. Illus. by Albert Williams. Crowell (0-690-28893-X), 1972. 41p. B/W illus. (Interest level: 2-4).

From childhood poverty and work to courageously making stands as a leader in the civil rights movement, Fannie Lou Hamer's biography is an inspiring story of the value and significance of a single individual's acts and influence upon multitudes. Simply written and generously illustrated, this important story is relevant to most ages.
♦ Students may wish to research the Mississippi Freedom Democratic Party.
1. Hamer, Fannie Lou 2. African-Americans—Mississippi—Biography 3. Mississippi—Biography.

92 Handy, William C.
Montgomery, Elizabeth Rider. *William C. Handy: Father of the Blues*. Illus. by David Hodges. Garrard (No ISBN), 1968. 96p. B/W illus. (Interest level: 3-6).

William C. Handy, musician and composer, made his major contribution to the world as the arranger who wrote down the blues music that was indigenous to the Mississippi Delta where he lived from 1903 to 1906. His "St. Louis Blues" and other songs changed popular music as they introduced America's original form of music to the world.
♦ Students may enjoy listening to some of W.C. Handy's original works.
1. Handy, William C. 2. African-Americans—Biography.

92 Henson, Jim
Woods, Geraldine. *Jim Henson: From Puppets to Muppets*. Dillon (0-87518-348-4), 1987. 54p. Color photos. (Interest level: 2-4).

This book recounts the life story of the native Mississippian whose creations, the Muppets, have had tremendous success in television and other media. This high-interest story is illustrated with color photographs of Mr. Henson and his famous characters.
♦ Children may want to write to the chamber of commerce in Mr. Henson's birthplace, Leland, Mississippi.
1. Henson, Jim 2. Puppets 3. Mississippi—Biography.

92 Jones, John Luther (Casey)
York, Carol Beach. *Casey Jones*. Illus. by Bert Dodson. (Folk Tales of America Series). Troll (0-89375-298-3), 1980. 46p. Color illus. (Interest level: 3-6).

Casey Jones, the engineer and folk hero, was travelling through Mississippi when his train collided with another one and he was killed. This simple, well-told tale engages the reader in this story of his desire to become an engineer, the biggest and best dream of the time.
♦ Students may wish to extend the story by learning the song about Casey Jones by Wallace Saunders or writing the Casey Jones Museum for more information.
1. Jones, John Luther (Casey) 2. Mississippi—Biography 3. Railroads—Biography.

92 Morris, Willie
Morris, Willie. *Good Old Boy: A Delta Boyhood*. Yoknapatawpha (0-916242-09-1), 1980. 143p. (Interest level: 5-8).

This is a delightful, well-written autobiographical book set in the 1940s in Yazoo City, Mississippi, by the small-town Willie Morris who would become a Rhodes scholar and the youngest editor-in-chief in the history of *Harpers* magazine. Later filmed by Disney, these entertaining and enchanting stories of friends, a car-driving dog, sports, and another time appeal to today's readers of all ages.
♦ Students may want to compare the life of a boy in the forties to that of today.
1. Mississippi—Biography.

92 Payton, Walter
Sufren, Mark. *Payton*. Charles Scribner's Sons (0-684-18940-2), 1988. 151p. B/W photos. (Interest level: 5-8).

This biography of the record-breaking and popular superstar football player describes his life from his Mississippi childhood to his retirement in 1988 from the Chicago Bears. The book also relates his business and personal life.
♦ Research a football player from the student's home state and chronicle his life after football.
1. Payton, Walter, 1954- 2. Football players 3. Chicago Bears (football team) 4. Mississippi—Biography.

92 Presley, Elvis
Rubel, David. *Elvis Presley: The Rise of Rock and Roll*. Millbrook (1-878841-18-1), 1991. 100p. B/W photos. (Interest level: 6+).

This biography of the Tupelo, Mississippi, recording artist relates his youth, career, and death, and it describes the social changes of the 1950s and 1960s. A recent account of this musical and social phenomenon,

the book is appropriate and engaging for middle grades.
♦ Students could outline some of the social changes that occured during the 1950s and 1960s.
1. Presley, Elvis, 1935-1977 2. Singers—United States—Biography 3. Rock musicians.

92 Presley, Elvis
Wootton, Richard. *Elvis!* Random (0-394-87046-8), 1985. 127p. B/W photos. (Interest level: 5-8).
This is a biography of the king of Rock 'n' Roll, Elvis Aaron Presley, who was born in Tupelo, Mississippi, in 1935, and died in Memphis, Tennessee, in 1977. This sympathetic portrait addresses the reasons for his success and early death.
♦ Students may enjoy writing the Elvis Presley Museum in Tupelo, Mississippi.
1. Presley, Elvis, 1935-1977 2. Singers—Mississippi—Biography 3. Rock musicians—United States—Biography 4. Mississippi—Biography.

92 Pride, Charley
Barclay, Pamela. *Charley Pride*. Illus. by Dick Brude. Creative Education (0-87191-397-6), 1975. 31p. Color illus. (Interest level: 3-6).
From a childhood of picking cotton in the Mississippi Delta to a career first in baseball and later as one of the world's most successful country music recording stars, Charley Pride has had a remarkable life and career. Color illustrations make this an appealing book about a famous African American.
♦ Students may enjoy listening to some of Mr. Pride's recordings.
1. Pride, Charley 2. African Americans—Mississippi—Biography 3. Mississippi—Biography.

92 Robinson, John C.
Simmons, Thomas E. *The Brown Condor: The True Adventures of John C. Robinson*. Bartleby (0-910155-7), 1988. 198p. B/W photos. (Interest level: 8+).
John C. Robinson, a pioneering African-American aviation hero, grew up in Gulfport, Mississippi, and dreamed of breaking the color barrier to a career in aviation. His career spans three decades and includes his courageous exploits in the World War II Ethiopian invasion.
♦ Students may wish to study more about the Ethiopian invasion of World War II.
1. Robinson, John C. 2. Air pilots—United States—Biography 3. Air pilots—Ethiopia—Biography 4. African-Americans—Mississippi—Biography.

92 Soto, Hernando de
Grant, Matthew G. *De Soto: Explorer of the Southeast*. Illus. by Harold Henriksen. Creative Education (0-87191-283-X), 1974. Unpaginated. Color illus. (Interest level: 2-4).
In the sixteenth century, Hernando de Soto became the first European to cross the Mississippi River in his unsuccessful search for gold in the New World. In simple text, the reader is told of his desire for power and money, the many battles with Native Americans, and his eventual death on the banks of the Mississippi.

♦ Students may enjoy making a map that traces de Soto's route through the southeastern region.
1. Soto Hernando de, 1500 (ca.)—1542 2. Explorers, Spanish.

92 Taulbert, Clifton L.
Taulbert, Clifton L. *Once Upon a Time When We Were Colored*. Council Oak Books (0-933-31-19-X), 1989. 153p. B/W photos. (Interest level: 7+).
Taulbert, a successful businessman/author, tells the story of his youth in the Mississippi Delta, affirming the roots and dignity of poor African Americans in the land of cotton and the joys discovered in family, friends, church, and home on the way up to full participation in the American dream. Black-and-white family photographs enhance this evocative and inspiring story.
♦ Young people could study the careers of other prominent native Mississippians.
1. African-Americans—Mississippi—Biography 2. Mississippi—Biography.

92 Winfrey, Oprah
Patterson, Lillie. *Oprah Winfrey: Talk Show Host and Actress*. Enslow (0-89490-289-X), 1990. 128p. B/W photos. (Interest level: 5+).
Oprah Winfrey spent her first six years in her birthplace of Attala County, Mississippi, with her grandmother before moving to Milwaukee and, later, Nashville. The biography of the television and film star relates African-American history and heritage, and tells of the many influences on her life and career.
♦ Students may enjoy researching the county from which Ms. Winfrey came.
1. Winfrey, Oprah 2. Television personalities 3. Actors and actresses 4. African-Americans—Biography.

Fiction

Awiakta, Marilou. *Rising Fawn and the Fire Mystery*. Illus. by Beverly Bringle. St. Luke's Press (0-918518-29-6), 1983. 43p. B/W illus. (Interest level: 3-6).
This book is based on actual events in 1833 when Rising Fawn, a Choctaw child, is kidnapped from her Mississippi Choctaw home during the "Removal of Indians" to California. In this poignant and triumphant story, she is adopted by a Memphis, Tennessee, family and comes to understand the ways of her new home and the unity of all things.
♦ Children might enjoy learning more about the "Removal of Indians."
1. Choctaw Indians—Fiction 2. Indians of North American—Fiction 3. Kidnapping—Fiction.

Ball, Zachary. *Bristle Face*. Holiday (No ISBN), 1962. 206p. (Interest level: 5-8).
Turn-of-the-century foxhunting in the Mississippi countryside is the setting for this humorous and touching story about 14- year-old Jase Landers, his homely dog who develops into a great trail dog, and a storekeeper friend named Lute Swank.
♦ Young people might study hunting in Mississippi.
1. Dogs—Fiction 2. Fox hunting—Fiction 3. Mississippi—Fiction.

Ball, Zachary. *Sputters*. Holiday (No ISBN), 1963. 220p. (Interest level: 5-8).

Jase's non-barking dog, Sputters, may not be much to look at, but he helps the young boy aid the sheriff in the apprehension of moonshiners in this humorous book set in the countryside of turn-of-the-century Mississippi. This work is a sequel to *Bristle Face* (*see* preceding entry).
♦ As a reading follow-up, students might want to research prohibition in Mississippi.
1. Dogs—Fiction 2. Mississippi—Fiction.

(Easy)
Birchman, David. *Brother Billy Bronto's Bygone Blues Band*. Illus. by John O'Brien. Lothrop (0-688-10423-1), Unpaginated. Color illus. (Interest level: 1-3).

This story, in humorous verse, tells of dinosaurs who perform in a band that plays the blues, the music started in the Mississippi Delta. This is a book that is fun for children and adults with colorful illustrations throughout to delight the eye, as the poetry enchants the ears.
♦ As a reading follow-up, children may choose to draw the instruments used by blues musicians.
1. Blues (Music)—Fiction 2. Stories in rhyme.

(Easy)
Bullock, Judy Broadus. *Uncle Wiley Whiskers Tells How the Catfish Got Its Name*. Illus. by Liz Ann Barber. Quail Ridge Press (0-937552-49-6 pbk), 1992. Unpaginated. B/W illus. (Interest level: 1-3).

Catfish, having been popular in Mississippi for many years, are now a major crop being exported throughout the world. Written in rhythm and rhyme by a former Mississippi elementary school teacher, this small paperback book tells the story of the adventures of a Mississippi catfish named "Uncle Wiley."
♦ Students may enjoy writing for more information about catfish from the Catfish Institute.
1. Catfishes—Fiction 2. Stories in rhyme.

Burchard, Peter. *Jed: The Story of a Yankee Soldier and a Southern Boy*. Illus. by the author. Coward-McCann & Geoghegan (No ISBN), 1960. 94p. B/W illus. (Interest level: 4-8).

Set during the Civil War, this story tells how a Wisconsin boy, Jed, survives the bloody Battle of Shiloh and is stationed in war-ravaged Mississippi. In this moving story, he suffers homesickness that is alleviated by his "enemies" when he takes an injured Mississippi boy back to the latter's home and family.
♦ Students may research other Civil War battles in Mississippi.
1. Mississippi—Fiction.

Faulkner, William. *The Wishing Tree*. Illus. by Don Bolognese. Random (No ISBN), 1967. 82p. B/W illus. (Interest level: 4-6).

The only published children's story by Mississippi's Nobel Prize winning author, William Faulkner, this book is a dream fantasy featuring a mysterious boy named Maurice who leads Dulcie and her friends on an enchanting search for the Wishing Tree. In this vivid and warm tale told in Southern dialect, they discover that "you don't need a Wishing Tree to make things come true."
♦ Students may want to study about the famous Mississippi author of this tale.
1. Fantasy

Fichter, George S. *First Steamboat Down the Mississippi*. Illus. by Joe Boddy. Pelican (0-88289-715-2), 1989. 112p. B/W illus. (Interest level: 5-8).

A 14-year-old orphan, Tim Collins, joins the crew of the *New Orleans* on the first steamboat on the Mississippi River from Pittsburg to Natchez in 1811. This is an exciting, historical story with river pirates, hostile Indians, a treacherous river, and the most powerful earthquake ever recorded in North America that will keep the reader interested.
♦ Students could pretend that they were on this voyage with Tim and write a letter home.
1. New Orleans (Steamboat)—Fiction 2. Mississippi River—Fiction.

(Easy)
Flournoy, Valerie. *The Patchwork Quilt*. Illus. by Jerry Pinkney. Dial (0-8037-00970-0), 1985. Unpaginated. Color illus. (Interest level: 2-4).

With the help of her mother and whole family, young Tanya finishes the quilt of memories that her ill grandmother began with pieces of the family's old clothing. Telling the family's story, the quilt making tale affirms family values.
♦ Children may want to draw a quilt with pieces telling their own family story.
1. Quilting—Fiction 2. Grandmothers—Fiction 3. Family life—Fiction 4. African-Americans—Fiction.

(Easy)
Greenberg, Polly. *Oh Lord, I Wish I Was a Buzzard*. Illus. by Aliki. Macmillan (No ISBN), 1968. Unpaginated. Color illus. (Interest level: K-3).

This is a delightful story of a little girl and her brother who go to work in the cotton field with their father. Simple and rhythmic lyrics enhanced by Aliki's beautiful pictures make it a perennial favorite.
♦ Children may participate in the telling of the story or act it out.
1. Cotton—Fiction 2. Mississippi—Fiction.

Herndon, Ernest. *Backwater Blues: A Novel of Faith and Fury*. Zondervan (0-310-53621-9 pbk.), 1991. 192p. (Interest level: 7+).

This is a story of an aging Mississippi blues artist, Nick Rose, whose nephew escapes from jail, taking Nick and his granddaughter on a terror-filled murder and crime spree through Mississippi swamp lands. The three must learn to work together to survive, and all must confront their darkest fears.
♦ Students may extend the story by writing a "wanted" poster for Calvin.
1. Mississippi—Fiction.

Holling, Holling C. *Minn of the Mississippi*. Illus. by the author. Houghton Mifflin (0-395-17578-X), 1951. 85p. Illus. (Interest level: 4-6).

Through the story of a snapping turtle, Minn, the reader is told of the history, climate, and geography of the Mississippi River. This Newbery Honor Book describes the background of this great river.

♦ Students may wish to study the wildlife found on the Mississippi River.

1. Turtles—Fiction 2. Mississippi River—Fiction.

(Easy)

Maxner, Joyce. *Nicholas Cricket*. Illus. by William Joyce. Harper & Row (0-06-024222-1), 1989. Unpaginated. Color illus. (Interest level: K-3).

America's original music form, the blues, which gave birth to jazz and rock 'n' roll, had its roots in the Mississippi Delta. This whimsical and entertaining celebration of the rhythms of that folk music, southern landscape, and language with wonderful color illustrations and the Bug-A-Wug Cricket Band "is just so grand!"

♦ As a follow-up to this story, children may want to find out about crickets and how they make their noises.

1. Crickets—Fiction 2. Bands (Music)—Fiction 3. Animals—Fiction 4. Stories in rhyme.

(Easy)

Mayer, Mercer. *Liza Lou and the Yeller Belly Swamp*. Illus. by the author. Parents, 1976. 46p. Color illus. (Interest level: K-2).

This story relates the adventures of the resourceful title character who outwits the haunts, witches, gobblygooks, and other critters and creatures of the swamp. Fun is enhanced with Mayer's delightful illustrations throughout.

♦ Children may enjoy studying real animals who inhabit the swamps and marshes.

1. Monsters—Fiction.

McKissack, Patricia. *The Dark-Thirty: Southern Tales of the Supernatural*. Illus. by Brian J. Pinkney. Knopf (0-679-81863-4), 1992. B/W illus. (Interest level: 4+).

This collection of original stories is inspired by African-American history and southern storytelling. One of the 10 stories is set in Tallahatchie County, Mississippi, and describes the Ku Klux Klan of the 1930s. The black-and-white drawings serve as fitting illustrations for each story.

♦ Reading ghost stories from the student's own region would be an interesting follow-up.

1. Ghosts—Fiction 2. Horror stories 3. African-Americans—Fiction 4. Short Stories.

(Easy)

McKissack, Patricia. *Nettie Jo's Friends*. Illus. by Scott Cook. Knopf (0-394-99158-3), 1988. Unpaginated. Color illus. (Interest level: K-3).

Southern folklore and excellent story-telling characterize this tale of a fanciful young girl's search for a needle to sew a new dress for her doll. With a colorful cast of animals beautifully painted by Mississippi artist/illustrator Scott Cook, this book will delight children.

♦ Children may want to read and compare this book to other southern tales such as Br'er Rabbit.

1. Animals—Fiction 2. Dolls—Fiction.

(Easy)

Miles, Miska. *Mississippi Possum*. Illus. by John Schoenherr. Little, Brown (No ISBN), 1965. 41p. B/W illus. (Interest level: K-4).

A young girl befriends a possum when both are forced to seek higher ground during a flood. This simply told story's strong themes of family love and concern make it an important book.

♦ Children may want to study the wild animals of this region.

1. Mississippi River—Fiction 2. Opossums—Fiction.

Morris, Willie. *Good Old Boy and the Witch of Yazoo*. Yoknapatawpha (0-916242-60-9), 1989. 164p. (Interest level: 6+).

Small-town Mississippi of 1946 is the setting for this tale of mischievous boys, an endearing dog named Skip, and the rumors of witches that enliven the town of Yazoo. Young Willie investigates and contributes to hysteria with pranks that entertain readers of all ages.

♦ Students could write the Yazoo City Chamber of Commerce for information about the town of today.

1. Mississippi—Fiction.

Searcy, Margaret Zehmer. *The Charm of the Bear Claw Necklace*. Pelican (0-88289-821-3), 1990. 67p. B/W illus. (Interest level: 4-8).

Based on actual archaeological evidence from 7000 years ago in the southeastern region of North America, this story relates the adventures of a group of Native American children and the dangers they faced from nature and men.

♦ After sharing the book, students may wish to collect stones to make their own necklace.

1. Indians of North America—Fiction 2. Stone Age—Fiction.

Searcy, Margaret Zehmer. *Ikwa of the Mound Builder Indians*. Pelican (0-88289-762-4), 1989. 73p. B/W photos. (Interest level: 4-8).

The rich history of Lower Mississippi Valley Native Americans known as the Mound Builder Indians is related through the fictional story of Ikwa, a girl of 12, and her family, who lived more than 800 years ago. Photographs and drawings illustrate the way of life, culture, and beliefs of the builders of the temple mounds typical of Mississippi, Alabama, and other states.

♦ Students may want to create a piece of clay pottery.

1. Mound Builders—Fiction 2. Indians of North America—Fiction.

Taylor, Mildred D. *The Friendship*. Illus. by Max Ginsburg. Dial (0-8037-0418-6), 1987. 53p. B/W illus. (Interest level: 2-4).

Set in 1933, this haunting story features young Cassie Logan, her three brothers, and Mr. Tom Bee, the elderly African-American man shot in the leg for calling a white storekeeper by his first name. This moving tale with strong characters and beautiful illustrations is unforgettable.

♦ Students may prepare a grocery list of items that they could purchase during the 1930s.

1. African-Americans—Fiction 2. Southern States—Race relations 3. Race relations—Fiction 4. Prejudices—Fiction.

Taylor, Mildred D. *The Gold Cadillac*. Illus. by Michael Hays. Dial (0-8037-0343-0), 1987. 43p. B/W illus. (Interest level: 3-5).

When an African-American family brings its new shiny gold cadillac from Ohio to Mississippi, the two sisters, Wilma and Lois, encounter the ugliness of racial prejudice for the first time. The sepia illustrations effectively demonstrate the social and emotional environment in which African Americans lived during this period.
♦ Students may want to discuss/research the various forms of racial prejudices.
1. Blacks—Fiction 2. Prejudices—Fiction 3. Race relations—Fiction 3. Mississippi—Fiction.

Taylor, Mildred D. *Let the Circle Be Unbroken*. Dial (0-8037-4748-9), 1981. 384p. (Interest level: 6+).

This powerful sequel to the author's *Roll of Thunder, Hear My Cry* (*see* page 98) continues the saga of the Logan Family in rural Mississippi. The story exemplifies how they are able to maintain dignity with courage in the face of prejudice in the 1930s.
♦ Students may research the effects of the Depression on farmers.
1. African-Americans—Fiction 2. Mississippi—Fiction 3. Prejudices—Fiction 4. Race relations—Fiction.

Taylor, Mildred D. *Mississippi Bridge*. Illus. by Max Ginsburg. Bantam (0-553-15992-5), 1990. 62p. B/W illus. (Interest level: 3-5).

Set in Mississippi in the 1930s, this insightful story shows young white Jeremy Simms' growing awareness of the price of prejudice as he participates in a tragic day in the lives of his African-American and white neighbors at a rural crossroads store.
♦ Students might list evidences of progress made in integration since the 1930s.
1. African-Americans—Fiction 2. Mississippi—Fiction 3. Southern States—Race relations 4. Race relations—Fiction.

Taylor, Mildred D. *The Road to Memphis*. Puffin (0-14-036077-8 pbk), 1990. 291p. (Interest level: 6-8).

Winner of the Coretta Scott King Award, this third book in the Logan family saga is set in 1940s Mississippi. This engaging book is about 17-year-old Cassie and her brother and friend's efforts to accompany their friend Moe to safety in Memphis after he fights racist attackers.
♦ Students may wish to compare this book with other Coretta Scott King Award winners.
1. Race relations—Fiction 2. Prejudices-Fiction 3. African-Americans—Fiction 4. Mississippi—Fiction 5. Southern States—Race relations.

Taylor, Mildred D. *Roll of Thunder, Hear My Cry*. Dial (0-8037-7473-7), 1976. 276p. (Interest level: 4-8).

This Newbery Award winner, set in Mississippi in 1933, begins the saga of Cassie Logan and her family as they try to maintain their independence as the only African-American people in their hometown to own their own land. Strong characters offer insight into the lifestyle and values of this southern family.
♦ Students may wish to compare the effects of the Depression on blacks and whites.

1. Blacks—Fiction 2. Depressions, Economic—Fiction 3. Mississippi—Fiction.

Taylor, Mildred D. *Song of the Trees*. Illus. by Jerry Pinkney. Dial (0-8037-5453-1), 1975. 48p. B/W illus. (Interest level: 4-8).

This book, first in the Logan Family saga, introduces eight-year-old Cassie Logan and her family, proud but poverty-stricken African-Americans in Mississippi. The illustrations enhance the story of this family being cheated into selling Cassie's beloved forest for very little money during the Depression.
♦ Students might study the various types of trees found in Mississippi.
1. Blacks—Fiction 2. Depressions, Economic—Fiction 3. Mississippi—Fiction.

Wallin, Luke. *The Slavery Ghosts*. Bradbury (0-02-792380-0), 1983. 121 p. (Interest level: 5-8).

In this ghost story by a Mississippi author, Livy and Jake James encounter Civil War ghosts while living in a large southern mansion. A good novel for boys and girls about the tragic events of the past that plague those living in the same mansion, in the same place, today.
♦ Students may follow up the story by researching a Civil War battle.
1. Ghosts—Fiction.

Wells, Dean Faulkner. *The Ghosts of Rowan Oak: William Faulkner's Ghost Stories for Children*. Illus. by John F. Davis. Yoknapatawpha (0-916242-7-1), 1980. 63p. B/W illus. (Interest level: 3-6).

The author recounts three of the ghost stories told to her as a child by her uncle the Nobel Prize winner, William Faulkner. She recaptures the magic of his storytelling and shares the feeling of what it was like to listen to the tales of the man she called "Pappy."
♦ Students may want to research more about William Faulkner's life in Rowan Oak.
1. Ghost stories 2. Faulkner, William 3. Mississippi—Fiction.

Periodicals

799.09762
Mississippi Outdoors. Mississippi Department of Wildlife, Fisheries, and Parks. Color photos. Six issues/year. $6.00. (Interest level: 4+).

This magazine contains beautiful color photography, informative articles, and occasional poems about out-of-doors, wildlife, and careers in the Magnolia State. Mississippi's natural beauty is highlighted with the lovely photos.
♦ Students may enjoy contrasting an outdoor sport from Mississippi with one from their own state.
1. Mississippi 2. Hunting—Mississippi—Periodicals 3. Fishing—Mississippi—Periodicals.

Professional Materials

810.8
Mississippi Writers: An Anthology. University Press of Mississippi (0-87805-479-0), 1991. 519p.

Selected from the four-volume set, *Reflections of Childhood and Youth*, this is an anthology of fiction, nonfiction, poetry, and drama by scores of Mississippi authors from Eudora Welty, William Faulkner, Richard Wright, and Margaret Walker Alexander to Barry Hannah, Lerone Bennett, Anne Moody, Shelby Foote, and Richard Ford. This excellent collection also includes 28 pages of biographical and bibliographical information.

♦ Teachers may wish to pursue additional works by these writers.

1. Mississippi—Literary collections 2. American literature—20th century 3. American literature—Mississippi 4. Children—Literary collections 5. Youth—Literary collections.

973

Lemann, Nicholas. *The Promised Land*. Knopf (0-394-56004-4), 1991. 410p.

This ALA Notable Book engagingly tells the stories—over fifty years—of several representative African-American families which left rural Mississippi Delta and moved to Chicago. It describes how the migration "changed the United States" from a country where race and African-American culture were primarily regional and rural issues into one where race relations affect life, society, politics, and culture of all U.S. society.

♦ Students may wish to explore the migration of peoples from their own regions.

1. African-Americans—Migrations—History—20th century 2. Rural-urban migration—United States—History—20th century.

975

Wilson, Charles Reagan and **Ferris, William**, eds. *Encyclopedia of Southern Culture*. University of North Carolina Press (0-8078-1823-2), 1989. 1634p.

Sponsored by the Center for the Study of Southern Culture at the University of Mississippi, this acclaimed award-winning reference book is organized "around twenty-four thematic sections, including history, religion, folklore, language, art, and architecture . . . literature, music . . ." etc. Over 800 scholars and writers in a variety of fields define, address and illuminate "the forces that have supported either the reality or the illusion of the southern way of life—people, places, ideas, institutions, events, symbols, rituals, and values."

♦ Students and teachers may wish to use this to supplement various topics in the classroom.

1. Southern States—Civilization—Dictionaries 2. Southern States—Dictionaries and encyclopedias.

976.2

Ethnic Heritage in Mississippi. University Press of Mississippi (0-87805-578-0), 1992. 212p. B/W illus. (Interest level: Professional).

This intriguing and comprehensive survey of the diverse heritage of the state uses essays by scholars to enhance a valuable multicultural study of the wide variety of ethnic groups in the state, beginning with Native Americans and including African Americans and a variety of Europeans and Asians. This is an excellent southern study with important national concerns of cultural identity and acculturation.

♦ Students may wish to research an ethnic groups from their own area.

1. Minorities—Mississippi—History 2. Mississippi—Race relations 3. Mississippi—Ethnic relations.

North Carolina

by Linda Veltze

Nonfiction

133.1
Smith, Beth Craddock. *Mystery Tour, A Student Guide to North Carolina Ghosts & Legends*. Broadfoot's (0-916107-94-9), 1992. 135p. B/W illus. (Interest level: 3-8).

This student centered book contains a collection of 25 legends and ghost stories from ancient times to the present day. Each story contains a vocabulary section, and at the end of the book, "Expanding" activity and "Understanding" sections that provide an opportunity for added dimensions of comprehension.
♦ Students can choose their favorite story and retell it in their own words, being prepared to introduce the story by explaining why it brings them enjoyment.
1. Ghosts—North Carolina. 2. Legends—North Carolina.

133.10
Carter, Catherine T. *Ghost Tales of the Moratoc*. John F. Blair (0-89587-091-6), 1992. 150p. (Interest level: 6-8).

The northeastern part of North Carolina, the Moratoc region, is the source of the tales told in this book, many of them passed on by the authors' now deceased relatives, and many retold from Native American tradition with local folklore intertwined. Each tale is different and unique and sprinkled with North Carolina local history.
♦ Students can read the story of White Feather, and the contemporary Native American woman who was visited by him, and then put their own thoughts in writing as to whether they believe we can be visited by people who have died years ago.
1. Ghost stories, American. 2. Ghosts—North Carolina.

133.10
Russell, Randy. *Mountain Ghost Stories and Curious Tales of Western North Carolina*. John F. Blair (0-89587-064-9), 1988. 109p. (Interest level: 6-8).

The Blue Ridge and Smoky Mountain areas have given rise to ghost stories of Native American and Anglo origin and are collected in this work. They would appeal to the reader who enjoys mystery and the supernatural with the background of a mountain society of yesteryear.
♦ Students may choose their favorite story and video themselves retelling it in their own words, and, if possible, adapting it to a geographical setting where they live.
1. Ghosts—North Carolina. 2. Witchcraft—North Carolina. 3. Ghosts—Appalachian Mountains. 4. Witchcraft—Appalachian Mountains.

371.10
Houston, Gloria. *My Great-Aunt Arizona*. Illus. by Susan Condie Lamb. HarperCollins (0-06-022606-4; 0-06-022607-2 lib bind), 1922. 16p. (Interest level: 2-8).

This story of a woman from birth to her death at 93 years of age is replete with luscious details of Blue Ridge Mountain life and the enjoyment of a life fully lived. The illustrations allow one to read in between the lines and see how an empowered woman of yesteryear made her mark on the world through her global vision, her affection for children, and her dedication to the teaching profession, which was her vehicle for expressing these gifts.
♦ Just as Gloria Houston tells about a favorite relative of hers, children can write a story (a shorter version than this one) about one incident when a favorite relative that they love, helped them in a special way.
1. Hughes, Arizona Houston, 1876-1969—Juvenile literature. 2. Teachers—Appalachian Region—Biography—Juvenile literature.

398.20
Brown, Virginia Pounds and **Owens, Laurella**. *Southern Indian Myths and Legends*. Illustrated by Nathan H. Glick. Beechwood (0-912221-02-X), 1985. 159p. B/W illus. (Interest level: 4-8).

Eighteen Cherokee legends are included among these stories from seven southern tribes, many of which were collected between 1887 and 1989 and told by people who as children associated with the myth-keepers and priests of the tribes. The similarities of story between the different tribes is noted and the evolution of the story as it is presented provides a special type of information as to how oral tradition becomes a written one.

♦ Students may read the Cherokee story of Spear-finger and compare it with such stories as Hansel and Gretel and Little Red Riding Hood and decide which story is the most frightening and why.

1. Indians of North America—Southern States—Legends.

398.20
Caduto, Michael J. and **Bruchac, Joseph**. *Native American Stories Told by Joseph Fruchac* (from *Keepers of the Earth*). Illus. by John Kahionhes Fadden. Fulcrum Publishing (1-55591-094-7 pbk), 1991. 145p. B/W illus. (Interest level: 3-8).

Sixteen Native American tribal traditions and their histories are represented in this collection of stories, including two Cherokee stories from North Carolina. This important work chronicles the importance of story-telling in our lives and the special contribution of stories from the Native American tradition that reinforce the wisdom of humans seeking a balance with nature.

♦ Students may explore the relationship that the "Coming of the Corn" describes between humans and the plants that give them food, and in "Awi Usdi, the Little Deer," which describes the relationship between humans and the animals that give them food. They may then compose a new story wherein the old Grandmother of the first story meets Awi Usdi, the deer, in the second.

1. Indians of North America—Legends. 2. Indians of North America—Religion and mythology.

398.20
Goode, Diane. *The Diane Goode Book of American Folk Tales & Songs*. Collected by Ann Durell. Illus. by the author. E.P. Dutton (0-525-44458-0), 1989. 63p. (Interest level: 1-8).

In addition to the Appalachian story of "The Three Girls with the Journey-Cakes," the song "On Top of Old Smokey," and a story about Davy Crockett, the book also recounts an African-American tale from North Carolina called "The Talking Mule." Notable for its inclusion of several African-American folktales and its delightful illustrations, this book spans several regions and cultures to provide an introduction to the American oral tradition of story and song.

♦ Extending the theme of "The Talking Mule," students can write a story about what their pet or one in their neighborhood would say if he or she could talk.

1. Tales—United States—Juvenile literature 2. Folk songs, English—United States—Juvenile literature.

398.20 (Reference)
Lankford, George E., comp. and ed. *Native American Legends, Southeastern Legends: Tales from the Natchez, Caddo, Biloxi, Chickasaw, and Other Nations*. (American Folklore Series). August House (0-87483-039-7 pbk), 1987. 265p. B/W illus. (Interest level: 7-8).

Twelve narratives of the Cherokees are included in this work, which provides valuable scholarly materials on the origins of the Native American peoples of the

Southeast, and discusses one tribe's influence upon another. Narratives are divided into two chapters called "The Ways of the World," and "Adventures," and introductions to each chapter include valuable information for the study of the Native Americans of this region.

♦ The class may form groups, each group choosing an animal to represent them and then conduct a storytelling festival, using a Native American narrative, whose main character is the animal from that group.

1. Indians of North America—Southern States—Legends. 2. Indians of North America—Legends.

398.20
Walser, Richard. *North Carolina Legends*. Division of Archives and History/North Carolina Department of Cultural Resources (0-86526-139-3 pbk), 1980, 1986. 76p. Available from Broadfoot's. (Interest level: 6-8).

Over 40 diverse legends and tales are portrayed here with something to please, enchant, and entertain almost anyone. They range from Native American tales to those depicting famous characters (Daniel Boone, George Washington, etc.) to Jack tales and ghost stories to stories of magical and legendary happenings. In the chapter, "Notes and Sources," the origin of each legend is described along with the books containing the earliest known versions of these legends.

♦ Each student can choose a favorite tale or legend, and make a poster illustrating or symbolizing the legend. This can form the basis for an in-class storytelling festival where, in their own words, students can recount their chosen tale, and those hearing the tale can summarize the historical, geographical, or cultural facts learned from these recountings.

1. North Carolina—Legends 2. Folklore—North Carolina

398.21
Compton, Kenn and **Compton, Joanne**. *Jack and the Giant Chaser, an Appalachian Tale*. Illus by Kenn Compton. Holiday House (0-8234-0998-8), 1993. Unpaginated. Color illus. (Interest level: 2-5).

Set in the Appalachian Mountains of North Carolina, this is a tale of a smart young boy, and an easily duped giant. It is fast moving, told in a type of cleaned-up mountain dialect, and celebrates Jack's courage, his ability to think on his feet, and his ability to trick the giant into fearing the worst.

♦ The story reveals Jack's thoughts: "since everybody thought he was a hero, he figured he'd have to try and act like one." Students should decide whether the events of the entire story lead them to think Jack was a real hero; they will need to justify their opinions.

1. Folklore—United States. 2. Giants—Folklore.

398.21
Haley, Gail E. *Jack and the Bean Tree*. Illus. by author. Crown (0-517-55717-7), 1986. 43p. (Interest level: 1-5).

The source of this story is the legacy of Jack Tales found in the mountains of North Carolina today that tells of the familiar Jack in the Beanstalk in an Appalachian environment. Nature and magic abound throughout this story of Jack's curiosity and daring.

♦ Two students can work together imagining they have just come into possession of a giant's magic tablecloth and seeing if they can agree on foods that are so delicious they can never get enough of them. The team should work together to create a poster showing their favorite foods.
1. Fairy tales 2. Folklore—England 3. Giants—Fiction.

398.21

Haley, Gail E. *Jack and the Fire Dragon*. Illus. by author. Crown (0-817-56814-4), 1988. 35p. (Interest level: 1-5).

The teller of this spellbinding tale, Poppyseed, was modeled after the author's North Carolina grandmother, the vehicle for a story that enchants listeners and readers with the adventures of Jack who ventured down into the Fire Dragaman's hole and ends up with a beautiful wife, gold, and wives for his two brothers. Dynamic and authentic, the work has as its source the tales of North Carolina's most famous storytellers, Ray Hicks and the late Cratis Williams.
♦ By renaming themselves Jack or Jacqueline, students can tell a tale of a real life adventure, changing what they need to of the real life story to make it spooky, scary, and adventurous.
1. Fairy tales 2. Folklore—United States.

398.22

Haley, Gail E. *Mountain Jack Tales, as Told and Illustrated by Gail E. Haley*. Dutton Children's Books (0-525-44974-4), 1992. 131p. B/W illus. (Interest level: 3-8).

Containing a wealth of information about life in the North Carolina Appalachians, this wonderful collection of "Jack Tales" is written as though the tales were spoken from the mouth of the expert storyteller, Poppyseed. They include nine different "Jack" tales, the author's comments about universal sources of the tales, rationale for the use of the lemon woodblock engravings used to illustrate the story, and a glossary of words still used in the mountains of North Carolina today.
♦ The children can tell a simple story of their own choosing, using as many of the expressions contained in the glossary or that they found in the "Jack" tales, as they comfortably can.
1. Tales—United States. 2. Folklore—United States.

398.22

Hunter, C.W. *The Green Gourd: A North Carolina Folktale*. Illus. by Tony Griego. G.P. Putnam's Sons (0-399-22278-2), 1992. 32p. (Interest level: K-8).

Based on a North Carolina folktale that may have Native American origins, this humorous adventure tells of a woman who defies local wisdom by choosing a gourd before it's ripe to replace the dipper she lost, is chased by the green gourd gone mad with witchery, and is finally saved by a young boy who smashes it. Retold in local dialect, the green gourd, with a personality all its own, is rivaled in interest only by the spry old woman whom the illustrations show to be energetic, fun-loving, and not above celebrating her victory with the rest of the "critters" over biscuits and butter.
♦ The class should decide on a list of common sayings that offer a type of advice or warning; individuals can then create a story on their own about what happened to them one day when they decided to do the opposite of the advice contained in the saying.
1. Folklore—North Carolina.

508.75

Dean, Jim and **Earley, Lawrence S**., eds., *Wildlife in North Carolina*. University of North Carolina Press (0-8078-1751-1), 1987, 201p. B/W and Color photos. (Interest level: 4-8).

This book is a collection of articles and photos spanning 50 years from the North Carolina magazine, "Wildlife in North Carolina." Lovely photos and a variety of writing styles make this a captivating book that speaks of sports, flora and fauna, special places in North Carolina, and hunting and fishing.
♦ Students can read about the possum in "The Ultimate Survivor" and learn how the possum was not a favored character in North American Native American legends but was a type of bearer diety in some South American cultures. Students may learn to recount from memory one of the Cherokee legends about the possum.
1. Natural history—North Carolina. 2. Nature conservation—North Carolina. 3. North Carolina—Description and travel.

582.13 (Reference)

Batson, Wade T. *Wild Flowers in the Carolinas*. University of South Carolina Press (0-87249-504-3), 1990. 153p. (Interest level: 4-8).

This authoritative work describes the wild flowers of North and South Carolina with photographs, categories, and locations where they can be found. The introduction discusses endangered plant species and the factors causing the proliferation of endangered species; it also provides an explanation for each plant's common and scientific name and an illustrated glossary to help the reader understand the context in which many terms throughout the book are used.
♦ Students may pay a visit to a craft shop or a florist that features dried wild flower arrangements to obtain the names of the flowers that make up an arrangement; they may then see how many of the flowers are native to North Carolina and in what areas and seasons they flourish.
1. Wild flowers—North Carolina—Identification 2. Wild flowers—South Carolina—Identification.

582.16 (Reference)

Duncan, Wilbur and **Duncan, Marion**. *Trees of the Southeastern United States*. University of Georgia Press (0-8203-0954-0), 1988. 322p. Color photos. (Interest level: 4-8).

This well-organized reference work includes introductory chapters, a glossary, and detailed information about 11 major groups of trees in this area of the United States. Each tree in the major groups has a map of the U.S. alongside its entry, which shows the states where the tree is found.
♦ Students can make a list of all the trees found in North Carolina and put an interesting fact by the name of each tree, i.e., the tree comes from Asia or is eaten as food by wildlife.
1. Trees—Southern States—Identification.

597.92
Cutchins, Judy and **Johnston, Ginny**. *Scoots the Bog Turtle*. Illus. by Frances Smith. Atheneum (0-689-31440-X), 1989. 32p. Color illus. (Interest level: 2-4).

The chain of life in the bog of North Carolina is revealed through the story of Scoots the turtle. The illustrations and text will capture the magic of the bog for the young child and tell the story of a myriad of animals: owls, bats, bees, birds, butterflies, insects, chickadees, foxes, frogs, honeybees, mice, raccoons, salamanders, skunks, snails, and snakes.
♦ Each child should select one animal to talk about in order to create a "class" story. The teacher will open with the beginning sentence, and then each student will add a sentence mentioning the animal selected but creating the plot of the story as it goes along, with the teacher providing an ending to the story if one has not already surfaced.
1. Bog turtle—Juvenile literature. 2. Bogs—Juvenile literature. 3. Bog turtle. 4. Bogs. 5. Turtles.

629.13
Freedman, Russell. *The Wright Brothers, How They Invented the Airplane*. Photos by Wilbur and Orville Wright. Holiday House. (0-8234-0875-2), 1991. 129p. B/W photos. (Interest level: 4-8).

This Newbery Honor Book recounts the story of the Wright brothers in the context of worldwide scientific inquiry into the principles of flying, and does so in a tale filled with joy, frustration, and adventure. Historic photographs and details about the several successful flights at Kitty Hawk, North Carolina, make this section of the book memorable and impressive.
♦ The students can pretend they are Madame Hart O. Berg, the first woman to fly as a passenger in an airplane (p. 94), and describe their impressions of this amazing experience to their dearest friend.
1. Wright, Orville, 1871-1948—Juvenile literature.
2. Wright, Wilbur, 1867-1912—Juvenile literature.
3. Aeronautics—United States—Biography— Juvenile literature.

629.13
Hook, Jason. *The Wright Brothers* Illus. by Peter Lowe. Bookwright (0-531-18279-7), 1989. (Great Lives Series). 32p. Colored illus.; B/W photos. (Interest level: 3-5).

The story of the Wright Brothers is told making a strong connection between the scientific curiosity of their youth, inventions in their later years, scientific research, and the success of their airplane and airflight. It also describes the close relationship between the two brothers within the Wright family, making possible such a successful working relationship. Also mentioned are the ups and downs of the acceptance of this invention, until finally its success was heralded all over the world. It includes a listing of important dates, a glossary, and a list of books to read.
♦ Students should make a note of all the city names mentioned as they read the story and then locate these on a large map, placing a marker to call attention to its location. Students can tell the story of the Wright brothers in their own words using these geographical locations to show the spread of their influence around the world.

1. Wright, Wilbur, 1867-1912—Juvenile literature 2. Wright, Orville, 1871-1948—Juvenile literature 3. Aeronautics—United States—Biography—Juvenile literature.

629.13
Schulz, Walter A. *Will and Orv*. Illustrated by Janet Schulz. Carolrhoda Books (0-87614-669-8), 1991. 48p. Color illus. (Interest level: 1-3).

Based on historical records, the story of the first historic flight with a motor aircraft at Kitty Hawk, North Carolina, is told as though it were through the eyes of an actual witness, Johnny Moore, a young boy who grew to know the Wright brothers from their frequent visits to the area. The color illustrations help to make it an exciting and moving story of a successful scientific experiment.
♦ Students can imagine themselves the neighbors of another important inventor and tell of their reactions to witnessing the success of a new invention.
1. Wright, Orville, 1871-1948—Juvenile literature.
2. Wright, Wilbur, 1867-1912—Juvenile literature.
3. Aeronautics—History—United States— Juvenile literature.

629.13
Stein, R. Conrad. *The Story of the Flight at Kitty Hawk*. Illus. by R. Conrad Stein. Children's (0-516-04614-4), 1981. (Cornerstones of Freedom Series). 31p. (Interest level: 3-6).

Tells the story of the Wright Brother's success at Kitty Hawk, North Carolina, along with the events following their success.
♦ The story documents Orville's disappointment that his invention made possible the use of aircraft in World War I. Students may give an example from their own life when something they did, which was not bad in and of itself, resulted in a terrible consequence.
1. Wright, Orville, 1871-1948—Juvenile literature
2. Wright, Wilbur, 1867-1912—Juvenile literature.

629.13
Taylor, Richard L. *The First Flight: The Story of the Wright Brothers*. Watts (0-531-10891-0), 1990. 64p. Color illus. (Interest level: 3-6).

This book describes the challenges facing the Wright brothers and the research that led to their triumph at Kitty Hawk, North Carolina, in 1903. The text is highlighted by historical photographs that hint at the dynamism and tenacity of these famous brothers.
♦ Students may read the biography of a modern day inventor and compare and contrast his or her life to that of the Wright brothers.
1. Wright, Wilbur, 1867-1912—Juvenile literature
2. Wright, Orville, 1871-1948—Juvenile literature.

641.59
Tartan, Beth. *North Carolina and Old Salem Cookery*. New and rev. ed. University of North Carolina Press (9-8078-2035-0), 1992. 382p. (Interest level: 6-8).

The compiler of this cookbook sees the twenties and thirties as a "gentler, kinder life." This treasury of details about that way of life and the recipes that fortified it is well researched and tells the reader about

the way of life that gave birth to these recipes. Unfortunately, this way of life was a racially segregated one.
♦ Students should read about Lulu Rucker, the Herb Woman in Chapter 17, and then draw a picture of how they would imagine her to be, listing some of the herbs she might be selling to her customers on Saturday mornings.
1. Cookery, American—Southern style 2. Cookery—North Carolina.

709.75

Manley, Roger. *Signs and Wonders: Outsider Art Inside North Carolina*. North Carolina Museum of Art (0-88259-957-7), 1989. Available from University of North Carolina Press. 135p. Color and B/W photos. (Interest level: 7-8).

The concept of "outsider" art is compared and contrasted with the artistic process as it is more commonly conceived. The work contains photographs of the North Carolina artists with their work and a description of the lifestyle that supports such creativity.
♦ Students can reflect on the dream-like aspect of "outsider" art and make a sketch of some "outsider" art that would fit in their school.
1. North Carolina Museum of Art—Catalogs. 2. Folk art—North Carolina—Exhibitions—Catalogs. 3. Folk artists—North Carolina—Exhibitions—Catalogs. 4. North Carolina Museum of Art.

781.62

Cotten, Elizabeth. *Freight Train and Other North Carolina Folk Songs and Tunes* (Sound recording). Smithsonian Folkways Records (No ISBN), 1989. Smithsonian #C-SF 40009. (30 min.). $9.50 for cassette tape, $14.00 for C.D. (Interest level: 3-8).

This recording by an African-American woman in her early sixties includes songs sung in the style of southeastern North Carolina country ragtime picking, church songs, blues, and traditional songs from the state. Elizabeth Cotten, winner of a Grammy and many other awards, records these regional songs in an authentic and unpretentious manner.
♦ Elizabeth Cotten cleaned houses for many years until she was discovered by chance; after several years she began giving concerts and making recordings. Students should try to convince someone they know who is over 60 to record a song that they sang in their childhood. Students can then try to discover the hidden beauty in the songs of an ordinary person.
1. Folksongs—North Carolina.

790

Ide, Eleanor. *Lost Colony Games, First English Games Brought to America*. Sparks Press (0-916822-12-5 pbk), 1984. 36p. B/W illus. (Interest level: 3-8).

This well-researched and clearly written book is a compilation of games that could have been played by the sixteenth-century Roanoke voyagers and is interspersed with history of the early colonists to North Carolina. Three type of games are described: games for the crowded conditions on board ships, games for the closely built settlement houses, and games for the open space of field or beach.
♦ Students may choose their favorite game in the book and play it with the necessary number of friends. The players should give themselves first and last names that might have been held by those early colony voyagers.
1. Games—England. 2. Games—North Carolina. 3. Roanoke Colony (N.C.)

809

Buckner, Sally. *Our Words, Our Ways, Readings and Writing in North Carolina*. Carolina Academic Press (0-89089-401-9), 1991. 616p. B/W photos. (Interest level: 8+).

This multicultural and varied anthology of North Carolina authors is organized into themes of "heritage" and "home" with each work prefaced by a general introduction, biographical sketch of the author, a "language alert" to explain outdated dialect or unfamiliar words, and a "reflecting" section to extend the theme or ideas of the piece. The work is outstanding for its scope and richness of presentation.
♦ Students should read the 1952 poem "Sharecropper" and then compose a short poem about a "have-not" of the present day.
1. Authors, American 2. North Carolina 3. North Carolina—Literatures.

810.992

Broadfoot, Jan and **Barrow, Joyce**, comp. *Contemporary North Carolina Authors*. Broadfoot's (No ISBN), 1989, 1990. 25+p. per packet. B/W photos. (Interest level: 5-8).

In a three-ring binder format, this work features 150 North Carolina authors who speak about their personal backgrounds, their working environment, their previous jobs, and their work and how the people and places of North Carolina are reflected in it. This work supplies a wealth of information, difficult to locate elsewhere, and also offers, on the part of each author, advice to aspiring young writers.
♦ Students can impersonate their favorite author and give a booktalk on one of his or her books, including autobiographical details from this work.
1. Authors, American—North Carolina—Biography 2 Authors, American—20th century—Biography.

813.54

Carter, Forrest. *The Education of Little Tree*. University of New Mexico Press (0-8263-0879-1 pbk.), 1976. (Interest level: 7-8).

Forrest Carter recalls his upbringing by his Eastern Cherokee grandparents from North Carolina in this well-written account of his boyhood in the 1930s. This griping and memorable story will fascinate young people and give them an understanding, through literature, of the differences in outlook between the Native American and white worlds.
♦ Students can read the account of the Trail of Tears and discuss as to whether it was properly named, or whether they would have preferred a different one.
1. Carter, Forrest—Biography—Youth. 2. Novelists, American—20th century—Biography. 3. Cherokee Indians—Biography.

813.54
Davis, Donald D. *Barking at a Fox-Fur Coat, Family Stories and Tall Tales*. August House (0-87483-141-5), 1991. 206p. Interest level: 5-8).

In the "Notes," Donald Davis indicates the development of each of his 17 stories from a family happening in his rural North Carolina home until it reached its final form. Humorous, dramatic, and suspenseful, Davis' portrayal of real people out of his childhood is such that one can relate to, chuckle over, be amazed at, and finally envy Davis for this rich heritage of memories.
♦ Students may read all of the "pet" stories in the book, especially the Tall Tale of "Uncle Gudger's First Pet," and then write a newspaper article (using a Tall Tale twist) with an attention-getting headline about the amazing activities they have witnessed of a pet in their neighborhood.
1. Davis family—Folklore—Fiction 2. Tales—North Carolina.

813.54
Davis, Donald D. *Listening for the Crack of Dawn*. August House (0-87483-153-9), 1990. 220p. (Interest level: 5-8).

Fourteen stories are told about Donald Davis's youth in the North Carolina mountains. Humorous, poignant, and enthralling, they serve both as an inspiration for teachers who attempt to fashion student-centered education, and for students who, through these stories, are charmed into realizing that real adventure, courage, and fun are packed into the ordinary events of life.
♦ Students should read the last story about "A Different Drummer" and think about what being a hero really means. They can then write a letter to the soldier who deserted the Vietnam troops and let him know what they feel about the action he took.
1. Davis family—Folklore—Fiction 2. Tales—North Carolina.

813.54
Davis, Donald D. *Listening for the Crack of Dawn* (Audiocassette). August House, 1991. 2 audiocassettes, (2 hours). (Interest level: 5-8).

Four stories from the book of the same title are recorded in Davis's inimitable voice, serious in tone, yet subtle in its clever and witty way of remembering a young boy's discovery of the world. Characterizations of the important people in Davis's life make this recording one which transports the listener to the mountains of North Carolina.
♦ Students can listen to the LS/MFT story and imagine how Terrell's mother felt knowing that the neighborhood boys were needlessly afraid of her son; they can then record a telephone conversation between her and her best friend about the problem and what she wants to do about it.
1. Davis family—Folklore—Fiction 2. Tales—North Carolina.

917.56
Biggs, Walter C. *State Parks of North Carolina*. John F. Blair (0-89587-071-1), 1989. B/W illus. 339p. (Interest level: 7-8).

This systematic collection of data about the state parks of North Carolina provides not only important information of interest to the tourist, but maps, historical data, and information about regional products and plant and animal life that is of interest to students and teachers. Included are names and addresses of each state park and of various state agencies (private and governmental) that are related to the preservation and dissemination of information on state parks.
♦ The children may write a poem about some aspect of a particular state park in North Carolina, using as inspiration information obtained from this book, and color photographs of North Carolina state parks in *National Geographic* or other books of scenic photos.
1. Parks—North Carolina—Guidebooks. 2. North Carolina—Description and travel—1981—Guidebooks.

917.56
Fradin, Dennis B. *North Carolina*. (From Sea to Shining Sea Series). Childrens Press (0-516-03833-8), 1992. 64p. Color and B/W illus. (Interest level: 3-6).

This comprehensive history of North Carolina runs from the arrival, 12,000 years ago, of the Native American to 1992. This book, with its glossary, time line of North Carolina history, summary of North Carolina noteworthy information, gallery of famous North Carolinians, etc., manages to put even the trivial into an important context.
♦ After reading the book, students can study the picture map of North Carolina (p. 5) and identify all the people on the map, numbering them in chronological order for their appearance in North Carolina history and distinguishing those that represent actual personalities and those that represent groups of people.
1. North Carolina—Juvenile literature.

917.56
Leland, Elizabeth. *The Vanishing Coast*. John F. Blair (0-89587-092-4), 1992. 141p. B/W photos. (Interest level: 6-8).

A chapter is dedicated to each of the cities along the South and North Carolina coast, making the area and its history come to life in the stories of its people and their revealing photographs. One senses the preciousness of these tales because of the changes that modernization and development have imposed upon the trades and lifestyles of the island inhabitants.
♦ Students may read the story of the Menhaden Chanteymen, the African-American netpullers of Beaufort, North Carolina, and the honors they have received, and compose the lyrics to a similar question-and-answer song that could be sung by a group of people who do very hard physical work.
1. Atlantic Coast Region (S.C.)—Description and travel 2. Atlantic Coast Region (S.C.)—Social life and customs 3. Atlantic Coast Region (N.C.)—Description and travel 4. Atlantic Coast Region (N.C.)—Social life and customs 5. Leland, Elizabeth, 1954—Journeys—South Carolina—Atlantic Coast 6. Leland, Elizabeth, 1954—Journeys—North Carolina—Atlantic Coast.

917.56 (Reference)
Ockershausen, Jane. *The North Carolina One-Day Trip Book*. EPM Publications, Inc. (0-939009-38-2), 1990. 304p. B/W illus. (Interest level: 5-8).

With a view toward making a successful one-day trip filled with adventure, history, and folklore, the book offers trips in the Northwest and Southwest Mountains, the Northern and Southern Foothills, the Heartland, and the Northern and Southern Coast of North Carolina. In addition to the above, the guide makes interesting reading for the traveler who wishes to have a grasp on a situation before leaving, with details about schedules and seasonal events.
♦ Students can choose their favorite one-day trip and write a short play about it; some of the characters could tell about the history of the place and others could be people that they might meet while on the trip.
1. North Carolina—Description and travel—1981—Tours.

917.56
Sakowski, Carolyn. *Touring the Western North Carolina Backroads*. John F. Blair (0-89587-077-0), 1990. 305p. B/W illus. (Interest level: 6-8).

Twenty-one tours were created in this very popular mountainous region for their especially rich historical tradition, folklore, and legend as well as extraordinary scenery. Giving enough detail to follow on an actual trip, the book makes fascinating reading and gives a feel for why the author selected the backroads instead of the impersonal highway.
♦ Students can pretend they are Malinda Blalock, who joined the Confederate army pretending to be a man just so she could follow her husband, and that they have just arrived home and are beginning to tell their story (p. 234).
1. North Carolina—Description and travel—1981—Tours. 2. Historic sites—North Carolina—Guidebooks. 3. Automobiles—Road Guides—North Carolina. 4. North Carolina—History, Local.

917.56
Young, Claiborne S. *Cruising Guide to North Carolina*. John F. Blair (0-89587-074-6), 1983. 301p. B/W photos. (Interest level: 6-8).

The entire North Carolina coast, the largest area of inland waters on the East Coast of the U.S., is explored with navigational data and details about local setting, restaurants, lodging, and historical facts and folklore. Though intended as a manual for boaters exploring the coasts of North Carolina, the possibilities for vicarious voyages make this book an interesting one for younger adventurers.
♦ North Carolina students can make a poster depicting their coastal location, and all students can draw themselves as a crew member in the original Roanoke settlement, as an assistant in the Wright brothers expedition at Kitty Hawk, as a member of the Edenton Tea Party at Edenton, or as part of Blackbeard's crew in the Battle at Ocracoke.
1. Boats and boating—North Carolina—Guide-books 2. North Carolina—Description and travel—1981—Guidebooks.

917.68
Radlauer, Ruth. *Great Smoky Mountains National Park*. Photographs by Rolf Zillmer. Childrens Press (0-516-07489-X), 1985. 48p. Color photos. (Interest level: 3-8).

This book describes the area, way of life, and history of the Great Smoky Mountains and its National Park and what can be seen and experienced by the traveler of today. The beautiful photographs and artful narrative fuse to recreate a special mood peculiar to the region.
♦ Students may choose a section of the narrative that can be dramatized by groups of students (in costume) using a musical background and portraying the activities mentioned in the prose.
1. Great Smoky Mountains National Park—Juvenile literature

917.68
Walker, Steven L. *Great Smoky Mountains, the Splendor of the Southern Appalachians*. Camelback Design Group (1-879924-09-9), 1991. 64p. Color photos. (Interest level: 4-8).

The Great Smoky Mountains of eastern Tennessee and western North Carolina are described in geological, biological, ecological, and historical terms. These mountains are beautifully described and photographed as a governmentally protected area where wildlife can flourish.
♦ Students may do a special radio feature broadcast about the Great Smoky Mountains as the "Salamander Capitol of the World," and research some of these 26 different species to add facts to their presentation.
1. Great Smoky Mountains (N.C. and Tenn.) 2. Great Smoky Mountains (N.C. and Tenn.)—Pictorial works 3. Great Smoky Mountains National Park (N.C. and Tenn.) 4. Mountain ecology—Great Smoky Mountains (N.C. and Tenn.)

970
Perdue, Theda. *Native Carolinians, the Indians of North Carolina*. Division of Archives and History/North Carolina Department of Cultural Resources (0-86526-217-9 pbk), 1985. 73p. B/W photos. (Available from Broadfoot's). (Interest level: 7-8).

Much valuable information about the Cherokee, Lumbee, and lesser known tribes in North Carolina is contained in this work. The history begins with the earliest arrival of the Native Americans to North Carolina and continues to the current decade. Black-and-white photographs and drawings provide excellent documentation.
♦ Students may examine the listings of "Important Dates of North Carolina Indian History," choosing one date (from the 1940s to the present) and make a short radio announcement detailing the facts surrounding the event.
1. Indians of North America—North Carolina 2. North Carolina—History.

971.68
Walker, Steven L. *Great Smoky Mountains, the Splendor of the Southern Appalachians*. Camelback/Elan

Venture (1-879924-02-1 pbk), 1991. Unpaginated. Color photos. (Interest level: 3-8).

Wonderful maps, breathtaking views poetically photographed, and clear science instruction, aided by well done color illustrations and diagrams, make this book on the Smoky Mountains National Park an enjoyable and instructional work. The park covers two states, and students of North Carolina will learn little-known information about the area from this attractive book.

♦ Students may begin an imaginary trip to the Smoky Mountains and write the first page of their diary telling how their trip began and what their impressions were.

1. Great Smoky Mountains (N.C. and Tenn.) 2. Great Smoky Mountains (N.C. and Tenn.)—Pictorial works. 3. Great Smoky Mountains National Park (N.C. and Tenn.) 4. Mountain ecology—Great Smoky Mountains (N.C. and Tenn.).

973

Perdue, Theda. *The Cherokee* Chelsea House (1-55546-695-8), 1988. (Indians of North America Series). 111p. Color and B/W photos. (Interest level: 6-8).

This substantive and sensitive portrayal of the Cherokee tribes relates their history in the context of their rich culture. Chronicled in the story are the early intermarriages with white traders, the influence of the missionary schools, and the forced migration in the "Trail of Tears." Two chapters deal with the Eastern Band of the Cherokees in northwestern North Carolina (the Oconaluftee Cherokees) and the Cherokee story (Eastern and Western Bands) of the twentieth century.

♦ Students may prepare a mural depicting the myths of the Cherokee people, their traditional way of life (including crafts and social organization), the Trail of Tears, and the geographical location of the Cherokee Bands in the twentieth century.

1. Cherokee Indians

973.6

Lillegard, Dee. *James K. Polk, Eleventh President of the United States*. Childrens Press (0-516-01351-3), 1988. (Encyclopedia of Presidents Series). 98p. B/W photos and illus. (Interest level: 3-7).

Featured in this book is the story of James Polk, a North Carolina son, with family and educational roots in North Carolina, and how his life influenced the political life of the country at that time. Historical photographs and a chronology of American history from 1492 to 1987 are provided and serve to set the story in its historical framework.

♦ Students may contrast the election campaign of James Polk with recent presidential election campaigns and contrast the positive and negative features of each.

1. Polk, James K. (James Knox), 1795, 1849—Juvenile literature. 2. Presidents—United States—Biography—Juvenile literature.

974

Cheek, Pauline Binkley. *Appalachian Scrapbook: An ABC of Growing Up in the Mountains*. Appalachian Consortium Press (0-913239-44-5 pbk), 1988. 161p. B/W illus. (Interest level: 3-6).

Delightful charcoal illustrations punctuate each page of this North Carolina family's history. After the enticing introduction, the highlights of the scrapbook are organized according to the alphabet (A-Z). Within these confines, all the folklore and fun, the history of Native Americans and later settlers, and the folktales, foods, and language of the mountain people are experienced through the eyes and ears of a child.

♦ Students may wish to, in a personal scrapbook, use the letters of the alphabet to guide them as they tell the story of their family.

1. Appalachian Region, Southern—Juvenile literature.

975

Brown, Virginia Pounds and **Owens, Laurella**. *The World of the Southern Indians*. Illus. by Nathan H. Glick. Beechwood Books (0-912221-00-3), 1990. 176p. B/W illus. (Interest level: 5-8).

This work identifies North Carolina as one of the five states with the largest Native American populations; it is home to the Hatteras, Tuscaroras, Catawbas, Cheraws, Cherokees, Lumbees. The reader is treated to an interesting, clear discussion of Native American life in North Carolina, Alabama, Florida, Georgia, Mississippi, South Carolina, and Tennessee, along with maps showing Native American tribal settlements, illustrations of their way of life, portraits of famous historical figures, place names of today drawn from the original Native American languages, and lists of important historical sites to visit.

♦ Students may write to the different museums and historical sites listed for North Carolina, asking for any information about North Carolina Indian history and the exhibits that they have, and use this information to make a collage, attaching any representations of diet, tools, pictures and clothing that they are able to collect for each of the tribes.

1. Indians of North America—Southern states—Juvenile literature.

975

Lepthien, Emilie. *The Cherokee*. Children's Press (0-516-01938-4), 1985. (New True Books). 48p. Color and B/W photos. (Interest level: 1-3).

The arrival of the Native Americans to this continent is described in easy-to-read terms. The history and customs of the Cherokee are described and a section is provided on the Eastern Band of the Cherokee who reside in North Carolina.

♦ Students may learn more about the Trail of Tears and pretend they are Cherokee elders telling their grandchildren about what happened on this march, describing the hardships in their own words and how they felt having to leave the land to go to a new one.

1. Cherokee Indians—Juvenile literature.

975

Mancini, Richard E. *Indians of the Southeast*. Facts of File (0-8160-2390-5), 1992. (The First Americans Series). 96p. Color and B/W photos and illus. (Interest level: 3-8).

Several tribes of Native Americans in North Carolina are discussed in detail throughout this work. Information about the various tribes of southeastern Indians are integrated under common themes of "roots," "living," "ritual, religion, and traditions," and "change" and discussed in an interesting and thorough fashion.

♦ Students can check the business directory of the phone company in their city and see how many businesses are listed under "wood carving" and "wood working" to determine how common the wood carving traditions of such peoples as the North Carolina Cherokees (p. 92) are in cities today.

1. Indians of North America—Southeastern States—Juvenile literature.

975
Moore, Warren. *Mountain Voices: A Legacy of the Blue Ridge and Great Smokies*. Globe Pequot Press (0-87106-671-8), 1988. 276p. Color photos. (Interest level: 7-8).

This carefully crafted story of a journey through the mountains attests to the culture of its peoples, folklore, history, and their firsthand accounts of survival. The work includes the names and photos of over 150 of its contributors. The book dispels many stereotypes about mountain culture and gives meaning to well-known customs.

♦ Students can make a list of all the new things they have learned that they haven't read about in any other history book. Students can also speak with an elderly friend or relative and find out if they learned anything from their ancestors about the Civil War, or the Depression, or Native American traditions, and share this with the class.

1. Blacks—Fiction 2. Slavery—Fiction 3. Magic—Fiction.

975 (Reference)
Wilson, Charles Reagan and **Ferris, William**, eds. *Encyclopedia of Southern Culture*. University of North Carolina Press (0-8078-1823-2), 1989. 1634p. B/W photos. (Interest level: 6+).

This interdisciplinary study of the South provides a synthesis of current scholarship running the gamut from "Agriculture" to "Violence" and "Women's Life." This well-written multi-cultural work yields much information on North Carolina: biographies on well-known politicians, newscasters, presidents, and authors. Hundreds of references to the state are contained in this fascinating volume.

♦ In the section about the "Mythic South," students can read about some of the "myths" that seem to be in vogue today. The class can write to the North Carolina State Department of Tourism and see if the literature they receive (the photographs and the language used) give evidence of the continuation of some of the southern myths they have read about.

1. Southern States—Civilization—Dictionaries 2. Southern States— Dictionaries and encyclopedias.

975.6
Aylesworth, Thomas G. and **Aylesworth, Virginia L.**. *Lower Atlantic, North Carolina, South Carolina*. Chelsea House (1-55546-556-0), 1988. (Let's Discover the States Series). 64p. Color illus. (Interest level: 3-5).

Thirty-five pages are dedicated to North Carolina with important information about the state's past and present, including descriptions of famous natives. The

colored photos and illustrations entice the reader to learn more about this area.

♦ Beginning with the information this book provides about the state's nickname "The Tar Heel State," students may research the nicknames of the other southeastern states and their origins, and put the conclusions of their research on a poster that can be displayed in class.

1. South Atlantic States—Juvenile literature. 2. North Carolina—Juvenile literature. 3. South Carolina—Juvenile literature.

975.6
Bushong, William. *North Carolina's Executive Mansion, the First Hundred Years*. Executive Mansion Fine Arts Committee and Executive Mansion Fund, Incorporated (LC 91-071639), 1991. 190p. B/W and Color illus. Available from the Executive Mansion Fund, Inc. 301 North Blount Street, Raleigh, NC 27601. (Interest level: 5-8).

More than just a story of the mansion and its architecture and renovations, this work tells the story of the governors and their families and how the times shaped their lives and the decisions they made in the mansion. The tale of the executive mansion is a fascinating one, with historical and human interest photographs embellishing the story, and the "Notes" providing a wealth of human interest and historical detail.

♦ After reading the citations given in the Index about David Haywood, students may analyze the photograph showing the mansion's butler and his image on the artist's palette, and write an essay making a case for what they feel were the impact of the times upon the life of this humble but well-known man.

1. North Carolina Executive Mansion (Raleigh, N.C.) 2. Raleigh (N.C.) 3. Buildings, structures, etc.

975.6
Clayton, Thomas H. *Close to the Land: The Way We Lived in North Carolina, 1820-1870*. University of North Carolina Press (0-8078-1551-9), 1983. 100p. B/W photos. (Interest level: 5-8).

This work describes the changes in North Carolina society brought about by the Civil War and its aftermath (changes in social relationships between black and white, planter and freedman, women and men, and great economic changes). The multiplicity of contributions of the African-American slaves to the North Carolina economy is well noted, with quotes from little-known manuscripts accompanied by illustrations of historical documents. The adoption of public school education in the 1850s and the growth and influence of religious denominations are also included.

♦ In the chapter on "Rural Community," students should note the proposed salary for a rural teacher, listed by subject. From the central office of their school district, they can obtain data on the average salary in their school district and calculate how many subjects are taught and what the approximate cost per subject would be over a three-month period so that they may compare it with that of the Burn's Creek teacher's proposal.

1. North Carolina—History

975.60

Clements, John. *Flying the Colors: North Carolina Facts, a Comprehensive Look at North Carolina Today, County by County*. Clements Research (0895-8106), 1988. 375p. (Interest level: 7-8).

This comprehensive work provides a wealth of information on each county in North Carolina; discusses the government structure, land resource regions, and major market areas; and outlines a chronological history of the state.

♦ Using the 35-page chronological history of North Carolina, students may trace the multicultural heritage of North Carolina and contrast this data with the information on ancestry groups mentioned in the 1980 county population totals for the state.

1. North Carolina—Miscellanea—Periodicals.
2. North Carolina—Statistics—Periodicals.

975.6

Conway, Cece, Gosling, Maureen, and **Blank, Les.** *Julie: Old Time Tales of the Blue Ridge* (Videocassette). Flower Films (0-933621-54-X), 1991. Color, (11 min.). $100.00. (Interest level: 6-8).

This film is set against the spectacular scenery of the Blue Ridge Mountains with songs and music of the region interspersed with the story of "Julie." Julie is a real person who was born in 1903 and who answers the questions of the interviewer to reveal the real person within and the life she has led.

♦ Julie analyses her own character, revealing that she really was a sensitive person, but acted hard hearted and mean sometimes to hide this quality. Students should think of their own character and describe a time when they may have appeared differently to others than they really were inside.

1. North Carolina—Social life and customs. 2. North Carolina—History, Local. 3. Appalachian Region—History.

975.6

Couch, Ernie and **Couch, Jill**. *North Carolina Trivia*. Rutledge Hill (0-934395-37-3 pbk), 1986. 191p. (Interest level: 6-8).

Approximately 500 questions and answers are contained in this book with sections relating to geography, entertainment, history, arts and literature, sports and leisure, and science and nature. Facts gleaned from many sources make this small paperback book a valuable source of information.

♦ Students may use photographs from books, periodicals, tourist information, etc., to make a class collage about North Carolina.

1. North Carolina—Miscellanea 2. Questions and answers.

975.6

Fenn, Elizabeth A. *Natives and Newcomers: The Way We Lived in North Carolina Before 1770*. University of North Carolina Press (0-8078-1549-7), 1983 103p. B/W photos. (Interest level: 5-8).

This well-done, scholarly work was made possible not only by the more well-known historical resources but by the author's public appeal for additional information and location of previously unknown sites. Generously illustrated by black-and-white photographs of historical documents, paintings and historical sites, the story of the settling of North Carolina, from its earliest Native American colonists to the last wave of European immigrants, is told. Included in these narratives is the historical basis of the "Lost Colony" legend, and sympathetic treatment of the contributions of African-American slaves to the development of North Carolina. A bibliography and map of historic places is included in each book of these series.

♦ Students may choose a photograph of a historical site and make a drawing depicting a person who might have lived in one of these buildings. Assuming the character of one of these inhabitants, students can write a first-person account of their daily life in this building.

1. North Carolina—History

975.6

Fradin, Dennis B. *The North Carolina Colony*. Childrens Press (0-516-00396-8), 1991. 159p. B/W illus. (Interest level: 4-7).

From the early Native Americans who arrived almost 12,000 years ago to the Norwegians arriving about 982 to the 1791 Bill of Rights, this book on North Carolina describes the main events and the people and forces influential in bringing North Carolina from proprietary colony to royal colony to statehood. Detailed biographies of Sir Walter Raleigh, John White, John Lawson, Blackbeard, Daniel Boone, Cornelius Harnett, James Iredell, and Richard Dobbs Spaight; reproductions of historical documents and illustrations; and a "Colonial America Time Line" add to the well-documented historical accounts that provide fascinating reading.

♦ Students may choose the role of a runaway, mistreated slave, or a woman involved in the Edenton Tea Party, and tell their side of the story in the first person.

1. North Carolina—History—Colonial period, ca. 1600-1775—Juvenile literature. 2. North Carolina—History—Colonial period, ca. 1600-1775—Biography—Juvenile literature.

975.6

Garrison, Webb. *A Treasury of Carolina Tales*. Rutledge Hill Press (0-934395-75-6), 1988. 157p. B/W illus. (Interest level: 6-8).

Combining tales of North Carolina and South Carolina in one collection, this work uses a two- to five-page format to tell a lively story about some unusual, little-known piece of history dealing with the past of the Carolinas. Because it deals with personal-interest stories of many known and unknown people, it is livelier than most historical chronicles, and as such will appeal to the age group mentioned.

♦ Students may select the stories about women and analyze what situation or personal qualities enabled them to become important enough to have been written about, and why, even today, there are so few women written about in the history books.

1. North Carolina—History, Local. 2. South Carolina—History, Local. 3. Legends—North Carolina. 4. Legends—South Carolina.

975.6
Hales, Cheyney. *Archeology in North Carolina.*
(Film). North Carolina Department of Cultural Re-
sources and U.N.C. Center for Public Television (no
ISBN), 1989. (29 min.). Available for viewing from the
Film Services Branch Division of the State Library,
Raleigh, NC. (Interest level: 6-8).

This film describes the purpose of archeology digs
and the various cultures of North Carolina that are
currently being studied (pre-colonial Native Americans, plantation, and early twentieth century). Adventure, discovery, and respect for the past as a link to the
future are the themes of this excellent film.
♦ Students may interview someone from their local
museum and find out the most recent archeological
discovery nearest their home and the estimated age
of the artifacts or sites encountered. The class can
prepare a radio news show to tell their listeners about
what they have learned.
1. Excavations (Archaeology)—North Carolina.
2. North Carolina—Antiquities. 3. Indians of North
America—North Carolina—Antiquities.

975.6
Hurmence, Belinda, ed. *My Folks Don't Want Me to
Talk About Slavery. Twenty-one Oral Histories of For-
mer North Carolina Slaves.* John Blair (0-89587-038-
X), 1992. 103p. (Interest level: 6-8).

Twenty-one first person accounts of people who
were slaves in the South were recorded by paid federal
government workers in the 1930s. Edited for clarity,
they were first published in 1984 by the editor who
wanted recognition for the true African-American pioneers of the South.
♦ After reading about the numerous accounts prohib-
iting slaves from learning to read, students should
think about how reading has personally enriched
their life, and make a list of all the ways that it makes
their life a better one.
1. Slaves—North Carolina—Biography. 2. African-
Americans—North Carolina—Biography. 4. Oral history.

975.6
Kuralt, Charles and **McGlohon, Loonis**. *North Carolina Is My Home.* Edited by Patty Davis. Fast & McMil-
lan (0-88742-107-5), 1986. 103p. Color illus. (Interest
level: 5-8).

As Kuralt states, "the reality of any place is what
its people remember of it." His memories of North
Carolina, accompanied by a variety of photographs, are
the bulk of the book, supplemented by artful weavings
of historical description and ample renditions of historical drawings and documents. His accounts mention
such North Carolina sons as Thomas Wolfe, O. Henry,
and presidents Andrew Jackson, James K. Polk, and
Andrew Johnson.
♦ Students may determine the percentage of photographs in the book that depict a rural society.
1. North Carolina—Social life and customs 2. North
Carolina—Description and travel—1981.

975.6
Nathans, Sydney. *The Quest for Progress: The Way
We Lived in North Carolina, 1870-1920.* University of

North Carolina Press (0-8-89-1552-7), 1983. 112p.
B/W photos. (Interest level: 5-8).

The period between 1870-1920 saw great changes
in North Carolina society, which are chronicled and
illustrated with historical documents and narratives of
the lives of many important change agents. Such
changes came about because of new inventions, in-
creasing population, transportation opportunities,
growth of the tobacco industry, unionism, industriali-
zation, growth of the middle class, new opportunities
in higher education, the abolistion of slavery for the
African American, and the changes that came about
because of World War I.
♦ In the chapter, "Industry Comes of Age," students
can read about the incident that took place at the
Haw River mill, when a woman was fired and another woman commanded to take her place, and the
subsequent decisions of the union to defy this order.
Each student may choose a character to assume—
the woman fired, the replacement, the foreman, or a
union official—and write a letter to a friend telling
their point of view.
1. North Carolina—History

975.6 (Reference)
The Old North State Fact Book. North Carolina Division of Archives and History (0-86526-099-0), 1990.
268p. Color photos. (Available from Broadfoot's). (Interest level: 8).

This valuable source of information about North
Carolina includes a concise description of the state's
early history, a description of the capitol and legislative
buildings and executive residences, and a listing of all
the governors. All the state symbols are described and
many are illustrated.
♦ Students may choose one of the state symbols (seal,
flag, bird, flower, insect, tree, mammal, shell, salt
water fish, toast, precious stone, reptile, rock, bev-
erage, historic boat, dog, nicknames, motto, colors,
or song) and work in groups to prepare multi-media
presentations on these symbols, perhaps using a
story-line, a song, or poem, etc., and using realia,
photographs, overheads, music, slides, or videos.
1. North Carolina—History 2. North Carolina—Statistics.

975.6
Parramore, Thomas C. *Express Lanes and Country
Roads: The Way We Lived in North Carolina, 1920-
1970.* University of North Carolina Press (0-8078-
1553-5), 1983. 110p. B/W photos. (Interest level: 5-8).

The transformation of cultural life during this period of North Carolina's history is described as a struggle between urban development and individualism,
between isolationism and entry into the American
mainstream. This period saw a change in farming
methods, the growth of manufacturing, and the transformation of farming methods, communications, and
transportation. The Great Depression, the New Deal,
and the conditions of life after World War II, all affected
North Carolina in unique ways. In addition to coming
to terms with the rest of the region, nation, and the
world, North Carolina experienced internal struggles
to meet the needs of its own citizens, namely African
Americans, Native Americans, women, children, the

aged, the poor, and the disabled. These major issues are well documented through significant accounts of important and lesser-known personalities, photographs, and a bibliography.

♦ Students may analyze the photograph depicting a Greensboro sit-in in 1960 (p. 86) and assume the personality of one person in the photograph, telling what they felt like on the day of the sit-in, what events led up to it, what events happened that day, and what their fears or hopes are about the future.

1. North Carolina—Economic Conditions 2. North Carolina—Social Conditions.

975.6

Thompson, Kathleen. *Portrait of America, North Carolina*. Raintree (0-86514-454-0), 1987. 48p. Color photos. (Interest level: 3-6).

This book includes several pages of historical and contemporary information. People, representative of the state, record their thoughts in interview form. Things "special" to North Carolina, the first symphony, first arts council, etc., are highlighted.

♦ Students may review the products that are produced or crops grown in North Carolina and make a note of any that are used in their home, and especially if they are made in North Carolina.

1. North Carolina—Juvenile literature.

975.6

Watson, Harry L. *An Independent People: The Way We Lived in North Carolina, 1770-1820*. University of North Carolina Press (0-8078-1550-0), 1983. 120p. B/W photos. (Interest level: 5-8).

This period is amply recorded by focusing on individuals from various classes and racial and ethnic groups. The status of Native Americans and African-American slaves is examined at length. The status of women and their lack of equality with men is described in the social setting of the day. Violence as a characteristic of all socio-economic groups of the time and the emergence of the urban setting are also examined.

♦ In the chapter on "Towns in the Rural Society," students should note the apprenticeships that children began at age 12, when they left their families to learn a trade. Students can imagine that they are at that point in their life where they are ready to leave home and that the night before their departure, they write a letter to their parents telling them of their feelings at having to leave home and the future they hope to build for themselves.

1. North Carolina—History

975.61

Bosco, Peter I. *Roanoke, the Story of the Lost Colony*. Millbrook Press (1-56294-111-9), 1992. (Spotlight on American History Series). 72p. Color illus. (Interest level: 4-8).

The story of the Roanoke colony is filled with adventure and drama and such colorful characters as Sir Walter Raleigh, Sir Francis Drake, Sir Richard Grenville, Queen Elizabeth I, Governor Lane, John White, Thomas Hariot, King Wingina, and Manteo. Historical portraits of royalty and the colonizers, White's sensitive portrayal of the Native American cultures of early North Carolina, the beautiful color

maps and the chronology tables, and a listing of historical sources and recommendations for further reading make this an excellent choice for a beginning student of colonial history.

♦ Students may compare the full color portraits of Sir Walter Raleigh and his son, Sir Francis Drake, and Sir Richard Grenville and draw some conclusions about what the artist felt about their character from their depicted expressions, posture, and clothing.

1. Roanoke Colony (N.C.)—Juvenile literature.

975.61

Ehringhaus, Ann Sebrell. *Ocracoke Portrait, Photographs and Interviews*. John F. Blair (0-89587-060-6), 1988. 107p. B/W photos. (Interest level: 6-8).

The author interviewed people who live on the island and captured their unique sense of place and contentment with island life. The photographs and interviews are divided according to the seasons, which the islanders proclaim are very important to them.

♦ Students should pick their favorite season and then choose their favorite photo of Ocracoke in that season, writing a description of the feelings they have after looking at that photograph.

1. Ocracoke Island (N.C.)—Description and travel— Views. 2. Ocracoke Island (N.C.)—Social life and customs—Pictorial works.

976.9

Greene, Carol. *Daniel Boone, Man of the Forests*. Childrens Press (0-516-04210-6), 1990. (Rookie Biography Series). 47p. Color and B/W photos. (Interest level: 2-4).

This adventure story about Daniel Boone devotes a chapter to the time spent in the Yadkin Valley in North Carolina. The entire book is quick moving and conveys the image of Boone as a sturdy explorer, who settles in various places with his family, but eventually moves on to new experiences.

♦ Daniel Boone's story describes several unpleasant encounters with Native Americans. Students should assume that they are Native Americans who feel their hunting grounds are being threatened by the Boone invasion and tell in their own words what they feel about this situation and what they did to resolve it.

1. Boone, Daniel, 1734-1820—Juvenile literature. 2. Pioneers—Kentucky—Juvenile literature 3. Frontier and pioneer.

Biography

See also biographical entries in the North Carolina Nonfiction section, especially udner 371.10, 629.13, 813.54, and 973.6.

920

Greenfield, Eloise and **Little, Lessie Jones**. *Childtimes: A Three-Generation Memoir*. Thomas Y. Crowell (0-690-03875-5), 1979. 175p. B/W photos. (Interest level: 3-8).

An important African-American author, Eloise Greenfield depicts life in Parmele, North Carolina, through the lives of three women and their generations, is a touching tribute to the importance of families and the memories of childhood. Simply but eloquently written, the story is in first person, with a "landscape" introduction to the lives of each of the women as it related to the history of African Americans and their civil rights struggle.

♦ Students may read the description of Leslie Blanche Jones Little's "papa" and try to describe their "papa," uncle, or grandfather, and write about some of same type of experiences as they apply to their family.

1. Jones, Pattie Ridley—Juvenile literature 2. Little, Lessie Jones—Juvenile literature 3. Greenfield, Eloise—Juvenile literature 4. Parmele, N.C.—Biography—Juvenile literature 5. Washington, D.C.—Biography—Juvenile literature 6. African-American children—Biography—Juvenile literature.

920
Ravi, Jennifer. *Notable North Carolina Women*. Bandit Books, 1992. 156p. B/W photos. (Interest level: 5+).

This is an easy-to-read collection of biographies of 31 North Carolina women in the fields of popular culture, education, politics, publishing, entertainment, science, and reform. Though many are not well known by today's children, the book does include several African Americans, and perhaps expands the thinking of young children about the wide range of accomplishments for which a woman can be considered notable.

♦ Students may check the sources listed at the back of each notable woman and locate one to see how the author used it to compile the information listed in the book.

1. Women—North Carolina—Biography 2. North Carolina—Biography.

920.07 (Reference)
Powell, William Stevens, ed. *Dictionary of North Carolina Biography*. 4 vols. University of North Carolina Press. (0-8078-1329-X, 0-8078-1656-6, 0-8078-1806-2, 0-8078-1918-2), Vol. 4 published in 1991. 415p. (Interest level: 5-8).

Volume four of this series provides information on notable North Carolina figures with names from L-O, and cross references to other articles. This scholarly edition spans the last 400 years and chronicles the famous and infamous from all walks of life.

♦ Students may choose to read the biographies of five famous women, chosen from a certain section of the book, and have their classmates do the same in different sections of the book. Then the group can get together and come to a consensus as to what type of life a women had to lead to get included in a book of this type.

1. North Carolina—Biography—Dictionaries

92 Dole, Elizabeth
Mulford, Carolyn. *Elizabeth Dole, Public Servant*. Enslow Publishers, Inc. (0-89490-331-4), 1992. 144p. B/W photos. (Interest level: 5+).

This is an easy-to-read biography detailing the childhood-to-adult story of a North Carolinian who was a Republican presidential cabinet member and who is now director of the Red Cross. Though it paints

her as a near perfect person destined for success, it provides an opportunity for young people to see how political offices are aspired to and won by hard-working women.

♦ Students may wish to discuss in class the expectations for women in the days that Elizabeth Dole was growing up and how she was able to carve out a new role for herself.

1. Dole, Elizabeth 2. Women—North Carolina—Biography 3. North Carolina—Biography.

Fiction

Beatty, Patricia. *Who Comes with Cannons?* Morrow Junior Books (0-688-11028-2), 1992. (Interest level: 4-8).

The story of the underground railroad comes alive in the story of the Bardwell family who are Quakers living on a North Carolina farm. Truth, a cousin who comes to live with them becomes unwittingly involved in this dangerous cause. Beatty, an award-winning author, supplements this gripping drama with additional sections of factual information on the Quakers, the Underground Railroad, and the history of North Carolina and people and places in the book.

♦ Students can recount other periods in history when persecuted peoples had to hide, and discuss how this formidable task was made harder or easier based on the circumstances and the people who risked their lives to help them.

1. United States—History—Civil War, 1861-1865—Juvenile fiction.

Cleaver, Vera and **Cleaver, William J.** *Trial Valley*. J.B. Lippincott Company (0-397-31722-0), 1977. 158p. (Interest level: 5-8).

Set in the mountains of western North Carolina where hard work and courage are required to survive, this sequel to *Where the Lilies Bloom* follows the story of the family of orphans headed by Mary Call. This is a touching story of a young girl coming of age who serves as mother to a brother and sister who, as they grow in years and independence, resent her control over their lives.

♦ Students may analyze the statement that Mary Call makes when she rejects her Virginian suitor ("I have my kids and I believe in them.") and then have her write a letter to the children saying, "Dear Romey and Ima Dean. You are so important in my life, and I believe in you because. . . "

1. Brothers and sisters—Fiction 2. Great Smoky Mountains—Fiction 3. Orphans—Fiction.

Hooks, William H. *The Ballad of Belle Dorcas*. Illus. by Brian Pinkney. Knopf (0-394-8465-1, 0-394-94645-6), 1990. 40p. Color illus. (Interest level: 4-8).

This is a tale from the African-American oral tradition of eastern North Carolina, passed on by the descendants of the community called "East Arcadia." This captivating story with its beautiful color illustrations recreates the mystique of century-old beliefs and traditions. The story is about the love between a free-issue black woman, Belle Dorcas, and her slave boyfriend, Joshua, and tells of a "cunger" spell put on

Joshua by Granny Lizard to keep him from being sold. Unfortunately, it also keeps Belle from the romance she yearns for.
♦ Students may tell the same story from the point of view of Joshua, the fiddle player. When he is turned into a smokehouse, let him tell, with as much humor as possible, how he views the fright that other people have of him in his new form.
1. Blacks—Fiction 2. Slavery—Fiction 3. Magic—Fiction.

Hooks, William H. *The Legend of the White Doe.* Illus. by Dennis Nolan. Macmillan (0-02-744350-7), 1988. 44p. (Interest Level: 4-7).

The English colony on Roanoke Island, North Carolina, which disappeared in the late sixteenth century, is the setting for this story. It provides an account of a still-existing legend as to what became of this lost colony. It tells about Virginia Dare, the first English child born in America and others who went with her to escape unfriendly natives threatening their original settlement and their eventual assimilation into the Native American culture at Croatoan. Virginia, renamed Ulalee, was turned into a white doe by a medicine man who wished to marry her and foil her younger suitor. At the end of the story she is turned back from doe to human, only to be mortally wounded by the older medicine man.
♦ Students may stage a mock interview session with Wanchese and hear firsthand why he was motivated to shoot the deadly arrow that killed Ulalee.
1. Dare, Virginia, b. 1587—Juvenile fiction 2. Raleigh's Roanoke colonies, 1584-1590—Juvenile fiction 3. Indians of North America—Juvenile Fiction.

Houston, Gloria. *But No Candy.* Illus. by Lloyd Bloom. Philomel (0-399-22142-5), 1992. 30p. Color illus. (Interest level: K-4).

Lee matures to become aware of the world beyond her father's store, even though she never leaves her hometown in North Carolina. The muted dark-color illustrations seem to depict memories of the war years of the 1940s and the changing of Lee's candy centered world to one where she is aware and appreciative of her family, relatives, and their place in the world.
♦ Students should check the number of illustrations in the book that refer to candy and the ones that don't, and then determine whether this accurately reflects the importance that candy plays in the story.
1. World War, 1939-1945—United States—Fiction 2. Candy—Fiction 3. Stores, Retail—Fiction 4. Uncles—Fiction.

Houston, Gloria. *The Year of the Perfect Christmas Tree.* Illus. by Barbara Cooney. (0-8037-0300-7 lib bind), 1988. (Dial Books for Young Readers). 29p. (Interest level: 1-4).

Set in the Blue Ridge Mountains of North Carolina, the story of Ruthie, her mother and father, and the Christmas tree they donated to their church is passed down to the granddaughter who narrates the story. The story and the illustrations give a glimpse of Appalachian life, and of the love of family members for each other.

♦ Students may compose a letter as though it were written by Ruthie's father, telling his family that he will make it home for Christmas after all.
1. Christmas trees—Fiction. 2. Christmas—Fiction. 3. Appalachian Region—Fiction. 4. World War, 1914-1918—United States—Fiction.

Lyons, Mary. *Letters from a Slave Girl, the Story of Harriet Jacobs.* Charles Scribner's Sons (ISBN 0-684-19446-5), 1992. (Interest level: 5-8).

Set in Edenton, North Carolina, the true story of Harriet Ann Jacobs, a slave, is told by the author through a series of recreated letters written by Harriet to the important people in her life from 1825 to 1897. The book contains photographs illustrating the historical basis for the story, family trees, a glossary of nineteenth-century words, and a bibliography of works that the young reader can turn to for extended reading.
♦ Students can discuss why the author chose this format to tell the true story of Harriet Ann Jacobs, and why so few stories of women in this time period have been told.
1. Jacobs, Harriet A. (Harriet Ann), 1813-1897—Juvenile fiction.

Miller, Ruth White. *The City Rose.* McGraw-Hill (0-07-941950-7), 1977. 171p. (Interest level: 4-8).

A child's worst fears are set to print in this story. Dee's whole family, except her brother, died in a fire, and she was sent to live with her aunt and uncle in North Carolina. The plot has enough mystery in it to cause both the reader and Dee to temporarily forget her troubles and become involved in the mysterious happenings taking place in the woods, all of which lead her to an even closer place in the heart of the aunt and uncle with whom she now lives.
♦ Dee experiences what it is to change from an urban to a rural setting. Students can pretend as though they have moved to the opposite type of life they are experiencing now (urban to rural, or rural to urban) and describe what they see in this imaginary setting that they are witnessing for the first time.
1. Orphans—Fiction

Periodicals

North Carolina Libraries. North Carolina Library Association. (ISSN 0029-2540), Quarterly. $32 per year. (Interest level: Professional).

Though the principle audience is librarians, this journal also contains many materials of interest to teachers. Regular features include "North Carolina Books" where the latest books and other publications of interest dealing with subjects related to North Carolina are reviewed. "Lagniappe*North Caroliniana," also features reviews of North Carolina materials in various non-book formats.
♦ Teachers may wish to review several of the non-print materials on North Carolina for use in their classes.
1. North Carolina—Library services.

070.4

NCFLC Newsletter. North Carolina Foreign Language Center, Quarterly. Color and B/W photos. Free. (Interest level: Professional).

This newsletter contains valuable information on North Carolina ethnic groups and their activities and resources. Information is also included on their collections in 150 different languages, including Cherokee. Valuable for media specialists, foreign language teachers, and teachers wishing to give a multicultural emphasis to their teaching.
1. North Carolina—Library Services.

639.9

Wildlife in North Carolina. North Carolina Wildlife Resources Commission (ISSN 0043-549x), Monthly. Color and B/W illus. $7.50 per year. (Interest level: 6-8).

Materials on wildlife are beautifully illustrated and provide plenty of opportunity for young people studying North Carolina to extend what is learned in the classroom or to pursue further research.
♦ Students can use the many colored photos of wildlife as guides to making their own illustrations for use in oral reports.
1. Natural history—North Carolina. 2. Nature conservation—North Carolina. 3. North Carolina—Description and travel.

975.6

Advisory List of Instructional Media, North Carolina. Media Evaluation Services, North Carolina Department of Public Instruction. Annually/Biannually. Free. (Interest level: Professional).

The list is an annotated bibliography of K-12 print and nonprint materials on North Carolina currently available for purchase. Inclusion in the list constitutes a recommendation.
1. North Carolina—Bibliography—Catalogs. 2. North Carolina—Audiovisual aids—Catalogs.

975.6

North Carolina Historical Reviews. North Carolina Division of Archives and History, State Library. (ISSN 0029-2494), Quarterly. B/W Illus. $25 per year. (Interest level: Professional).

Suitable for teachers who wish to pursue the latest in historical findings about North Carolina topics and to avail themselves of information on historical issues of a multicultural nature. The articles contain footnotes and bibliographies that point to additional resources.
♦ Teachers may wish to use these materials to challenge students to understand that history is constantly being rewritten.
1. United States—North Carolina.

975.6

Tar Heel Junior Historian, The State History Journal for Inquiring Students. Tar Heel Junior Historian Association, North Carolina Museum of History. (ISSN 0496-8913). B/W illus. $3 per year. (Interest level: 4-8).

Filled with written and photographic material to excite the young student learning about North Carolina, the journal also carries student-authored articles and contains ideas for activities to use in lessons. Issues also feature a theme, e.g., North Carolina's Coastal Plain.
♦ Students should choose an article dealing with a topic interesting to them and report on it to the class.
1. North Carolina—History—Periodicals. 2. North Carolina—History—Societies, etc.—Periodicals.

Professional Materials

398.20

Caduto, Michael J. *Teacher's Guide to Keepers of the Earth.* Fulcrum (1-55591-040-8), 1988. 48p. (Interest level: Teachers of Grades 3-8).

This guide includes a section on the Cherokee tribes of Tennessee, Georgia, Alabama, and North Carolina, gives reading lists for adults and children that correspond with the chapters, and indicates the book's philosophy as it relates to values education and environmentalism. This Teacher's Guide reflects the quality of *Keepers of the Earth (see* page 115) and carefully illustrates how teacher can use these ideas in the classroom.
♦ Using the material that relates to the importance of story-telling in the Native American cultures, teachers can discuss with students how story-telling influenced the disciplining of young children and determine the students' views about this practice.
1. Indians of North America—Legend 2. Indians of North America—Religion and mythology—Juvenile literature 3. Creative activities and seat work.

398.20

Caduto, Michael J. and **Bruchac, Joseph.** *Keepers of the Animals, Native American Stories and Wildlife Activities for Children.* Illus. by John Kahionhes Fadden, Melody Lightfeather, D.D. Tyler, and Carol Wood. Fulcrum (1-55591-088-2), 1991. 266p. B/W illus. (Interest level: 3-8; Professional).

Native American stories from several tribal traditions, including the Cherokee from North Carolina, are the focal point of this book with accompanying suggested extending activities to enable the student to study about animals, to understand them, to care for them, and to develop a wildlife conservation ethic. The teacher or librarian is well prepared by the various chapters to get the most from the rich source of Native American traditions through the tips offered for telling stories, leading the "guided fantasjes," performing puppet shows, and the explanations of the philosophy inherent in the conducting of these activities.
♦ After reading the Cherokee story about "Why Possum Has a Naked Tail," which describes the difference between the possum's tail in the "old days" as compared to how it is now, students can find three other animals that scientists say had a different form many years ago, and create a story about one of them as to "Why the——had a ——."
1. Indians of North America—Legends. 2. Animal ecology—Study and teaching (Elementary) 3. Human ecology—Study and teaching (Elementary).

398.20
Caduto, Michael J. and **Bruchac, Joseph.** *Keepers of the Earth, Native American Stories and Environmental Activities for Children.* Illus by John Kahionhes Fadden and Carol Wood. Fulcrum (1-55591-027-0), 1989. 209p. B/W illus. (Interest level: 3-8; Professional).

This book provides an interdisciplinary approach to environmental and values education through the use of Native American legends, including two North Carolina legends, "The Coming of Corn" and "Awi Usdi, The Little Deer." Each chapter's discussion, questions, activities, and experience extenders provide a unique and valuable view of the world for the students who use them.

♦ Keeping in the spirit of the supposed times when animals and humans talked to each other (from the Awi Usdi legend), students can record a message to an endangered animal mentioning why they think it is needed on this earth and what message they hope to pass on to other human beings about the need for its survival.

1. Indians of North America—Legends 2. Indians of North America—Religion and mythology—Juvenile literature 3. Creative activities and seat work.

497.50
Holmes, Ruth Bradley and **Smith, Betty Sharp**. *Beginning Cherokee* (Kit). University of Oklahoma Press (0-8061-1463-0), 1976. 2 sound cassettes; text. $17.95. (Interest level: Professional).

North Carolina is the origin of one of the two main dialects spoken on the Qualla reservation today by about 3,000 people, and these recordings provide the opportunity for the teacher of North Carolina units to enable the students to hear what the language of contemporary Cherokees sounds like, to see its alphabet, and to speculate as to how the language frames "an outlook and an intellect." Valuable information is contained in the introduction and appendices, and gives the student the chance to learn some of the language and understand why it has survived.

♦ Students may discuss why the language has survived despite all odds.

1. Cherokee Languages. 2. Indians of North America—Languages.

781.64
Lomax, Alan, narrator. *Appalachian Journey.* (Videocassette). Cultural Equity, Inc. (0-7936-0604-7), 1991. (PBS's American Patchwork Series, PBS Video Distributor). (60 min.). $39.95. (Interest level: Professional).

The Appalachian mountains of North Carolina are the setting for this superb sociological exploration of the way of life that was inherited by present-day mountain dwellers of North Carolina. The teacher will not lack for material from the video to share with any age students, as Native American, African-American, English, Scotch, and Irish contributions are discussed and interviews with contemporary story-tellers, musicians, and everyday people are done with Alan Lomax's folklorist wisdom punctuating the documentary.

♦ Students may view the segment on the African-American contributions to Appalachian dance customs, and research the notion that Lomax presents,

namely that the African slaves of the area came from as sophisticated a background as the European settlers of that time.

1. Folk songs—Southern States. 2. Appalachian Region—Country Music. 3. Folklore—Southern States.

810.09
McNeil, Nellie and **Squibb, Joyce**. eds. *A Southern Appalachian Reader.* Appalachian Consortium Press (0-913239-50-X), 1989. 529p. (Interest level: 7-Adult).

This excellent source of Appalachian poetry, short stories, ballads and history offers questions at the end of each selection to encourage critical thinking and discussion. The selections provide an excellent background for a teacher preparing to teach the upper elementary grades about the North Carolina region of Appalachia (though the book contains works from several states); several would be valuable to the elementary student (such as the story of the death of Tsali, the Cherokee leader, told to the author by Tsali's granddaughter).

♦ After reading the injustice described in the story of Tsali, students should explore the reasons why they think certain ethnic and racial groups have been denied the right to life, liberty, and the pursuit of happiness, and they should explore what can be done to prevent this in the future.

1. American literature—Appalachian Region. 2. Appalachian Region—Literary collections. 3. Young adult literature, American—Appalachian Region.

917.56
Alexander, John and **Lazell, James**. *Ribbon of Sand.* Algonquin Books of Chapel Hill (0-945575-32-7), 1992. 238p. B/W illus. (Interest level: 7-8; Professional).

Maps, diagrams, and narrative make this a valuable source of information about the Outer Banks of North Carolina. Historical and ecological information abound in this lovingly told account of the Outer Banks, which includes a valuable chapter on "Flight," telling of "Kitty Hawk," and the story of the Wright brothers and how they utilized the winds of this area to finalize their historic experiments.

♦ Students may prepare a presentation on the story of flight using the quotations given from letters of the Wright brothers, and the poem written by Robert Frost about them.

1. Outer Banks (N.C.)—History. 2. Outer Banks (N.C.)—Geography. 3. Ecology—North Carolina—Outer Banks.

973.08
Vanderbilt, Arthur T. *Fortune's Children: The Fall of the House of Vanderbilt.* Quill William Morrow (0-688-10386-3), 1989. 496p. B/W photos. (Interest level: Professional).

This comprehensive history of the Vanderbilt family, one of the richest families in the United States, is chronicled in terms of interesting family dynamics, work ethic, and building and spending patterns. It covers the period 1794 until 1955, and Chapter 7 tells of the Biltmore Castle, situated in the mountains of Asheville, North Carolina.

♦ Students may wish to act out a typical afternoon or evening conversation between members of the Vanderbilt family that might have taken place at the Biltmore. The teacher may wish to use information from Chapter 7 to set the scene as to the type of life led there.

1. Vanderbilt family. 2. United States—Biography. 3. Upper classes—United States—Biography. 4. Wealth—United States—History.

South Carolina

by Pamela Barron

Nonfiction

016.9701 (Reference)
Blumer, Thomas J. *Bibliography of the Catawba.*
Scarecrow Press (0-8108-1986-4), 1987. (Native
American Bibliography Series). 547p. (Interest level:
5-Adult).

This fully annotated bibliography covers more than
300 years of the history of the Catawba, a native South
Carolina tribe. This comprehensive work includes
monographs, periodicals, and newspaper articles, as
well as manuscripts.
♦ Using the bibliography to identify titles, students
can read and report on books and articles about the
Catawba.
1. Catawba Indians—Bibliography 2. Indians of North
America—South Carolina—Bibliography

016.9757 (Reference)
South Carolina Department of Archives and History. *South Carolina Department of Archives and History: A Guide to the Local Government Records in the
South Carolina Archives.* University of South Carolina
Press (0-87249-609-0), 1988. 315p. (Interest level:
7-Adult).

Local government records are among South Carolina's most valuable historical sources. This guide,
organized by county, identifies local government records that are available at the state archives. This work
makes this information available for the first time.
♦ Students can find out what kinds of records are kept
by different agencies and discuss how these records
might be useful in research.
1. Public records—South Carolina 2. South Carolina—
History—Sources

069.09757 (Reference)
South Carolina Museum Directory. South Carolina
Federation of Museums (No ISBN), 1988. 54p. (Interest level: 4-Adult).

All of the museums in South Carolina are covered
in this comprehensive guide. Entries are listed in alphabetical order by county. Each entry includes address,
telephone number, hours of operation, and a brief
description of the museum's holdings.

♦ Using the information in the directory, students can
plan a trip to a museum they would like to visit.
1. Museums—South Carolina—Directories 2. Historic
buildings—South Carolina—Directories

070.025 (Reference)
Hendricks, Sue. *1992, S.C. Guide: Media and Legislative Information.* Hendricks (No ISBN), 1992. 93p.
(Interest level:4-Adult).

This is a directory of newspapers, magazines, television and radio stations, and state elected officials in
South Carolina. To enhance accessibility, this ready-reference guide is arranged geographically by type of
information.
♦ Students can make a list of the media sources in their
town and visit some of these sources.
1. Television stations—South Carolina 2. Radio stations—South Carolina 3. Newspapers—South Carolina

328.757 (Reference)
1992 South Carolina Legislative Manual. 73d ed. General Assembly of South Carolina (No ISBN), 1992.
600p. B/W and Color photos. (Interest level: 3-Adult).

This guide to the organization of the South Carolina
state government includes elected officials, rules and
committees, and special legislative data. Annual updates make this ready-reference work a good source for
recent information on the state's governance.
♦ Students can use this guide to find out if their
representatives serve on any committees.
1. South Carolina—General Assembly

398.2
Faulkner, William J. *The Days When Animals Talked:
Black American Folktales and How They Came to Be.*
Illus. by Troy Howell. Follett (0-695-40755-4), 1977.
190p. B/W illus. (Interest level: 4-8).

This collection of more than 30 tales is divided into
two parts. Part 1 is a collection of African-American
slave tales. All of the tales in part 2 are authentic
narratives told to the author by elderly men and women
who lived around Darlington County, South Carolina.
The author attempts to put these tales in their proper
perspective to show the African-American struggle

against injustice and oppression, as well as to establish their place as important contributions to storytelling.

♦ Students may want to try their hand at writing similar tales about different animals.

1. Folklore—African-American 2. Animals—Fiction

398.209757
Daise, Ronald. *De Gullah Storybook.* (Audiocassette). G.O.G. Enterprises (No ISBN)., 1991. 1 sound cassette, (20 min.); 1 book. 29p. B/W illus. $21.95. (Interest level: 3-Adult).

A collection of 10 short verses are read first in the Gullah dialect, then in English, and the words are written in Gullah, then in English. The audio recording gives the audience the opportunity to hear a language that is fast disappearing.

♦ Before playing the tape, let students try to translate the verses into English using the illustrations as a guide.

1. African-Americans—Folklore—South Carolina 2. Tales—South Carolina

398.209757
Rhyne, Nancy. *More Tales of the South Carolina Low Country.* John F. Blair (0-89587-042-8), 1984. 121p. (Interest level: 5-Adult).

As a follow-up to *Tales of the South Carolina Low Country* (*see* following entry), Rhyne has collected 22 more tales set in the Low Country of South Carolina. This is a wonderful assortment of entertaining stories, which range from the tragic story of a young girl who died on Edisto Island more than 100 years ago to Clark Gable's visit to Hampton Plantation.

♦ See if students can recall hearing any stories with plots or themes similar to those in this collection.

1. Tales—South Carolina 2. Legends—South Carolina

398.209757
Rhyne, Nancy. *Tales of the South Carolina Low Country.* John F. Blair (0-89587-027-4), 1982. 93p. (Interest level: 5-Adult).

Using bits of folklore and oral narratives, Rhyne has put together a collection of 14 tales set in the area known as the Low Country of South Carolina. Archivists at the Library of Congress claim that South Carolina is richer in folklore than any other state, and the range of tales in this collection adds support to that claim.

♦ As folklore communicates the "flavor" of a region, encourage students to collect superstitions, customs, and folk expressions from family, friends, and others in their community.

1. Tales—South Carolina 2. Legends—South Carolina

398.21
Sans Souci, Robert D. *Sukey and the Mermaid.* Illus. by Brian Pinkney. Four Winds (0-02-778141-0), 1992. Unpaginated. Color illus. (Interest level: 2-5).

Sukey, a young girl living with her mother and stepfather, is forced to do all of the household chores until the day she is befriended by a mermaid. The author has expanded an earlier tale appearing in Elsie C. Parsons' 1923 work *Folklore of the Sea-Islands, South Carolina* (American Folk-Lore Society), which

is one of the few authenticated African-American tales about mermaids.

♦ Students can locate other stories about mermaids and compare them with this story to see if there are any common characteristics.

1. Mermaids. 2. Folklore, African-American

398.25
Martin, Margaret Rhett. *Charleston Ghosts.* University of South Carolina Press (8-7249-091-2), 1963. 105p. Illus. (Interest level: 4-8).

This is a collection of 18 stories from Charleston, South Carolina, about real people, real places, and "real" ghosts. All of the stories have been carefully researched and documented by the author as to their authenticity.

♦ Students can locate the settings for these stories on a map of Charleston. Is there any "pattern" to their locations?

1. Ghosts 2. Legends—South Carolina—Charleston

398.25
Roberts, Nancy. *South Carolina Ghosts: From the Coast to the Mountains.* University of South Carolina Press (0-87249-428-4), 1983. 152p. B/W photos. (Interest level: 4-8).

This is a collection of 18 ghost stories, all based on actual events, from the famous Gray man of Pawley's Island, who warns of approaching storms, to the phantom horseman of Columbia. An appendix with notes and commentaries on the stories and a bibliography of related works are included.

♦ Students can explore their own communities for stories surrounding "unexplained events."

1. Ghost stories 2. Ghosts—South Carolina

507
Nature Scene. South Carolina Educational Television Network (No ISBN), n.d. 47 programs, (30 min.). Available on 1/2" VHS videocassettes. Series broadcast free in South Carolina; otherwise prices vary according to broadcast rights. Viewer's guide available. (Interest level: 3-Adult).

This series of programs chronicles the richness and diversity of South Carolina's natural history. These programs help the audience to explore and appreciate the beauty of our natural environment.

♦ Take students on a nature walk to see what they can discover.

1. Nature study—South Carolina 2. South Carolina—Nature study

574.90946
Meyer, Peter K. *Nature Guide to the Carolina Coast: Common Birds, Crabs, Shells, Fish, and Other Entities of the Coastal Environment.* Avian-Cetacean Press (0-9628186-0-7), 1991. 148p. Color photos. (Interest level: 4-Adult).

This is a practical identification guide to the most common birds, crabs, shells, fish, and other animals that are to be found along the coasts of the Carolinas. The author, a naturalist, uses the common names of plants and animals in the text, making this guide easy to use. The scientific names and other definitions are given in the back of the book.

♦ Ask students to learn about 10 animals found along the coast.
1. Marine animals

582.13
Batson, Wade T. *Wild Flowers in South Carolina*. University of South Carolina Press (0-87249-257-5), 1980. 146p. Color photos. (Interest level: 4-Adult).

This field guide can be used to identify more than 500 native South Carolina plants. This work begins, rather than ends, with a glossary and includes nontechnical descriptions of plants to facilitate identification.
♦ Challenge students to learn to identify at least 10 new species of wildflowers.
1. Wild flowers—South Carolina

594.0975
Rhyne, Nancy. *Carolina Seashells*. East Woods Press (0-914788-531), 1982. 95p. B/W photos. (Interest level: 4-Adult).

This is a very clear and concise identification guide to the most common Carolina shells. The detailed, realistic black-and-white drawings; glossary of related terms; bibliography; and comprehensive index make this a useful book.
♦ Ask students to identify shells they have found.
1. Shells—North Carolina 2. Shells—South Carolina

598.29756
Carter, Robin M. *Finding Birds in South Carolina*. University of South Carolina Press (0-87249-837-9), 1992. 208p. Color illus. (Interest level: 4-Adult).

This book includes a listing of bird species in South Carolina and identifies approximately 200 prime birding sites arranged by county. The author gives explicit instructions for locating the sites; describes the birds, flora, and fauna to be found in the area; and devotes special attention to rare and unusual species, such as the painted bunting.
♦ Students can keep track of how many different birds they see over a given time period.
1. Birds—South Carolina

615.882 (Reference)
Morton, Julia F. *Folk Remedies of the Low Country*. E. A. Seeman Publishing (0-912458-46-1), 1974. 176p. Color photos. (Interest level: 5-Adult).

This guide describes 62 plants used in folk remedies. Descriptions include botanical and common names, habitat, range, current use in South Carolina, historical medical uses, etc. This work is useful from a historical perspective and as a guide to native plants.
♦ Students can look up remedies described for common ailments, such as a cold or a fever.
1. Botany, Medical—South Carolina 2. Folk Medicine—South Carolina 3. Plants, Medicinal—South Carolina

641.3318
Hess, Karen. *The Carolina Rice Kitchen: The African Connection, Featuring a Facsimile of the Carolina Rice Cookbook*. Carolina Press (0-87249-666-X), 1992. 214p. (Interest level: 8-Adult).

This engaging work, packed with fascinating historical details, chronicles the history of rice in South

Carolina, documents its connection to slavery, and offers hundreds of recipes. The author presents a serious study of culinary history and explores a region and a culture that have not received a great deal of attention in the past.
♦ This work discusses the variations in cooking rice. Students can find out how rice is most frequently prepared in their community.
1. Cookery (Rice)—History 2. Rice—South Carolina—History 3. Cookery—South Carolina—History

641.59757
Geraty, Virginia Mixon. *Bittle en' T'ing: Gullah Cooking with Maum Chrish'*. Sandlapper (0-87844-107-7), 1992. 78p. B/W illus. (Interest level: 4-Adult).

This collection of recipes from the South Carolina Low Country is written in Gullah with English translations and includes an extensive glossary of Gullah words. The recipes are "told" in the voice of a character based on the granddaughter of a Yoruba-descended slave. This narrative format weaves together a collection of lore from a nearly vanished culture.
♦ See how well students can "translate" a recipe without looking at the glossary, then let them check to see how well they did.
1. Cookery—American—Southern Style 2. Cookery—South Carolina

700
Conversations with Artists. South Carolina Educational Television Network (No ISBN), n.d. 30 programs, (varying from 6 to 20 min.). Available on 1/2" VHS videocassettes. Series broadcast free in South Carolina; otherwise prices vary according to broadcast rights. Teacher's guide available. (Interest level: 7-12).

This is a series of intimate and informal interviews with artists who either currently live and work in South Carolina or have their roots there. The series provides students with valuable insights and information about artists and their work.
♦ Students can experiment with some of the artistic media employed by these artists.
1. Artists—South Carolina 2. South Carolina—Artists

720.92 (Reference)
Bryan, John M. *Robert Mills, Architect*. American Institute of Architects Press (1-55835-019-5), 1989. 196p. B/W illus. (Interest level: 7-Adult).

This book chronicles the life and accomplishments of Robert Mills, the South Carolina architect who designed the Washington Monument. An extensive collection of previously unpublished drawings and sketches is included in this work.
♦ Ask students to contrast the information about the Washington Monument in this work with that in another work to see what insights are gained.
1. Mills, Robert, 1781-1855 2. Architecture, Modern—19th Century—United States

720.9757 (Reference)
Ravenel, Beatrice St. Julien. *Architects of Charleston*. University of South Carolina Press (0-87249-828-X), 1992. 329p. B/W illus. (Interest level: 5-Adult).

This work chronicles the lives and accomplishments of the builders, engineers, and architects responsible for the historic city of Charleston, South Carolina. The subjects include Robert Mills, who designed the Washington Monument, as well as favored Charlestonians Gabriel Manigault and William Drayton.

♦ Students can visit some of the structures described in this work.

1. Architects—Charleston, South Carolina 2. Architecture—South Carolina—Charleston

729.4 (Reference)
Neuffer, Claude. *Correct Mispronunciations of Some South Carolina Names*. University of South Carolina Press (0-87249-424-1), 1983. 182p. (Interest level: 4-Adult).

This is an alphabetical listing of many of the most common names in South Carolina, including names of people, places, and things. The authors have included the correct spelling of each name, its phonetic equivalent, and a brief historical explanation of the pronunciation, making this an invaluable resource.

♦ Students can check to see if names from their regions are included and if not, make a pronunciation guide of their own.

1. Names—Geographical—South Carolina 2. Names, personal—South Carolina—Pronunciation 3. English language—South Carolina—Pronunciation 4. South Carolina—History, local

739.47
Vlach, John Michael. *Charleston Blacksmith: The Work of Philip Simmons*. University of South Carolina Press (0-87249-835-2), 1992. 172p. B/W photos. (Interest level: 6-Adult).

Charleston, South Carolina, is known for its beautiful ironwork, and this book is a guide to the work created by the city's best-known blacksmith, Philip Simmons. This book includes more than 100 photos of the artist's works, as well as methods, materials, motifs, and personal recollections of this gifted individual.

♦ Students can research blacksmithing to see if there have been any changes over the years.

1. Simmons, Philip 2. Blacksmiths—South Carolina

741.5975
Ariail, Robert. *Ariail View: Cartoons*. The State Printing Co. (No ISBN), 1990. Unpaginated. B/W illus. (Interest level: 4-Adult).

This is a collection of political cartoons drawn by the cartoonist of *The State* newspaper in Columbia, South Carolina. This gifted and award-winning cartoonist has a knack for finding the humor in any political issue. This volume contains a separate section of cartoons relevant to South Carolina.

♦ Using this book as a guide, students can try drawing a political cartoon about a current issue.

1. Caricatures and cartoons 2. South Carolina—Politics and government

745.075 (Reference)
Stanton, Gary. *Collecting South Carolina Folk Art: A Guide*. University of South Carolina. McMissack Museum (No ISBN), 1989. 42p. B/W illus. (Interest level: 6-Adult).

This brief guide outlines the rich and culturally diverse folk heritage of South Carolina by describing some of the folk life and folk arts to be found. The book illustrates many traditional arts, gives examples of historical and contemporary art, gives suggestions for collecting, and describes state agencies to contact for assistance.

♦ Students can explore their communities to discover the kinds of folk art available.

1. Folklore—South Carolina 2. Folk Art—South Carolina 3. South Carolina—Social life and customs

746.41
Rosengarten, Dale. *Row upon Row: Sea Baskets of the South Carolina Low Country*. University of South Carolina, McKissick Museum (0-938983-02-4), 1986. 64p. B/W illus. (Interest level: 6-Adult).

This work describes in great detail the coiled sea grass basketry that still flourishes today in the coastal regions of South Carolina. These baskets have evolved from an African folk art introduced into the state in the late seventeenth century. This book gives this art form the recognition it deserves and describes its present-day use.

♦ As an art project, students may want to create coiled baskets using rope and string.

1. Basket making—South Carolina 2. Grasswork

746.46 (Reference)
Horton, Laurel. *Social Fabric: South Carolina's Traditional Quilts*. University of South Carolina, McKissick Museum (No ISBN), n.d. 56p. B/W illus. (Interest level: 5-Adult).

This study of more than 1,300 traditional quilts created in South Carolina includes a brief description of textiles and quiltmaking traditions. This work, filled with photographs of quilts and of the women who created them, demonstrates that quilts are not just objects, but part of a family's life and heritage.

♦ Students can create a display of quilts belonging to members of their community.

1. Quilts—South Carolina

759.13
Everett, Gwen. *Li'l Sis and Uncle Willie: A Story Based on the Life and Paintings of William H. Johnson*. Rizzoli (0-8478-1462-9), 1991. Unpaginated. Color illus. (Interest level: 2-5).

This is a fictionalized account of the life of the South Carolina painter William Johnson, as told by his six-year-old niece. The artist's own paintings accompany the text, and they fit the text so well that it seems as though the artist illustrated his own story.

♦ Ask students to research the lives of other African-American artists.

1. Johnson, William H. 2. Artists 3. African-Americans—Biography 4. Painting—American

782.92
Rose, Cynthia. *Living in America: The Soul Saga of James Brown*. Serpent's Tail (1-85242-209-2), 1990. 182p. (Interest level: 6-Adult).

This work presents a comprehensive look at the life and music of South Carolina resident James Brown.

The author has interviewed James Brown and captures his personality, as well as his accomplishments.

♦ Play a recording of James Brown's music so students can appreciate his title as "King of Soul Music."

1. Soul Music 2. Brown, James

800

Conversations with S.C. Writers (Revised). Columbia: South Carolina Educational Television Network (No ISBN), n.d. 8 programs, (15 min.). Available on 1/2" VHS videocassettes. Series broadcast free in South Carolina, otherwise prices vary according to broadcast rights. Teacher's guide available. (Interest level: 4-12).

This series consists of interviews with authors, such as Tom Feelings and Eleanora Tate who either live and work in South Carolina or who have roots there, and who write for children and young adults. In these interviews, the authors read excerpts from their books and explain how they write, where they get ideas, and what writing skills an author needs.

♦ After viewing an interview, students can discuss how their perceptions of the writing process have changed.

1. South Carolina—Writers 2. Writers—South Carolina

912.757 (Reference)

Puetz, C.J., ed. *South Carolina County Maps*. Rev. ed. County Maps Puetz Place (0-916514-14-5), 1989. 128p. B/W illus. (Interest level:4-Adult).

This is an atlas of maps for each of the counties in South Carolina, arranged in alphabetical order. Brief information about each county is included. This book is oversized, making it very easy to read.

♦ Children can draw maps of their schoolyard, neighborhood, or town.

1. South Carolina—Maps

917.57 (Reference)

Kovacik, Charles F. *South Carolina: The Making of a Landscape*. University of South Carolina Press (0-87249-684-8), 1989. 235p. B/W illus. (Interest level: 6-Adult).

The state of South Carolina, though small in actual land area, encompasses a great deal of geographic diversity. This work, which describes the state's economic and cultural geography, is divided into three parts: the physical setting, the historical setting, and contemporary South Carolina. Ten regional subdivisions based on population are also identified.

♦ Take students on a field trip to observe firsthand the geography surrounding them.

1. South Carolina—Geography

917.57

Neuffer, Claude and **Neuffer, Irene**. *The Name Game: From Oyster Point to Keowee*. Sandlapper Press (0-87844-009-7), 1972. 60p. B/W illus. (Interest level: 4-8).

This is a compilation of the stories behind many of the place names in South Carolina, along with the appropriate historical context. The authors have an established reputation and have devoted years to researching the correct origins of these place names.

♦ Have students try to discover the origins of some of the names in their communities.

1. Names, Geographical 2. South Carolina—History 3. South Carolina—History

917.57 (Reference)

Pitzer, Sara. *Traveling in South Carolina: A Selective Guide to Where to Go, What to See, What to Do*. University of South Carolina Press (0-87249-868-9), 1992. 160p. B/W Illus. (Interest level: 4-Adult).

For the first-time traveler to South Carolina, as well as current residents, this guide provides detailed information on food, accommodations, and interesting places to visit. The book is divided into the three major geographic regions of upcountry, midlands, and low country and includes historical background, major attractions, little-known surprises, day trips, and places to stay and eat.

♦ Students can be critics and evaluate places and restaurants mentioned in this guide.

1. South Carolina—Description and travel

917.57

Rhyne, Nancy. *Touring the Coastal South Carolina Backroads*. J. F. Blair (0-89587-090-8), 1992. 276p. B/W illus. (Interest level: 4-Adult).

This guide describes 13 automobile tours created by the author through the Low Country of South Carolina, indicating the mileage and points of interest for each. This is more than just a tour book, because it is filled with little-known historical tidbits about out-of-the-way places like Frogmore, as well as more popular cities like Charleston, Beaufort, Myrtle Beach, and Georgetown.

♦ Students can take one of the tours described and make a list of, or take photographs of, their discoveries.

1. Automobile travel—South Carolina—Guidebooks
2. South Carolina—Description and travel—Tours

917.57

South Carolina Geography. South Carolina Educational Television Network (No ISBN), n.d. 7 programs, (20 min.). Available on 1/2" VHS videocassettes. Series broadcast free in South Carolina; otherwise prices vary according to broadcast rights. Teacher's guide available. (Interest level: 6-9).

This on-location production provides an in-depth study of South Carolina's geographic regions. The series is a good instructional resource for middle and junior high school teachers of South Carolina geography.

♦ Using terminology learned from this series, students can describe the geography of their town.

1. Geography—South Carolina 2. South Carolina—Geography

917.57 (Reference)

South Carolina Wildlife Facilities Atlas. South Carolina Wildlife Marine Resources Department (No ISBN), 1988. 128p. B/W and Color illus. 61 maps. (Interest level:4-Adult).

This is a county-by-county directory of the public wildlife facilities in South Carolina, including fishing piers, boat ramps, nature study areas, etc. The detailed

maps for each county, which identify the various types of facilities, make this an invaluable resource.
♦ Students can practice their map-reading skills by locating some of the facilities listed for their counties.
1. Boats and boating—South Carolina 2. Fishing—South Carolina 3. Outdoor Recreation—South Carolina

917.5771 (Reference)
Edwards, Ann Darlington. *The Governor's Mansion of the Palmetto State*. State Printing Co. (No ISBN), 1978. 124p. B/W and Color photos. (Interest level: 4-Adult).
This work describes and traces the history of the Governor's Mansion of South Carolina, including some of its famous former residents. A very readable text and photographs on almost every page give the reader an in-depth look at this stately old building.
♦ Students might want to create a guide for another historic building in their community.
1. Historic buildings—South Carolina 2. South Carolina—Governors

917.57915
Bill Settlemyer's Touring Charleston South Carolina. (Videocassette). The Settlemyer Company(No ISBN), 1987. 1 videocassette, 1/2" VHS, Color, (30 min.). $21.95. (Interest level: 4-Adult).
This tour of the historic city of Charleston includes nearby plantations, gardens, and beaches. The video lives up to its title, and viewers feel as though they are really touring Charleston.
♦ If a video camera is available, students may want to showcase their own towns using this video as a model.
1. Automobile travel—South Carolina—Guidebooks 2. South Carolina—Description and Travel—Tours.

923.2757 (Reference)
Governors of South Carolina: 1776-Present. 2nd ed. Piedmont Co. (No ISBN), 1988. 44p. B/W illus. (Interest level: 3-Adult).
This ready-reference work puts concise biographical information about each of the governors of South Carolina at the reader's fingertips. The authors have tried to include a photograph or portrait for each biography, as well as a selective bibliography of useful sources for further research.
♦ Using only their photographs, see how many of the governors students are able to recognize.
1. South Carolina—Governors

970.1 (Reference)
Bierer, Bert W. *South Carolina Indian Lore*. The State Printing Co. (No ISBN), 1972. 164p. B/W and Color illus. (Interest level: 6-Adult).
This is a detailed account of South Carolina's Native American population, including its history, archaeology, ceramics, trade paths, etc. This well-researched book is filled with maps and photographs that clearly illustrate the influence the native peoples exerted on this state.

♦ Students might want to write a paper or lead a discussion about contributions made by these tribes.
1. Indians of North America—South Carolina—Antiquities

970.3
Merrell, James Hart. *The Catawbas*. New York: Chelsea House (0-55546-694-X), 1989. Indians of North America. 112p. Color Illus., (includes B/W photos). (Interest level: 6-8).
This very thorough presentation of the history and culture of the Catawba, a tribe indigenous to South Carolina, begins with their first contact with Spanish explorers and ends with their very recent legal attempts to reclaim their homeland. This is one of the few books available to this age group devoted solely to the Catawba.
♦ Ask students to find out what has transpired since this book was published concerning the Catawba's legal attempts to regain their traditional homeland.
1. Catawba Indians

973.337
Daybreak at the Cowpens: Turning Point in the Revolution.(Videocassette). Spectrum South, Inc. (No ISBN), 1990. 1/2" VHS, Color, (20 min.). $29.95. (Interest level: 4-Adult).
This is a dramatic re-creation of the Battle of Cowpens, January 17, 1781, as recounted by a survivor. This story is based on the poem "Battle of the Cowpens" by Arthur Magill.
♦ Locate the poem on which this video was based and have students contrast the two.
1. Cowpens, Battle of, 1781 2. South Carolina—History—Revolution, 1775-1783 3. United States—History—Revolution

975.6 (Reference)
Gaillard, Frye. *Becoming Truly Free—300 Years of Black History in the Carolinas*. Charlotte Observer (0-9614-6030-X), 1985. 80p. B/W illus. (Interest level: 6-Adult).
This is an expansion of a series of articles, which first appeared in the *Charlotte Observer*, that chronicle how the status and circumstances of African Americans have changed in the Carolinas during the last 300 years. This is not a scholarly work, but rather a synopsis of events arranged in 50-year increments.
♦ Students can pick a period in American history and contrast the status of African Americans then to their status now.
1. African-Americans—North Carolina—History 2. African-Americans—South Carolina—History

975.7 (Reference)
Clements, John. *More Than an Almanac, South Carolina Facts: A Comprehensive Look at South Carolina Today, County by County*. Clements Research II, Inc. (ISSN 1056-960X), 1991. 278p. Color Illus. (Interest level: 4-Adult).
This work presents an overview of current information about South Carolina in an expanded almanac format. It is not indexed, but it contains an easy-to-use table of contents designed to put statistics at the reader's fingertips.

♦ Using this work as a resource, students can create a trivia game.

1. South Carolina

975.7 (Reference)
Edgar, Walter B. *South Carolina in the Modern Age.* University of South Carolina Press (0-87249-830-1), 1992. 272p. B/W Illus. (Interest level: 6-Adult).

This book, the first history of contemporary South Carolina to appear in more than 25 years, chronicles the events of the last 100 years, as the state emerged from the devastation of the Civil War into mainstream America. This volume, written by a University of South Carolina history professor, includes a chronology of South Carolina history, notes, a list of suggested readings, and more than 70 illustrations, many not previously published.

♦ Students can compare the chronology of events listed in this work with one listed in another source to see if they agree.

1. South Carolina—History—1865-

975.7 (Reference)
Fort Sumter: Anvil of War, Fort Sumter National Monument South Carolina. National Park Service, U.S. Department of the Interior. (I 29.9/5:127), 1984. 63p. Color photos. (Interest level: 4-Adult).

This compact guide to Fort Sumter, located near Charleston, South Carolina, includes both historical and contemporary maps. This book clearly and concisely presents the historical significance of Fort Sumter and outlines its role in the Civil War.

♦ Ask students to pretend they are soldiers on the eve of the Civil War and write an imagined account of their experiences.

1. Fort Sumter (Charleston, S.C.)—History 2. Charleston (S.C.)—History—Civil War, 1861-1865

975.7 (Reference)
Heisser, David C. R. *The Seal of the State of South Carolina: A Short History.* South Carolina Department of Archives and History (1-880067-11-0), 1992. 36p. B/W illus. (Interest level: 6-Adult).

The history of the development of the seal used to represent the state of South Carolina is presented in a concise and readable text. Black-and-white illustrations enhance the text and clearly delineate the changes that were made to the seal.

♦ As a follow-up activity, students might want to design a seal that represents their own personal attributes.

1. South Carolina—History

975.7 (Reference)
Landler, Ernest McPherson. *South Carolina: An Illustrated History of the Palmetto State.* Windsor Publications (0-89781-262-X), 1988. 232p. B/W photos. (Interest level: 6-Adult).

This is a brief illustrated history of South Carolina, from its early inhabitants to contemporary culture. More than 150 portraits, maps, drawings, and photos, each with a detailed caption, enhance this readable text.

♦ Students can compile an album of photographs about their geographic region and write captions to accompany them.

1. South Carolina—History

975.700496 (Reference)
Ferguson, Leland G. *Uncommon Ground: Archeology and Early African America, 1650-1800.* Smithsonian Institute Press (1-56098-059-3), 186p. B/W illus. (Interest level: 7-Adult).

The author, an archaeologist, pieces together the culture of the early slaves in South Carolina and shows how they used skills from their homeland to create a new life. The author spent more than 10 years in the field collecting the artifacts upon which this work is based.

♦ Compare the descriptions of the lives of slaves in this work with those in other sources to check for discrepancies.

1. Slavery—South Carolina 2. Slave—South Carolina—Social conditions 3. Plantations—South Carolina 4. African-Americans—South Carolina—Antiquities 5. South Carolina—Antiquities 6. South Carolina—History—Colonial Period, ca 1600-1775

975.700496073 (Reference)
To Walk the Whole Journey: African-American Cultural Resources in South Carolina. South Carolina Department of Parks, Recreation and Tourism: South Carolina State Museum (No ISBN), 1992. 35p. (Interest level: 4-Adult).

This directory of resources on the cultural heritage of African Americans in South Carolina includes a listing of colleges and universities, festivals, monuments, historic houses, museums, schools, businesses, research and archival resources, as well as others. Because the information is arranged both by type of resource and geographically by county, this is a useful guide.

♦ Students can use the directory to plan a holiday celebration or a trip to an interesting site.

1. African-Americans—South Carolina—History—Directories 2. South Carolina—Description and travel—Guidebooks

975.704 (Reference)
Moore, John H. *South Carolina in the Eighteen Eighties: A Gazetteer.* Sandlapper Publishing (0-87844-069-0), 1989. 322p. B/W photos. (Interest level: 6-9).

This is a collection of actual news reports from South Carolina's leading newspaper of the 1880s, Charleston's *News and Courier*, that present portraits of towns. These essays, arranged in alphabetical order, include details that in many cases can not be found anywhere else and give a glimpse into the day-to-day life of South Carolina more than 100 years ago.

♦ After reading one of these articles, students might want to write an article about their own town for readers 100 years in the future.

1. Cities and towns—South Carolina 2. South Carolina—Description and travel

975.7

Daise, Ronald. *Reminiscences of Sea Island Heritage.* Sandlapper Publishing (0-87844-081-X), 1986. 117p. B/W photos. (Interest level: 6-8).

The author, a native islander, documents the lifestyles and customs of St. Helena Island, gleaned from the memories of a group of its residents. This collection of folktales, spirituals, and beliefs, illustrated with photographs taken on the island in the late 1800s and early 1900s, helps to preserve a unique language and culture.

◆ In the *Foxfire* tradition, ask students to gather photographs, stories, tales, etc., similar to those included in this collection. Or the teacher could select one of the customs, tales, etc.—such as the "cakewalk"—and have students research it in their own community.

1. South Carolina

975.7

Fradin, Dennis B. *South Carolina.* Children's Press (0-516-03840-0), 1992. From Sea to Shining Sea. 64p. B/W illus. (Interest level: 4-6).

This book gives a brief overview of South Carolina, including its history, geography, economy, flora, fauna, and famous people. The size of the text, attractive illustrations, and tables make an inviting presentation of the information.

◆ This book includes a page of interesting facts about South Carolina called "Did You Know." Students can write additional items to be included.

1. South Carolina

975.7

Hurmence, Belinda, ed. *Before Freedom, When I Just Can Remember: Twenty-Seven Oral Histories of Former South Carolina Slaves.* John F. Blair (0-89587-069-X), 1989. 135p. (Interest level: 7-Adult).

This is a collection of carefully edited oral narratives about slavery and the Reconstruction era in South Carolina, as told by men and women who were in their eighties, nineties, and hundreds during the Great Depression. These sometimes brief and moving passages give a real sense of everyday life as experienced by African-Americans during the time of the Civil War through Reconstruction.

◆ Using these narratives as a model, students can gather stories from elderly people in the same age range (eighties to hundreds).

1. Slaves—South Carolina—Biography 2. African-Americans—South Carolina—Biography 3. Slavery—South Carolina—History sources 4. Oral history 5. South Carolina—Biography

975.7

Kent, Deborah. *America the Beautiful, South Carolina.* Children's Press (0-516-00486-7), 1990. 144p. Color Illus. (Interest level: 4-6).

This is a brief overview of the history, geography, culture, and people of the Palmetto state. "Facts at a Glance," which comprises the last 30 pages, includes basic general information, such as important dates and people, governors, etc., in an almanac form, which makes the information accessible.

◆ Students can compare the information presented in this book with the information found in a children's encyclopedia. Which source presents the information most clearly?

1. South Carolina

975.7

Lyman, Nancy. *The Colony of South Carolina.* Watts (0-531-00831-2), 1975. (A First Book). 81p. B/W illus. (Interest level: 4-8).

This work offers a description of the history, way of life, and important people and places of colonial South Carolina. The effective use of white space, numerous illustrations, catchy chapter headings, and listings of important people, places, and dates, make this a useful work.

◆ It might be interesting to have students locate the important places in colonial South Carolina on a contemporary map to see how they fared.

1. South Carolina—History—Colonial period, ca 1600-1775 2. South Carolina—Social life and customs—Colonial period—ca 1600-1775

975.7

Mary Long's Yesteryear. Rev. South Carolina Educational Television Network (No ISBN), n.d. 18 programs, (30 min.). Available on 1/2" VHS videocassettes. Series broadcast free in South Carolina; otherwise prices vary according to broadcast rights. Teacher's guide available. (Interest level: 8-12).

These programs, created by Mary Long, who has more than 40 years of experience in theater and teaching drama, present many of the historical sites in South Carolina. Students travel with Long to some of the places they study about in South Carolina history.

◆ Let students produce a historical video about their own town.

1. South Carolina—History

975.7

Osborne, Anne R. *The South Carolina Story.* Sandlapper Publishing (0-87844-083-6), 1988. 240p. B/W illus. (Interest level: 4-Adult).

This easy-to-read history of South Carolina highlights people, places, and events from South Carolina's prehistory to the present time. This work is not intended to be a scholarly text, but rather to appeal to a wide audience and to develop appreciation for the state's history.

◆ Encourage students to talk about some of the events that have had the most impact on South Carolina's development.

1. South Carolina—History

975.7

The Palmetto Special. South Carolina Educational Television Network (No ISBN). 39 programs, (20 min.). Available on 1/2" VHS videocassettes. Series broadcast free in South Carolina; otherwise prices vary according to broadcast rights. (Interest level: 6+).

This series of videos explores topics in South Carolina's history through dramatization, visits to locations, interviews, historic photographs, and other visuals. It is accompanied by a revised teacher's lesson guide that reflects the restructuring of the middle school curriculum.

♦ Have students shoot a short video describing their town and its history.

1. South Carolina—History

975.7
Pettus, Louise. *The Palmetto State: Stories from the Making of South Carolina*. Sandlapper Publishing (0-87844-097-6), 1991. 317p. (Interest level: 6-Adult).

This is a collection of 79 tales about South Carolina history, ranging from the sixteenth century up through the 1960s. The stories are arranged chronologically in sections and reflect the diversity of the state's cultural heritage.

♦ Using the style of this book as a model, students can write about events that have occurred in South Carolina since the late 1960s.

1. South Carolina—History

975.7042
Schultz, Constance B., ed. *A South Carolina Album, 1936-1948: Documentary Photography in the Palmetto State*. University of South Carolina Press (0-87249-816-6), 1992. 142p. B/W photos. (Interest level: 4-Adult).

This collection of photographs captures the people of South Carolina in the years of the Great Depression. All of the photographs have been printed from original negatives and arranged chronologically. The captions include date, place, and identifying remarks.

♦ Students can create a contemporary photograph album to show what life is like today.

1. Depressions—1929—South Carolina—Pictorial works 2. Documentary photography—South Carolina 3. South Carolina—Pictorial works 4. South Carolina—Social conditions—Pictorial works

975.771 (Reference)
Moore, John Hammond. *Columbia and Richland County: A South Carolina Community, 1740-1990*. University of South Carolina Press (0-87249-827-1), 1992. 544p. B/W illus. (Interest level: 6-Adult).

This work chronicles more than 250 years in the development of Columbia, the South Carolina state capitol, and is organized into five chronological sections. The author has done extensive research and bases this work on family papers, reminiscences, census returns, newspaper files, and documents.

♦ Students can research the history of their own town and create a slide/tape or video based on their research.

1. Columbia(S.C.)—History 2. Richland County (S.C.)—History

975.787
Gragg, Rod. *Pirates, Planters & Patriots: Historical Tales from the South Carolina Grand Strand*. Peace Hill Publishers (0-916253-00-7), 1985. 150p. B/W illus. (Interest level: 6-9).

This is a brief and very readable collection of stories about colorful characters from the Grand Strand—that 55 mile-long stretch from Little River to Georgetown, South Carolina. The author, a former television journalist, has compiled and organized this information for

the first time and has included an extensive bibliography of many primary sources.

♦ Involve students in creative dramatics, giving them the opportunity to role play the characters.

1. Myrtle Beach Region (S.C.)—History

Biography

See also biographical entries from the South Carolina Nonfiction section, especially under 700, 720.92, 800, and 923.2757.

920.72
Bodie, Idella. *South Carolina Women: They Dared to Lead*. 2nd ed. Sandlapper Publishing (0-87844-079-8), 1990. 154p. B/W illus. (Interest level: 6+).

This collection of biographies of 51 South Carolina women is written in an interesting and informative narrative form and arranged in chronological order, from colonial to contemporary times. The book includes a listing of many other South Carolina women who have distinguished themselves in their fields. The author's intent is to help young people appreciate the contributions women have made.

♦ Students can select one of the women listed in the last chapter and write a short biography.

1. Women—South Carolina—Biography 2. South Carolina—History 3. Leadership

92 Bethune, Mary McLeod
Halasa, Malu. *Mary McLeod Bethune: Educator*. Chelsea House (1-55546-574-9), 1989. (Black Americans of Achievement). 111p. B/W photos. (Interest level: 6-8).

This work chronicles the life and numerous achievements of Mary McLeod Bethune, the educator who was born in 1875 in Mayesville, South Carolina, and devoted her life to seeking equality for African Americans in education and political rights. The biography is well organized and includes a bibliography of related works and a chronology of Bethune's achievements.

♦ Students can create a time line of the civil rights movement. Where do Bethune's contributions fit?

1. Bethune, Mary McLeod, 1875-1955 2. Teachers 3. African-Americans—Biography

92 Gibson, Althea
Biracree, Tom. *Althea Gibson*. Chelsea House (1-55546-654-0), 1989. (American Women of Achievement). 109p. B/W photos. (Interest level: 5-8).

This work describes the life of Althea Gibson, the first African-American woman to win the women's tennis championship at Wimbledon, from her birth in Silver, South Carolina, in 1927. The judicious use of clear photographs and nice type make this an accessible biography.

♦ Students can identify other African-American athletes who were "firsts" in particular sports.

1. Gibson, Althea, 1927 2. Tennis players 3. African-Americans—Biography

92 Gillespie, Dizzy
Gentry, Tony. *Dizzy Gillespie*. Chelsea House (0-7910-1127-5), 1991. (Black Americans of Achievement). 110p. B/W photos. (Interest level: 6-8).

The life and accomplishments of Dizzy Gillespie, the great jazz musician who was born in Cheraw, South Carolina, in 1917, are presented. A readable text and good use of photographs make this a useful work.
♦ You might share a recording of Dizzy Gillespie's music, so students can appreciate his contribution.
1. Gillespie, Dizzy, 1917-1992 2. Musicians 3. African-Americans—Biography

92 Jackson, Jesse
Halliburton, Warren. *The Picture Life of Jesse Jackson*. 2nd ed. Watts (0-531-084808-X), 1984. 48p. B/W photos. (Interest level: 1-3).

This brief biography describes the life of Jesse Jackson, the African-American minister and civil rights worker, from his South Carolina childhood through his unsuccessful 1984 campaign for the Democratic presidential nomination. The large typeface and the photographs on every other page make this book appealing to the youngest readers.
♦ Jackson has had other accomplishments since this biography was written; help students bring this work up to date.
1. Jackson, Jesse, 1941- 2. African-Americans—Biography 3. Civil Rights workers

92 Jackson, Jesse
Jakoubek, Robert. *Jesse Jackson: Civil Rights Leader and Politician*. Chelsea House (0-7910-1130-5), 1991. (Black Americans of Achievement). 127p. B/W photos (Interest level: 6-8).

This is a good overview of the life and accomplishments of Jesse Jackson, the internationally known politician who was born in 1941 in Greenville, South Carolina. Many informative photographs and the catchy chapter headings help to engage the reader.
♦ Students may use newspaper and periodical indexes to find the most recent information on Jackson's career.
1. Jackson, Jesse, 1941- 2. Civil rights workers 3. African-Americans—Biography

92 McNair, Ronald E.
Naden, Corinne. *Ronald McNair*. Chelsea House (0-7910-1133-X), 1991. (Black Americans). 109p. B/W photos. (Interest level: 6-8).

The book covers the life and accomplishments of the second African-American astronaut, Ronald McNair, a native of Lake City, South Carolina, who was killed during the ill-fated Challenger space shuttle mission. Clear and expressive photos and an index extend the text.
♦ Students can imagine what it might be like to be an astronaut and write a description of a flight they took.
1. McNair, Ronald E. 2. Astronauts 3. African-Americans—Biography

92 Vesey, Denmark
Edwards, Lillie J. *Denmark Vesey: Slave Revolt Leader*. Chelsea House (1-55546-614-1), 1990. (Black Americans of Achievement). 109p. B/W photos. (Interest level: 6-8).

This is a biography of Denmark Vesey, the slave whose 1822 revolt failed and prompted South Carolina to pass even stricter laws limiting the education, movement, and occupations of slaves and free African Americans. The author is a history professor who has written extensively about the African-American experience.
♦ Lead a discussion about the consequences of this revolt. Do the students feel it accomplished anything?
1. Vesey, Denmark, 1767(ca)-1822 2. Slaves 3. African-Americans—Biography 4. Charleston(S.C.)—History—Slave insurrection

Fiction

Beatty, John and **Beatty, Patricia**. *Who Comes to King's Mountain?*. Morrow (0-688-22041-X), 1975. 287p. (Interest level: 6-8).

A young boy, Alec McLeod, who lives in the Highland Scots community of Ninety-Six Section, South Carolina, during the Revolutionary War, must decide which side he will follow, Loyalist or Rebel. This exciting novel presents both fictitious and historical characters in a clear and vivid manner while spanning events from the taking of Charles Towne in 1780 to the Battle of King's Mountain.
♦ Students can discuss the choice Alec had to make. Do they agree with his decision?
1. United States—History—Revolution, 1775-1783—Fiction

Bodie, Idella. *Ghost in the Capitol*. Sandlapper (0-87844-072-0), 1976. 118p. B/W illus. (Interest level: 4-6).

There seems to be a ghost inhabiting the South Carolina state capitol building, and three children are determined to meet him. The author includes historical events in the story through conversation and also shares incidental information on poltergeists and haunted houses.
♦ Students may want to write fictionalized accounts about other historical landmarks.
1. Ghost stories 2. South Carolina—Fiction

Edwards, Sally. *Isaac and Snow*. Coward (TR-698-20244-9), 1973. 123p. B/W illus. (Interest level: 4-6).

A young boy, Isaac, discovers a white porpoise and begins training her. But when others discover his secret, they begin to plan how the porpoise could be used to bring money and tourists to the isolated sea island community off the coast of South Carolina. This is a good presentation of life in an island community.
♦ Have students research the habits of porpoises to see how true-to-life the author's portrayal of them is in this book. See if students can discover what causes albinism.
1. Porpoises—Fiction 2. Sea islands—Fiction

Edwards, Sally. *When the World's on Fire*. Illus. by Richard Lebenson. Coward, (No ISBN), 1972. 125p. B/W illus. (Interest level: 4-6).

Annie, a nine-year-old slave, matches wits against the British soldiers who are occupying Charleston, South Carolina, during the American Revolution. The excellent characterization brings this period of history to life for younger readers.

♦ Annie had a difficult decision to make; students can discuss her options and whether they agree with her decision.

1. United States—History—Revolution, 1775-1783—Fiction

Hansen, Joyce. *Out from This Place*. Walker & Co. (0-8027-6816-4), 1988. (Walkers American History Series for Young People). 135p. (Interest level:6-8).

This sequel to the 1987 Coretta Scott King Honor Book, *Which Way Freedom?*, continues the story of Easter and Obi. In the sequel, the Civil War has ended and Reconstruction is the result of a country turned upside down. This time period in our history is presented from a special perspective—that of former slaves.

♦ Encourage students to choose another period or event in history and write about it from another perspective.

1. African-Americans—History—1863-1877—Fiction 2. Reconstruction—Fiction 3. United States—History—1865-1898

Hansen, Joyce. *Which Way Freedom?*. Walker (0-8027-6623-4), 1986. (Walkers American History Series for Young People). 120p. (Interest level: 6-8).

Although 200,000 African Americans fought in the Civil War, historically their contributions have been neglected. This realistically written story of three slaves from a plantation near Charleston, South Carolina, is based on quotes from original sources and was the Coretta Scott King Honor Book for 1987.

♦ Students might want to contrast this work of fiction with a nonfiction work to check its accuracy.

1. Fort Pillow, Battle of, 1864—Fiction 2. African-American soldiers—Fiction 3. United States—History—Civil War, 1861-1865—Participation, African-American—Fiction

Hooks, William F. *The Ballad of Belle Dorcas*. Illus. by Brian Pinkney. Knopf (0-394-84645-1), 1990. Unpaginated. Color illus. (Interest level: 2-5).

Belle Dorcas, a freeborn African-American woman, gives up her freedom to marry Joshua, a slave. When a cruel master tries to separate them, a conjure woman's spell reunites them. This tale is based on those that abound in the tidewater sections of the Carolinas, where conjure men or women may still be found today among the Gullah people who live in the offshore islands of the Carolinas.

♦ Ask students to see if they can find a similar tale among the European tradition of Grimm and Perrault.

1. African-American—Fiction 2. Slavery—Fiction 3. Magic—Fiction

Rhyne, Nancy. *Alice Flagg: The Ghost of the Hermitage: A Novel*. Pelican Publishing Company (0-88289-760-8), 1990. 255p. (Interest level: 7-Adult).

This work of historical fiction, set in Murell's Inlet, South Carolina, in the 1800s, is based on the true story of the ill-fated love between Alice Flagg, a 15-year-old planter's daughter, and a common lumberman. Alice is a legendary and well-known figure in South Carolina, and the author does a good job of documenting her life and afterlife, as people still claim to see her ghost today, more than 140 years after her death.

♦ Since this is a work of fiction based on fact, students can discuss what constitutes the difference between this work and a biography.

1. Flagg, Alice Belin, 1833-1849—Fiction 2. South Carolina—History—Fiction

Rhyne, Nancy. *Once upon a Time on a Plantation*. Illus. by Joan Holub. Pelican Publishing Co. (0-88289-702-0), 1988. 159p. B/W illus. (Interest level: 4-6).

This is a collection of nine short stories, which center around two twelve-year-old boys who live on an antebellum plantation in South Carolina. The author, a South Carolina resident, was inspired to write these stories after hearing tales told by Will Alston of Hampton Plantation in South Carolina.

♦ Since these stories are written from a boy's perspective, children can imagine and discuss what girls' lives might have been like during this time.

1. Plantation life—South Carolina—Fiction 2. South Carolina—Fiction

Rumsey, Marian. *Carolina Hurricane*. Morrow (0-688-22128-9), 1977. 157p. B/W Illus. (Interest level: 4-6).

A boy and his dog are at the mercy of a hurricane after they become stranded on a remote marsh island off the coast of South Carolina. This story presents a chilling firsthand account of the fury of a hurricane.

♦ Students can pretend that they are at the mercy of some act of nature and write an account of the experience.

1. Hurricane—Fiction

Tate, Eleanora E. *The Secret of Gumbo Grove*. Watts (0-553-27226-8), 1987. 266p. (Interest level: 4-6).

In this novel, set in the fictitious beach town of Gumbo Grove, South Carolina, we meet 11-year-old Raisin. Raisin has learned in school that African Americans never did anything "worth talking about," so she decides to become involved in her community and discovers that African-Americans have indeed made important contributions. This book provides a good portrait of a small southern town and promotes the importance of uncovering one's history.

♦ Students may wish to interview people in their communities who have made important contributions.

1. African-Americans—Fiction 2. South Carolina—Fiction 3. Mystery and detective stories

Tate, Eleanora E. *Thank You, Dr. Martin Luther King, Jr!*. Watts (0-531-15151-40), 1990. 237p. (Interest level: 4-6).

The children of Gumbo Grove, a fictitious beach town in South Carolina, discover during Black History Month that African Americans have made many important contributions. This is a sequel to Tate's *The Secret of Gumbo Grove* and reinforces the same themes.

♦ Students can write thank you letters to other people (famous or otherwise).
1. African-Americans—Fiction 2. African-Americans—History—Fiction

Periodicals

507
South Carolina Wildlife. South Carolina Wildlife and Marine Resources Department (ISSN 0038-3198). Bimonthly. Color photos. $10.00 per year. (Interest level: 6-Adult).
The articles in this journal deal with state parks and forests, natural flora and fauna, and recreation. A listing of events throughout the state is included as a regular feature. The aim is to promote public awareness and educate people about the importance of conserving, protecting, and restoring South Carolina wildlife.

590.744
Riverbanks. Riverbanks Zoological Society, P.O. Box 1060, Columbia, SC 29202. Quarterly. Subscription provided to members of the Zoological Society. $25.00 per year. (Interest level: 2-Adult).
This journal includes a range of articles, from general interest stories about animals to articles specifically related to Riverbanks Zoo. A calendar of events and a listing of new animals either born or acquired by the zoo are included. *Parade* selected this zoo as one of the 10 best for its size in the country.

917.57
Pee Dee Magazine. Pee Dee Magazine, Inc., P.O. Box 5070, Florence, SC 29502. Bimonthly. $18.90. (Interest level: 4-Adult).
The articles in this journal range from historical to contemporary and include events, places, economy, people, etc.. A regular feature, "Pee Dee Profile," features an interview with a resident who is making an interesting contribution to the region. This journal's purpose is to celebrate the history, lifestyle, and culture of the Pee Dee region of South Carolina.

917.57
Sandlapper: The Magazine of South Carolina. RPW Publishing Corp., 334 Old Chapin road, Lexington, SC 29072. (ISSN 1046-3267). Quarterly. $14.95 per year. (Interest level: 4-Adult).
The articles in this journal cover a wide range of topics of general interest to residents of South Carolina. The topics may be of either contemporary or historical focus and include people, places, events, etc., along with a regular feature entitled "Place Names in South Carolina."

Professional Materials

016.9757
Epps, Edwin C. *South Carolina Literature: A Reading List for Students, Educators, and Laymen.* Rev. ed. Woodspurge Books (No ISBN), 1989. 31p. (Interest level: 6-Adult).

This is a partially annotated bibliography of South Carolina materials that fit into three categories: those written by South Carolina natives, those written by longtime residents, and those about some aspect of the state's history or culture. The author has used the same chronology as Dr. Lewis P. Jones in his textbook, *South Carolina: One of Fifty States* (Sandlapper Publishing, 1991)
1. South Carolina—Bibliography 2. South Carolina—History—Bibliography

025.1734
Government Documents in South Carolina: A Directory of Collections of Federal, State, Local and Council of Government Libraries in South Carolina. 2nd ed. Government Documents Round Table, South Carolina Library Association (No ISBN), 1992. 72p. (Interest level: 8-Adult).
This guide to government documents in South Carolina is arranged alphabetically by city, then alphabetically by institution. Each entry includes the kinds of documents in the collection, services provided, and whether fees are charged.
1. Government publications—South Carolina 2. State government publications—South Carolina

975.7
The Civilian Conservation Corps in South Carolina, 1933-1942. Public Programs Division, South Carolina Department of Archives and History (1-80067005-6 series), 1990. (Public Programs Document Packet No. 4). B/W illus. (Interest level: 6-8).
This packet of resource material for teachers is designed to introduce students to the Civilian Conservation Corps and to help them appreciate its impact on the South Carolina economy during the Great Depression. This is a self-contained unit that gives students the opportunity to handle reproductions of archival material.
1. Civilian Conservation Corps (U.S.)—South Carolina 2. Public Service Employment—South Carolina 3. South Carolina—History—Study and Teaching

975.7
Copp, Roberta. *Community as Classroom: An Oral History Resource Publication.* Public Programs Division, South Carolina Department of Archives and History (1-880067-06-4), 1991. (Public Programs Document Packet No. 7). 38p. B/W illus. (Interest level: 6-8).
This is a collection of resources designed to introduce students and teachers to the concept of using oral history projects to link their curriculum to their community and bring history to life. The packet is basically a "how to" manual full of useful ideas and procedures and includes suggestions for possible projects.
1. Oral History

975.7
Copp, Roberta. *Jones: Time of Crisis, Time of Change.* Public Programs Division, South Carolina Department of Archives and History (1-880067-05-6 series), 1989. (Public Programs Document Packet No. 2). 24p. Illus.; Maps. (Interest level: 6-8).

This packet, a follow-up to the first packet in this series, continues the story of the Jones family to cover the years from 1835 to 1860. This unit also includes reproductions of primary source archival materials for students to utilize in their research.
1. Jones, Jehu 2. South Carolina—History—Study and teaching

975.7
Copp, Roberta. *South Carolina African-Americans in the Civil War: Two Sides to a Story*. South Carolina Public Programs Division Department of Archives and History (1-880067-05-6 series), 1990. (Public Programs Document Packet No. 6). Illus.; Maps. (Interest level: 6-8).

This collection of materials presents the choices that African Americans had to make during the Civil War, whether to remain loyal to the state of South Carolina or to fight for the Union. This teaching packet, like the others in this series, contains learning activities for students and suggestions for teachers.
1. South Carolina—History—Study and teaching
2. South Carolina—History—Civil War 1861-1865
3. United States—History—Civil War 1861-1865—African-Americans

975.7
Copp, Roberta. *The Spanish in South Carolina: Unsettled Frontier*. Public Programs Division, South Carolina Department of Archives and History (1-880067-05-6 series), 1989. (Public Programs Document Packet No. 3). Maps. (Interest level: 6-9).

This is a teacher's packet of reproductions of archival materials to help students understand the Spanish influence in South Carolina, and why the colony became an English rather than a Spanish colony. A strength of this packet, like the others in this series, is the opportunity it affords students to develop their critical thinking skills.
1. South Carolina—History—Study and teaching 2. Spaniards—South Carolina

975.7
Heritage Education. Public Programs Division, South Carolina Department of Archives and History (1-80067-05-6 series), 1990. (Public Programs Document Packet No. 5). B/W illus. (Interest level: 6-8).

This teaching packet is designed to help children begin to look more critically at various types of architecture and put architecture into its proper historical perspective. The packet contains a variety of learning activities, an extensive bibliography, and suggestions for further research.
1. South Carolina—History—Study and teaching
2. Architecture—South Carolina—Study and teaching

975.7
Jehu Jones: Free Black Entrepreneur. Public Programs Division, South Carolina Department of Archives and History (1-80067-05-6 series), 1989. (Public Programs Document Packet No. 1). B/W illus. (Interest level: 6-8).

This packet of reproductions of primary source archival materials can help students understand the life and times of Jehu Jones, a free African American in early nineteenth-century Charleston, South Carolina. This self-contained packet includes suggestions for the teacher, as well as ideas for possible research projects.
1. Jones, Jehu 2. Charleston (S.C.)—History—Study and teaching 3. Archives—South Carolina—Study and teaching

975.7
Jones, Lewis P. *Books and Articles on South Carolina History*. 2nd ed. University of South Carolina Press (0-87249-649-X), 1991. 177p. (Interest level: 6-Adult).

This comprehensive annotated bibliography, arranged in chronological order, is designed to provide readers "enough good reading" to satisfy their interest and curiosity about South Carolina and to reach teachers, students, and laymen. The book lists generally available titles and articles in periodicals that are often overlooked.
1. South Carolina

975.7
Schulz, Constance B. *The History of South Carolina Slide Collection: Master Guide: Uses, Captions, Index*. Sandlapper Publishing (No ISBN), 1989. 124p. (Interest level: 4-Adult).

This is a guide to a commercially available collection of more than 1,000 slides of South Carolina divided into ten general categories and distributed by the same publisher. This book includes detailed information about each slide in the collection, as well as a comprehensive index.
1. South Carolina—History—Audiovisual aids
2. South Carolina—History—Sources

Tennessee

by David Mielke

Nonfiction

016.91768 (Reference)
Smith, Sam. *Tennessee History: A Bibliography*. BKS Demand (087049158X), 1990. 498p. (Interest level: 4-8+).

This is the standard historical bibliography on Tennessee. It consists of the full range of Tennessee historical interest and will be useful for the fourth through eighth grade student.

♦ Students can find out what the oldest books are on Tennessee, who wrote them, and why.

1. Tennessee—History.

026.941
Marsh, Carole. *The Tennessee Library Book*. Gallopade Publishing Group (0-7933-3131-5), 1992. 36p. (Interest level: All Ages).

This guide to the many unusual special collections in libraries across Tennessee is useful for students, teachers, and other writers. It includes a reproducible research form, glossary, and activities for young readers.

♦ Students may invite a librarian to their class to tell them how libraries develop special collections of materials like the ones described in this book.

1. Tennessee—Libraries.

031
Marsh, Carole. *Tennessee Quiz Bowl Crash Course!* Gallopade Publishing Group (0-7933-2059-3), 1992. 36p. (Interest level: 4-6+).

This book has questions and answers about Tennessee on a variety of topics. It would be great for academic competition preparation or just for fun.

♦ Students may divide into two teams and have their own quiz bowl using the questions in this book.

1. Tennessee.

133.1
Shebar, Sharon Sigmond and **Mirrill, Leslie H**. *The Bell Witch*. J. Messner (0-671-44005-5), 1983, 63p. Illus. (Interest level: 3-6).

This book traces the history of "Old Kate," the ghost that haunted the Bell family of Tennessee between 1817 and 1820. This is a suspenseful and well-written book.

♦ Students may discuss their belief or lack of belief in the existence of ghosts.

1. History—Tennessee 2. Tennessee—Folklore.

133.1
Windham, Kathryn Tucker. *Thirteen Tennessee Ghosts and Jeffrey*. Strode Publishers (0-87397-108-6), 1977, 159p. B/W illus. (Interest level: 5-6).

This book provides accounts of spiritual happenings that are a part of Tennessee history and folklore. It was written for a general audience and is very appropriate for upper grades.

♦ Students may bring community stories of "local ghosts" into the classroom.

1. Tennessee—Folklore.

305.5
Haskins, James. *The Day Martin Luther King, Jr., Was Shot: A Photo History of the Civil Rights Movement*. Scholastic (0-590-43661-9), 1992. 96p. B/W photos. (Interest level: 3-9).

The history of the civil rights struggle is chronicled from the beginning of slavery through today. Particular emphasis is placed on the 1968 Martin Luther King assassination at the Lorraine Motel in Memphis and how that affected the civil rights movement.

♦ Students may ask their parents where they were and what they remember of specific major events in the civil rights struggle, particularly what their thoughts were concerning the assassination of Dr. King.

1. Civil rights—History 2. African-Americans—Folklore.

305.90697
Bailey, Fred A. *Class and Tennessee's Confederate Generation*. University of North Carolina Press (0-8078-1703-1), 1987. 205p. (Interest level: 7-8+).

This book looks at life in Tennessee for the Confederate veterans and sympathizers following the Civil War. Although written for adults, this work will be valuable for junior high school history students.

♦ Students may research the veterans benefits received by former soldiers of the Confederacy following the Civil War.
1. Tennessee—Civil War 2. Tennessee—Civil War and Reconstruction.

328.73
Hillin, Hank. *Al Gore Jr., Born to Lead*. Pine Hall Press (0-9615022-1-5), 1988. 200p. (Interest level: 5-8+).
This biography of Vice-President Gore of Tennessee tells his life from growing up in Carthage, going to college, and following his father's footsteps into politics. A very good biography of a contemporary Tennessee political figure.
♦ Students may write Vice-President Gore to tell him they have read Hank Hillin's biography of him and ask for his opinion of the biography.
1. Tennessee—Politics.

331.88
Werstein, Irving. *Labor's Defiant Lady: The Story of Mother Jones*. Thomas Y. Crowell Co. (069018667), 1969. 146p. (Interest level: 5+).
This is a biography of the turn-of-the-century radical labor organizer, Mother Jones, who is known for her statement, "Pray for the dead and fight like hell for the living." This book could offend those with anti-labor sentiments.
♦ Students may research current labor/management problems in the United States and compare them to the problems faced by Mother Jones and her labor activists nearly 100 years ago.
1. History — Tennessee 2. Tennessee — The economy.

353.0082
Van Fleet, Alanson. *Tennessee Valley Authority*. Chelsa House (1-55546-123-9), 1987. 96p. (Interest level: 4-6).
This book tells the story of the founding of the Tennessee Valley Authority and its purpose and work through today. The emphasis is on flood control, electricity generation, and recreation.
♦ Students may research how dams assist in flood control.
1. Tennessee—Tennessee Valley Authority.

394.268
Marsh, Carole. *Tennessee Classic Christmas Trivia*. Gallopade Publishing Group (0-7933-1061-X), 1992. 36p. (Interest level: 2-6+).
This is a joyous potpourri of Tennessee holiday trivia, including events, recipes, ways of celebrating, etc.
♦ Students may write about the ways Christmas is celebrated in Tennessee that differ from the way that holiday is celebrated in their home (if Christmas is celebrated in their home).
1. Tennessee—Holidays.

398.2
Justus, May. *Eben and the Rattlesnake*. Garrard Publishing Co. (0811640159), 1969. 48p. (Gr. 4-6).
A hoe used to kill a rattlesnake on a Tennessee mountain farm swells into the size of a giant log from

the snake's poison. It is downright troublesome telling this story to people who come by just to see the corncrib that was built out of the log.
♦ People's arms swell when they are bitten by a poisonous snake. Students may investigate why the same thing does not happen when a snake bites a log.
1. Tennessee—Folklore.

398.2
Justus, May. *It Happened in No-End Hollow*. Illus. by Mimi Korach. Garrard Publishing Co. (0811640124), 1969. 48p. Illus. (Interest level: 4-6).
This book is the retelling of three traditional tales from the Great Smoky Mountain region of Tennessee. They are "Old Ben Bailey Meets His Match," Little Lihu's Lucky Day," and "Don't Be a Silly-Billy." These are excellent folktales for middle school readers.
♦ Students may research traditional tales in their community and present them to the class.
1. Tennessee—Folklore.

597.96
Gove, Doris. *Water Snakes Year*. Illus. by Beverly Duncan. Atheneum (0-689-31597-X), 1991. 32p. Color illus. (Interest level: 4+).
This story of a harmless water snake's life in the world of water, woods, and shade brings the reader to admiration of both snake and environment. The author, a biologist, wrote her doctoral dissertation on snakes and is recognized in Tennessee as "the snake lady."
♦ Students may obtain a harmless snake from a pet store or zoo, share the snake with their class, and discuss feelings they may have about handling snakes.
1. Tennessee—Wildlife 2. Reptiles.

720.97688
Hagaman, Clara. *Governor John Sevier's Farm Home, Marble Springs: Home of Tennessee's First Governor, John Sevier*. Governor John Sevier Memorial Association (Knoxville) (No ISBN), 1987. 64p. Color and B/W photos and illus. (Interest level: 3+).
This descriptive book of a 225-year-old home and how people at that time lived is useful in portraying the style of living of the wealthy on the early U. S. frontier.
♦ Children may list the differences between living in 1790 and today.
1. Tennessee—History 2. Tennessee—Buildings.

784.5
Love, Robert. *Elvis Presley*. F. Watts (0-531-10239-4), 1986. 126p. B/W and Color photos. (Interest level: 3-8).
The rock and roll singer's life is chronicled from early days in Mississippi until his death in 1977. This attractively illustrated book presents an "introduction" to Elvis that may be needed by those born since his death.
♦ Students can learn more about Elvis Presley by renting a music video.
1. Music—Rock and Roll.

784.5

Saunders, Susan. *Dolly Parton, Country Goin' to Town*. Illus. by Rodney Pate. Puffin Books (0-14-032162-4), 1986. 56p. Color illus. (Interest level: 5+).

This biography of the country music singer focuses on her roots, growing up in Sevier County, Tennessee. It illustrates the poverty of possessions, yet wealth of family love that existed among the Partons.

◆ Children could discuss Dolly Parton, the singer, and play some of her songs, such as "The Coat of Many Colors," which relates to her childhood.

1. Tennessee—Music, Country Music.

811.5

Giovanni, Nikki. *Ego-tripping and Other Poems for Young People*. Illus. by George Ford. L. Hill (Distributed by Independent Publishers Group) (0-88208-020-2), 1974, 37p. (Interest level: 5-8).

This book offers poems for and about young people, particularly Tennessee African Americans, by one of Tennessee's premier African-American poets.

◆ Students may write a poem on what it means to be a young boy or girl in today's world.

1. Poetry—African-American authors 2. African-Americans—poetry.

811.54

Carson, Jo. *Stories I Ain't Told Nobody Yet: Selections from the People Pieces*. Orchard Books (0-531-05808-5), 1989. 84p. (Interest level: 7+).

Forty-nine poems taken from the conversations of East Tennessee Appalachian people as they discuss neighbors, kin, work, relationships, and themselves reveal the inside thoughts of mountain people.

◆ Students may discuss how poetry sometimes can be the best medium for understanding the thoughts and aspirations of other people.

1. Tennessee—Poetry.

811.54

Giovanni, Nikki. *Spin a Soft Black Song; Poems for Children*. Illus. by Charles Bible. Hill and Wang (0-8090-8795-2), 1971, 64p. (Interest level: 3-8).

Thirty-five poems recount the feelings of African-American children concerning their neighborhoods, society, and themselves. The Tennessee poet's Knoxville College experiences add to the flavor of the poetry.

◆ Students may write a poem about a neighbor of theirs.

1. Poetry—African-American authors 2. African-Americans—poetry.

811.54

Marsh, Carole. *Tennessee Coastales for Kids!* Gallopade Publishing Group (0-7933-2063-3), 1992, 72p. (Interest level: 4-6+).

This is a collection of dramatic stories, poetry, and even recipes centered around the waterways of Tennessee and the child's own imagination. They are very useful as spin-offs for children to write their own stories.

◆ Students may find out about the Tennessee-Tombigbee waterway and describe their findings to the class.

1. Tennessee.

813.3

Harris, George Washington. *Sut Lovingood's Yarns, Edited for the Modern Reader by M. Thomas Inge*. College and University Press , 1966 (out of print). 336p. (Interest level: 6+).

This volume includes the complete text of Sut Lovingood and most of the author's previously uncollected pieces that appeared in Tennessee newspapers. This is Tennessee folklore published in newspapers to entertain Tennessee readers.

◆ Students may tell how they would respond if they read such outrageous accounts in their newspaper. Would they accept it as truth as many Tennesseeans did after reading these stories?

1. Fiction—Folklore.

912.768 (Reference)

DeLorme Staff. *Tennessee Atlas and Gazateer*. Delorme Map Co. (0-89933-240-4), 72p. 1989. Maps; Tables. 72p. (Interest level: 3-6).

This collection of maps and facts about Tennessee is useful for children studying Tennessee social sciences.

◆ Students can use the Tennessee map to determine how far it is from Mountain City to Memphis,and then see which U.S. cities are the same distance as Mountain City is from Memphis.

1. Tennessee—Geography.

917

Radlauer, Ruth and **Zillmer, Rolf**. *Great Smoky Mountains National Park*. Childrens Press (0-516-07489-X), 1976. 48p. Color illus. (Interest level: 3-6).

This book, with its attractive illustrations, introduces the Great Smoky Mountains National Park and the variety of attractions there for people to enjoy. Even though this book is older, it is not dated and still in print.

◆ Students can discuss and compare the attractions of the Great Smoky Mountains National Park with those of several other national parks.

1. Tennessee—National Parks.

917.68

American World Geography. *Tennessee: A Photographic Celebration*. American World Geography (0-938314-90-4), 1991, 96p. Color photos. (Interest level: K-8).

This book is a collection of Tennessee photographs with only a small amount of written text. Students will enjoy seeing photographs of what they are studying in Tennessee social studies.

◆ The class may discuss the notion: "One picture is worth one thousand words."

1. Tennessee.

917.68 (Reference)
Appalachian Trail Guide to Tennessee-North Carolina, 9th Edition. Appalachian Trail Conference (0-917953-31-2), 1989. B/W illus.; Maps. 268p. (Interest level: 5-6).

This is the revised edition of the guide to the Appalachian Trail in Tennessee and North Carolina, including the Great Smoky Mountains. This classic guide is invaluable in describing the wilderness of East Tennessee.
♦ Students can find out how many people walk the Appalachian Trail each year and reasons why they do so.
1. Tennessee—Appalachian Trail.

917.68
Carpenter, John Allan. *Tennessee.* Childrens Press (0-516-04142-8), 1978. 96p. Color illus. (Interest level: 2-8).

The volume discusses the history, geography, resources, and sites of interest in Tennessee and describes the achievements of many historically prominent Tennesseeans. It is an excellent generic source of facts on Tennessee, although the older student may require more depth.
♦ The class may pursue the question of where in Tennessee prominent Tennesseans hailed, and why.
1. Tennessee—History.

917.68
Clark, Joe. *Tennessee Hill Folk.* B/W photos and captions by Joe Clark and an essay by Jesse Stuart. Vanderbilt University Press (0-8265-1183-X), 1972. Unpaginated. B/W photos. (Interest level: 6-8+).

Narratives of the lives of Appalachian mountain people are told in a very human and descriptive way. The lavish black-and-white photographs add tremendously to children's understanding of the role of folkways and old time practices in the lives of these people.
♦ Some people say "Hill Folk" should change and do things the modern way. The class may consider if there is anything about the life of these people that attracts them.
1. Tennessee—Folklore.

917.6804
O'Brien, Tim. *Tennessee: Off the Beaten Path.* Globe Pequot (0-87106-484-7), 1990. 149p. Illus. (Interest level: 5-6).

The approach of this book of stories about unusual and interesting places in Tennessee reminds the reader of the work of Charles Kuralt as he travels across the United States.
♦ Students may discover some interesting and little known facts about places in their community, especially out-of-the-way places.
1. Tennessee—Geography.

970.004
Steele, William O. *The Cherokee Crown of Tannassy.* J.F. Blair Co (0-910244-99-5), 1977. 162p. (Interest level: 5-8+).

While attempting to charm the Cherokees into loyalty to England, Sir Alexander Cuming is offered the crown of the Cherokee kingdom, Tannassy. "Tan-nassy" is the source for the state name, Tennessee. This book presents a Revolutionary War point of view not often expressed in American books.
♦ Students may determine why the Cherokees usually favored the British side during the American Revolution.
1. Tennessee—Native Americans 2. Tennessee—Revolutionary War.

973.91
Blos, Joan W. and **Dixon, Tennessee**. *The Heroine of the Titanic.* Morrow Junior Books (0-688-07547-9), 1991. 132p. (Interest level: 3-8).

The stories in this book are anecdotal accounts of Tennessee heroine, Molly Brown (1867-1932). There is a special emphasis on her survival of the sinking of the luxury liner, Titanic. This is an excellent source on a prominent Tennessee woman who accomplished great goals and lived an exciting life.
♦ Students may answer the questions: How did the lives of women differ 100 years ago from the women of today. What hurdles did they have to cross that women today do not?
1. Tennessee—Women.

976 (Reference)
Aylesworth, Thomas G. *The Southeast: Georgia, Kentucky, Tennessee.* Chelsa House Publishers (1-55546-557-9), 1988. (Let's Discover the States). 64p. Maps. (Interest level: 3-6).

This descriptive resource book contains a major section on Tennessee history, geography, and points of human interest.
♦ Each child should share with classmates one new and exciting thing about Tennessee that she or he discovered while reading this book.
1. Tennessee—Facts.

976.4
Driskill, Frank A. *Davy Crockett: The Untold Story.* Eakin Press (0-89015-298-5), 1981. 56p. (Interest level:3-8).

This book traces the life of Davy Crockett from Tennessee to Texas, where he died at the Alamo in 1836. Though the title addresses an "untold story," there is little told that will add to other biographies of this important Tennessean.
♦ Students can research Davy Crockett's life and career in Tennessee and report their findings to the class.
1. History—Tennessee.

976.8
Bice, David A. *A Panorama of Tennessee.* Walworth Publishing Co. (0-940213-73-7), 1989. 153p. Illus., some color. (Interest level: 2-8).

This profusely illustrated book provides images from Mountain City to Memphis, giving a pictorial view of Tennessee from the Appalachians to the Mississippi. An excellent book for the entire elementary school.
♦ Students may discuss what the advantages would be in living in each of the three grand divisions of Tennessee.
1. Tennessee.

976.8

Bond, Octavia Louise. *Old Tales Retold; or Perils and Adventures of Tennessee Pioneers*. Vanderbilt University Press (042024884), 1972, 262p. (Interest level: 6-8+).

Stories of Tennessee's first settlers and later heroes are recounted in this book, first published in 1941. This is a classic introduction to Tennessee heroes.

♦ Students may find out why the early Tennessee settlers left their homes in the East to journey to the Tennessee territory.

1. History—Tennessee.

976.8

Braden, Beulah Brummett. *When Grandma Was a Girl*. Illus. by Clifford Smith. Preface by John Rice Irwin. Oak Ridger, 1976 (out of print). (Interest level: 4-8).

This fictionalized account of the author's grandmother's childhood is an excellent depiction of turn-of-the century East Tennessee (Anderson County) rural social life and customs.

♦ Students may describe some of the ways life was harder for people when Grandma was a girl than it is today.

1. History—Tennessee.

976.8

Cimprich, John. *Slavery's End in Tennessee 1861-1865*. University of Alabama Press (0-8173-0257-3), 1985. 191p. (Interest level: 6-8+).

This volume discusses how the end of slavery in Tennessee came about. The focus is on the last days of Tennessee slavery, during the Civil War. The writing is for a general audience but could be very useful in the fifth and sixth grades.

♦ Students may investigate the reasons why slavery was never a big issue in the mountain region of Tennessee.

1. Tennessee—Slavery 2. Tennessee—Civil War.

976.8

Couch, Ernie and **Couch, Jill**. *Tennessee Trivia, Revised Edition*. Rutledge Hill Press (1-55853-109-2), 1991. 192p. (Interest level: 3-6).

This book contains little known facts about Tennessee. There is material in the volume for various grade and difficulty levels.

♦ Each student should come up with an interesting piece of trivia about his or her community.

1. Tennessee.

976.8

Crawford, Charles Warren. *Dynamic Tennessee: Land, History, and Government*. Steck-Vaughn Co. (0-8114-4168-7), 1990. 340p. Illus.; Charts; Photos; 15 color plates in a special section. (Interest level: 5-6).

This social studies text covers the history, geography, economics, and politics of Tennessee. It is lavishly illustrated and the text is very readable.

♦ The class will discuss the notion of being proud to be a Tennessean or being proud to be a resident of their state, if not Tennessee. What is unique in Tennessee's (or their state's) heritage that could give one pride?

1. Tennessee—History.

976.8

Dixon, Max. *The Wataugans*. Overmountain Press (0-923807-47-X), 1989. 80p. (Interest level: 4-6).

This book tells the story of the people who first settled in East Tennessee and the trials and tribulations they suffered. This book for general audiences is still usable with middle school students.

♦ Students may research the "Proclamation of 1763" and report on the effect it had on the settlements west of the proclamation line.

1. Tennessee—History.

976.8

Eway, James. *A Treasury of Tennessee Tales*. Rutledge Hill Press (0-934395-04-7), 1985. 144p. Illus. (Interest level: 4-8).

Eway has collected fictionalized tales based on actual Tennessee events. His style of writing is very entertaining and historically informative. Much of the material could be classified as folk tales.

♦ Each child should share other fictionalized tales of actual historical figures.

1. Tennessee—History 2. Tennessee—Folklore.

976.8

Ewing, James. *It Happened in Tennessee*. Rutledge Hill Press (0-934395-31-4), 1986. 144p. Illus. (Interest level: 5-6).

This book tells of Tennessee events with national implications. It is assumed the readers have heard of the events prior to reading about them but they may not have known their Tennessee connection.

♦ Students may evaluate the event in the book they think is the most important in the development of our country as a whole.

1. Tennessee—History.

976.8

Fradin, Dennis B. *Tennessee*. Childrens Press (0-516-03842-7), 1992. 64p. Color illus.; Maps. (Interest level: 2-6).

This book discusses Tennessee historically, from geographic points of interest and the lives of famous residents. This is a beautifully illustrated volume, small in size, and appropriate for beginning readers who are interested in social studies.

♦ Students may discuss who they believe is the most famous Tennessean of all times, and why they believe that.

1. Tennessee—Geography 2. Tennessee—Famous People.

976.8

Gerson, Noel Bertram. *Franklin, America's "Lost State."* Crowell-Collier Press (088416413), 1968. 167p. B/W illus. (Interest level: 4+).

During the late 1700s, a proposal was introduced in Congress to admit the state of Franklin, territory which is now part of Tennessee and North Carolina. The author explores the reasons why the proposal was introduced and why it failed. This book provides an introduction to an oft overlooked act in the early United States, the refusal to admit a state to the Union.

♦ Students should find out if any other proposed states were not admitted to the Union.

1. Tennessee—State of Franklin.

976.8

Jones, Billy Mac, ed. *Heroes of Tennessee*. Memphis State University Press (No ISBN), 1979. 160p. (Interest level: 5-8).

This book provides the biographies of prominent Tennessee historical figures, including William Blount, Davy Crockett, and Sam Houston. This is an excellent biographical source with each entry written by different authors.

♦ Students may write a biography of a modern day Tennessee hero in the same style as the authors of these biographies.

1. History—Tennessee.

976.8

Landry, Bill. *The Heartland Series*. WBIR-TV, 1513 Hutchinson Ave., Knoxville, TN 37917, (No ISBN). VHS, (20+ hours). $377.00 or $29.00 per tape. (Interest level: K-8+).

This is a series of 13 videos with each approximately one and one half to two hours in length. Each video contains 35-minute segments exploring the history, traditions, and folkways of East Tennessee.

♦ Using video equipment, individual children could make five-minute vignettes of people, events, or places in their home town.

1. Tennessee—Journalism 2. Tennessee—Folklore.

976.8

Marsh, Carole. *"Avast, Ye Slobs!": Tennessee Pirate and Treasure Trivia*. Gallopade Publishing Group (0-7933-1076-8), 1992. 36p. (Interest level: 3-6+).

Pirates appear to be one of children's favorite subjects to study. This book includes some excellent activities and an original short story.

♦ Students may discuss how Captain Hook in Peter Pan compares to the pirates in these stories.

1. History—Tennessee.

976.8

Marsh, Carole. *"Chill Out!": Scary Tennessee Stories Based on Frightening Tennessee Truths*. Gallopade Publishing Group (0-7933-4780-7), 1992. 36p. (Interest level: 4-6+).

This collection of amazing tales of Tennessee is told side-by-side with real-life historic or scientific facts that lend credibility to their possible truth. Children will be fascinated by these stories.

♦ Students may write their thoughts about what makes a story "scary" and share their thoughts with their classmates.

1. Tennessee—Folklore.

976.8

Marsh, Carole. *Christopher Columbus Comes to Tennessee*. Gallopade Publishing Group (0-7933-3746-1), 1992. 36p. (Interest level: 3-6+).

This book contains many "you are Columbus" scenarios to let readers explore the impact early settlers

had on Tennessee. It puts the student in the shoes of the early explorers and lets them role play the importance of exploration.

♦ With their parents, children can explore a part of their community that they have never visited and write their impressions of that exploration.

1. History—Tennessee.

976.8

Marsh, Carole. *The Hard-to-Believe-But-True! Book of Tennessee History, Mystery, Trivia, Legend, Lore & More*.Gallopade Publishing Group (0-7933-1073-3), 1992. 36p. (Interest level: 3-6+).

This is a book of fascinating, factual trivia, oddities, curiosities, and tales about Tennessee. Children love trivia and other unusual facts and will find this is a very entertaining book.

♦ Each student should share with his or her classmates the one fact learned that seemed more unusual or unbelievable than the others.

1. History—Tennessee 2. Tennessee—Folklore.

976.8

Marsh, Carole. *How to Start a Tennessee Library—At Home or School!*. Gallopade Publishing Group (0-7933-4358-5), 1992. 36p. (Interest level: 4-6+).

This is a clear guide for all ages on how to start, catalog, and share a collection of state resources in all formats: books, magazines, clippings, art, music, etc. It is an excellent source on how to start your own personal book collection.

♦ Students can begin gathering books on Tennessee for their home room, using the information from this book to organize this class collection.

1. Libraries.

976.8

Marsh, Carole. *If My Tennessee Mama Ran the World*. Gallopade Publishing Group (0-7933-2065-8), 1992. 36p. (Interest level: K-6+).

This book of short humorous essays gives children insight into the difference that kindness, cleanliness, diplomacy, ethics, beauty, and other positive attitudes and attributes can make. This is an excellent source for spin-off writing activities, focusing on the notion of how Tennessee would be different if your mother/father "ran the world."

♦ Students may write a short story on what the world would be like if their mother were in charge.

1. Tennessee.

976.8

Marsh, Carole. *My First Book About Tennessee! Why Wait to Learn About Our Great State?* Gallopade Publishing Group (0-7933-5695-4), 1992. 36p. Interest level: K-4).

This is a great introduction to Tennessee's history, geography, people, birds, minerals, insects, etc. It contains several activities for children.

♦ Students may find out about Tennessee's state bird and why that particular bird has been designated as such.

1. History—Tennessee.

976.8
Marsh, Carole. *Sex Stuff for Tennessee Teachers of Kids 7-17.* Gallopade Publishing Group (0-7933-2699-0), 1992. 150p. (Interest level: 2-6+).

This volume is not only a complete guide to questions children ask, but it contains a section of addresses and phone numbers for sex education information resources in Tennessee. This is one of the few sources that particularizes its content to a state or region.
♦ Students may make a list of the sources of information, local or in another city, that are available by toll free phone.
1. Sex Education.

976.8
Marsh, Carole. *Tennessee Bandits, Bushwackers, Outlaws, Crooks, Devils, Ghosts, Desparados & Other Assorted & Sundry Characters.* Gallopade Publishing Group (0-7933-1058-X), 1992. 36p. (Interest level: 3-6+).

A variety of Tennessee people and stories are illustrated in this book. It provides an excellent and unique way to learn Tennessee social studies.
♦ Students can decide which character in this book Tennesseans would be least proud of for being from Tennessee? Why?
1. History—Tennessee 2. Tennessee—Folklore.

976.8
Marsh, Carole. *The Tennessee Bookstore Book.* Gallopade Publishing Group (0-7933-2981-7), 1992. 36p. (Interest level: All Ages).

This useful guide to Tennessee bookstores and their specialties is helpful for students, teachers, and other writers in discovering the fun of collecting books. It includes a reproducible research form, glossary, and activities for young readers. This volume would be great in assisting students to discover the fun of collecting books, especially in the many used bookstores.
♦ Tennessee students may visit a Tennessee bookstore and look through and report on the Tennessee books they find. Students in other states may visit a local bookstore and look for books on their state.
1. Tennessee.

976.8
Marsh, Carole. *Tennessee Dingbats! Book 1: A Fun Book of Games, Stories, Activities, and More About Our State That's All in Code! for You to Decipher.* Gallopade Publishing Group (0-7933-3900-6), 1992. 138p. (Interest level: 2-6).

This fun, educational, challenging book of games, stories, and activities in a "dingbat" computer code for readers to decipher includes the key to the code. Excellent for critical-thinking and concentration skills.
♦ Students may invent their own code, write an important message, and challenge their classmates to "break" their code.
1. Tennessee—Folklore.

976.8
Marsh, Carole. *Tennessee Festival Fun for Kids!* Gallopade Publishing Group (0-7933-4052-7), 1992. 36p. (Interest level: K-6).

The fairs, festivals, and other public events of Tennessee are listed and described in this book. Festivals range from the Tennessee State Fair to industrial and special interest festivals emphasizing geography and history.
♦ Students may visit one of the listed festivals.
1. Tennessee.

976.8
Marsh, Carole. *The Tennessee Hot Air Balloon Mystery.* Gallopade Publishing Group (0-7933-2696-6), 1992. 36p. (Interest level: 3-6+).

This book is a geography skill-builder based on a real-life runaway hot air balloon adventure. It is a fast-paced story featuring geographic clues to help readers determine where in Tennessee they are floating, bouncing, or zooming over.
♦ Students may obtain some old Tennessee maps and cut small squares from the maps. They can paste 10 or so of them on a sheet and ask classmates to figure out where in Tennessee they are, encouraging them to use clues, such as mountains, waterways, highways, and small towns.
1. Tennessee—Geography.

976.8
Marsh, Carole. *Tennessee "Jography": A Fun Run Thru Our State?* Gallopade Publishing Group (0-7933-2046-1), 1992. 36p. (Interest level: 3-6+).

This book covers all aspects of Tennessee geography, including physical, topography, weather, economic, historic rivers, and even how to get to the "big game."
♦ Students may write an essay on what part of the study of Tennessee geography they like the best.
1. Tennessee—Geography.

976.8
Marsh, Carole. *The Tennessee Media Book.* Gallopade Publishing Group (0-7933-3287-7), 1992. 36p. (Interest level: All Ages).

This book is a guide to the print, broadcast, and online media of Tennessee. It is updated as necessary and includes a reproducible research form, glossary, and activities for young readers.
♦ Students may invite a local television, radio, or newspaper personality to their class to inform them how news is gathered for print or broadcast.
1. Tennessee—Media.

976.8
Marsh, Carole. *Tennessee School Trivia: Surprising Stuff About Our Schools, Teachers & Students!* Gallopade Publishing Group (0-7933-1067-9), 1992, 36p. (Interest level: 2-6+).

This delightful hodgepodge of trivia, statistics, people, events, stories, etc. in Tennessee's schools in the past and present is something teachers and students may enjoy together.
♦ Students may try to discover a bit of trivia about their teacher that none of the other students knows.
1. Tennessee—Education.

976.8
Marsh, Carole. *Tennessee Silly Trivia*. Gallopade Publishing Group (0-7933-2044-5), 1992. 36p. (Interest level: 2-6+).

This book provides an entertaining way to sharpen Tennessee knowledge and critical thinking skills with a multiple choice quiz covering Tennessee history, geography, people, legends, folklore, and more.
♦ Students can construct a set of multiple choice questions and answers on the history, geography, people, legends, and folklore of a Tennessee town or county.
1. Tennessee.

976.8
Marsh, Carole. *Tennessee Timeline: A Chronology of Our State's History, Mystery, Trivia, Legend, Lore & More!* Gallopade Publishing Group (0-7933-6001-3), 1992. 36p. (Interest level: 3-6+).

This book helps children make connections between when and what in Tennessee's history and information about people, business, science, politics, medicine, minorities, culture, exploration, technology, literature, wars, disasters, the future, etc. Activities, such as creating a time capsule for Tennessee, a personal time line, and other projects, are presented.
♦ Students can find out and write about the events that took place in Tennessee during the year of their birth.
1. Tennessee.

976.8
Marsh, Carole. *Tennessee's (Most Devastating!) Disasters & (Most Calamitous!) Catastrophes*. Gallopade Publishing Group (0-7933-2068-2), 1992, 36p. (Interest level: 3-6+).

History, geography, science, and more are covered in this book in the context of natural disasters and upheavals.
♦ Students may find out about the Flood of 1940 and what happened to the ET&WNC Railroad.
1. History—Tennessee.

976.8
Marsh, Carole. *"Uncle Rebus": Tennessee Picture Stories for Computer-Age Kids!* Gallopade Publishing Group (0-7933-4627-4), 1992. 36p. (Interest level: K-6).

This book contains stories, poems, riddles, etc. about Tennessee in a charming rebus format using computer "dingbat" rebus art. There are fun activities especially for the younger student.
♦ Students can construct their own rebus using a story from their community.
1. Tennessee—Folklore.

976.8
Marsh, Carole. *"Yum, Yum!": The Tennessee Kid's Cookbook*. Gallopade Publishing Group (0-7933-1070-9), 1992, 36p. (Interest level: 2-6+).

This collection is a clever concoction of culinary heritage, cooking, and food lore. In addition to lots of recipes, there is advice on nutrition and cooking safety.
♦ Students can cook some of the recipes given in this book, or obtain a simple recipe from their grandmothers to share with the class.
1. Tennessee—Food.

976.8
McKissack, Patricia and **McKissack, Fredrick**. *Tennessee Trailblazers*. March Media (09863482408), 1993. 106p. Color plates. (Interest level: 3-6).

The lives of Tennesseans "Big Foot" Spencer, Nancy Ward, Ella Shepherd, and Cordell Hull are chronicled. Each of these historically significant individuals has an ethnic background very different from the other three. These are excellent short biographies of individuals not often encountered.
♦ Students may learn more about prominent Native Americans whose lives were similar to that of Nancy Ward.
1. Tennessee—History.

976.8
McNair, Sylvia. *America the Beautiful, Tennessee*. Childrens Press (0-516-00488-3), 1990. 143p. Color illus.; maps. (Interest level: 3-6).

This general reference book for the elementary school introduces the geography, history, and famous people of Tennessee.
♦ Students should imagine they are given the opportunity to live anywhere in Tennessee. Where would they live, and why?
1. Tennessee.

976.8
Sirvaitis, Karen. *Tennessee*. Lerner Publications (0-8225-2711-1), 1991. 72p. Some color illus. (Interest level: 3-6).

This book introduces the geography, history, people, industries, and other highlights of Tennessee to students. This small but comprehensive volume covers the entire state.
♦ Students may research what the music industry means to Tennessee, not only Nashville, but Memphis, Bristol, and other cities where music is an industry.
1. Tennessee.

976.8
Wehling, Susan. *Mountain Vision*. Appalshop Film & Video, 306 Madison Street, Whitesburg, Ky 41858 (No ISBN), 1991, VHS, (27 min.). (Interest level: 6-8+).

This video examines examples of "homegrown" television video and features East Tennessee video pioneers, Broadside Television, who put video events on East Tennessee's first public video access channel. The film is excellent in depicting television as a means of communicating local events.
♦ The class may design, produce, and tape a television program focusing on their locality. Then they should request the program be shown over the local cable access channel.
1. Tennessee—Media.

976.855
Deegan, Paul and **Bauer, Marion**. *Nashville, Tennessee*. Crestwood House (0-89686-468-5), 1989. 48p. Color illus. (Interest level: 3-6).

This volume highlights the attractions of Nashville with a special emphasis on the country music industry, Opryland, and other landmarks. The book contains excellent color plates of the city.

◆ If a camera and a roll of film can be obtained, each student may shoot one picture that tells the story of his or her town. The pictures should be logged so there is no repetition.
1. Tennessee—Cities.

976.855
Lynch, Amy. *Nashville*. Dillon Press, Inc. (0-87518-453-7), 1991.(A Downtown America Book). 60p. Color photos.; Maps. (Interest level: 5-9).

The author has provided an introduction to the city of Nashville, highlighting places to visit and things to do while there. In addition to providing excellent color photographs that bring life to the narrative, the book glorifies the city while also dealing with its urban problems of poverty, crime, and drugs.
◆ This good introduction to city description should allow children to develop a descriptive and illustrated document of their home town.
1. Tennessee—Cities.

976.87
Brachey, Doug. *Rugby: Tennessee's Victorian Village*. JM Productions (0939298619 pbk), 1987. 72p. B/W and Color illus. (Interest level: 4-8+).

This book contains stories and descriptions of the buildings in the town of Rugby, Tennessee. The Victorian structures have been preserved and are an object of curiosity.
◆ The class could compare the buildings illustrated in this book with those of 100 years earlier. What kind of progress was made during that 100 years?
1. Tennessee—History 2. Tennessee—Buildings.

976.9003 (Reference)
Crutchfield, James A. *Tennessee Almanac and Book of Facts*. Rutledge Hill Press (0-934395-59-4), 1990. 320p. (Interest level: 3-6).

This book is the standard source for information published on Tennessee. It should assist the teacher in answering any question a child might have on Tennessee facts.
◆ Students may divide into two groups with each group using the book to develop a set of 10 questions. The questions of one group can be answered by the other group using the book as a reference.
1. Tennessee.

Biography

See also biographical entries in Tennessee Nonfiction section, especially under 328.73, 331.88, 784.5, 973.91, and 976.4.

920.0768
Marsh, Carole. *Tennessee State Greats!*Gallopade Publishing Group (0-7933-1055-5), 1992. 36p. (Interest level: 3-6+).

This book offers multi-format, multi-cultural biographies on the famous and infamous of Tennessee. There is a special focus on their early lives and the obstacles they overcame, especially educational obstacles.

◆ Students may write a story on the person they believe to be the most famous Tennessee African-American.
1. Tennessee—Biography 2. History—Tennessee.

92 Handy, William C.
Montgomery, Elizabeth Rider. *William C. Handy: Father of the Blues*. Illus. by David Hodges. Garrard Publishing Co.(0879491129), 1968, 95p. (Interest level: 3-7+).

This is a biography of Tennessee's most famous blues musician. Handy died in 1958 and lived his life entirely during the racial segregation era. This book offers interesting illustrations depicting the life of a blues artist.
◆ Students may find out more about the "blues" and its place in American music.
1. Folklore—Tennessee 2. Music—Jazz.

Fiction

Bontemps, Arna Wendell. *Chariot in the Sky: A Story of the Jubilee Singers*. Illus. by Cyrus Leroy Baldridge. Beacon Press (0-8705-330-1), 1947. 238p. (Interest level: 6-8+).

This is a fictionalized account of the famous Fisk University Jubilee Singers. Arna Bontemps was the librarian at Fisk for many years and was intimately acquainted with this touring group.
◆ Students may obtain historical recordings of the Fisk Jubilee Singers and share them with their class.
1. History—Tennessee 2. History—African-American 3. African-American—music 4. African-American—Higher Education.

(Easy)
Bulla, Clyde Robert. *Daniel's Duck*. Pictures by Joan Sandin. Harper and Row (0-06-020908-9), 1979. 60p. Photos. (Interest level: K-3).

A novice wood carver is momentarily defeated when people laugh at the result of a winter of work. A good example of how feelings may be hurt by others and yet how one can be victorious in the end.
◆ Students may share a time when their feelings may have been hurt by someone making fun of what they have done.
1. Crafts—Woodcarving.

(Easy)
Carson, Jo. *Pulling My Leg*. Pictures by Julie Downing, Orchard Books (A Richard Jackson Book). (0-531-05817-4), 1990. 32p. (Interest level: K-6).

When a joking uncle collects hammer, pliers, and a screwdriver to help a young Tennessee mountain child with her loose tooth, the tooth amazingly comes out by itself.
◆ Students may describe the ways they have "helped" their baby teeth come out.
1. Tennessee—Fiction.

Caudill, Rebecca. *The Best Loved Doll*. Henry Holt and Co. (0-8050-2103-5), 1992. 64p. Illus. (Interest level: 2-6).

For a doll contest at a party, a little girl chooses to enter a doll that seems least likely to win a prize, but it does win a special one. A good illustration of how children value objects and determine what is beautiful.

♦ The children will share with each other possessions they have that may not appear to be beautiful or valuable in the eyes of others, but are in their eyes.

1. Tennessee—Fiction.

Caudill, Rebecca. *A Certain Small Shepherd*. Henry Holt and Co. (0-8050-1323-7), 1965. 48p. Color illus. (Interest level: K-8).

Jamie, a mute Tennessee mountain child, is able to play the role of a good shepherd at Christmas despite his handicap. This book is poignant and should have the children in tears of joy over Jamie's achievement.

♦ Children may bring examples of people they know who have functional disabilities and give examples as to how these people meet the challenges in their daily lives.

1. The Physically Handicapped.

Caudill, Rebecca. *A Pocketfull of Cricket*. Hentry Holt and Co. (0-8050-1200-1), 1989. 48p. Illus. (Interest level: 3-6).

This is the story of a young Tennessee farm boy named Jay, who finds a cricket and makes it his summer companion. When school begins, the cricket accompanys Jay to school and makes a chirping noise. This book is an excellent portrayal of the relationship between a boy and his animal friend, in this case a cricket.

♦ This book presents an opportunity for children to voice their feelings about their pets and what they mean to them.

1. Tennessee—Fiction.

Caudill, Rebecca. *Saturday Cousins*. Dell (0-440-40208-5,YB), 1989. 117p. (Interest level: 4-8).

Two Tennessee mountain familes, who are cousins, take turns visiting each other's homes on Saturday. No matter what they do on Saturday, they always have a good time. This is an excellent source on building positive extended family relationships.

♦ The children should write about their cousins, what they do together, and compare them to the families in the book.

1. Tennessee—Fiction.

Caudill, Rebecca. *Schoolhouse in the Woods*. Illus. by Decie Merwin. Dell (0-440-40170-4), 1989. 120p. (Interest level: 4-8).

A Tennessee mountain child, Bonnie, goes to school and learns readin', ritin', and 'rithmetic from Miss Cora in a one-room school. She values the lessons learned and the experiences of a one-room school education. Both the writing and Decie Merwin's pictures capture the flavor of what it was like to attend a one-room school.

♦ The class should research and find out about former one-room schools in their district. They may interview someone who either attended or taught in a one-room school.

1. Tennessee—fiction.

Caudill, Rebecca. *Up and Down the River*. Dell (0-440-40191-7), 1989. 115p. (Interest level: 3-6).

The Fairfield children earn summer money caring for pets of people on vacation. They find themselves with a yard full of pets and possibly more responsibility than they can handle. Caudill focuses on the responsibility of their making a decision to care for pets and then carrying through with that responsibility, even though the result is very entertaining.

♦ Students may explore some of the ways children may make extra money during summer vacation.

1. Tennessee—Fiction.

Caudill, Rebecca and **Ayars, James**. *Contrary Jenkins*. Illus. by Glen Rounds. Holt, Rinehart and Winston (0-03-015046-9), 1969. 40p. B/W illus. (Interest level: 4-6).

Stories are told of episodes in the life of Contrary Jenkins as he lived by what he called the "law of contrary" in Tennessee. These are humorous stories by a gifted Appalachian story teller.

♦ Students may discuss what it means to be contrary and give examples of how people in their life are sometimes that way.

1. Tennessee—Folklore.

Cole, Norma. *The Final Tide*. McElderry Books (0-68950-510-8), 1990. 153p. (Interest level: 5-8).

When the Tennessee Valley Authority builds a dam at Wolf Creek to bring electricity to Toller's Ridge, everyone in Geneva's family prepares to move to higher ground except for Granny who refuses to leave her home. The author describes a phenomenon that was very common in the establishment of TVA lakes.

♦ Students may discuss the reasons they think Granny did not wish to give up her home even though she was getting much better living quarters than before.

1. Tennessee—Tennessee Valley Authority.

Cross, Helen Reeder. *Isabella Mine*. Illus. by Catherine Stock. Lothrop, Lee and Shepard Books (0-688-00885-2), 1982. 147p. Color illus. (Interest level: 4-8).

Eleven-year-old Molly finds life in a small rural community in East Tennessee's Copper Basin to be full of activities and adventures. The author is very sympathetic to Appalachian mountain life.

♦ Students may discuss both the necessities and the dangers of living on Copper Basin land.

1. Tennessee—Fiction 2. Appalachian Mountain Life.

Green, Connie Jordan. *The War at Home*. Macmillan Publishing Company (0-68950-470-5), 1989, 136p. (Interest level: 4-8).

Young Mattie and her family move to Oak Ridge, Tennessee, during World War II where her father is involved with a secret government project. This was a straight-forward story of adjustments made by children during war time.

♦ Students may read further about what was happening in Oak Ridge during World War II. How would the students feel if their father or other close relative had been a part of what was happening there?

1. Tennessee—Fiction.

Hansen, Joyce. *Which Way Freedom?* Walker Press (0-8027-6623-4), 1986. 120p. (Interest level: 4-8).

During the Civil War, Obi escapes from slavery and joins a Union Army African-American regiment. He ultimately becomes involved with the bloody fighting at Fort Pillow, Tennessee.

♦ Students should research the Battle of Fort Pillow and explain why it was such a terrible ordeal for African-American soldiers fighting for the Union.

1. African-American Studies 2. Tennessee—Slavery 3. Tennessee—The Civil War.

Haun, Mildred and **Gower, Hershel Gower**, eds. *The Hawk's Done Gone, and Other Stories.* Vanderbilt University Press (0-8265-1213-5), 1985. 328p. (Interest level: 6+).

These folk tales of life in the Appalachian mountain region can be used to better understand Appalachian culture.

♦ Students should find a folk story from their ethnic heritage that could be used to help an "outsider" understand their way of life.

1. Fiction—Folklore.

Justus, May. *Holidays in No-End Hollow.* Garrard Publishing Co.(0811640248), 1970. 63p. Color illus. (Interest level: 4-6).

Four short stories tell how Thanksgiving, Christmas, a housewarming, and a school's birthday are celebrated in Tennessee's Great Smoky Mountains. The author emphasizes the differences between Smoky Mountain celebrations and the celebrations of most other people.

♦ Students may describe how their celebrations are different from those described in this book.

1. Tennessee—Folklore 2. Tennessee—Great Smoky Mountains.

Justus, May. *Jumping Johnny Outwits Skedaddle.* Garrard Publishing Co.(0811640280), 1971. 62p. Illus. (Interest level: K-3).

A young Tennessee mountain boy's high-jumping mule proves its worth on a stormy ride to fetch a doctor. This is a great adventure book.

♦ Students may discuss how calling a doctor to help someone in their family would be a different situation for them than it was for Johnny.

1. Tennessee—Folklore.

Justus, May. *New Boy in School.* Hastings House (0-81164031-1), 1963. 56p. Illus. (Interest level: 3-8).

When his family moves from Louisiana to Tennessee, seven-year-old Lennie discovers he is the only African American in his classroom. He must overcome conflict and find his place at the school. This book is a good item for race relations assignments.

♦ Each member of the class should write how they would have reacted if they had been in Lenny's place.

1. Tennessee 2. African-Americans —Education.

(Easy)
Justus, May. *Surprise for Perky Pup.* Garrard Publishing Co. (0811667049), 1971. 39p. (Interest level: K-3).

When he is hit on the head while sleeping, Perky Pup becomes convinced that someone doesn't like him

and he soon has all the other dogs in his Tennessee neighborhood roaring in sympathy. A fine pre-school to early elementary story.

♦ The class can discuss why Perky Pup acted so strange.

1. Tennessee—Literature.

Justus, May. *Tales from Near-Side and Far.* Illus. by Herman B. Vestal. Garrard Publishing Co. (0811640183), 1970. 63p. (Interest level: 2-6).

Four stories set in Tennessee's Great Smoky Mountains tell about a troublesome pup, a peddler named Step-Along, a pet mule, and a boy who knew how to use his legs.

♦ Students may discuss how these stories differ from the stories of life in their neighborhoods.

1. Tennessee—Folklore.

(Easy)
Justus, May. *You're Sure Silly, Billy.* Garrard Publishing Co. (0811669580), 1972. 63p. Illus. (Interest level: K-3).

Billy's judgements cause trouble in adventures with a runaway pig and a bean pot. This is a good example of an Appalachian childrens story set in Tennessee.

♦ Students can tell what they would have done about that pig if they had been Billy.

1. Tennessee—Literature.

Kassem, Lou. *Listen for Rachel.* McElderry Books (0689503962), 1986. 164p. (Interest level: 5+).

Moving up into the mountains of Tennessee introduces Rachel to a possible calling, as she learns about folk medicine from a local nature doctor. She puts aside this study as the Civil War divides her family and romance enters her life. The author provides an unusual description of family life at the beginning of the Civil War.

♦ Students may describe a calling they may have some time in their lives. Is it similar to Rachel's?

1. Folklore—Medicine 2. Tennessee—Civil War.

Marsh, Carole. *Tennessee Silly Basketball Sportsmysteries, Volume 1.* Gallopade Publishing Group (0-7933-1064-4), 1990. 36p. (Interest level: 2-6+).

The author calls this a collection of "swishy" stories based on the exploits of various Tennessee basketball teams. After reading the stories, children can choose their own endings. It is a great source for reluctant readers.

♦ Students can give the nicknames of five of the college basketball teams in Tennessee.

1. Tennessee—Sports.

Marsh, Carole. *Tennessee Silly Basketball Sportsmysteries, Volume 2.* Gallopade Publishing Group (0-7933-2071-2), 1992. 36p. (Interest level:2-6+).

A continuation of the Tennessee basketball stories found in Volume 1 (*see* preceding entry).

♦ Students can describe the mystery they enjoyed the most, and tell why.

1. Tennessee—Sports.

Marsh, Carole. *Tennessee Silly Football Sportsmysteries, Volume 1.* Gallopade Publishing Group (0-7933-2050-X), 1990. 60p. (Interest level: 2-6+).

This book of choose-your-own-ending humorous stories based on Tennessee state teams is a great source for reluctant readers.
♦ Students may find out who General Robert Neyland was and why he is so important to football in Tennessee?
1. Tennessee—Sports.

Marsh, Carole. *Tennessee Silly Football Sportsmysteries, Volume 2*. Gallopade Publishing Group (0-7933-2053-4), 1992. 60p. (Interest level: 2-6+).

This is a continuation of the Tennessee football mysteries found in Volume 1.
♦ Students may find out the name of the football stadium in Memphis and the event that is held there at the end of every year.
1. Tennessee—Sports.

Martin, Katherine McConnell. *Night Riding*. Knopf Publishing Co. (0679800646), 1989. 197p. (Interest level: 7+).

Eleven-year-old Prin's secure world in a small Tennessee town during the 1950s is turned upside down when she discovers that her new friend and neighbor is being abused by the girl's own father. Child molestation in the mountains, as well as elsewhere, is a very real problem.
♦ If they were Prin, how would the students respond to this problem?
1. Tennessee—Fiction 2. Child Molestation.

Miles, Miska. *Hoagie's Rifle-Gun*. Illus. John Schoenherr. Little, Brown Co. (0525360117), 1970. 40p. (Interest level: 4-6).

Hoagie hunts animals for food to feed his Appalachian family but that act becomes very difficult when he is confronted with game that has a name. This book explores the question of how we define our relationships with the animal world.
♦ Children may discuss the positive and negative aspects of our society's views of hunting animals with guns.
1. Tennessee—Fiction.

Miller, Jim Wayne. *Newfound: A Richard Jackson Book*. Orchard Books (0-531-05845-X), 1989. 213p. (Interest level: 7+).

A boy growing up in his grandparents' house in the Appalachian Mountains learns about the town and the people around him, their habits, stories, and lore. This highly descriptive book of Appalachian mountain life was written by a gifted novelist.
♦ Students can describe how they would learn about the people around them if they moved into a new area.
1. Tennessee—Fiction.

Savoldi, Gloria Root. *Tennessee Boy*. Westminster Press (0-664-32513-0), 1972. 159p. (Interest level: 5-8+).

Two 13-year-old boys, one African American, one white, discover things about each other and the Civil War, as they travel from Tennessee to Washington, D.C., in 1865. This is an excellent story of what it might have been like for African Americans and whites to learn about each other at a time when slaves were being emancipated.
♦ Students may imagine themselves going a long distance with a person of another race. Would topics relevant to race enter into their personal conversations?
1. African-Americans 2. Tennessee—The Civil War.

Steele, William O. *Flaming Arrows*. Harcourt, Brace, and Jovanovich (0-15-228427-3), 1990. 146p. (Interest level: 5-6).

An Indian attack on a fort in the Tennessee wilderness makes young Chad Rabun realize that it is wrong to condemn one person for the misdeeds of another. This book gives an excellent account of life on the early Tennessee frontier and the delicate issues of relationships between the settlers and Native Americans.
♦ Students may look for reasons why there was so much animosity between the early settlers and Indians and try to determine how conflict could have been avoided.
1. Native American Studies 2. Tennessee—History.

Steele, William O. *The Man with the Silver Eyes*. Harcourt, Brace, and Jovanovich (0-15-251720-0), 1976. 147p. Illus. (Interest level: 4-8).

Until he learns the reason for the arrangement, a young Cherokee boy has mixed emotions about living for a year with a white man. This is another good book for exploring race relations.
♦ Students may discuss how they would feel if they were in the young boy's place.
1. Tennessee—Cherokees 2. Native Americans.

Steele, William O. *The Perilous Road*. Harcourt, Brace, and Jovanovich (0-15-260647-5), 1990. 156p. (Interest level: 4-6).

Fourteen year old Chris hates the Yankees for invading his Tennessee mountain village. He learns a difficult lesson when he reports a Yankee supply train to the Confederates, only to learn that his brother is part of the Yankee unit attached to the train. This is one of the best books on the division of family loyalties in Tennessee during the Civil War.
♦ The Civil War in East Tennessee could be researched by the students and analyzed as to why a majority of East Tennessee citizens supported the Union cause.
1. Tennessee—Civil War.

Steele, William O. *Triple Trouble for Hound Dog Zip*. Illus. by Mimi Korach. Garrard Press (081164037X), 1972. 64p. (Interest level: 2-5).

This is the entertaining story of Tennessee farmer Tom, and Zip, a most unusual dog, who was very adept at doing "human work," but not at staying out of trouble. This is a very entertaining book.
♦ Students may discuss what they would do if their dog were just like Zip.
1. Tennessee—Folklore.

West, Emmy and **Govan, Christine**. *Danger Downriver*. Illus. by Christine Govan. Viking Press (0-670-25575-0), 1972. 175p. Illus. (Interest level: 5-8+).

When his father mysteriously disappears from the tavern where they spent the night, a 10-year-old boy finds he has no choice but to stay and work for the surly tavern keeper.

♦ Students may research the idea of indentured work among colonial children and adults.

1. Tennessee—History.

White, Alana J. *Come Next Spring*. Clarion Books (0-395-52593-4), 1990. 170p. (Interest level: 5+).

In 1949, in the Great Smoky Mountains of Tennessee, Salina struggles to accept the inevitability of change—a highway cutting through the farmland, a brother and sister starting their own lives, and nothing left in common with her best friend.

♦ Students may discuss change and how one copes with great changes in life.

1. Tennessee—Fiction 2. Tennessee—Great Smoky Mountains.

Periodicals

398.05
Tennessee Folklore Society Bulletin. Middle Tennessee State University (ISSN 0040-3253), Quarterly. $25.00 per year. (Interest level: 6+).

A general periodical on all aspects of Tennessee folklore, from the mountains to the Mississippi River.

♦ Students should compare one aspect of Tennessee folklore, with a similar item of folklore from another state.

1. Folklore—Tennessee 2. Tennessee—Social life and customs

976.005
Now and Then. Center for Appalachian Studies at East Tennessee State University (ISSN 0029-5361), Tri-annually. $10.00 per year. (Interest level: 6+).

A general interest journal focusing on Tennessee's Appalachian Region. Topics include folklore, language and other areas unique to Appalachian culture.

♦ Using material from this publication and any other evidences collected, students should prove or disprove the notion that regional differences in speech are becoming more acceptable on a national level.

1. Appalachian Region, Southern—Periodicals.

976.8
Journal of East Tennessee History. East Tennessee Historical Society, Quarterly. $25.00 per year. (Interest level: Professional).

This journal focuses on the history of the eastern third of Tennessee. It contains general historical reports aimed at adult readers.

♦ Teachers may select certain articles for advanced students to read and report to the rest of the class.

1. Tennessee—History—Periodicals.

Professional Materials

011.62
Martin, Judy. *Choosing Books for Appalachian Children*. Berea College (No ISBN), 1982. 300p. (Interest level: Adult)

This is a definitive, though dated, source on books published on Appalachian themes. It is not organized by state, though a goodly portion of the material is directly related to Tennessee.

1. Appalachian Region.

451.3
Mertins, Barbara, ed. *Ready for Young People: Kentucky, Tennessee, and West Virginia*. American Library Association (0-8389-0426-2), 1985. 157p. (Interest level: Adult).

One-third of this reference source deals with books on Tennessee. A new edition is forthcoming.

1. Tennessee—books.

976.8
Weeks, Terry and **Womack, Bob**. *A History of Tennessee: Teacher Guide*. Clairmont Press (0-9623319-0-3), 1990, 149p. (Interest level: Professional).

This guide to the teaching of Tennessee history is divided into three parts: teacher's guide, workbook, and tests. It is an excellent generic teaching guide, applicable to available middle school Tennessee history texts.

1. Tennessee—History.

Virginia

by Suzanne Sprenger

Nonfiction

394.26
The Washington's Birthday Surprise (Sound Filmstrip). Society for Visual Education, 1981. (More Holiday Adventures of the Lollipop Dragon). 1 filmstrip, 35mm, Color; 1 audiocassette, (13 min.). $39.00. (Interest level: K-2).

Apple Blossom and Lollipop Dragon take the viewers on a visit to Mount Vernon, Virginia, in 1796 to chat with the George Washington. This animated filmstrip's color and music will delight students.
♦ This filmstrip could be viewed as a class activity to use with a celebration of George Washington's birthday, followed by viewing authentic photographs of Mount Vernon and of the Washingtons.
1. George Washington, 1732-1799—Juvenile films

398.2
Barden, Thomas, ed. *Virginia Folk Legends*. University Press of Virginia (0-8139-1335-7 pbk), 1991. 347p. Illus. (Interest level: 7-8).

Folktales of various sections of Virginia for older readers are retold with credit for the town, city, or county of origin. The use of dialect in many of the stories may be difficult reading for some students.
♦ Students might write a folktale of their own town by researching old newspapers of the area for interesting stories to recount, or by interviewing older members of their family for interesting tales.
1. Legends—Virginia 2. Tales—Virginia

582.078
Wyler, Rose. *Science Fun with Peanuts and Popcorn*. Illus. by Pat Stewart. J. Messner (0-671-55572-3), 1986. 48p. Color illus. (Interest level: 2-3).

This simple, straightforward book shows experiments using seeds and plants, root formations, and plant growth. The uncluttered illustrations will appeal to the younger readers.
♦ Students might try various simple experiments with peanuts. Teachers could emphasize the peanut's im-

portance to Virginia's agriculture, and why the peanut is grown in southside Virginia.
1. Peanuts—Experiments 2. Botany—Experiments 3. Plants—Experiments.

582.16 (Reference)
Gupton, Oscar and **Swope, Fred**. *Trees and Shrubs of Virginia*. University Press of Virginia (0-8139-0886-8), 1981. 205p. Color photos. (Interest level: 3-8).

Oscar Gupton and Fred Swope have given the readers a look at the trees and shrubs found across Virginia. The organization and color photographs of this resource are exceptional.
♦ The students might collect leaves of area trees to label and display, with team effort recognized for the most varieties gathered.
1. Trees—Virginia 2. Shrubs—Virginia

591 (Reference)
Virginia's Endangered Species. Sponsored by Virginia Department of Game and Inland Fisheries. McDonald and Woodward Publishing (0-939923-17-3), 1991. 672p. Illus., some color; Maps. (Interest level: 4-8).

This comprehensive resource guide identifies and describes more than 250 rare and endangered plants and animals in Virginia. This monograph is an excellent resource for ecological research topics.
♦ Students could research at least three endangered or rare plants or animals close to their home county/city and write a letter to the editor of the local paper suggesting ways the community might support these species.
1. Endangered species—Virginia—Congresses. 2. Nature conservation—Virginia—Congresses.

599
Freschet, Berniece. *Possum Baby*. Illus. by Jim Anorsky. Putnam (0-399-61105-3), 1978 (out of print). *(see and Read Nature Story Series)*. 45p. Illus., some color. (Interest level: K-2).

This is a delightful presentation of the life of a baby opossum from birth to first experience "playing possum". The emphasis on the nocturnal habits and dangers of this common Virginia animal will delight the young reader.

Students could tell about a time that they "played possum," draw a picture of the event, and have a class discussion of ways animals protect themselves from danger.

1. Virginia opossum 2. Opossums. 3. Animals—Infancy.

599
Grosvenor, Donna. *The Wild Ponies of Assateague Island*. Photos by James L. Stanfield. National Geographic Society (0-87044-166-3), 1975. 30p. (Books for Young Explorers Series). Color illus., photos. (Interest level: 2-5).

The text and colorful photographs describe the lives of the wild ponies of Assateague, including the annual pony penning on nearby Chincoteague Island. The large photographs of these endearing wild ponies make this book an excellent read aloud.

♦ Before reading the book, students could illustrate how they think the ponies came to live on this sandy reserve.

1. Chincoteague pony—Assateague Island (Md. and Va.) 2. Ponies.

635.6
Watts, Franklin. *Peanuts*. Illus. by Gene Sharp. Childrens Press (0-516-03689-0), 1978. 31p. Illus. (Interest level: K-4).

This book includes full-color photographs to help explain the origin, characteristics, cultivation, and uses of the peanut. Its concise, but thorough coverage of the peanut will be very helpful in class research.

♦ After hearing the book about one of Virginia's popular agricultural products, students could develop a class collection of peanut recipes. Each recipe would be written on a peanut-shaped paper and the cover would be colored to resemble a peanut. These shapebooks would be a fun gift to send home along with a sample of class-made peanut butter.

1. Peanuts.

636.1
Henry, Marguerite. *A Pictorial Life Story of Misty*. Illus. by Wesley Dennis. Rand McNally (0-02-743626-8), 1976. 112p. Illus.; Photos. (Interest level: 3-7).

In this book, Marguerite Henry tells how she came to win the famous pony, Misty of Chincoteague, and what became of Misty and her offspring. The wonderful illustrations and sincerity of her writing will endear this book to students.

♦ Students might write a letter to relate various experiences they have had with pets, or with a pet they wish they had and share these letters with a local retirement home.

1. Misty (Horse) 2. Henry, Marguerite 3. Chincoteague pony.

636.1
Marguerite Henry's Misty-Famous Chincoteague Pony (Model). Breyer Animal Creations, 1986. Plastic 7" model. $25.00. (Interest level: K-8).

This model is part of the Breyer collectible models and is a replica of Marguerite Henry's famous Misty of Chincoteague Island, Virginia. It is available at toy stores, as is Stormy, Misty's foal. The color, size, and durability of the model will make it an asset to any unit on Marguerite Henry, Chincoteague, or horses.

♦ The model pony could be used for writing motivation and in creative displays about the Marguerite Henry stories and the life of the wild ponies of Chincoteague Island.

1. Misty (Horse) 2. Chincoteague pony.

636.5
Patent, Dorothy. *Wild Turkey, Tame Turkey*. Photo. by William Munoz. Clarion Books (0-89919-704-3), 1989. 57p. Color illus. (Interest level: 3-5).

This book relates the colorful history of the native American turkey and compares that proud bird with its domesticated cousin. This book's value is enhanced by the informative text and beautiful photographs.

♦ After discussing the poultry business of the Rockingham County, Virginia, area, students could construct a colorful bulletin board turkey with tail feathers that contain facts about the turkey.

1. Wild turkeys 2. Turkeys.

646
Colonial Clothing, 1760-1770 (Videorecording). Colonial Williamsburg Foundation (LC 76-703964), 1976. VHS, Color, Full motion, (17 min.). $25.95. (Interest level: 5-8).

This video focuses on clothing worn by Virginians and most of the American colonists in the eighteenth century. It shows an upper class couple of that time rising in the morning and dressing for the day. Since the video shows only one well-to-do family, teachers might stress that all colonists did not dress as well as those portrayed.

♦ A colonial fair day with students dressing the parts, discussing crafts of the day, and having a picnic or outing featuring colonial foods could be planned.

1. Costume—History—18th century 2. Costume—United States—History

780.9
Music of Williamsburg (Videorecording). Colonial Williamsburg Foundation, nd. VHS, Color, Full motion, (40 min.). $25.95. (Interest level: 6-8).

Through a day's activities, this video recreates the music and rhythm of colonial Williamsburg with a sailor, slave, laborer, student, aristocrat, child, and trained musician. This is a beautifully crafted video.

♦ Before viewing the video, the class might participate in a group activity using a knowledge chart transparency, completing "What I Know About Colonial Music/Instruments." After viewing the video, complete another section of the knowledge chart labeled, "What I Learned About Colonial Music/Instruments." The next activity, completing a section of the chart "What I Would Like to Know About Colonial Music," could be done individually and could precede research time in the library.

1. Music—History—18th Century 2. Music—United States—History

800
Literature to Enjoy and Write About: Series 1 (Videorecording). Pied Piper Productions, 1989. 3 videocas-

settes, VHS, Color, (98 min.). Includes 5 guides. $195.00. (Interest level: 5-8).

These videos introduce trade books as a springboard to literature-based writing projects and include the book, *The Double Life of Pocahontas* by Jean Fritz (*see* page 151) in a unit on teaching interviewing skills using biographies. These videos are professionally presented and will encourage students to read the featured books.

♦ Student actors portraying historical Virginians could be interviewed by classmates.

1. Reading—Language experience approach 2. Books and reading 3. English language—Study and teaching

800

Literature to Enjoy and Write About: Series 2 (Videorecording). Pied Piper Productions, 1990. 3 videocassettes, VHS, Color, (98 min.). Includes 5 guides. $195.00 (Interest level: 5-8).

These videos demonstrate a literature-based program using trade books to introduce students to such writing types as the friendly letter, persuasive writing, book review, sequels, and readers theater. *Bridge to Terabithia* by Katherine Paterson (*see* page 155) is used to teach friendly letter, and *Charley Skedaddle* by Patricia Beatty (*see* page 154) is used to demonstrate readers theater. Both selections are set in Virginia.

♦ Students might develop letters written from one character within a book, or between two characters of different books.

1. Reading—Language experience approach 2. Books and reading 3. English language—Study and teaching

821

Read, Thomas Buchanan. *Sheridan's Ride*. Illus. by Nancy Winslow Parker. Greenwillow Books (0-688-10873-3), 1993. 32p. Illus. (Interest level: 4-6).

This book is an illustrated version of the nineteenth-century narrative poem about the frantic ride by Union General Philip Sheridan to join his troops at Cedar Creek, Virginia, in 1864. The book will delight students with its tribute to the horse, Rienzi, who carried General Sheridan to this important Civil War battle.

♦ By researching the battle, students might find the incorrect information in the poem when compared to the true events surrounding the Battle of Cedar Creek. Some students might prepare a readers theater or choral reading of the selection.

1. Sheridan, Philip Henry, 1831-1888—Poetry 2. Cedar Creek (Va.), Battle of, 1864—Poetry 3. United States—History—Civil War, 1861-1865—Poetry

912

USA GeoGraph. (Computer Software). Minnesota Educational Computing Consortium, 1992. Apple IIgs, 786K or Macintosh Plus, 1 megabyte, 3.5" disk. For Apple IIgs $59.00; for MAC $69.00. (Interest level: 5-8).

By using the 1990 United States Census with a "living map" theme, this program allows students to learn about American history and the nature of their state with 100 demographic, social, environmental, and economic categories.

♦ Using bar graph presentations, students might compare Virginia with another state or with their own state.

1. United States—Description and travel 2. United States—Maps

912

VA Indian Wall Map. (Map). Rand McNally & Co. (Catalog No. 314-19144-5). Two-sided wall map, spring roller, 50" x 68". $103.00. (Interest level: 4-6).

This Indian map of Virginia displays state boundaries, tribal names and range lines, and historical information and text on such aspects of tribal life as village living, food sources, and education. This resource would be an invaluable addition to the multicultural study of Virginia.

♦ Students might recreate a typical Virginia Indian village of a specific time period.

1. Indians of North America—Virginia—Maps

912

Virginia State Map. (Map). Rand McNally & Company (Cat. No. 114-10862-5). 65" x 50" wall map. $103.00. (Interest level: 4-8).

This visual relief state map has inset maps depicting population and economic activities of Virginia. The additional information surrounding the colorful map will be a helpful resource.

♦ Students might select trivia cards created by the teacher using the map as the answer source. Examples of the trivia might include locating the highest mountain in Virginia, finding specific towns, finding a town that includes a part of the student's name, or locating the closest state park.

1. Virginia—Maps

917.5

Geography of the United States, III. (Sound Filmstrip). National Geographic Society (LC 78-731223), 1979. 2 filmstrips, Color, 35mm; 2 audiocassettes (29 min.). Includes 2 guides. $68.00. (Interest level: 4-6).

This set of filmstrips and audiocassettes offers a description of the upper and lower South with emphasis on the points of interest, economy, and geographic features. Virginia's location and role in its region is a strong feature of the filmstrip, "The Upper South".

♦ Students might be encouraged to note Virginia's regional location and create a clay or dough relief map of the region depicted in the filmstrip. Each team of students might create a relief map that emphasizes a different aspect of the region, such as agriculture, industry, recreation, or population.

1. Southern States—Description and travel

917.55 (Reference)

The Encyclopedia of Virginia. Somerset Publishers, Inc. (0-403-09902-1), 1992. (Encyclopedia of the United States). 587p. Illus.; Maps; Photos. (Interest level: 4-8).

This resource includes biographical information of governors since 1607, a chronology of events in Virginia, a directory of state services and agencies, a dictionary of places in Virginia, and a description of historical places by county and city. The photographs are of poor quality, but the county/city information is very useful.

♦ The description of famous old residences could be recreated in drawings by the students, or used as a setting in a mystery or ghost story.

1. Virginia—Encyclopedias.

917.55 (Reference)

Hagemann, James. *The Heritage of Virginia; The Story of Place Names in the Old Dominion.* Donning Press (0-89865-255-3 pbk), 1986. 297p. Illus., pbk.; Bibliography; Index. (Interest level: 3-8).

This reference book gives the origins of the names of Virginia localities. This is an excellent source for research for most place names in Virginia.

♦ After creating posters about the names of their hometown or county and surrounding localities, students could have a charades-type game to act out area names for classmates.

1. Names, Geographical—Virginia 2. Virginia—History, Local

917.55

Peters, Margaret. *A Guidebook to Virginia's Historical Markers.* University Press of Virginia (0-8139-1047-1), 1985. 269p. Index. (Interest level: 4-8).

This guidebook describes both significant and little known historical markers on Virginia's highways, including Revolutionary War and Civil War activities, historic homes, and churches. This guide is an excellent reference for writing activities about Virginia and for information about Virginia students' local area history.

♦ Students could draw several area markers on the computer or on posters and share the information with the class.

1. Historical markers—Virginia—Guidebooks. 2. Virginia—Description and travel—1981—Guidebooks.

917.55

Radlauer, Ruth. *Shenandoah National Park.* Photos by Ed and Ruth Radlauer. Childrens Press (0-516-07744-9), 1987. 48p. Color photos. (Interest level: 3-6).

This work describes one of Virginia's national parks, with flora and fauna, history and ecology of the area, and trail terms for hikers. The full-color illustrations and variety of information make this book an excellent resource.

♦ Students might plan an overnight hike by making a diagram or list of backpack contents as they plan for food, sleeping, first aid, and water. Students also might read *Grandpa's Mountain* by Carolyn Reeder (*see* page 155).

1. Shenandoah National Park (Va.)

917.8

Lewis and Clark Stayed Home. (Computer Software). Minnesota Educational Computing Corporation (0-7929-0168-1), 1991. For: Apple II series computers;

128K RAM; 1 disk drive; Monochrome or color monitor. $59.00. (Interest level: 5-8).

In this interactive computer program, students get to explore the Louisiana Purchase in place of Virginia's Lewis and Clark. To have a successful mission, students are challenged to map the Louisiana Purchase, establish friendly contact with the Native American tribes, and attempt to find a route to the Pacific Ocean.

♦ Students could research the lives of Virginians Lewis and Clark, map their travels across the United States, and use the interactive computer game for involvement.

1. Explorers 2. Louisiana Purchase

921 (Reference)

Oakley, Ruth. *The Marshall Cavendish Illustrated History of the Presidents of the United States.* Illus. by Steve Lucas and Tim Woodcock-Jones. Marshall Cavendish Corp. (1-85435-144-3 set), 1990. 8 vols. Illus., some color.; Indexes. (Interest level: 4-8).

This eight-volume set details the life of each president with emphasis on his political activity in historical context. Students will find this colorful set an excellent source for Virginia presidents and related time line activities.

♦ Teams of students could develop a time line for each of the Virginia presidents with emphasis on events in the country during that president's life. Chronologically displayed, these time lines could be an informative focus of the school halls.

1. Presidents—United States—Biography

970.3

Feest, Christian. *The Powhatan Tribes.* Chelsea House (1-55546-726-1), 1990. 111p. (Indians of North America Series). Illus; Photos; Maps. (Interest level: 7-8).

This book examines the culture, history, and changing fortunes of the Powhatan Indians of Virginia. This valuable resource covers the history of the Powhatan tribes from before the settlement of Jamestown on into modern day.

♦ As group activities, students could research the early culture of the Powhatan tribes, covering such topics as clothing, food, religion, and pottery. Other groups could research the present-day status and condition of the Powhatan tribes.

1. Powhatan Indians 2. Indians of North America

973.2

Colonial Life in the South. (Videorecording). Zenger Video Distributors. VHS, Color, (11 min.). $59.00. (Interest level: 4-8).

In this video, a surveyor on his way to Williamsburg from the Blue Ridge Mountains stops at a small farm and at a large plantation. This video gives a view of the social and economic climate before the Revolutionary War.

♦ Students could view this video and then read the book, *Journey to Monticello: Traveling in Colonial Times* by James Knight (*see* following entry). After reading, students could compare the early travel adventures and hardships to a trip to Williamsburg today.

1. United States—Social life and customs—Colonial period, ca. 1600-1775

973.2
Knight, James. *Journey to Monticello: Traveling in Colonial Times*. Illus. by George Guzzi. Troll Associates (0-89775-736-5), 1982. 31p. (Adventures in Colonial America Series). Illus. (Interest level: 4-7).

In this book, the reader follows a young man as he uses different modes of transportation to make the long and difficult trip from Massachusetts to Virginia in the spring of 1775.

◆ Using a comparison chart, students might compare a business trip today with one in 1775.

1. United States—Description and travel—To 1783 2. Transportation—History

973.3
Yorktown—Independence Achieved. (Sound Filmstrip). Troll Associates, nd. 1 filmstrip, Color, 35mm; 1 cassette (approx. 9 min.). $28.00. (Interest level: 4-7).

This filmstrip depicts the surrender at Yorktown, offering students an opportunity to see actual landmarks and historical sites.

◆ Students could create a replica of the Yorktown battle on a large flat piece of cardboard.

1. Yorktown, Battle of, 1781—Juvenile film 2. United States—History—Revolution, 1775-1789—Juvenile film

973.46
Fisher, Leonard Everett. *Monticello*. Illus. with photographs and drawings by the author. Holiday House (0-8234-0688-1), 1988. 64p. Illus, Photos. (Interest level: 6-8).

This is the story of Thomas Jefferson's remarkable home near Charlottesville, including its planning, building, downfall, and restoration. The illustrations of inventions, floor plans, and grounds make the book very understandable.

◆ Students might design a real estate advertisement for Monticello that could be advertised in a large magazine for the wealthy reader. The ad should focus on the major features of the home and its historic significance.

1. Monticello (Va.) 2. Jefferson, Thomas, 1743-1826—Homes and haunts

973.5
Haley, Gail E. *Jack Jouett's Ride*. Illus. by the author. Viking (0-670-40466-7), 1973 (out of print). 31p. Color illus. (Interest level: 3-5).

This book recaptures the 1781 incident during the American Revolution when Jack Jouett rode to warn Thomas Jefferson and others of the coming of Tarleton's Raiders. This book, with it's delightful linoleum cut illustrations is a good read-aloud to motivate research.

◆ Students might write and illustrate a short report on why John (Jack) Jouett was called the "Paul Revere of the South." Some students could choose to write

from the viewpoint of Jack Jouett's famous horse as he carried Jack to warn the colonists.

1. Jouett, John, 1754-1822 2. United States—History—Revolution, 1775-1783

973.5
Jack Jouett's Ride. (Sound Filmstrip). Weston Woods Studios (LC 75-735596), 1975 (out of print). 1 filmstrip, Color, 35mm; 1 cassette, (7 min.). (Interest level: 3-5).

This filmstrip is based on the book of the same title by Gail E. Haley (*see* preceding entry). Linoleum cuts are used to recount the incident during the American Revolution when Jack Jouett rode to warn Thomas Jefferson and others of Tarleton's approach. Music is done by the Williamsburg Fife and Drum Corps. This filmstrip is out of print, but is very possibly available in local Virginia libraries. The combination of wonderful visuals and music make it an excellent resource.

◆ After reading the book and viewing the filmstrip, several students could report on music and instruments of the colonial period.

1. Jouett, John, 1754-1822—Juvenile films 2. United States—History—Revolution, 1775-1783

973.5
Robertson, James, Jr. *Civil War Sites in Virginia: A Tour Guide*. The University Press of Virginia (0-8139-0907-4 pbk), 1982. 108p. Illus.; Maps; Index, pbk. (Interest level: 6-8).

Virginia towns and counties involved in the Civil War are described in short readable form. Battlefields are located by areas of Virginia, and include present-day highway directions. This is a simple to use, but very comprehensive reference source for students and teachers.

◆ Students could research Civil War sites, with Virginia students looking at those nearest their home. Pretending that they were there at the battle or skirmish, students could write several diary entries before and after the incident.

1. Historic sites—Virginia—Guide-books. 2. Virginia—Description and travel 3. Virginia—History—Civil War, 1861-1865

973.7
Beller, Susan Provost. *Cadets at War: The True Story of Teenage Heroism at the Battle of New Market*. Illus. by the author. Shoe Tree Press (1-55870-196-6), 1991. 95p. Illus. (Interest level: 7-8).

This work discusses the role of the Virginia Military Institute cadets in the Battle of New Market in 1864.

◆ Students might read Chapter 9, "Screaming, Fighting, Dying," from *Voices from the Civil War: A Documentary History of the Great American Conflict* by Milton Meltzer (*see* following entry). After becoming familiar with selections from both works, students could create letters to families of a cadet who participated at New Market.

1. New Market, Battle of, 1864. 2. Virginia Military Institute—History—19th century. 3. United States—History—Civil War, 1861-1865—Campaigns

973.7
Meltzer, Milton. *Voices from the Civil War: A Documentary History of the Great American Conflict*. Edited by Milton Meltzer. Thomas Y. Crowell (0-690-04802-5), 1989. 203p. Illus.; Index. (Interest level: 7-8).

Letters, diaries, journal entries, ballads of the period, speeches, and newspaper articles are intertwined to depict the feelings and events of the Civil War's four years. This book is an excellent introduction to any activity dealing with the Civil War and those who were a part of it.
♦ Students might create a newspaper that could have been written during the Civil War. Towns and cities that were established before the 1860s may be able to provide examples of original Civil War period newspapers.
1. United States—History—Civil War, 1861-1865.

973.7
Murphy, Jim. *The Boys' War: Confederate and Union Soldiers Talk About the Civil War*. Clarion Books (0-89919-893-7), 1990. 110p. Illus. (Interest level: 6-8).

This work uses diaries, personal letters, and archival photos to describe the experiences of boys 16 and younger who fought in the Civil War.
♦ Students might use this work with the books *Shades of Gray* by Carolyn Reeder (*see* page 155) or *Charley Skedaddle* by Patricia Beatty (*see* page 154) as research and motivational material for creating their own journals and diary entries.
1. United States—History—Civil War, 1861-1865—Children 2. United States—History—Civil War, 1861-1865—Personal narratives

975.5
Ashabranner, Brent. *A Grateful Nation: The Story of Arlington National Cemetery*. Illus. by Jennifer Ashabranner. Putnam (0-399-22188-3), 1990. 117p. Illus.; Photos. (Interest level: 6-8+).

The author traces the history of our national burial ground and shrine to American heroes. This impressive site is located in Arlington, Virginia, on the grounds of Robert E. Lee's home. The book is fully illustrated with black-and-white photographs.
♦ After a discussion of the Tomb of the Unknowns, students might debate why there should or should not be such a tomb.
1. Arlington National Cemetery (Va.)

975.5
Aylesworth, Thomas. *Atlantic: District of Columbia, Virginia, West Virginia*. Illus. by Virginia L. Aylesworth. Chelsea House (0-7910-1041-4), 1991. (States Reports Series). 64p. Illus.; Maps. (Interest level: 4-7).

Featured in this work are the geographical, historical, and cultural aspects of Virginia. This book allows the reader the opportunity to understand the regional aspects of the state, with special emphasis on cultural offerings.
♦ Students could plan a one-week tour of the state to include at least 10 historical or cultural sites to visit. Groups would present their planned tour to other

students in a competitive spirit to "sell" them on the merits of their tour "package."
1. Virginia 2.West Virginia 3. District of Columbia

975.5 (Reference)
Dabney, Virginius. *Virginia: The New Dominion, a History from 1607 to the Present*. University Press of Virginia (0-8139-1015-3), 1987. 629p. Illus. (Interest level: 4-8; Professional).

This resource, written by a Pulitzer Prize-winning author, covers the major developments in Virginia history. This history would be most useful as a professional reference.
♦ Students and teachers might use this reference for background information for projects.
1. Virginia

975.5
Fradin, Dennis B. *Virginia*. Childrens Press (0-516-03846-X), 1992. (From Sea to Shining Sea Series). 64p. (Interest level: 3-5).

This book gives an introduction to the interesting sites, geographical features, and important people of Virginia. This colorful series is an easy-to-use source of basic information about the states with an interesting trivia section entitled, "Did You Know?"
♦ Students might create a "fact book" about Virginia written on pages in the shape of the state and having an interesting fact on each page emphasized with a dot for location.
1. Virginia.

975.5
Fradin, Dennis B. *The Virginia Colony*. Childrens Press (0-516-00387-9), 1986. (The Thirteen Colonies Series). 158p. Illus.; Ports.; Bibliography. (Interest level: 6-8).

This work presents the history, economy, and culture of early Virginia from Powhatan to Thomas Jefferson. The black-and-white photos and drawings will assist students in creating posters and time lines of the early colony.
♦ The class can create an illustrated, over-sized time line of major events of early Virginia history.
1. Virginia—History—Colonial period, ca. 1600-1775
2. Virginia—History—Revolution, 1775-1783

975.5
Kalman, Bobbie. *Colonial Town: Williamsburg*. Crabtree Publishing Co. (0-86505-489-4), 1991. (Historic Communities Series). 32p. Photos. (Interest level: K-8).

A visit to colonial Williamsburg is the focus of this colorful book. This book and the others in the Historic Communities Series are excellent resources for colonial life in Virginia.
♦ Students might design their own colonial home and garden as if they were building it during the eighteenth century in Williamsburg.
1. Williamsburg, Virginia

975.5
McNair, Sylvia. *Virginia*. Childrens Press (0-516-00492-1), 1989. (America the Beautiful Series). 144p. Illus., some color; Index. (Interest level: 4-8).

McNair's work introduces the geography, history, government, economy, culture, famous people, and historic sites of the Old Dominion.

♦ After creating a large 4' x 8' outline map of Virginia on white paper for a wall of the classroom, students could choose a place of interest in the state, create a 5" x 7" facts card about the location, and draw an original art design about the site on the wall map.

1. Virginia

975.5
Sirvaitis, Karen. *Virginia*. Lerner Publications (0-8225-2702-2), 1991. (Hello U.S.A. Series). 72p. Illus., some color; Maps. (Interest level: 3-5).

This book introduces the geography, history, people, industries, and other highlights of Virginia. This work has an inviting section covering a number of famous Virginians and an excellent focus on the ecosystem of the Chesapeake Bay.

♦ Students may use this book as a reference to create an acrostic of the word "Virginia"; they can put the acrostic on a poster and decorate it with a major event in the history of Virginia.

1. Virginia.

975.5
Stein, R. Conrad. *The Story of Arlington National Cemetery*. Illus. by Richard Wahl. Children's Press (0-516-04610-1), 1979. (Cornerstones of Freedom Series). 31p. Color illus. (Interest level: 3-5).

This brief history of Arlington National Cemetery describes the famous and less well-known people buried there. This book is written in a story form, making it a pleasant read aloud selection.

♦ After having the book read to them, students might illustrate a selection from the book and participate in a discussion of why scientific advancements may help prevent unknown soldiers in the future.

1. Arlington National Cemetery (Va.)

975.5
Thompson, Kathleen. *Virginia*. Raintree (0-86514-447-8), 1985. (Portrait of America Series). 48p. Illus.; Maps. (Interest level: 4-5).

Thompson discusses the history, economy, culture, and future of Virginia. The cultural and historical aspects of this book make it a strong resource for class projects, and the annual events calendar for the state will be a complement to any unit.

♦ Students might create a modern time line of events of Virginia's nineteenth and twentieth centuries, with special emphasis on Virginia's war heroes, entertainers, and sports figures.

1. Virginia

Biography

921
Fitz-Gerald, Christine Maloney. *Meriwether Lewis and William Clark*. Childrens Press (0-516-03061-2), 1991. (World's Great Explorers Series). 126p. Color photos, illus. (Interest level: 4-8).

This book describes the early life of the Virginians, Meriwether Lewis and William Clark, and the expedition they made from St. Louis to the Pacific. The extraordinary illustrations in this book and its creative format make it a wonderful resource.

♦ Journals were kept by both Lewis and Clark and by other members of the exploration party. After researching the Shoshoni and Mandan tribes, students could write several journal entries as though they were on the expedition and were observing these tribes.

1. Explorers—West (U.S.)—Biography 2. Lewis, Meriwether, 1774-1809 3. Clark, William, 1770-1838

92 Ashe, Arthur
Weissberg, Ted. *Arthur Ashe—Tennis Great*. Illus. by the author. Chelsea House (0-7910-1141-0 pbk), 1991. (Black Americans of Achievement Series). 109p. Introductory essay by Coretta Scott King. Illus. (Interest level: 5-8).

This work presents the life of an important African-American athlete and tennis player from Virginia, Arthur Ashe. This book pre-dates Arthur Ashe's death, but includes many of the major contributions that he made to this country.

♦ Students could create a mobile about Arthur Ashe including words and items relating to his life (tennis racket, tennis trophies, etc.) as part of the mobile. Other outstanding Virginians of achievement could also be featured in mobile displays.

1. Ashe, Arthur—Biography 2. Tennis players—United States—Biography. 3. African-Americans—Biography

92 Bailey, Pearl
Brandt, Keith. *Pearl Bailey: With a Song in Her Heart*. Illus. by Gershom Griffith. Troll Associates (0-8167-2921-2), 1992. 48p. Color illus. (Interest level: 4-6).

This is a biography of the singer born in Newport News, Virginia, who entertained audiences with her performances on Broadway, television, and the concert stage. This illustrated biography will appeal to students and will also be an excellent multicultural selection.

♦ Students might watch the movie, *Porgy and Bess,* in which Pearl Bailey starred.

1. Bailey, Pearl 2. African-Americans—Biography 3. Singers—Biography

92 Fitzgerald, Ella
Kliment, Bud. *Ella Fitzgerald*. Chelsea House (1-55546-586-2), 1988. (Black Americans of Achievement Series). 112p. Illus.; Ports. (Interest level: 7-8).

This work depicts the life of singer Ella Fitzgerald who was born in Newport News, Virginia, and who has won numerous Grammy Awards. This selection is an excellent multicultural addition, as well as one that portrays the artistic contributions made by a Virginian.

♦ Students could study the growth of jazz in the United States, listen to jazz selections, and construct a time line of the stars of jazz with Ella Fitzgerald prominently featured.

1. Fitzgerald, Ella 2. Singers—United States—Biography 3. African-American singers—Biography

92 Harrison, William Henry
Fitz-Gerald, Christine Maloney. *William Henry Harrison: Ninth President of the United States.* Children's Press (0-516-01392-0), 1987. (Encyclopedia of Presidents Series). 98p. Illus.; Ports. (Interest level: 6-8).

This is a biography of our ninth president who was born at Berkeley Plantation in Virginia, and who died one month after taking office. This is a good resource on an often overlooked Virginian.
♦ Students might research the Battle of Tippecanoe and the Shawnee chief Tecumseh, illustrating the role Harrison took in the events with a cartoon or slogan-type poster typical of Harrison's era.
1. Harrison, William Henry, 1773-1841 2. Presidents— United States—Biography

92 Henry, Patrick
Fritz, Jean. *Where Was Patrick Henry on the 29th of May?* Illus. by Margot Tomes. Coward, McCann & Geoghegan (0-698-20307-0), 1975. 47p. Illus. (Interest level: 3-4).

This is a humorous, yet well researched biography of the fiery orator from Virginia's Revolutionary period. In this biography, as in her other works, Jean Fritz has delightfully portrayed history's characters with lively style and attention to funny details in their lives.
♦ Students might create a cartoon-style series of pictures illustrating the events of May 29 of several of the years of Patrick Henry's life, beginning with his birth on May 29, 1736.
1. Henry, Patrick, 1736-1799

92 Henry, Patrick
Reische, Diana. *Patrick Henry.* Illus. by author. Watts (0-531-10305-6), 1987. (First Book Series). 92p. Illus.; Bibliography; Index. (Interest level: 3-5).

This biography presents the life and career of the Virginian who was an orator, lawyer, statesman, and framer of the Bill of Rights. An excellent index and bibliography complement this book.
♦ Students might use clear 35mm filmstrip material and very fine overhead pens to illustrate several frames of a filmstrip about Patrick Henry. An audiotape to accompany the filmstrip could be created by the student(s). Old filmstrips can be bleached to use for this activity.
1. Henry, Patrick, 1736-1799

92 Jackson, Thomas J. "Stonewall"
Fritz, Jean. *Stonewall.* Drawings by Stephen Gammell. Puffin Books (0-14-032937-4 pbk), 1989. 152p. llus., pbk. (Interest level: 6-8).

This is a biography of the brilliant Civil War general who earned the nickname "Stonewall" at the Battle of Bull Run. This biography is written in the readable manner characteristic of Jean Fritz's historical books.
♦ Students might research the Battle of Bull Run or view a video of the battle before reading the book.
1. Jackson, Stonewall, 1824-1863 2. United States— History—Civil War, 1861-1865—Campaigns

92 Jefferson, Thomas
Adler, David. *A Picture Book of Thomas Jefferson.* Illus. by John and Alexandra Wallner. Holiday House

(0-8234-0791-8), 1990. (Picture Book Biography Series). 32p. Illus. (Interest level: 2-4).

This biography of Thomas Jefferson traces the life and achievements of the Virginia architect, president, and author of the Declaration of Independence. This is an excellent beginning biography for young readers.
♦ Students might illustrate their favorite event or invention from Jefferson's life and attach the creation to a silhouette of Monticello or of Jefferson for display.
1. Jefferson, Thomas, 1743-1826 2. Presidents— United States—Biography

92 Jefferson, Thomas
Adler, David. *Thomas Jefferson: Father of Our Democracy.* Illus. by Jacqueline Garrick. Holiday House (0-8234-0667-9), 1987. (First Biography Series). 48p. Illus. (Interest level: 3-5).

This account of Jefferson's life highlights many of his accomplishments as governor, architect, gardener, inventor, and president. The emphasis on Jefferson's inventive talents make this book a valuable resource.
♦ As an inventor, Jefferson was recognized even in foreign countries. Students could design an advertisement for one of the colonial newspapers for one of his inventions.
1. Jefferson, Thomas, 1743-1826 2. Presidents—Biography

92 Jefferson, Thomas
Johnson, Ann Donegan. *The Value of Foresight: The Story of Thomas Jefferson.* Illus. by Steve Pileggi. Value Communications (0-916392-42-2), 1979. 63p. Color illus. (Interest level: 2-4).

This biography of Thomas Jefferson emphasizes his lasting contributions to his country. These "Values" books have been a part of many libraries for several years and have contributed insight into the characters of many famous personalities.
♦ Students might relate to Thomas Jefferson's use of foresight by illustrating a scene of someone who did not think ahead and who suffered for it.
1. Jefferson, Thomas, 1743-1826 2. Presidents— United States—Biography

92 Jefferson, Thomas
Meltzer, Milton. *Thomas Jefferson: The Revolutionary Aristocrat.* Franklin Watts (0-531-11069-9), 1991. 256p. Illus. (Interest level: 7-8).

The Virginia author of the Declaration of Independence and third president of the United States is presented in this biography. The length of this biography makes it most suitable for the more capable readers.
♦ After reading selections from this book about Thomas Jefferson, students might critique the selection for information that they discovered to be entertaining, as well as informative.
1. Jefferson, Thomas, 1743-1826 2. Presidents— United States—Biography

92 Jefferson, Thomas
Quackenbush, Robert. *Pass the Quill, I'll Write a Draft: A Story of Thomas Jefferson.* Illus. by the author.

Pippin Press (0-945912-07-2), 1989. 36p. Color illus. (Interest level: 2-4).

This biography follows the life and accomplishments of the third president, Thomas Jefferson, from his birth to his retirement to Monticello. This is one of the entertaining biographies of famous personalities done by Quackenbush that features humorous text and illustrations.

♦ After they are introduced to simple political cartoons from area newspapers, students might create a simple political cartoon about one of the Virginia-born presidents .

1. Jefferson, Thomas, 1743-1826 2. Presidents—United States—Biography—Juvenile humor

92 Lee, Robert E.
Bains, Rae. *Robert E. Lee, Brave Leader.* Illus. by Dick Smolinski. Troll Associates (0-8167-0545-3 lib bind; 0-8167-0546-1 pbk), 1986. 43p. Illus. (Interest level: 2-3).

This book traces the life of the leader of the Confederate forces, Robert E. Lee, with emphasis on his difficult childhood in Virginia. The briefness of this book makes it an excellent choice to use with reluctant readers.

♦ Students could complete a compare/contrast chart to discuss toys of the children of the early 1800s and those of today's nine-year-olds. Students might draw both a toy of the 1800s and one of the favorites of today.

1. Lee, Robert E., 1807-1870—Biography

92 Lee, Robert E.
Greene, Carol. *Robert E. Lee: Leader in War and Peace.* Childrens Press (0-516-04209-2), 1989. (Rookie Biography Series). 45p. Illus., some color. (Interest level: K-3).

This work is a simple biography of the Virginia general who commanded a Confederate Army during the Civil War. The material presented in this book allows the reader to see more of Robert E. Lee than just his Civil War experiences.

♦ Students could draw a picture of something they have done that was very hard, but which made them proud, using as an example Robert E. Lee's hard work to take care of his widowed mother and their house.

1. Lee, Robert E., 1807-1870—Biography 2. Generals—United States—Biography 3. United States—History—Civil War.

92 Madison, James
Fritz, Jean. *The Great Little Madison.* Putnam (0-399-21768-1), 1989. 159p. Illus. (Interest level: 6-8).

This highly acclaimed biography explores the life of the fourth president of the United States, a Virginian who overcame childhood illness to become a powerful leader. This book is as entertaining as it is enlightening.

♦ Students might create a short play depicting the events surrounding the British attack on Washington in 1814.

1. Madison, James, 1751-1836. 2. Presidents—United States—Biography

92 Monroe, James
Fitz-Gerald, Christine Maloney. *James Monroe: Fifth President of the United States.* Childrens Press, 1987. (Encyclopedia of Presidents Series). 98p. Illus. (Interest level: 6-8).

This work explores the life and political career of the fifth president of the United States, best remembered for his Monroe Doctrine denying further European control in the western hemisphere. The format of this series of biographies offers an excellent look at the political impact of the president featured.

♦ Monroe traveled to many countries while serving his own. Students could enlarge a map of the world and color the countries that he visited, adding notes about what he accomplished for the United States.

1. Monroe, James, 1748-1831 2. Presidents—United States—Biography

92 Moses, Grandma
Oneal, Zibby. *Grandma Moses, Painter of Rural America.* Illus. by Donna Ruff; paintings by Grandma Moses. Viking Kestrel (0-670-80664-1), 1986. (Women of Our Time Series). 58p. Illus.; Ports. (Interest level: 4-7).

This is a biography focusing on the early years of Grandma Moses, who is known for her paintings of rural America and who lived in Staunton, Virginia. This is an excellent source to use with a focus on Virginia women.

♦ Students could research a number of famous women artists of our time, including P. Buckley Moss, and compare their styles by using a variety of art books.

1. Moses, Grandma, 1860-1961 2. Painters—United States—Biography

92 Pocahontas
Fritz, Jean. *The Double Life of Pocahontas.* Illus. by Ed Young. Putnam (0-399-21016-4), 1983. 96p. Illus.; Map; Bibliography; Index. (Interest level: 5-6).

This book depicts the life of the famous Native American princess with sufficient realities to dispel many of the myths of this intriguing girl caught between two cultures. This book will bring the character of Pocahontas alive for the reader.

♦ Students could create a short play based on research of the life of Pocahontas. The emphasis of this project should be on the true cultural aspect of her "saving" Captain John Smith, not on the myths.

1. Pocahontas, d. 1617—Biography 2. Powhatan Indians—Biography.

92 Pocahontas
Greene, Carol. *Pocahontas: Daughter of a Chief.* Childrens Press (0-516-04203-3), 1988. (Rookie biography Series). 45p. Color illus. (Interest level: K-3).

This is a brief biography of the Native American princess who became involved with the Virginia colonists at Jamestown. The time line in each of the books in this Rookie Biography Series can be an excellent resource for students.

♦ Students might develop a "Virginia Native American Celebration" complete with a meal and attire made from large brown paper bags with support for the project from pictures of early Virginia Native Americans at work and play.

1. Pocahontas, d. 1617—Biography 2. Indians of North America—Virginia—Biography 3. Jamestown (Va.)—History

92 Poe, Edgar Allan

Edgar Allan Poe. (Videorecording). January Productions; Dist. by Zenger Video, 1985. Color, (18 min.). Includes guide. $39.95. (Interest level: 7-8).

This video from a filmstrip uses dramatic watercolors, factual narration, and poetic readings to explore the life and career of American writer Edgar Allan Poe of Virginia. This production is a filmstrip to video enhancement.

♦ Students could select one of Poe's short stories or poems to read as a small group and then retell to the class with readers theater performance.

1. Poe, Edgar Allan, 1809-1849 2. Authors, American—19th century—Biography.

92 Smith, John

Graves, John Parlin. *John Smith.* Illus. by Al Fiorentino. Chelsea House (0-7910-1499-1), 1991. 96p. Illus. (Interest level: 4-6).

John Smith is idealized as a famous hero in this fictionalized biography of the famous Jamestown leader reprinted from the original series, World Explorer Books, by Garrard Pub. (1965). Teachers will welcome this reprint of a well-used resource about John Smith.

♦ Students could research the Powhatan Indians of Virginia and report on John Smith's contact with them and his reports on their lifestyles.

1. Smith, John, 1580-1631 2. Explorers—Virginia—Biography 3. Jamestown (Va.)—History

92 Taylor, Zachary

Collins, David. *Zachary Taylor, 12th President of the United States.* Garrett Educational Corp. (0-944483-17-8), 1989. 121p. Illus. (Interest level: 6-8).

This biography details the childhood, education, and employment of the president from Virginia nicknamed "Old Rough and Ready", Zachary Taylor. This resource is suited for upper elementary and middle school readers.

♦ Near the end of Zachary Taylor's life, two great novels were written, Charles Dickens' *David Copperfield* and Nathaniel Hawthorne's *The Scarlet Letter*. Students might become familiar with these works and report on what life was like in the late 1800s as pictured in these novels.

1. Taylor, Zachary, 1784-1850 2. Presidents—United States—Biography

92 Tyler, John

Lillegard, Dee. *John Tyler: Tenth President of the United States.* Childrens Press (0-516-01393-9), 1987. (Encyclopedia of Presidents Series). 98p. Illus.; Ports. (Interest level: 6-8).

This is a biography of the Virginian who became tenth president upon the death of William Henry Harrison. Black-and-white prints and photos are abundant throughout the work.

♦ The telegraph was invented during Tyler's term; students might send several "telegraphs" relating events of Tyler's term in office, putting them chronologically on a "telegraph wire" across the classroom.

1. Tyler, John, 1790-1862 2. Presidents—United States—Biography

92 Washington, Booker T.

Gleiter, Jan. *Booker T. Washington.* Illus. by Rick Whipple. Raintree Childrens Books (0-8172-2663-X), 1988. 32p. Color illus. (Interest level: 2-4).

This biography traces the life of the African-American educator, Booker T. Washington, who rose from a birth into slavery near Bedford, Virginia, to establish Tuskegee Institute in Alabama. The large print and color illustrations in this biography will motivate even reluctant readers to complete this book.

♦ Students might present short dramatic skits of Booker T. Washington's life, with each group doing a different event, such as his trips to the mill as a tiny boy or sweeping the school to be accepted at Hampton.

1. Washington, Booker T., 1856-1915 2. Educators—United States—Biography 3. African-Americans—Biography

92 Washington, Booker T.

McKissack, Pat. *The Story of Booker T. Washington.* Childrens Press (0-516-04758-2), 1991. (Cornerstones of Freedom Series). 31p. Illus.; Photos; Index. (Interest level: 5-8).

This book traces the life of the Virginia-born African-American educator who had such a vital part in the beginning of Tuskegee Institute. McKissack examines many facets of Booker T. Washington's life, making this one of the more reliable sources for a complete picture of his life.

♦ After reading or hearing this book, students could create a collage of drawings about the life of Booker T. Washington, perhaps focusing on the hardships he faced as he strived to educate himself.

1. Washington, Booker T., 1856-1915—Biography 2. African-Americans—Biography 3. Educators—United States—Biography

92 Washington, George

D'Aulaires' George Washington. (Sound Filmstrip). Spoken Arts, 1983. 1 filmstrip, 35mm, Color; 1 cassette, (8 1/4 min.). $45.00. (Interest level: 2-3).

This is a colorful telling of George Washington's life through the book by Ingri D'Aulaire. This retelling of the book shows Washington as student, scout, soldier, and president. The illustrations are a delight.

♦ Students could read a short biography of Washington, watch the filmstrip, and work together to complete a Venn diagram of what information was common to both works, and what was unique to each work.

1. Washington, George, 1732-1799—Juvenile films

92 Washington, George

Greene, Carol. *George Washington, First President of the United States.* Childrens Press (0-516-04218-1), 1991. (Rookie Biography Series). 42p. Illus., some color. (Interest level: K-3).

Written for the beginning reader, this colorful life story of George Washington has well-spaced text and a good balance of full-page illustrations that will appeal to the primary student.

♦ Students might create a black silhouette of each student using a filmstrip or overhead projector as the light source and display each silhouette with a short research report about George Washington with his silhouette as the center.

1. Washington, George, 1732-1799 2. Presidents—United States—Biography

92 Washington, George

The Life of George Washington. (Sound Filmstrip). Society for Visual Education (LC 78-740366), 1971. (Lincoln and Washington: Why We Celebrate Their Birthdays Series). 1 filmstrip, Color, 35 mm; 1 cassette, (12 min.). $39.00. (Interest level: 2-4).

This filmstrip describes the childhood of George Washington in colonial Virginia, his military and political leadership, and his election as the first president of the United States. The animated illustrations make this filmstrip an inviting addition to any unit dealing with the American colonial period.

♦ Students might watch this filmstrip in conjunction with reading the book, *George Washington's Mother* by Jean Fritz (*see* page 153), and create an acrostic of the word "Washington."

1. Washington, George, 1732-1799 2. Presidents—United States—Biography

92 Washington, George

Osborne, Mary Pope. *George Washington: A Leader of a New Nation.* Dial Books for Young Readers (0-8037-0949-8), 1991. 117p. Illus.; Maps; Index. (Interest level: 4-6).

This portrayal of George Washington is a reliable resource for middle level readers. This is a well-documented biography of the first President and includes a time line of interesting events of Washington's life that can serve as an excellent resource.

♦ Using the time line of Washington's life, students might create a mock TV screen and scrolling story of some of the events of his life. A script could be written to be read as the story of his life "scrolls" across the make-believe screen made of a large box, two dowel sticks, and some butcher paper.

1. Washington, George, 1732-1799—Biography 2. Presidents—United States—Biography.

92 Washington, George

Quackenbush, Robert. *I Did It with My Hatchet: A Story of George Washington.* Illus. by the author. Pippin Press (0-945912-04-8), 1989. 36p. Color illus. (Interest level: 2-4).

This humorous rendition of George Washington's life includes famous and little known anecdotes. The cartoon-type drawings will delight the readers.

♦ Students might create a cartoon drawing of the humorous events in Washington's life using additional resources such as Quackenbush's *Pass the Quill, I'll Write a Draft: A Story of Thomas Jefferson* (*see* page 150) or Jean Fritz's series of humorous biographies of famous figures of the American Revolution (*see* pages 150-151).

1. Washington, George, 1732-1799—Anecdotes 2. Presidents—United States—Biography

92 Washington, George

The Story of George Washington. (Videorecording). Robert Quackenbush Studios; Dist. by Charles Clark Co., 1990. VHS, Color, (15 min.). $49.95. (Interest level: 2-6).

Robert Quackenbush focuses on his book about George Washington, *I Did It with My Hatchet* (*see* preceding entry), as he retells the story in this full motion video.

♦ Students could compare this video with several other humorous biographies by Robert Quackenbush and keep an illustrated chart listing Quackenbush's available biographies as a reading log.

1. Washington, George, 1732-1799 2. Presidents—United States—Biography

92 Washington, Mary Ball

Fritz, Jean. *George Washington's Mother.* Illus. by DyAnne DiSalvo-Ryan. Grosset & Dunlap (0-448-40384-6), 1992. 48p. Color illus. (Interest level: 2-3).

This work describes the mother of our first president and her relationship with her children. The book relates that George Washington's father died when George was only 11 years old, leaving a large estate and many children to be cared for by his wife, Mary Ball Washington. Students will be delighted with the style and humor of this unique biography.

♦ After students hear or read both this book and *George Washington's Breakfast* by Jean Fritz (*see* page 154), they can create a Mother's Day card that George could send to his mother in 1745, or plan and cook a meal typical of George Washington's era.

1. Washington, Mary Ball, 1708-1789 2. Presidents—Family 3. Washington, George, 1732-1799

92 Wilson, Woodrow

Collins, David. *Woodrow Wilson, 28th President of the United States.* Garrett Educational Corp. (0-944483-18-6), 1989. 121p. Illus. (Interest level: 6-8).

This biography traces the life of the Virginia-born president who grew up in the Civil War South, led the United States during World War I, helped found the League of Nations, and was buried in Washington Cathedral.

♦ During Wilson's term, prohibition and women's right to vote were established. Students might have a debate on either or both of the issues as they relate to the United States today.

1. Wilson, Woodrow, 1856-1924 2. Presidents—United States—Biography

92 Woodson, Carter G.

McKissack, Pat. *Carter G. Woodson: The Father of Black History.* Illus. by Edward Ostendorf. Enslow Publishers (0-89490-309-8), 1991. (Great African-Americans Series). 32p. Illus. (Interest level: 5-6).

This work describes the life of the Virginian who first pioneered the study of African-American history. Pat McKissack's research and careful attention to detail make this an excellent multicultural selection.

◆ Students might make a model of an African American's invention and describe its contribution to our way of life.
1. Woodson, Carter Godwin, 1875-1950 2. African-Americans—Biography 3. Historians—United States—Biography

Fiction

Alphin, Elaine Marie. *The Ghost Cadet*. Henry Holt and Co. (0-8050-1614-7), 1991. 182p. (Interest level: 5-6).

This book tells how a family gold watch is recovered with the help of the ghost of a Virginia Military Institute cadet killed at the Battle of New Market over 130 years ago. The events occur while 12-year-old Benjy is visiting his grandmother in Virginia.
◆ Students could research the heroism of the cadets who fought in the Battle of New Market and create an historical "marker" to acknowledge the soldiers' bravery and to recognize the annual ceremony of the "Roll Call of the Dead" at VMI. Students might survey their own families to ask if there have been family possessions that have been inherited.
1. New Market, Battle of, 1864—Fiction 2. Ghosts—Fiction 3. Grandmothers—Fiction

Beatty, Patricia. *Charley Skedaddle*. Morrow (0-688-06687-9), 1987. 186p. (Interest level: 5-7).

During the Civil War, a 12-year-old Bowery Boy from New York City joins the Union Army as a drummer, deserts during a battle in Virginia, and encounters a hostile old mountain woman.
◆ Students might read sections from *The Boys' War: Confederate and Union Soldiers Talk About the Civil War* by Jim Murphy (*see* page 148) to support the reading of Charley Skedaddle. After these introductory experiences, students might write a letter from Charley to his sister explaining his desertion from the Union Army.
1. United States—History—Civil War, 1861-1865—Fiction 2. Virginia—Fiction 3. Mountain life—Fiction

Brooks, Kenneth. *Chesapeake Sleighride*. Illus. by Joshua Tolford. Chilton Book Co. (0-8019-5549-1), 1970 (out of print). 120p. llus. (Interest level: 4-5).

This book takes place during a winter storm on the Chesapeake Bay in 1904. A 14-year-old boy is responsible for bringing a 90-foot schooner safely into port ahead of a rival boat. Though out of print, this title is still available in some older media centers.
◆ A reading center about the Chesapeake Bay might be created, including a water scene drawn by students, pictures of marine animals of the region, and books about the Bay and the Bay Bridge Tunnel.
1. Sea stories 2. Chesapeake Bay—Fiction

Fritz, Jean. *George Washington's Breakfast*. Illus. by Paul Galdone. Coward-McCann (LC 69011475), 1969. 47p. Color illus. (Interest level: 3-4).

Having the same name and birthday as George Washington, a young boy wants everything else in his life just as Washington had it, but he has to work to find out what Washington had for breakfast. This is a short fun book for elementary students.
◆ After reading this title and *George Washington's Mother* (*see* page 153), students might cook a breakfast as a class project, including foods that George Washington would have eaten in early Virginia.
1. Washington, George, 1732-1799—Fiction

Henry, Marguerite. *Misty of Chincoteague*. Illus. by Wesley Dennis. Aladdin Books (0-689-71492-0 pbk), 1991. 173p. Illus. (Interest level: 4-6).

This work is the classic story of the Chincoteague pony round-up and the determination of two youngsters to own a pony of their own. Set on Chincoteague Island, Virginia, this story continues to excite its readers.
◆ Students might create a scene from the book in a shoebox "diorama" format.
1. Ponies—Fiction 2. Chincoteague Island (Va.)—Fiction

Henry, Marguerite. *Stormy, Misty's Foal*. Illus. by Wesley Dennis. Aladdin Books (0-689-71487 pbk), 1991. 222p. Illus. (Interest level: 4-6).

A foal, born in the aftermath of a great storm, and her famous mother help raise money to repair the storm damage on Chincoteague Island, Virginia, and to restore the herds of wild ponies on Assateague Island.
◆ Students might research the National Seashore system of the United States, allowing students to create a comparison chart of Chincoteague National Seashore and another national seashore.
1. Horses—Fiction 2. Chincoteague Island (Va.)—Fiction

Holmes, Mary. *Two Chimneys*. Illus. by Geri Strigenz. Raintree Steck-Vaughn (0-8114-3506-7), 1992. 48p. Color illus. (Interest level: 4-5).

Having lived in Virginia for six years since 1622, Katherine does not want to trade her exciting life on the tobacco plantation for a prearranged marriage to an English heir. This book is adequate in presenting a look at the very early period in Virginia's colony.
◆ This book was written about a dangerous time in the Virginia Colony. By creating a news program about the events in 1622 and another for the year 1644, students could depict the dangerous times of the mid-1600s in Jamestown.
1. Jamestown (Va.)—History—Fiction 2. Virginia—History—Colonial period, ca. 1600-1775—Fiction

Kassem, Lou. *A Haunting in Williamsburg*. Avon Books (0-380-75892-X pbk), 1990. (Avon Camelot Book). 104p. (Interest level: 5-7).

Revolutionary war ghosts enliven the summer 12-year-old Jayne spends trying to solve a family mystery in Williamsburg, Virginia.
◆ Using the map of Williamsburg in the *World Book Encyclopedia* as a guide, students might describe a walking tour of the town, being careful to give directions for travel, i.e., "north on Waller Street", etc. The "tour" could start at William and Mary College and end at the Peyton Randolph House.
1. Williamsburg (Va.)—Fiction 2. Ghosts—Fiction

Kyle, Louisa Venable. *The Witch of Pungo and Other Historical Stories of the Early Colonies*. Illus. by Jan Dool. Four O'Clock Farms Publishing Co., 1973. 87p. Illus.; Map. (Interest level: 3-5).

This book is a collection of stories, each with historical background, from the Virginia Beach, Virginia, area and is used as part of classroom studies in Virginia Beach area schools. Some stories are "Swift-Foot—A Brave Indian Boy," "Blackbeard's Treasure," "The Lighting of Cape Henry Lighthouse," "Christmas at Adam Thoroughgood's House," "Little Ella and the Windmill," and others. The map that pinpoints the location of each story is a fascinating study for students.
♦ Students might research how a windmill works after hearing the story "Little Ella and the Windmill," make a pinwheel to show how the wind operates the blades, and draw a poster of how wind power is used today.
1. United States—History—Colonial period, ca. 1600-1775—Fiction

Lenski, Lois. *Peanuts for Billy Ben*. Illus. by the author. Lippincott (LC 52005103), 1952 (out of print). (Roundabout America Series). 128p. Illus. (Interest level: 2-4).

This is the story of a farm family of southern Virginia whose work and play is regulated year-round by their peanut crop. Though out of print, this work should be available in older libraries.
♦ This work could be used in connection with a peanut unit studying the peanut as a plant and a crop. Talk about other nations that grow peanuts as a crop and use Franklin Watts' book *Peanuts* (*see* page 144) as support material.
1. Farm life—Fiction 2. Virginia—Fiction

Misty of Chincoteague. (Videorecording). Random House (LC 88709028), 1988. 1 videocassette (enhanced), VHS or Beta, Color, (27 min.). Includes guide. $69.00. (Interest level: 3-7).

Based on the book *Misty of Chincoteague* by Marguerite Henry (*see* page 154), this work tells the story of one of the ponies rounded up for the yearly auction on the Eastern Shore of Virginia. The video has been made from an enhanced filmstrip.
♦ Students might use the *National Geographic* article (June 1980 pp. 810-29) about Chincoteague Island as a reference to write an essay about life on this island.
1. Chincoteague pony—Juvenile films 2. Chincoteague Island (Va.)—Fiction 3. Ponies—Fiction

O'Dell, Scott. *The Serpent Never Sleeps*. Illus. by Ted Lewin. Houghton Mifflin (0-395-44242-7), 1987. 227p. Map. (Interest level: 7-8).

In the early seventeenth century, Serena Lynn follows the man she has loved since childhood to the New World and comes to know the hardships of colonial life and the extraordinary Princess Pocahontas. This book is for older middle school readers.
♦ As a pre-reading activity, a prepared list of words relating to the story and characters could be presented to the students along with such categories as agriculture, defense, geography, transportation, or others. Students would group the words by category and listen for them in the book.
1. Jamestown (Va.)—History—Fiction 2. Pocahontas, d. 1617—Fiction 3. Virginia—History—Colonial period, ca. 1600-1775—Fiction

Paterson, Katherine. *Bridge to Terabithia*. Illus. by Donna Diamond. Crowell (0-690-01359-0), 1977. 128p. Illus. (Interest level: 5-8).

In this Newbery Award-winning book, a 10-year-old Virginia boy must face the untimely death of his close friend. This moving book is one that students will eagerly read.
♦ Students could write an eyewitness news report of the events leading up to the death.
1. Friendship 2. Death

Paterson, Katherine. *Park's Quest*. Lodestar Books (0-525-67258-3), 1988. 148p. (Interest level: 5-7).

Eleven-year-old Park makes some startling discoveries when he travels to his grandfather's farm in Virginia to learn about his father who died in the Vietnam War. The reading level makes this book a challenge for most fifth grade readers.
♦ Park daydreams about the King Arthur legend through much of the book. Students could research knight's armor and create a shield with a coat of arms for Park.
1. Farm life—Fiction 2. Vietnamese Americans—Fiction

Reeder, Carolyn. *Grandpa's Mountain*. Macmillan (0-02-775711-7), 1991. 171p. (Interest level: 4-6).

During the Depression, 11-year-old Carrie makes her annual summer visit to her relatives in the Blue Ridge Mountains of Virginia and watches her determined grandfather fight against the government's attempts to take his farm land for a national park. This is a beautifully written work.
♦ Students could have a class debate on whether the government should have the right to take land for national parks.
1. Eminent domain—Fiction 2. Land use—Fiction 3. Mountain life—Fiction

Reeder, Carolyn. *Shades of Gray*. Macmillan (0-02-775810-9), 1989. 152p. (Interest level: 6-8).

At the end of the Civil War, 12-year-old Will, having lost all of his immediate family, leaves his city home to live in the Virginia countryside with his aunt and uncle, whom he considers to be traitors. This is a well written historical fiction selection.
♦ Students could view a filmstrip or video of *Across Five Aprils*, the Newbery Award-winning book about a family torn apart by the Civil War and discuss the similarities and differences of the two books' settings and characters.
1. Orphans—Fiction 2. United States—History—Civil War, 1861-1865—Fiction

Rylant, Cynthia. *The Relatives Came*. Illus. by Stephen Gammell. Bradbury Press (0-02-777220-9), 1985. 32p. Color illus. (Interest level: K-2).

Children will relate to the relatives' visit from Virginia and to the wonderful time had by all. The rhythm of the text and the beauty of the illustrations make this book a winner for all who read it.

♦ Students might share trip stories and illustrate them for a display centered with a drawing of a map of Virginia with stars marking the places visited, or where students hope to visit. Arrows pointing in the direction of places out of state and clearly marked north, south, east, and west direction letters will help introduce map skills.

1. Family life—Fiction

Sargent, Sarah. *Secret Lies*. Crown (0-517-54291-9), 1981. 118p. (Interest level: 6-8).

Thirteen-year-old Elvira arrives at her aunt's home in the hills of Virginia full of fantasies about the father she has never known and her mother's prejudices about life in a small town. This story will keep the interest of middle school girls.

♦ As a pre-reading activity, have students complete a comparison chart of life in the country and in a city like Chicago, allowing students the opportunity to research a rural Virginia county and the city of Chicago as to population, crime, schools, arts and entertainment, etc.

1. Family life— Fiction 2. Mothers and daughters—Fiction 3. Virginia—Fiction

Tripp, Valerie. *Felicity Learns a Lesson; A School Story*. Illus. by Dan Andreasen. Pleasant Co. (1-56247-007-8 pbk), 1991. (American Girls Collection). 69p. Color illus. (Interest level: 2-4).

Shortly before the Revolutionary War, nine-year-old Felicity, who lives in Williamsburg, is torn between supporting the tariff-based tea boycott and saving her friendship with Elizabeth, a young loyalist from England. Miniature illustrations of period items brighten the book and serve as marvelous annotations on the text.

♦ Students could prepare a colonial tea party after researching the traditions and proper manners of the colonial period.

1. Virginia—Social life and customs—Colonial period, ca. 1600-1775—Fiction 2. Friendship—Fiction

Tripp, Valerie. *Felicity Saves the Day*. Illus. by Dan Andreasen. Pleasant Co. (1-56247-034-5 pbk), 1992. (American Girls Collection). 69p. Color illus. (Interest level: 2-4).

During a visit to her grandfather's plantation in Virginia in 1775, Felicity's loyalty is torn between her father and Ben, her father's apprentice, who needs her help as he runs away to join George Washington's army of patriots. The illustrations complement the text and highlight items mentioned on the page.

♦ Students could view a video on George Washington's life or on the Revolutionary War and then write Ben a letter telling him about the life he faces in Washington's army.

1. Plantation life—Virginia—Fiction 2. Virginia—Social life and customs—Colonial period, ca. 1600-1775—Fiction

Tripp, Valerie. *Felicity's Surprise*. Illus. by Dan Andreasen. Pleasant Co. (1-56247-010-8 pbk), 1991. (American Girls Collection). 69p. Color illus. (Interest level: 2-4).

Christmas in Williamsburg means a dancing party at the Governor's Palace for Felicity, but her mother becomes very ill and cannot finish the special blue gown. A satisfying ending to this story makes it a reading pleasure and the illustrations on each page are delightful visual annotations.

♦ After researching colonial dress, students might create paper dolls that they can dress in colonial costume showing how they would like to have dressed to go to the Governor's Palace with Felicity.

1. Christmas—Fiction 2. Williamsburg (Va.)—Fiction 3. Virginia—Social life and customs—Colonial period, ca. 1600-1775—Fiction

Turner, Ann Warren. *Nettie's Trip South*. Illus. by Ronald Himler. Macmillan (0-02-789240-9), 1987. 30p. Illus. (Interest level: 3-5).

A 10-year-old northern girl encounters the ugly realities of slavery when she visits Richmond, Virginia, and sees a slave auction. This extraordinary book is based on a real diary, but is written in letter form.

♦ Reacting to problems in their neighborhoods or to articles in the local papers, students should create a diary of injustices that they encounter personally, or in the news.

1. Slavery—Fiction

Periodicals

051

Virginia Cavalcade. Virginia State Library (ISSN 0042-6474), 1951-. Illus., part color; Maps. (Interest level: 7-8).

This magazine about Virginia history has been published by the Virginia State Library since 1951. An inexpensive periodical of less than $10 a year, this magazine offers quarterly, colorful coverage of Virginia's past.

♦ Articles of interest to the students could be prominently displayed to heighten student awareness about Virginia with an emphasis on researching past issues for articles about local history.

1. Virginia—History—Periodicals 2. Virginia State Library.

051

Virginia Wildlife. Virginia Commission of Game and Inland Fisheries (ISSN 0042-6792), Sept. 1937. Illus.; ports. (Interest level: 3-8).

A colorful magazine for all ages. A classroom section is a very frequent pull-out section for teachers and students. This section is called "Wild in the Woods" and offers excellent support ideas for teachers and students.

♦ Pictures of Virginia birds from back issues of *Virginia Wildlife* could be used by students as a cover for a research booklet about the bird. Students could research its habitat, location in Virginia, distinct features, and food. Students might find additional information on the electronic encyclopedia, if available.

1. Wildlife management—Virginia—Periodicals 2. Game and game-birds—Virginia—Periodicals

West Virginia

by Harold M. Forbes

Nonfiction

331.89
Even the Heavens Weep: The West Virginia Mine Wars.
(Videocassette). Humanities Foundation of West Virginia (No ISBN), 1985. 1/2", B/W with color sequences, (60 min.). $24.95. (Interest level: 6-8).

The efforts of West Virginia coal miners to gain better working conditions were resisted by coal mine operators, leading to the mine wars at Cabin Creek and Paint Creek in 1912-13 and the Battle of Blair Mountain in 1921. The growth of company towns and the conditions that confronted the labor movement in West Virginia are documented in hundreds of historical photographs.
♦ Young people might study labor movements in other industries to find out whether disputes were handled in a violent or a cooperative manner.
1. Coal Mines and Mining—West Virginia 2. Strikes and Lockouts—Coal Mining

338.272
Cohen, Stan. *King Coal: A Pictorial Heritage of West Virginia Coal Mining.* Pictorial Histories (0-933126-53-0), 1984. 146p. B/W photos. (Interest level: 6-8).

The history, economic development, and political life of West Virginia have been dominated by the mining of coal, the state's most important natural resource. Hundreds of photographs portray and document every aspect of life and work in the West Virginia coal fields.
♦ Young people might develop a display or create a pictorial catalog of the products and processes that are obtained from coal.
1. Coal Miners—West Virginia 2. Coal Mines and Mining—West Virginia

385
Cass Scenic Railroad: Cass, West Virginia. (Videocassette). Pictorial Histories (No ISBN), 1985. Color, B/W, 1/2", (30 min.). $29.95. (Interest level: 4-8).

A booming lumber industry began with the completion of railroads up rugged Cheat Mountain from the town of Cass, West Virginia, in 1901. Film of 1950s lumbering operations and shay steam engines is featured along with the scenic wonders of a modern trip on the 11 miles of the Cass Scenic Railroad.
♦ Young people might visit scenic railways as a fun way of learning about the importance of the railroad in the history and economy of the region.
1. Railroads—West Virginia 2. Lumbering—West Virginia 3. Cass Scenic Railroad

398.2
Cober, Mary E. *The Remarkable History of Tony Beaver, West Virginian.* Illus. by William D. Hayes. McKay (No ISBN), 1953. 142p. (Interest level: 4-8).

Tony Beaver, woodsman folk hero, helped create the state of West Virginia, stopped a maple sugar geyser, invented matches and clothespins, and performed numerous other remarkable feats in these 17 tall tales. Tony's larger-than-life adventures are interwoven with nineteenth-century historical events and illustrated in lively caricature.
♦ As an activity, young people might study other American folk heroes to discover how their adventures were influenced by the places they lived or the work they performed.
1. Tony Beaver 2. Folklore

398.2
Preble, Jack. *Land of Canaan...Plain Tales from the Mountains of West Virginia.* McClain (No ISBN), 1965. 105p. Illus.; Map (Interest level: 7-8).

The land of Canaan is a beautiful but rugged area in the mountain counties of Tucker and Randolph in West Virginia. These entertaining tales of historical and legendary characters capture the adventurous spirit of mountain life and the fascination of numerous geographical wonders.
♦ Young people in West Virginia might plan a trip to Canaan Valley and to the various geographical attractions in that area. Students in other states might plan a trip to a nearby wilderness area.
1. Tales—West Virginia 2. Folklore—West Virginia

398.22
Felton, Harold W. *John Henry and His Hammer.* Illus. by Aldren A. Watson. Knopf (No ISBN), 1950. 84p. Illus. (Interest level: 4-8).

Folk hero John Henry worked at several jobs developing his strength and endurance before he began hammering spikes for the railroads. Fine storytelling and powerful illustrations relate John Henry's adventures leading up to his fatal contest with the steam drill at the Big Bend Tunnel in West Virginia.
♦ Young people might imagine what machines John Henry or other folk heroes would compete against today.
1. John Henry (Legendary Character) 2. African-American—Music 3. Folklore—West Virginia

398.22
Shapiro, Irwin. *John Henry and the Double-Jointed Steam Drill*. Illus. by James Daugherty. Messner (No ISBN), 1956. Unpaginated. Illus. (Interest level: 4-8).

John Henry survived his hammering contest with a steam drill and, with his wife Pollie Ann's help, recovered his strength and learned to work with the drill. The numerous illustrations convey John Henry's energy and power in this imaginative interpretation of the West Virginia folk hero's life.
♦ Young people might analyze how various machines help people with their work, so that they don't need to be as strong as John Henry.
1. John Henry (Legendary Character) 2. Folklore—West Virginia

398.23
Brown, Stephen D. *Haunted Houses of Harpers Ferry, Second Edition*. Illus. by Joseph D. Osmann. Little Brown House (0-915782-04-9), 1977. 69p. Illus. (Interest level: 4-12).

Western Maryland and northern Virginia meet West Virginia at Harpers Ferry, where tales abound of ghosts, mysterious occurrences, and haunted houses. Brown presents 17 stories of the supernatural, illustrated with appropriately spooky drawings.
♦ Young people might construct their own haunted house, as a Halloween activity or at any time of year.
1. Ghosts—West Virginia

398.23
Dougherty, Shirley. *A Ghostly Tour of Harpers Ferry*. Illus. by Suzanne Randell. EIGMID (No ISBN), 1982. 39p. Illus. (Interest level: 6-8).

The long and violent history of Harpers Ferry, West Virginia, includes many tales of mysterious occurrences, some explainable and others apparently supernatural. These chilling stories are told by the guide of the popular ghostly tour of Harpers Ferry.
♦ Young people might imagine they are reporters investigating an unusual, unexplainable event and write an account of their findings.
1. Tales—West Virginia 2. Ghosts—West Virginia 3. Harpers Ferry, West Virginia

398.4
Gainer, Patrick. *Witches, Ghosts and Signs: Folklore of the Southern Appalachians*. Seneca Books (0-89092-006-0), 1975. 177p. (Interest level: 6-8).

Through five decades, Patrick Gainer collected West Virginia's traditional speech and customs, ghost stories, folk cures, nature lore, superstitions, and witch tales. This excellent presentation of Appalachian folk-

lore and folklife is the work of one of West Virginia's most prominent folklorists.
♦ Young people might collect the lore of their own community by asking elderly people to recite stories and sayings from many years ago.
1. Tales—West Virginia 2. Ghosts—West Virginia 3. Folklore—West Virginia

398.4
Jones, James Gay. *Appalachian Ghost Stories, and Other Tales*. McClain (87012-203-7), 1975. 109p. (Interest level: 6-8).

Appalachian oral tradition has preserved numerous tales of ghosts, witches, murder, and legendary characters. Jones has selected 30 fascinating tales of unusual occurrences in West Virginia.
♦ Young people might take the role of a newspaper reporter investigating a haunted house and write an account of their discoveries.
1. Ghosts—West Virginia 2. Folklore—West Virginia 3. Tales—West Virginia

398.4
Jones, James Gay. *Haunted Valley, and More Folk Tales*. McClain (87012-341-6), 1979. 156p. (Interest level: 6-8).

Ghosts, monsters, and a host of unexplainable occurrences are encountered in the folklore of West Virginia. These 25 tales add interesting dimensions to everyday happenings and to various historical events.
♦ Young people might research some well-known event and try to find anecdotal stories related to it.
1. Ghosts—West Virginia 2. Folklore—West Virginia 3. Tales—West Virginia

398.4
Musick, Ruth Ann. *Ballads, Folk Songs & Folk Tales from West Virginia* West Virginia University Library (No ISBN), 1960. 71p. Music. (Interest level: 6-8).

This is a small collection of child ballads, American folk songs, European folktales, ghost stories, omen and token lore, rhymes and riddles for children, coal miners' tales, and fortune telling superstitions. Musick collected all this folk literature in West Virginia.
♦ Young people might collect folklore of their region from elderly people who have lived in their community for years.
1. Tales—West Virginia 2. Ballads, American—West Virginia 3. Folklore—West Virginia

624.2
Cohen, Stan. *West Virginia's Covered Bridges: A Pictorial Heritage*. Illus. by Bill Wintz & Steve Shaluta, Jr. Pictorial Histories (0-929521-55-2), 1992. 108p. Illus., Maps. (Interest level: 6-8).

Hundreds of covered bridges were constructed in West Virginia, but only 17 remained in 1992. In addition to the extant bridges documented with photographs, historical and technological data, and location maps, this work includes photographs and historical sketches of nearly 40 vanished covered bridges.
♦ Young people might build a model of a covered bridge using one of the truss designs described in this book.
1. Covered Bridges—West Virginia

719
Where People and Nature Meet: A History of the West Virginia State Parks. Pictorial Histories Publishing Company (0-933126-91-3), 1988. 183p. B/W photos; Maps. (Interest level: 7-8).

West Virginia's state parks protect the state's natural beauty, preserve historic sites, and provide outdoor recreational opportunities. Numerous photographs accompany an historical introduction to each state park.
♦ Young people may plan a family vacation to a local state park by mapping the route and determining what to do and see there.
1. Parks—West Virginia 2. West Virginia

784.49754
Boette, Marie, ed. *Sing a Hipsy Doodle and Other Folk Songs of West Virginia.* Illus. by Marcia Ogilvie. Music notes drawn by John Laflin. McClain (87012-091-3), 1971. 177p. Music; Illus. (Interest level: K-8).

Child ballads, colonial and early American songs, Appalachian folk songs, spirituals and religious songs, childrens' and play party songs, and parlor songs are all part of West Virginia's musical heritage. Over 100 songs are presented with musical notations, introductory and source information, title and first line indexes, and line drawings.
♦ Young people might learn and sing some of the old songs that are part of West Virginia's heritage.
1. Folk Songs, American—West Virginia

784.49754
Gainer, Patrick. *Folk Songs from the West Virginia Hills.* Seneca Books (0-89092-001-X), 1975. 236p. Music. (Interest level: 4-8).

Over 100 ballads, folk songs, fiddle tunes, hymns, and spirituals, collected by West Virginia's foremost folklorist, are presented with an historical introduction for each type of song and an anecdotal introduction for each tune. This fine presentation of West Virginia folk music includes a brief bibliography, an index to song titles, and an index to first lines.
♦ With many of the songs in conversation format, young people might sing or recite the dialogue while dramatizing the story.
1. Folk songs, American—West Virginia

793.34
Dalsemer, Robert G. *West Virginia Square Dances.* Country Dance & Song Society of America (No ISBN), 1982. 85p. B/W photos, music. (Interest level: 6-8).

Traditional square dancing, with distinctive local characteristics and with live music, is popular and thriving in West Virginia. This is a detailed examination of square dancing in five West Virginia communities.
♦ Young people might invite local dancers to teach them to square dance and organize square dancing as a regular school or club activity.
1. Square Dancing—West Virginia

811
McNeill, Louise. *Elderberry Flood: The History, Lore, and Land of West Virginia Written in Verse Form.* Elderberry Books (0-89459-066-9), 1979. 175p. (Interest level: 4-8).

Over 100 poems by West Virginia's Poet Laureate recount the state's history, culture, and lore. The quintessential spirit of West Virginia is conveyed in this factual yet poetic work, the crowning achievement of the region's finest poet.
♦ Young people might compose a poem about an important event, either historic or recent, in their own community.
1. West Virginia—Poetry

811
McNeill, Louise. *Gauley Mountain.* Harcourt Brace (No ISBN), 1939, 1960. Reprint. 98p. (Interest level: 7-8).

Memorable people, local yet universal, are the history, legend, and lore of West Virginia's Gauley—mountain and river and town. The historical essence of Gauley is transformed into verse by West Virginia's Poet Laureate.
♦ Young people might compose a poem or create an artwork based upon images and events in their community or their family.
1. West Virginia—Poetry

811
Milnes, Gerald. *Granny Will Your Dog Bite and Other Mountain Rhymes.* Illus. by Kimberly Bulcken Root. Knopf (0-394-84749-0), 1990. 45p. Color illus., plus 1 sound cassette. $18.95. (Interest level: K-6).

As they have been passed along through oral tradition, rhymes, riddles, and nonsense verse have entertained West Virginia mountain dwellers for many generations. The appeal of these lively Appalachian rhymes and riddles is enhanced by the delightful illustrations and the spirited performances on the recording.
♦ Young people might help preserve oral tradition by learning traditional rhymes, riddles, and folk tales and teaching them to their family and friends.
1. Mountain Life—Poetry 2. Children's Poetry, American 3. American Poetry

917.54
Cohen, Stan. *Historic Sites of West Virginia: A Pictorial Guide.* Pictorial Histories (0-933126-05-0), 1979. 240p. B/W photos. (Interest level: 4-8).

Notable historic sites, such as mills, taverns, banks, iron furnaces, oil wells, courthouses, post offices, forts, battlefields, houses, bridges, schools, and churches, are found throughout West Virginia. Brief explanations of their historical significance provide the captions for photographs of over 200 historic places.
♦ Young people might prepare a guide to historic sites in their community or county, illustrating it with photographs or drawings.
1. Historic Sites—West Virginia 2. West Virginia—Description and Travel

917.54
Wilkerson, Ellen S. and **Stowers, Ann W**. *Adventures in West Virginia: Day Trips & Longer Travels.* Aegina Press (0-916383-59-8), 1988. 306p. B/W photos; Maps. (Interest level: 6-8).

West Virginia offers numerous opportunities for the whole family to enjoy its natural beauty and vibrant history: museums, parks, festivals, wildlife, skiing, whitewater rafting, outdoor theater, resorts, glass factory tours, and more. Brief but informative descriptions of a couple hundred attractions include hours, locations, services, and handicapped accessibility.

♦ Young people might plan a West Virginia vacation to visit the places of greatest interest to them and their family.

1. West Virginia—Description and Travel

973.68

To Do Battle in the Land. (Videocassette).National Park Service (No ISBN), 1985. 1/2", Color, (27 min.). $110.00. (Interest level: 6-8).

Ossie Davis narrates this examination of slavery in the United States, John Brown's raid on Harpers Ferry to free the slaves, and the impact of the raid in igniting the Civil War. Of particular interest are the water-color paintings portraying historical events and the issue of whether John Brown was a violent abolitionist or a martyr with a heroic mission.

♦ Young people might stage a debate to discuss whether John Brown was justified in his approach to attempting to free the slaves.

1. John Brown, 1800-1859 2. Abolitionists 3. United States—History—Civil War

973.73

Cohen, Stan. *The Civil War in West Virginia: A Pictorial History.* Rev. Ed. Pictorial Histories (0-933126-02-6), 1982. 150p. Illus.;Maps. (Interest level: 6-8).

A border region of strategic interest to both sides during the Civil War, West Virginia did not experience many major battles but was the scene of over 600 minor battles, skirmishes, and raids. An amazing collection of historic photographs, drawings, and maps document the people, places, and events that made the Civil War such a significant era in West Virginia's history.

♦ As an activity, young people might create a diorama of a Civil War battle.

1. West Virginia—History—Civil War, 1861-1865

974

Rylant, Cynthia. *Appalachia: The Voices of Sleeping Birds.* Illus. by Barry Moser. Harcourt Brace Jovanovich (0-15-201605-8), 1991. 21p. Color illus. (Interest level: 4-8).

Appalachia can be characterized by dogs, coal miners, quilts, country churches, shy but friendly people, wintertime hunting, cornbread, buttermilk, and cherry cobbler. The essence of Appalachian life is captured in lyrical description and in illustrations adapted from the photographs of men and women whose photographic studies documented Appalachia.

♦ Young people might create a picture book of those aspects of everyday life that characterize their family or their community.

1. Appalachian region, Southern—Social Life and Customs. 2. Appalachian Region, Southern—Description and Travel

975.2

Graham, Frank, Jr. *Potomac: The Nation's River.* Illus. by Edward Schell. Lippincott (0-397-01139-3), 1976. 128p. Color illus. (Interest level: 7-8).

The Potomac River originates in the mountains of West Virginia, forms the boundary between West Virginia and Maryland, and flows through Virginia and the District of Columbia to the Chesapeake Bay. The history and beauty of West Virginia's Potomac Valley constitute a substantial portion of this book's essays and color photographs.

♦ Young people might develop a book of pictures and essays highlighting the appeal of their community or geographical area.

1. Potomac River Valley—History

975.4

Anderson, Joan. *Pioneer Children of Appalachia.* Illus. by George Ancona. Clarion (0-89919-440-0), 1986. Unpaginated. B/W photos. (Interest level: 4-8).

Appalachian pioneer life in the early nineteenth century is recreated in scenes photographed at Fort New Salem in West Virginia, a living history museum. Interesting narrative and photographs provide an appealing portrayal of the lifestyles of West Virginia's pioneer children.

♦ As an activity, young people might act out or write about various aspects of daily life as if they were pioneer children living on the frontier.

1. Pioneer Children 2. Frontier and Pioneer Life 3. Appalachia—Social Life and Customs

975.4

Carpenter, Allan. *West Virginia.* Children's Press (0-516-04148-7), 1979. (The New Enchantment of America State Books). 96p. Color photos. (Interest level: 4-8).

Anecdotes flesh out this account of the geography, history, natural resources, interesting people, educational institutions, and scenic attractions of The Mountain State. The balanced and readable narrative is enhanced by color photographs, an appendix of useful facts, and an index that includes references to illustrations.

♦ As an activity, young people might determine what geographical features and historical events resulted in the unusual shape of West Virginia's boundaries.

1. West Virginia

975.4

Cohen, Stan. *A Pictorial Guide to West Virginia's Civil War Sites and Related Information.* Pictorial Histories Publishing Co. (0-9299521-34-X), 1990. 120p. Maps; B/W photos. (Interest level: 7-8).

West Virginia was a border region claimed and intensely fought over by the United States and the Confederate States throughout the four years of the Civil War. This is a well-illustrated guidebook to numerous Civil War sites in this area of divided loyalties and constant military conflict.

♦ As an activity, young people might select and study a Civil War site; West Virginia students might then visit it with family or friends.

1. Historic Sites—West Virginia 2. West Virginia—Civil War, 1861-1865—Movements

975.4

For Liberty and Union. (Videocassette). Larry Keating Productions (No ISBN), 1977. 1/2", Color, (21 min.). $24.95. (Interest level: 4-8).

West Virginia attained statehood during the Civil War by breaking away from its parent state of Virginia, which had seceded from the United States to join the Confederate States. This film is a dramatization of the personalities, the issues, and the events that were involved in the creation of the thirty-fifth state.

♦ Young people might imagine what their community and their lives would be like if the Confederacy had won the Civil War, and West Virginia students might consider what their lives would be like if West Virginia had remained part of Virginia.
1. West Virginia Independence Hall Foundation
2. West Virginia—History—Civil War, 1861-1865.
3. West Virginia—Statehood, 1863.

975.4

Hyde, Arnout, Jr. *A Portrait of West Virginia.* Rev. ed. Illus. by the author. Cannon Graphics (0-9623153-0-3), 1989. 128p. Color photos. (Interest level: K-8).

West Virginia's natural beauty, scenic architecture, and people involved in special activities are captured in color photographs of every area of the state. This collection of superb photographs, all precisely identified, was created by the state's best-known photographer.

♦ Young people may take photographs and create a photographic portrait of their own community or neighborhood.
1. West Virginia—Description and Travel

975.4

Smith, J. Lawrence. *The High Alleghenies: The Drama and Heritage of Three Centuries.* Illus. by Bill Pitzer. Allegheny Vistas (No ISBN), 1982. 196p. Illus. (Interest level: 7-8).

The human history of the Allegheny Mountains of West Virginia is interwoven with their natural history. Drawings and photographs accompany accounts of fascinating historical events and engaging descriptions of the flora, fauna, caves, springs, and rivers of the mountains.

♦ Young people might determine how the history of their community is interrelated to its geography and natural environment.
1. Allegheny Mountains—History 2. West Virginia—Social Life and Customs

975.4

Thrash, Mary. *West Virginia Courthouses: A Pictorial History.* M. Thrash (0-9613021-0-0), 1984. 112p. Illus.; Photos. (Interest level: 4-8).

Many important official functions and activities are carried on within the 55 county courthouses in West Virginia. A photograph and historical sketch of each county's courthouse are accompanied by a brief history of the county and the county seat.

♦ Young people might tour their local courthouse to discover all the ways the occupants serve the community.
1. Courthouses—West Virginia 2. West Virginia—History

975.401

Wavra, Grace. *The First Families of West Virginia.* Illus. by the author. University Editions (1-56002-007-5), 1990. 70p. B/W illus.; Maps. (Interest level: 4-6).

Archeological evidence, rather than written records, provides information about the life of Native Americans who lived in West Virginia before the Europeans arrived. Maps and drawings of prehistoric sites and artifacts complement the discussions of Native cultures and artifacts as well as archeological techniques.

♦ Young people might compare utensils, clothing, and houses with those of today, noting similarities and differences.
1. Archaeology 2. Indians of North America 3. West Virginia—Antiquities

975.437

Cohen, Stan and **Andre, Richard.** *Capitols of West Virginia: A Pictorial History.* Pictorial Histories Publishing Co. (0-929521-18-8), 1989. 106p. B/W photos. (Interest level: 7-8).

This work documents the three moves of West Virginia's State Capital, the burning of the old capitol building, and the construction of the present Cass Gilbert-designed capitol building. The profusely illustrated account captures the political drama of relocating the capital and the architectural heritage of West Virginia's capitol buildings.

♦ As an activity, young people might examine the architecture of old or important buildings in their community to identify the features that make them attractive and then design a new capitol building with all the architectural features they like best.
1. West Virginia—Capital and Capitol 2. Architecture—West Virginia

975.48

Forks of Cheat. ((Videocassette). West Virginia Public Broadcasting (No ISBN), 1990. 1/2", Color, (58 min.). $24.95. (Interest level: 4-8).

Adventurous explorers and settlers, diverse natural resources, and disastrous pollution and flooding are documented in West Virginia's scenic Cheat River Valley. This excellent film captures the beauty and power of the largest untamed river in the eastern United States and the special qualities of the people living near it.

♦ Young people might examine how the river nearest their home has influenced the historical and economic development of the surrounding region.
1. Cheat River, West Virginia 2. West Virginia—History

975.5

Cohen, Stan. *Historic Springs of the Virginias: A Pictorial History.* Pictorial Histories (0-933126-14-X), 1981. 199p. Illus.; B/W photos. (Interest level: 6-8).

At many natural springs in Virginia and West Virginia, resorts and health spas were developed to attract visitors on the premise that spring waters would cure common diseases. Over 50 springs, most thriving in the 1800s and early 1900s, are documented in hundreds of photographs, drawings, and maps.

♦ As an activity, young people might create a diorama of a springs resort, designing their own hotel, cottages, baths, and landscapes.
1. Springs 2. Health Resorts 3. Mineral Waters

977
Klein, Benjamin F., ed. *The Ohio River Handbook and Picture Album*. Young and Klein (No ISBN), 1969, 1979. 448p. Illus.; Charts, Maps. (Interest level: 7-8).

The Ohio River, which forms the border between West Virginia and Ohio, has long been a thoroughfare for the movement of people and freight. Brief historical essays accompany hundreds of photographs, drawings, and maps documenting every aspect of the history of the Ohio River.
♦ Young people might enumerate the advantages of living near a river, such as recreation, transportation, and industry.
1. Ohio River

Biography

920.0754
Missing Chapters: West Virginia Women in History. West Virginia Women's Commission (No ISBN), 1983. 124p. (Interest level: Professional).

West Virginia women have made significant contributions in the roles of midwife, physician, journalist, photographer, educator, musician, civic activist, and social reformer. This work documents the lives and careers of nine women who have participated in West Virginia's history and development.
1. Women—West Virginia 2. West Virginia—History

920.0754
Missing Chapters II: West Virginia Women in History. West Virginia Women's Commission (0-9617031-0-5), 1986. 207p. (Interest level: Professional).

West Virginia women have made significant contributions in such roles as newspaper publisher, musician, educator, community leader, politician, playwright, business leader, extension agent, and folklorist. This work documents the lives and careers of 15 women who have participated in West Virginia's history and development.
1. Women—West Virginia 2. West Virginia—History

92 Bailey, Anne Hennis
Bice, David A. *Mad Anne Bailey*. Illus. by Rebecca Wilson. Jalamap (0-934750-06-8), 1980 (out of print). 35p. Color illus. (Interest level: 4-7).

After her husband was killed in a 1774 battle between the settlers and Native tribes in Western Virginia, Anne Bailey became a frontier scout and fighter based at Fort Lee, now Charleston, West Virginia. Brisk narrative and engaging color illustrations present various adventures in Bailey's long and exciting life on the frontier.
♦ Young people might examine the diverse roles that women performed on the frontier as it moved westward across the United States.
1. Bailey, Anne Hennis, 1742-1825 2. Frontier and Pioneer Life 3. Pioneers—West Virginia

92 Boarman, Andrew F.
Catching Up with Yesterday: Andrew F. Boarman—Craftsman, Musician, Teacher. (Videocassette). Cinema Guild (No ISBN), 1989. 1/2", Color with B/W sequences, (28 min.). $250.00. (Interest level: 4-8).

Andrew F. Boarman, born 1911, is a banjo maker, autoharp and banjo player, and proponent of traditional music. Beautiful West Virginia scenery provides the background for this enjoyable study of a multi-talented individual with genuine enthusiasm for traditional Appalachian music.
♦ Young people might invite a local folk musician to perform for their class or group and to discuss the instruments and tunes they play.
1. Boarman, Andrew F. 2. Musical Instrument Makers—West Virginia 3. Folk Music—West Virginia

92 Boyd, Belle
Scarborough, Ruth. *Belle Boyd, Siren of the South*. Mercer University Press (0-86554-065-9), 1983. 212p. Illus.; Photos.; Maps. (Interest level: 8).

Belle Boyd of Martinsburg, West Virginia, became a spy for the Confederate cause when she was 17 years old. Her dangerous exploits are reconstructed primarily from Boyd's autobiography and presented in the context of military and civilian life during the Civil War.
♦ Young people could re-enact Belle Boyd's adventures by presenting brief impromptu plays for other members of a class.
1. Boyd, Belle, 1844-1900 2. Spies—Southern States—Biography 3. United States—History—Civil War

92 Brown, John
Collins, James L. *John Brown and the Fight Against Slavery*. The Millbrook Press (1-56294-043-0), 1991. 32p. Illus., some color. (Interest level: 4-8).

John Brown and his men raided the federal arsenal in Harpers Ferry hoping to capture weapons to be used to free slaves in the area, who would join him in fighting against slavery everywhere. Historical and modern drawings and photographs portray the people and places involved in these events that helped start the Civil War.
♦ Young people might identify other abolitionists and determine what methods they used to oppose slavery.
1. Brown, John, 1800-1859 2. Abolitionists 3. United States—History—Civil War

92 Jackson, Thomas J. (Stonewall)
Fritz, Jean. *Stonewall*. Illus. by Stephen Gammell. Putnam (0-399-20698-1), 1979. 152p. Illus. (Interest level: 7-8).

Thomas J. Jackson's boyhood in West Virginia is presented as a prelude to a military career that culminated in distinguished service as a general in the Confederate Army. This narrative provides considerable insight into Jackson's personality, as well as a study of his role as a popular Civil War leader.

♦ Young people might prepare a brief biography of some other West Virginian who played an important part in the Civil War.

1. Jackson, Thomas Jonathan, 1824-1863 2. United States—History—Civil War, 1861-1865 3. Confederate States of America—Army—Stonewall Brigade

92 Jones, Mary Harris (Mother)

Atkinson, Linda. *Mother Jones: The Most Dangerous Woman in America.* Crown (0-517-53201-8), 1978. 246p. B/W illus. (Interest level: 7-8).

Mary Jones, "Mother" to the working class, was an outspoken labor leader devoted to improving the lives and working conditions of coal miners, railroad workers, steelworkers, and textile workers. This is a well-written and well-illustrated biography of an important figure in the American labor movement from the 1870s to the 1920s.

♦ Young people might examine the efforts of Mother Jones and other labor leaders to prohibit young children from working in factories and mines.

1. Jones, Mary Harris, 1830-1930 2. Labor Unions 3. Women in Trade Unions

92 McNeill, Louise

McNeill, Louise. *The Milkweed Ladies.* University of Pittsburgh Press (0-8229-3587-2), 1988. 122p. Illus. (Interest level: 7-8).

West Virginia's Poet Laureate tells of her youth on a Greenbrier Valley farm owned by her family for 200 years. Drawings of flowers and fruits decorate the margins of this lyrical account of rural life in the early twentieth century.

♦ Young people might explore their neighborhood and inventory the plants, flowers, and trees that are found in their area.

1. McNeill, Louise—Biography 2. Farm Life—West Virginia 3. West Virginia—Social Life and Customs

92 Pringle, John and Samuel

Bice, David A. *The Pringle Tree.* Illus. by Charles Fry. Jalamap (No ISBN), 1977 (out of print). Unpaginated. Illus. (Interest level: K-3).

John and Samuel Pringle were timid British soldiers who ran away from the French and Indian War and hid for four years, living in a big hollow sycamore tree in West Virginia. This is a humorous account of the unnecessary distress the Pringles brought upon themselves by running away from their fears rather than facing them.

♦ Young people might dramatize this story by making a hollow tree house from large boxes and pretending to live on the frontier.

1. Pringle, John—Biography 2. Pringle, Samuel—Biography 3. West Virginia—Discovery and Exploration

92 Retton, Mary Lou

Sullivan, George. *Mary Lou Retton: A Biography.* Wanderer Books (0-671-55472-5), 1985. 79p. B/W photos. (Interest level: 4-8).

Her superb performance at the 1984 Olympics made this West Virginia athlete the first American woman to win a gold medal in gymnastics. This illustrated biography is a balanced look at Mary Lou Ret-

ton's family, education, training, and athletic accomplishments.

♦ Young people might create a sports trading card with interesting facts about their favorite athlete.

1. Gymnastics—United States 2. Retton, Mary Lou

92 Rylant, Cynthia

Rylant, Cynthia. *Best Wishes.* Illus. by Carlo Ontal. Richard C. Owen (1-878450-20-4), 1992. (Meet the Author). 32p. Color photos. (Interest level: K-6).

West Virginia author Cynthia Rylant tells about the people, places, and animals that helped her be a writer of children's books. This appealing autobiography is nicely illustrated with color photographs of Rylant at home in Ohio and visiting family in West Virginia.

♦ Young people might write an autobiography that identifies the people, places, and animals that are important in their lives.

1. Rylant, Cynthia 2. Authors, American

92 Rylant, Cynthia

Rylant, Cynthia. *But I'll Be Back Again: An Album.* Orchard (0-531-05806-9), 1989. 54p. Illus. (Interest level: 5-8).

The author describes her childhood and adolescence in a small West Virginia town during the 1950s and 1960s. Some special photographs endear this bittersweet remembrance of Rylant's absent parents, her boy friends, the Beatles, and Robert F. Kennedy.

♦ Young people might describe in an autobiography those people who are most important in their lives.

1. West Virginia—Social Life and Customs 2. Rylant, Cynthia—Biography 3. Authors, American

92 Rylant, Cynthia

Cynthia Rylant. (Videocassette). American School Publishers (No ISBN), 1990. (Meet the Newbery Author Series). 1/2", Color, (20 min.). $45.00. (Interest level: 4-8).

As soon as Cynthia Rylant began working in the children's department of a public library at age 23, she knew she wanted to write books. Many of her books are based on Rylant's experiences growing up in southern West Virginia with people who liked to talk and tell stories.

♦ Young people might write and illustrate a story that is based upon one of their own memorable experiences.

1. Rylant, Cynthia 2. Authors, American

Fiction

Capote, Truman. *I Remember Grandpa: A Story.* Illus. by Barry Moser. Peachtree (0-934601-22-4), 1987. 37p. Illus. (Interest level: 6-8).

One of the saddest days of Bobby's life was moving from the mountains, so that he could attend school, and leaving his Grandpa and Grandma behind in West Virginia. The somber tone of this story of kindred separation is also conveyed in the dark, solemn portraits of Bobby's family.

♦ Young people might revive or strengthen a family connection by regularly writing letters to a favorite relative living in another community.

1. Family life—Fiction 2. West Virginia—Fiction

Carmer, Elizabeth and **Carmer, Carl**. *Tony Beaver, Griddle Skater*. Illus. by Mimi Korach. Garrard (No ISBN), 1965. Unpaginated. Color illus. (Interest level: K-6).

Wearing skates made of bacon-fat, Tony Beaver and Paul Bunyan race each other on Tony's Grandma's huge pancake griddle. Energetic illustrations accompany lively accounts of Grandma's pancake cooking feats and Tony's and Paul's pancake eating exploits.
♦ Young people might study other American folk heroes and imagine contests that they might have against each other.
1. Tony Beaver 2. Folklore—West Virginia

Gunter, Francis B. *The Golden Horseshoe*. Vantage (0-533-08523-3), 1990. 135p. Illus. (Interest level: 6-8).

Three teen-age West Virginia time travelers encounter the Mound Builders, Margaret Blennerhassett, John Brown's hanging, John Wilkes Booth, The Hatfield—McCoy feud, and the Miners' Battle at Blair Mountain. This fast-moving adventure story provides realistic glimpses into several fascinating episodes in West Virginia history.
♦ Young people might write a story of the adventures a time traveler would encounter visiting present-day West Virginia from the future.
1. West Virginia—History—Fiction

Naylor, Phyllis Reynolds. *Shiloh*. Atheneum (0-689-31614-3), 1991. 144p. (Interest level: 4-8).

In the hills near Friendly, West Virginia, 11-year-old Marty finds a lost Beagle and wants to keep it rather than return the dog to its harsh owner. The characters and their conflicts and the growing friendship of boy and dog are authentic and engrossing.
♦ Young people might learn about caring properly for different kinds of pets.
1. Dogs—Fiction 2. Animal—Treatment—Fiction 3. West Virginia—Fiction

Rylant, Cynthia. *A Blue-Eyed Daisy*. Bradbury (0-02-777960-2), 1985. 99p. (Interest level: 5-8).

This is a chronicle of events in the year leading up to the twelfth birthday of the youngest of five daughters of a disabled West Virginia coal miner. This story realistically depicts the ordinary and the unexpected in the life of an 11-year-old girl.
♦ Young people might begin to keep a daily journal of new activities, new experiences, and observations.
1. Family life—Fiction 2. West Virginia—Fiction

Rylant, Cynthia. *Miss Maggie*. Illus. by Thomas Di Grazia. Dutton (0-525-44048-8), 1983. Unpaginated. Illus. (Interest level: 2-6).

Young Nat was afraid of old Miss Maggie until he listened to his heart and not his head and discovered that concern for another person and a shared concern for all living beings is a good basis for friendship. Soft gray pictures of Nat, Miss Maggie, and various animal friends add to the appeal of this heartwarming story.
♦ Young people might create a story that demonstrates how old and new friendships can be based upon

shared interests and upon concern about other people.
1. Old Age—Fiction

Rylant, Cynthia. *Missing May*. Illus. by Orchard (0-531-08596-0), 1992. 89p. (Interest level: 5-8).

From her mountain home in West Virginia, 12-year-old Summer, her uncle Ob, and their unusual neighbor Cletus set out on a quest to contact the spirit of deceased Aunt May. This is a perceptive study of the emotional turmoil Summer experiences when she loses the Aunt who raised her.
♦ Young people might capture the memory of a lost loved one by collecting photographs and writing down special memories of them.
1. Death—Fiction 2. West Virginia—Fiction 3. Grief—Fiction

Rylant, Cynthia. *The Relatives Came*. Illus. by Stephen Gammell. Bradbury (0-02-777220-9), 1985. Unpaginated. Color illus. (Interest level: K-3).

Everyone enjoyed lots of hugs, lots of food, lots to talk about, and lots to do together as a family when the relatives came to visit from Virginia. Smooth narrative and lively, double-page illustrations evoke the excitement and enjoyment of being together as a big family.
♦ Young people might locate on a map all the places their relatives would come from if everyone gathered for a family reunion.
1. Family Life—Fiction 2. Appalachian Region, Southern

Rylant, Cynthia. *This Year's Garden*. Illus. by Mary Szilagyi. Bradbury (0-02-777970-X), 1984. Unpaginated. Color illus. (Interest level: K-3).

The planning and activities involved in gardening extend from late winter through spring and summer, then into late autumn. The chief attraction of this book is the vivid, double-page illustrations depicting the colors of the changing seasons.
♦ Young people might plant an indoor garden with sure-growing seeds (such as grass, lettuce, sprout beans) and observe their growth.
1. Gardens—Fiction 2. Seasons—Fiction

Rylant, Cynthia. *When I Was Young in The Mountains*. Illus. by Diane Goode. Dutton (0-525-42525-X), 1982. Unpaginated. (Interest level: K-3).

Fried okra, the Johnny-house, baptisms in the swimming hole, and Grandfather covered with coal dust are some memories of growing up in the mountains. The earth-tone illustrations evoke the atmosphere and the simplicity of life in the mountains of Appalachia.
♦ As an activity, young people might write about or draw those people and activities that probably will be special memories when they are older.
1. Mountain Life 2. Appalachia—Social Life and Customs

Smucker, Anna Egan. *No Star Nights*. Illus. by Steve Johnson. Knopf (0-394-99925-3), 1989. Unpaginated. Color illus. (Interest level: K-6).

Billowing smokestacks, factory whistles, slag heaps, and the glow of furnaces that turned night sky into red and orange, characterized steel-mill towns in

the 1950s. Richly colored illustrations realistically capture the atmosphere of growing up in a steel-mill town such as Weirton, West Virginia, the setting for this book.
♦ Young people might identify activities to do individually, or as a group, to make their community or neighborhood a cleaner, safer, more pleasant place to live.
1. Environmental Pollution 2. Steel Industry and Trade—West Virginia 3. West Virginia

Periodicals

016.975
Appalachian Outlook: New Sources of Regional Information Compiled by West Virginia University Library. West Virginia University Library (No ISBN), issued irregularly. No. 100 is February 1992. $10.00 per year (Interest level: 4-8).
Annotated bibliographic citations of books and articles pertaining to Appalachia are categorized by state names and numerous topics. Approximately 4000 citations in the last 33 issues will eventually be merged with the 8200 entries in the *Appalachian Bibliography* last published in 1980.
1. Appalachia

799
Wonderful West Virginia. West Virginia Division of Natural Resources (ISSN 0030-7157), Monthly. Volume 57 is 1993. Color photos. $12.00 per year. (Interest level: Adult).
Each issue presents five to ten illustrated articles on West Virginia history, wildlife, flora, and outdoor recreation. This periodical is noted for articles on unusual topics and for consistently exceptional photographs, most related to West Virginia's natural heritage.
1. Outdoor Recreation—West Virginia 2. Wildlife Conservation—West Virginia 3. Natural History—West Virginia

917.54
Goldenseal: West Virginia Traditional Life. West Virginia Division of Culture and History (ISSN 0099-0159), Quarterly. Volume 19 is 1993. Illus., mostly photos. (Interest level: Professional).
Ten to fifteen articles per issue focus upon every aspect of the life and culture of West Virginia. Each issue includes a calendar of fairs, festivals, and folklife events; reviews of books, recordings, films, and cultural events; and numerous illustrations.
1. West Virginia—History 2. West Virginia—Social Life and Customs

Professional Materials

016.9754
Forbes, Harold M. *West Virginia History: A Bibliography and Guide to Research.* West Virginia University Press (0-937058-03-3), 1981. 359p. Illus.; Map. (Interest level: Professional).

This bibliography is an indexed guide to published material dealing with the history of West Virginia. The 3106 sources listed include books, pamphlets, periodical literature, and unpublished theses.
1. West Virginia—History 2. West Virginia—Bibliography

309.1754
Maurer, B.B., ed. *Mountain Heritage.* 4th ed. McClain (87012-279-7), 1980. 344p. Illus. (Interest level: Professional).
This is a collection of essays on humans facing the wilderness, culture, arts and crafts, language, folklore and literature, music, dance, family and home, religion, and black culture in West Virginia. All contributions are by recognized authorities on their subjects.
1. West Virginia—Social Life and Customs 2. Folklore—West Virginia

574.9754
Core, Earl L. *The Wondrous Year: West Virginia Through the Seasons.* Seneca Books (0-89092-003-6), 1975. 208p. (Interest level: Professional).
Much local history, culture, and nature lore is woven through this month-by-month account of West Virginia's seasons. Written by an important botanist and local historian, this appealing work is useful for background reading or for reference.
1. Botany—West Virginia 2. Plants—Folklore 3. Natural History—West Virginia

975.4
Ash, Jerry Wayne and **Douthat, Stratton L**. *West Virginia USA.* Illus. by Bill Kuykendall and Harry Seawell. Seawell Multimedia (0-917040-00-7), 1976. 207p. Color illus. (Interest level: Professional).
West Virginia history is examined through studies of some of the state's most fascinating people, both historical and contemporary. This elegant book is profusely illustrated with photographs, both contemporary color and historical black and white, and includes a lengthy chronology of West Virginia history.
1. West Virginia—Description and Travel 2. West Virginia—History

975.4
Clagg, Sam. *West Virginia Historical Almanac: Bicentennial Publication.* McClain (0-87012-231-2), 1975. 172p. Illus. (Interest level: Professional).
In almanac fashion, over 1300 events spanning 300 years of West Virginia history are recorded date by date through the calendar year. A source is cited for every entry, providing a source for further investigation, and an index includes over 3000 references.
1. West Virginia—History—Chronology

975.4
Cometti, Elizabeth and **Summers, Festusp**, eds. *The Thirty-Fifth State: A Documentary History of West Virginia.* West Virginia University Library (No ISBN), 1966. 671p. Illus.; Map; ports. (Interest level: Professional).
This collection of 187 annotated West Virginia documents, taken from manuscripts, government publications, newspapers, and periodicals, spans the years

from 1609 to 1963. A thorough index lists hundreds of people, places, and events cited in documents that constitute the primary sources for much of West Virginia's history.
1. West Virginia—History

975.4
The Complete Catalog: Everything You Wanted to Know About West Virginia. West Virginia Library Commission (No ISBN), 1985. 92p. Illus.; Maps; Music. (Interest level: Professional).

This handbook includes basic geographical, population, and political facts, documentation of all the state symbols, a list of governors, summaries of major historical episodes, and a list of firsts and superlatives. This is a useful reference tool for basic data on many aspects of West Virginia history.
1. West Virginia

975.4
North, E. Lee. *The 55 West Virginias: A Guide to the State's Counties.* West Virginia University Press (0-937058-21-1), 1985. 117p. Illus.; Maps. (Interest level: Professional).

The individuality of each West Virginia county is presented in a brief history, an economic profile, a population profile, a selected bibliography, and a county map. This work is a very useful reference tool due to its clever approach to portraying each of West Virginia's 55 counties.
1. West Virginia 2. West Virginia—History

975.4
Rice, Otis K. *West Virginia: A History.* University of Kentucky Press (0-8131-1540-X), 1985. 326p. Illus. (Interest level: Professional).

This narrative history of West Virginia was written by a highly respected historian and author. A bibliography with suggested readings is provided for each chapter.
1. West Virginia—History

975.4
The West Virginia Heritage Encyclopedia. Jim Comstock (No ISBN), 1976. 25 vols. (Interest level: Professional).

Volumes 1-24 are an alphabetically arranged encyclopedia of people, places, events, and topics pertaining to West Virginia. Contents include "West Virginians Who Made Good Outside the State" in volume 24 and a collection of bibliographies in volume 25. "See also" references lead to more detailed information in *The West Virginia Heritage Encyclopedia. Supplemental Series,* 25 vols. in 23 books (*see* following entry).
1. West Virginia—History

975.4
The West Virginia Heritage Encyclopedia. Supplemental Series. Jim Comstock (No ISBN), 1974. 25 vols. in 23. (Interest level: Professional).

Reprints of standard works on West Virginia history and literature and new compilations on West Virginia literature, music, and women comprise the volumes in this set. "See" references in *The West Virginia Heritage Encyclopedia* (*see* preceding entry) refer to in-depth information in these Supplemental Series volumes, each of which can stand alone as an excellent historical resource.
1. West Virginia—History

975.4
West Virginia Picture Book. Jim Comstock (No ISBN), 1978. 301. Chiefly illus.; Maps; ports. (Interest level: Professional).

Described as volume 51 of *The West Virginia Heritage Encyclopedia* (*see* preceding entry), this collection of photographs and drawings depicts West Virginia people, places, and events. If a picture is worth a thousand words, these thousands of images speak volumes on West Virginia's heritage.
1. West Virginia—Description and Travel 2. West Virginia—History—Pictorial Works

975.4
Williams, John Alexander. *West Virginia: A Bicentennial History.* Norton (0-393-05590-6), 1976. (The States and the Nation Series). 212p. Illus.; B/W photos. (Interest level: Professional).

This is a study of seven places and their climactic historical events, each of which characterizes the values and attitudes of an era in West Virginia's history. This work concludes with a fascinating essay on the psychology of West Virginians and their history.
1. West Virginia—History

Directory of Publishers and Vendors

Below are the names and addresses of publishers and companies from whom materials cited in this book can be ordered.

Abraham Lincoln Birthplace National Historic Site
Rural Route #1
Hodgenville, KY 42748

Acadiana Profile
Acadiana News Agency, Ind.
P.O. Box 52247
Lafayette, LA 70505

Aegina Press, Inc.
59 Oak Lane, Spring Valley
Huntington, WV 25704

Alabama Bureau of Tourism and Travel
401 Adams Avenue
P.O. Box 4309
Montgomery, AL 36103-4309
1-800-ALABAMA

Alabama Conservancy
2717 7th Avenue South, Suite 201
Birmingham, AL 35233

Alabama Department of Economic and Community Affairs
Planning and Economic Development Division
P.O. Box 250347
Montgomery, AL 36125-0347
(205) 284-8630

Alabama Heritage (Magazine)
P.O. Box 870342
University of Alabama
Tuscaloosa, AL 35487-0342

Alabama Heritage Cookbook Publishers
P.O. Box 76072
Birmingham, AL 35253
Montgomery, AL 36130
(205) 242-4076

Alabama Museum of Natural History
University of Alabama
P.O. Box 870340
Tuscaloosa, AL 35487-0340

Alabama Natural History Society
Alabama Museum of Natural History
University of Alabama
Tuscaloosa, AL 35487-0342

Alabama Rural Electric Association
P.O. Box 244014
Montgomery, AL 36124

Alabama State Council for the Arts
One Dexter Avenue
Montgomery, AL 36130

Aladdin Publishing
P.O. Box 364
Palmer, AK 99645

Allegheny Vistas
P.O. Box 20
Tornado, WV 25202

Algonquin Books of Chapel Hill
P.O. Box 2225
Chapel Hill, NC 27515

American School Publishers
Princeton Road, Box 408
Hightstown, NJ 08520

American Library Association
50 East Huron Street
Chicago, IL 60611

Anchor Books
666 Fifth Avenue
New York, NY 10103

Appalachian Consortium Press
Appalachian State University
University Hall
Boone, NC 28608

Appalachian Trail Conference
P.O. Box 807
Harpers Ferry, WV 25425

Appalshop
P.O. Box 743
Whitesburg, KY 41858

APPLE Corps
250 Georgia Avenue, SE
Suite 205
Atlanta, GA 30312

Atheneum
833 Third Avenue
New York, NY 10022

Auburn Television
Thomas Causland, Marketing Director
Auburn University, AL 36849-3501

Audubon Park Press
P.O. Box 4327
New Orleans, LA 70178

Avon Books (Div. of the Hearst Corp.)
105 Madison Avenue
New York, NY 10019

Bandit Books, Inc.
P.O. Box 11721
Winston-Salem, NC 27106

Bantam Doubleday Dell
666 Fifth Avenue
New York, NY 10103

Bartleby Press
11141 Georgia Avenue, No. A6
Silver Spring, MD, 20902

Baton Rouge Visitors' Guide
P.O. Box 4149
Baton Rouge, LA 70821
1-800-527-6843

Beacon Press
25 Beacon Street
Boston, MA 02108

Beckley Films, Inc.
P.O. Box 28
Bradenton, FL 34206
(813) 748-3355

Berea College Press
Berea College, Box 2317
Berea, KY 40404

Birmingham Public Library
Linn Henley Research Library of
Southern History
2100 Park Place
Birmingham, AL 35203
(205) 226-3665

Bookabeast Series
512 Westerham Court
Louisville, KY 40222

Bookwright Press
387 Park Avenue, S.Fourth Floor
New York, NY 10016

Bradbury Press
866 Third Avenue
New York, NY 10022

Breyer Animal Creations
14 Industrial Road
Pequannock, NJ 07440

Briarfield Ironworks Park
Route 1, Box 147
Brierfield, AL 35035
(205) 665-1856

Broadfoot's of Wendell
6624 Robertson Pond Road
Wendell, NC 27591
1-800-444-6963

Camelback Design Croup, Inc. and Elan Publishing
6625 N. Scottsdale Road
Scottsdale, AZ 85250
(602) 948-4233

Cannon Graphics
418 Lehigh Terrace
Charleston, WV 25302

Carolina Academic Press
700 Kent Street
Durham, NC 27701

Carolrhoda Books
241 First Avenue North
Minneapolis, MN 55401

Cavendish, Marshall, Corp.
2415 Jerusalem Avenue
North Bellmore, NY 11710

Center for Louisiana Studies
University of Southwestern Louisiana
P.O. Box 40831
Lafayette, LA 70504
(318) 231-6027

Chatham Press, Inc.
Box A
Old Greenwich, CT 06870

Chelsea House Publishers
95 Madison Avenue
New York, NY 10016

Cherry Lane Books
110 Midland Avenue
Portchester, NY 10573

Chilton Book Co./Wallace Homestead Books
One Chilton Way
Radnor, PA 19089

Cinema Guild
1697 Broadway
New York, NY 10019

Clairmont Press, Inc.
P.O. Box 11743
Montgomery, AL 36111

Claitor's Law Books and Publishing Division
3165 South Acadian at I-10
Baton Rouge, LA 70808

Clarion Books
52 Vanderbilt Avenue
New York, NY 10017

Charles Clark Co., Inc.
170 Keyland Court
Bohemia, NY 11716

Classic Images Productions, Inc.
P.O. Box 239
Columbia, MD 21045

Clements Research II, Inc.
16850 Dallas Parkway
Dallas, TX 75248-1999

Cobblehill Books
375 Hudson Street
New York, NY 10014-3657

College and University Personnel Association
1233 20th Street NW
Suite 503
Washington, DC 20036

Colonial Williamsburg Foundation
P.O. Box 1776
Williamsburg, VA 23187-1776

Columbia Books Inc., Publishers
1212 New York Avenue NW
Suite 330
Washington, DC 20005

Columbia University Press
136 South Broadway
Irvington, NY 10533

Jim Comstock
4 Railroad Avenue
Richwood, WV 26261

Contemporary Books, Inc.
180 N. Michigan Avenue
Chicago, IL 60601

Council Oak Books
1428 S. St. Louis
Tulsa, OK 74120

Country Dance & Song Society of America
17 New South Street
Northampton, MA 01060

Coward-McCann and Geoghegan
200 Madison Avenue
New York, NY 10016

Crabtree Publishing Co.
350 Fifth Avenue Suite 3308
New York, NY 10118

Creative Education, Inc.
123 S. Broad Street
P.O. Box 227
Mankato, MN 56001

Creative Productions
P.O. Box 30515
Raleigh, NC 27612

Crescent Press
1916 Madison Rd.
Oakland, OR 97562

Crestwood House
866 Third Avenue
New York, NY 10022

Crowell-Collier Press
866 Third Avenue
New York, NY 10022

Crown Publishers
201 E. 50th Street
New York, NY 10022

Da Capo Press, Inc.
233 Spring Street
New York, NY 10013-1578

Data Courier, Inc.
620 South Fifth Street
Louisville, KY 40202

Dell Publishing
666 Fifth Avenue
New York, NY 10103

Delorme Mapping Co.
P.O. Box 298
Freeport, ME 04032

Delta Blues Museum
P.O. Box 280
Clarksdale, MS 38614

Dillon Press, Inc.
866 Third Avenue
New York, NY 10022

Donning Press
184 Business Park Drive #106
Virginia Beach, VA 23462-6533

Doubleday and Company, Inc.
666 Fifth Avenue
New York, NY 10103

Dutton Children's Books
375 Hudson Street
New York, NY 10014-3657

Eakin Press
P.O. Drawer 90159
Austin, TX 78709-0159

Educational Associates, Inc.
123 Polly Lane
Lafayette, LA 70508
1-800-960-2222

Elderberry Books
West Virginia Division of Culture and History
Cultural Center
Charleston, WV 25305

Enslow Publishers Inc.
Bloy Street and Ramsey Avenue
P.O.Box 777
Hillside, NJ 07205

EPM Publications
1003 Turkey Run Road
McLean, VA 22101

J.L. Estes
816 Pierremont Road
Shreveport, LA 71106

Executive Mansion Fund, Inc.
301 N. Blount Street
Raleigh, NC 27601-1007
(919) 733-1991

Experience America Inc.
P.O. Box 250
Cedar City, UT 84721-0250

Farrar, Straus, and Giroux
19 Union Square West
New York, NY 10003

Filson Club
1310 S. Third Street
Louisville, KY 40208

Flower Films & Video
10341 San Pablo Avenue
El Cerrito, CA 94530
(415) 525-0942

Four O'Clock Farms Publishing Co.
1422 N. Woodhouse Road
Virginia Beach, VA 23454

Four Winds Press
866 Third Avenue
New York, NY 10022

Friends of City Park
City Park Administration Bldg.
New Orleans, LA 70119

G.O.G. Enterprises
P.O. Box 2092
Beaufort, SC 29901-2092
(803) 524-9748

Gallopade: Publishing Group
235 E. Ponce de Leon Avenue Suite 100
Decatur, GA 30030

Garrett Educational Corp.
P.O. Box 1588
Ada, OK 74820

Gateway Productions, Inc.
3011 Magazine Street
New Orleans, LA 70115

George Washington Carver Museum
National Parks Service
Tuskegee University
Tuskegee, AL 36088

Georgia Conservancy
781 Marietta Street
Marietta, GA 30318

Georgia Department of Agriculture
Capitol Square
Atlanta, GA 30334
1-800-282-5852
(404) 656-3689

Georgia Department of Industry, Trade and Tourism
P.O. Box 1776
Atlanta, GA 30301-1776
(404) 656-3545

Georgia Department of Natural Resources
Film and Video
205 Butler Street SE
Suite 1258
Atlanta, GA 30334
(404) 656-0779

Georgia Department of Transportation
Public Affairs Office, Room 114
2 Capitol Square
Atlanta, GA 30334-1002
(404) 656-5267

David King Gleason
1766 Nicholson Drive
Baton Rouge, LA 70802

Globe Pequot Press
138 W. Main Street
Chester, CT 06412

Greater New Orleans Tourist and Convention Commission
1520 Sugar Bowl Drive
New Orleans, LA 70112
(504) 527-6900

Greenfield Review Press
2 Middle Grove Road
P.O. Box 308
Greenfield Center, NY 12833

Green Tiger Press
435 E. Carmel Street
San Marcos, CA 92069-4362

Greenwillow Books
1350 Avenue of the Americas
New York, NY 10019

Ben Griffith
330 Kramer Street
Carrollton, GA 30117
(404) 834-6386

Grimes Publications
624 S. Milledge Avenue
Athens, GA 30605
(404) 354-0463

Grossett and Dunlap, Inc.
200 Madison Avenue
New York, NY 10016

Hardy, Arthur, and Associates
P.O. Box 8058
New Orleans, LA 70182

Harcourt Brace Jovanovich
7555 Caldwell Avenue
Niles, IL 60648

Harmony Books
201 E. 50th Street
New York, NY 10022

HarperCollins Publishers, Inc.
10 East 53rd Street
New York, NY 10022-5299

Hastings House Book Publishers
141 Halstead Avenue
Mamaroneck, NY 10543

Hill and Wang, Inc.
19 Union Square W.
New York, NY 10003

Historic New Orleans Collection
533 Royal Street
New Orleans, LA 70130
(504) 523-4662

Holiday House, Inc.
18 E. 53rd Street
New York, NY 10022

Holt, Henry and Company
115 W. 18th Street
New York, NY 10011

Holt, Rinehart and Winston, Inc.
301 Commerce Street, Suite 3700
Fort Worth, TX 76102

W.S. Hoole Special Collections Library
University of Alabama
Tuscaloosa, AL 35487-0266

Horseshoe Bend National Military Park
Sean Gellett, Book and Information Officer
Daviston, AL 36256
(205) 234-7111

Houghton Mifflin Company
One Beacon Street
Boston, MA 02108

Humanities Foundation of West Virginia
Suite 800, Union Building
723 Kanawha Boulevard, East
Charleston, WV 25301

Independent Publishers Group
814 N. Franklin
Chicago, IL 60610

JM Productions
Box 1911
Brentwood, TN 37024-1911

Jefferson County Gazette
P.O. Box 3371
Louisville, KY 40201

Jove Publications, Inc.
200 Madison Avenue
New York, NY 10016

Larry Keating Productions
c/o West Virginia Independence
Hall Foundation
1528 Market Street
Wheeling, WV 26003

Kentucky Department for Libraries and Archives
300 Coffee Tree Road
Frankfort, KY 40601

Kentucky Derby Museum
704 Central Avenue
Louisville, KY 40208

Kentucky Educational Foundation (KEF)
3399 Tates Creek Road
Suite 101
Lexington, KY 40502

Kentucky Educational Television (KET)
600 Cooper Drive
Lexington, KY 40502-2296

The Kentucky Explorer
P.O. Box 227
1729 Hayes Valley Road
Jackson, KY 41339

Kentucky Heritage Council
State Historic Preservation Office
Frankfort, KY 40601

Kentucky Historical Society
Educational Resources
P.O. Box H
Frankfort, KY 40602

Kentucky Images
527 S. Upper Street
Lexington, KY 40508

Kentucky Sound
P.O. Box 43432
Louisville, KY 40253

Alfred A. Knopf
201 E. 50th Street
New York, NY 10022

L'Avant Studios
207 West Park Avenue
Tallahassee, FL 32301

Legacy Communications, Inc.
65 Roswell Street, Bldg. 400
Alpharetta, GA 30201
(404) 664-0641

Lerner Publications
241 First Avenue North
Minneapolis, MN 55401

Lexington-Fayette County Historic Commission
253 Market Street
Lexington, KY 40508

J.B. Lippincott Company
227 E. Washington Square
Philadelphia, PA 19106

Little, Brown and Co.
1271 Avenue of the Americas
New York, NY 10020

The Little Brown House
P.O. Box 179
Harpers Ferry, WV 25425

Lodestar Books
375 Hudson Street
New York, NY 10014

Lothrop, Lee and Shepard Books
1350 Avenue of the Americas
New York, NY 10019

Louisiana Conservationist
P.O. Box 98000
Baton Rouge, LA 70898

Louisiana Department of Economic Development
Communications Division
P.O. Box 94185
Baton Rouge, LA 70804-9185

Louisiana Department of Wildlife and Fisheries
(Publisher of Louisiana Conservationist)
2000 Quail Drive
Baton Rouge, LA 70808

Louisiana Secretary of State Office
P.O. Box 94125
Baton Rouge, LA 70804-9125
(504) 922-1000

Louisiana State Museum Complex
751 Chartres Street
New Orleans, LA 70116
504-568-6968
Included in the complex:
    The Arsenal
615 Saint Peter Street
    The Cabildo
701 Chartres Street
    Jackson House
619 Saint Peter Street
    The Lower Pontalba
523 Saint Ann Street
523-568-6968
    Madame John's Legacy
632 Dumaine Street
504-581-4321
    Old U. S. Mint Building
400 Esplanade Avenue
    The Presbytere
751 Chartres Street

Louisiana State Office of Tourism
529 Saint Ann Street
New Orleans, LA 70116
(504) 568-5661

Louisiana State Office of Tourism
Department of Culture, Recreation and Tourism
P.O. Box 94291
Baton Rouge, LA 70804
1-800-334-8626

Louisiana State University Press
Baton Rouge, LA 70893

Louisville Historical League, Books
Petersen-Dumesnil House
301 S. Petersen Avenue
Louisville, KY 40258

Macmillan Publishing Company
866 Third Avenue
New York, NY 10022

Mammoth Cave National Park
Superintendent
Mammoth Cave, KY 42259

McClain Printing Co.
212 Main Street
Parsons, WV 26827

McClanahan Publishing House, Inc.
P.O. Box 100
Kuttawa, KY 42055
(502) 388-9388
1-800-544-6959

McDonald and Woodward Publishing Co.
P.O. Box 10308
Blacksburg, VA 24062-0308

McElderry Books
866 Third Avenue
New York, NY 10022

McGraw-Hill Publishing Co.
1221 Avenue of the Americas
New York, NY 10020

McKay, David, Co.
201 E. 50th Street MD4-6
New York, NY 10022

MECC
6160 Summit Drive North
Minneapolis, MN 55430-4003

Meckler Corp.
11 Ferry Lane, W.
Westport, CT 06880

Mercer University Press
1400 Coleman Avenue
Macon, GA 31207

Julian Messner
190 Sylvan Avenue
Englewood Cliffs, NJ 07632

Mississippi Authority for Educational Television
P.O. Box 1101
Jackson, MS 39215-1101

Mississippi Department of Economic Development
The Division of Tourism
P.O. Box 849
Jackson, MS 39205

Mississippi Economic Council
P.O. Box 23276
Jackson, MS 39225

Mississippi Forestry Commission
301 N. Lamar Street S-300
Jackson, MS 39201

Mississippi Humanities Council
3825 Ridgewood Road
Jackson, MS 39211

Mississippi River Publishing Company
Route 2, Box 26
Leland, MS 38756

Modern Curriculum Press, Inc.
13900 Prospect Road
Cleveland, OH 44136

Montgomery Museum of Fine Art
One Museum Drive
P.O. Box 230819
Montgomery, AL 36123
(205) 244-5700

Morrow, William and Company
1350 Avenue of the Americas
New York, NY 10019

Mound State Monument
P.O. Box 66
Moundville, AL 35474
(206) 371-2572

John Muir Publications
P.O. Box 613
Santa Fe, NM 87504
(505) 902-4078

National Audiovisual Center
8700 Edgeworth Drive
Capitol Heights, MD 20743

National Geographic Society
P.O. Box 50096
Seattle, WA 98145-5096

National Park Service
Division of Publications
Harpers Ferry Center
Harpers Ferry, WV 25425

National Society of the Colonial Dames of America in the State of Georgia
"Georgia Illustrated, 1513-1793
c/o The Andrew Low House
329 Abercorn Street
Savannah, GA 31401

Native American Authors Distribution Project
The Greenfield Review Press
2 Middle Grove Road
P.O. Box 308
Greenfield Center, NY 12833

New Day Press
2355 E. 89th Street
Cleveland, OH 44106

New Orleans and the River Regions
Chamber of Commerce
P.O. Box 30240
New Orleans, LA 70190
(504) 527-6900

New Orleans Museum of Art
P.O. Box 19123
New Orleans, LA 70179-0123
504-488-2631

New World Recordings
701 7th Avenue
New York, NY 10036
(212) 302-0460

NIMCO, Inc.
P.O. Box 9
Calhoun, KY 42327

North Carolina Center for the Advancement of Teaching
Cullowhee, NC 28723-9062
(704) 227-7363

North Carolina Department of Cultural Resources
109 E. Jones Street
Raleigh, NC 27601-2807
(919) 733-2570
Fax (919) 733-8748

North Carolina Department of Public Instruction
Division of Social Studies
Division of Computer Services
116 West Edenton Street
Education Building
Raleigh, NC 27603-1712
(919) 733-3193

North Carolina Div. of Archives and History
109 E. Jones Street
Raleigh, NC 27601-2807

North Carolina Division of Travel and Tourism
Department of Economic and Community Development
430 North Salisbury Street
Raleigh, NC 27611
1-800-VISIT NC; in Raleigh, NC, call (919) 733-4171

North Carolina Historic Sites
North Carolina Department of Cultural Resources
109 E. Jones Street
Raleigh, NC 27601-2807
(919) 733-7862

North Carolina Museum of Art
2110 Blue Ridge Boulevard
Raleigh, NC 27607

North Carolina State Museum of Natural Sciences
Department of Agriculture
P.O. Box 27647
102 N. Salisbury Street
Raleigh, NC 27611
(919) 733-7450

Norton, W.W. and Company Inc.
500 Fifth Avenue
New York, NY 10110

Orchard Books
387 Park Avenue, S.
New York, NY 10016

Overmountain Press
P.O. Box 1261
Johnson City, TN 37605

Oxford University Press
2001 Evans Road
Cary, NC 27513

Oxmoor House
P.O. Box 2463
Birmingham, AL 35201

Pantheon Books
201 E. 50th Street
New York, NY 10022

PBS Video
Public Broadcasting Service
1320 Braddock Place
Alexandria, VA 22314-1698

PCR Publications
5985 West Pages Lane
Louisville, KY 40258

Peachtree Publishers Ltd.
494 Armour Circle, NE
Atlanta, GA 30324

Pee Dee Magazine, Inc.
P.O. Box 5070
Florence, SC 29502

Pelican Publishing Company
1101 Monroe Street
Gretna, LA 70053
(504) 368-1175

Philomel Books
200 Madison Avenue
New York, NY 10016

Pictorial Histories Publishing Co.
4103 Virginia Avenue, SE
Charleston, WV 25304

Pinaire Lithographing Corporation
1705 West Jefferson
Louisville, KY 40203

Pine Hall Press
P.O. Box 150657
Nashville, TN 37215-0657

Pippin Press
Gracie Station, Box 92
229 E. 85th Street
New York, NY 10028

Plantation Publishing Company
P.O. Box 17842
Natchez, MS 39122-842

The Pleasant Co.
Fairway Place
Middleton, WI 53562

Pleasant Hill Press
2600 Pleasant Hill Road
Sebastopol, CA 95472

Portals Press
P.O. Box 1048
Tuscaloosa, AL 35403

Portland Museum
2308 Portland Avenue
Louisville, KY 40212
(502) 776-7678

Presidio Press
31 Paramon Way
Novato, CA 94949

Puffin Books
375 Hudson Street
New York, NY 10014-3657

Putnam and Sons
200 Madison Avenue
New York, NY 10016

Puzzles and Such
P.O. Box 3188
Kutchenson, KS 67504

Quail Ridge Publishers
P.O. Box 123
Brandon, MS 39043

The Quest
3118 Magazine Street
New Orleans, LA 70115

Raintree Publishers, Inc.
310 W. Wisconsin Avenue
Milwaukee, WI 53203

Riverbanks Zoological Society
P.O. Box 1060
Columbia, SC 29202-1060
(803) 779-8730 or 779-8717

Rand McNally and Co.
P.O. Box 7600
Chicago, IL 60680

Random House, Inc.
201 E. 50th Street
New York, NY 10022

Rounder Records
One Camp Street
Cambridge, MA 02140
(617) 661-6308

Rourke Corp.
P.O. Box 3328
Vero Beach, FL 32964

RPW Publishing Corporation
334 Old Chapin Road
Lexington, SC 29072

Rudledge Hill Press, Inc.
513 Third Avenue, South
Nashville, TN 37210
(301) 290-9032

Scholastic, Inc.
730 Broadway
New York, NY 10003

Scribner
866 Third Avenue
New York, NY 10022

Seneca Books
Route 6, Box 81-B
Morgantown, WV 26505

The Settlemyer Company
P.O. Box 446
Charleston, SC 29402

Shakertown at Pleasant Hill Kentucky
3500 Lexington Road
Harrodsburg, KY 40330

Shoe Tree Press
Division of Betterway Publications, Inc.
P.O. Box 219
Crozet, VA 22932

Silver Burdette Press
190 Sylvan Avenue
Englewood Cliffs, NJ 07632

Simon and Schuster, Inc.
200 Old Tappan Road
Old Tappan, NJ 07675

Smithsonian Folkways Recordings
416 Hungerford Drive, Suite 320
Rockville, MD 20850
(301) 443-2314 (orders)
(202) 287-3262 (catalog)

South Carolina Educational Television Network
2712 Millwood Avenue
Columbia, SC 29205
(803) 737-3340

The South Carolina State Museum
301 Gervais Street
Columbia, SC 29201
(803) 737-4595

Sparks Press
900 W. Morgan Street
P.O. Box 26747
Raleigh, NC 27611

Spectrum South, Inc./Reedy River Press
P.O. Box 231
Shelby, NC 28151-0231
1-800 7 COWPENS

State Library of Louisiana
Louisiana Section
P.O. Box 131
Baton Rouge, LA 70821
(504) 342-4914

State of Alabama Department of Conservation
Administrative Division
Montgomery, AL 36130

Steck-Vaughn Company
8701 N. Mopac Blvd.
Austin, TX 78759

Gareth Stevens Inc.
River Center Bldg.
1555 N. River Center Drive
Suite 201
Milwaukee, WI 53212

Stewart, Tabori and Chang Publishers
740 Broadway, 11th Floor
New York, NY 10003

St. Luke's Press
4210 B.F. Goodrich Boulevard
Memphis, TN 38118

Strode Publishers
P.O. Box 626
Tomball, TX 77375

The Jesse Stuart Foundation
P.O. Box 391
Ashland, KY 41114

Texas A&M University Press
Drawer C
College Station, TX 77843

Thrash Publicationns
P.O. Box 4419
Los Angeles, CA 90051

Title Books, Inc.
3013 2nd Avenue South
Birmingham, AL 335233
(205) 324-2596

TRAVEL (Kentucky Department of Travel Development)
P.O. Box 2011
Frankfort, KY 40602
1-800-225-TRIP

Troll Associates
100 Corporate Drive
Mahwah, N.J. 07430

United States Army Corps of Engineers
New Orleans District, (Southern Louisiana Coastal District)
Public Affairs Office
P.O. Box 60267
New Orleans, LA 70160-0627
(504) 862-2201

United States Army Corps of Engineers
Vicksburg District, (North Louisiana Water Resources)
Public Affairs Office
Vicksburg, MS 39180-5191

University Editions, Inc.
59 Oak Lane, Spring Valley
Huntington, WV 25704

University of Alabama
Center for Public Television
Box 870150, Communication Building
Tuscaloosa, AL 35487-0150
(205) 348-6210

University of Alabama at Birmingham
Center for Labor Education and Research
1044 South 11th Street
Birmingham, AL 35294-4500

University of Alabama Press
University of Alabama
Tuscaloosa, AL 35487-0342

University of Chicago Press
5801 S. Ellis Avenue
Chicago, IL 60637

University of Georgia Press
Terrell Hall
Athens, GA 30602

University of Oklahoma Press
1005 Asp Avenue
Norman, OK 73019-0445

University of Pittsburgh Press
127 N. Bellefield Avenue
Pittsburgh, PA 15260

The University Press of Kentucky
663 S. Limestone Street
Lexington, KY 40508

University Press of Mississippi
3825 Ridgewood Road
Jackson, MS 39211

University Press of Virginia
P.O. Box 3608
Charlottesville, VA 22903

Value Communications
P.O. Box 119
Stamford, CT 06904-0119

Vanderbilt University Press
Box 1813, Station B
Nashville, TN 37235

Vanguard Institutional Pubs.
1011 Fourth Street, Suite 305
Santa Monica, CA 90403

Vantage Press, Inc.
516 W. 34th Street
New York, NY 10001

Vicksburg National Military Park
Box 349
Vicksburg, MS 39180

Carl Vinson Institute of Government
University of Georgia
201 N. Millage Avenue
Athens, GA 30602
(706) 542-2736

Walker and Company
720 Fifth Avenue
New York, NY 10019

Walt Disney Publishing Group
114 Fifth Avenue
New York, NY 10011

Wanderer Press, The
201 Ohio Street
St. Paul, MN 55107

Warner Books
666 Fifth Avenue
New York, NY 10103

Washington Square Press
1230 Avenue of the Americas
New York, NY 10020

Franklin Watts
387 Park Avenue, S.
New York, NY 10016

Westminster/John Knox Press
100 Witherspoon Street
Louisville, KY 40202-1396

Weston Woods Studios
389 New Town Turnpike
Weston Woods, CT 06883

West Virginia Division of Culture and History
Cultural Center
Charleston, WV 25305

West Virginia Division of Natural Resources
State Capitol
Charleston, WV 25305-0669

West Virginia Library Commission
Cultural Center
Charleston, WV 25305

West Virginia Public Broadcasting
WNPB-TV
191 Scott Avenue
Morgantown, WV 26505

West Virginia University Press
West Virginia University Library
P.O. Box 6069
Morgantown, WV 26506

West Virginia Women's Commission
Building 6, Room 637
State Capitol Complex
Charleston, WV 25305

Westcliffe Publishers
P.O. Box 1261
Englewood, CO 80150
(808) 523-3692

Albert Whitman and Company
6340 Oakton Street
Morton Grove, IL 60053

Windsor Publications, Inc.
1000 S. Bertilsen Road # 14
Eugene, OR 97402

Winston-Derek Publishers, Inc.
Pennywell Drive
P.O. Box 90883
Nashville, TN 37209

Wisconsin House Book Publishers
2 E. Mifflin, No. 100
Madison, WI 53703

Yoknapatawpha Press
Box 248
Oxford, MS 38655

Zenger Video
P.O. Box 802
Culver City, CA 90232-0802

Zondervan Publishing House
1415 Lake Drive SE
Grand Rapids, MI 49506

Author Index

Title Index

Subject Index

Compiled by Janet Perlman